World Economic and Financial Surveys

WORLD ECONOMIC OUTLOOK
April 2013

Hopes, Realities, Risks

International Monetary Fund

©2013 International Monetary Fund

Cover and Design: Luisa Menjivar and Jorge Salazar
Composition: Maryland Composition

Cataloging-in-Publication Data

World economic outlook (International Monetary Fund)
    World economic outlook : a survey by the staff of the International Monetary Fund. —
Washington, DC : International Monetary Fund, 1980–
    v. ; 28 cm. — (1981–1984: Occasional paper / International Monetary Fund, 0251-6365).
— (1986– : World economic and financial surveys, 0256-6877)

Semiannual. Some issues also have thematic titles.
Has occasional updates, 1984–

    1. Economic development — Periodicals. 2. Economic forecasting — Periodicals.
3. Economic policy — Periodicals. 4. International economic relations — Periodicals.
I. International Monetary Fund. II. Series: Occasional paper (International Monetary Fund).
III. Series: World economic and financial surveys.

HC10.80

ISBN 978-1-61635-555-5

Publication orders may be placed online, by fax, or through the mail:
International Monetary Fund, Publication Services
P.O. Box 92780, Washington, DC 20090, U.S.A.
Tel.: (202) 623-7430 Fax: (202) 623-7201
E-mail: publications@imf.org
www.imfbookstore.org
www.elibrary.imf.org

CONTENTS

Online Tables

Figures

ASSUMPTIONS AND CONVENTIONS

A number of assumptions have been adopted for the projections presented in the *World Economic Outlook*. It has been assumed that real effective exchange rates remained constant at their average levels during February 11–March 11, 2013, except for the currencies participating in the European exchange rate mechanism II (ERM II), which are assumed to have remained constant in nominal terms relative to the euro; that established policies of national authorities will be maintained (for specific assumptions about fiscal and monetary policies for selected economies, see Box A1); that the average price of oil will be $102.60 a barrel in 2013 and $97.58 a barrel in 2014 and will remain unchanged in real terms over the medium term; that the six-month London interbank offered rate (LIBOR) on U.S. dollar deposits will average 0.5 percent in 2013 and 0.6 percent in 2014; that the three-month euro deposit rate will average 0.2 percent in 2013 and 0.4 percent in 2014; and that the six-month Japanese yen deposit rate will yield on average 0.2 percent in 2013 and 2014. These are, of course, working hypotheses rather than forecasts, and the uncertainties surrounding them add to the margin of error that would in any event be involved in the projections. The estimates and projections are based on statistical information available through early April 2013.

The following conventions are used throughout the *World Economic Outlook:*

. . . to indicate that data are not available or not applicable;

– between years or months (for example, 2012–13 or January–June) to indicate the years or months covered, including the beginning and ending years or months;

/ between years or months (for example, 2012/13) to indicate a fiscal or financial year.

"Billion" means a thousand million; "trillion" means a thousand billion.

"Basis points" refer to hundredths of 1 percentage point (for example, 25 basis points are equivalent to ¼ of 1 percentage point).

For some countries, the figures for 2012 and earlier are based on estimates rather than actual outturns.

Data refer to calendar years, except for a few countries that use fiscal years. Please refer to the *country information* section of the WEO online database on the IMF website (www.imf.org) for a complete listing of the reference periods for each country.

Projections for Cyprus are excluded due to the ongoing crisis.

Mongolia is classified as Developing Asia (previously classified as a member of the Commonwealth of Independent States).

Afghanistan and Pakistan, previously classified as Developing Asia, have been added to the Middle East and North Africa (MENA) to create the Middle East, North Africa, Afghanistan, and Pakistan (MENAP) region. The MENA aggregate (excluding Afghanistan and Pakistan) will be maintained.

Data for the Marshall Islands and Micronesia are now included in the Developing Asia region.

As in the October 2012 *World Economic Outlook*, data for Syria are excluded for 2011 and later due to the uncertain political situation.

Starting with the April 2013 *World Economic Outlook*, the Newly Industrialized Asian Economies (NIEs) grouping has been eliminated.

If no source is listed on tables and figures, data are drawn from the World Economic Outlook (WEO) database.

When countries are not listed alphabetically, they are ordered on the basis of economic size.

Minor discrepancies between sums of constituent figures and totals shown reflect rounding.

As used in this report, the terms "country" and "economy" do not in all cases refer to a territorial entity that is a state as understood by international law and practice. As used here, the term also covers some territorial entities that are not states but for which statistical data are maintained on a separate and independent basis.

Composite data are provided for various groups of countries organized according to economic characteristics or region. Unless otherwise noted, country group composites represent calculations based on 90 percent or more of the weighted group data.

The boundaries, colors, denominations, and any other information shown on the maps do not imply, on the part of the International Monetary Fund, any judgment on the legal status of any territory or any endorsement or acceptance of such boundaries.

This version of the *World Economic Outlook* is available in full through the IMF eLibrary (www.elibrary.imf.org) and the IMF website (www.imf.org). Accompanying the publication on the IMF website is a larger compilation of data from the WEO database than is included in the report itself, including files containing the series most frequently requested by readers. These files may be downloaded for use in a variety of software packages.

The data appearing in the *World Economic Outlook* are compiled by the IMF staff at the time of the WEO exercises. The historical data and projections are based on the information gathered by the IMF country desk officers in the context of their missions to IMF member countries and through their ongoing analysis of the evolving situation in each country. Historical data are updated on a continual basis as more information becomes available, and structural breaks in data are often adjusted to produce smooth series with the use of splicing and other techniques. IMF staff estimates continue to serve as proxies for historical series when complete information is unavailable. As a result, WEO data can differ from other sources with official data, including the IMF's *International Financial Statistics*.

The WEO data and metadata provided are "as is" and "as available," and every effort is made to ensure, but not guarantee, their timeliness, accuracy, and completeness. When errors are discovered, there is a concerted effort to correct them as appropriate and feasible. Corrections and revisions made after publication are incorporated into the electronic editions available from the IMF eLibrary (www.elibrary.imf.org) and on the IMF website (www.imf.org). All substantive changes are listed in detail in the online tables of contents.

For details on the terms and conditions for usage of the WEO database, please refer to the IMF Copyright and Usage website, www.imf.org/external/terms.htm.

Inquiries about the content of the *World Economic Outlook* and the WEO database should be sent by mail, fax, or online forum (telephone inquiries cannot be accepted):

World Economic Studies Division
Research Department
International Monetary Fund
700 19th Street, N.W.
Washington, DC 20431, U.S.A.
Fax: (202) 623-6343
Online Forum: www.imf.org/weoforum

PREFACE

The analysis and projections contained in the *World Economic Outlook* are integral elements of the IMF's surveillance of economic developments and policies in its member countries, of developments in international financial markets, and of the global economic system. The survey of prospects and policies is the product of a comprehensive interdepartmental review of world economic developments, which draws primarily on information the IMF staff gathers through its consultations with member countries. These consultations are carried out in particular by the IMF's area departments—namely, the African Department, Asia and Pacific Department, European Department, Middle East and Central Asia Department, and Western Hemisphere Department—together with the Strategy, Policy, and Review Department; the Monetary and Capital Markets Department; and the Fiscal Affairs Department.

The analysis in this report was coordinated in the Research Department under the general direction of Olivier Blanchard, Economic Counsellor and Director of Research. The project was directed by Jörg Decressin, Deputy Director, Research Department, and by Thomas Helbling, Division Chief, Research Department.

The primary contributors to this report are Abdul Abiad, John Bluedorn, Rupa Duttagupta, Jaime Guajardo, Troy Matheson, Nkunde Mwase, Damiano Sandri, and John Simon.

Other contributors include Ali Al-Eyd, Alberto Behar, Samya Beidas-Strom, Paul Cashin, Luis Cubeddu, Alfredo Cuevas, Gabriel Di Bella, Frigyes Ferdinand Heinz, Dora Iakova, Joong Shik Kang, Padamja Khandelwal, M. Ayhan Kose, Prakash Loungani, Romain Ranciere, Julien Reynaud, Marina Rousset, Jay Shambaugh, Shane Streifel, Yan Sun, Marco E. Terrones, and Olaf Unteroberdoerster.

Gavin Asdorian, Shan Chen, Tingyun Chen, Angela Espiritu, Sinem Kilic Celik, Nadezhda Lepeshko, Ezgi O. Ozturk, Katherine Pan, Daniel Rivera-Greenwood, and Bennet Voorhees provided research assistance. Andrew Berg, Kevin Clinton, Olivier Coibion, Romain Duval, Douglas Laxton, Andrew Levin, Akito Matsumoto, Chris Papageorgiou, and Catherine Pattillo provided comments and suggestions. Mitko Grigorov, Mahnaz Hemmati, Toh Kuan, Rajesh Nilawar, Emory Oakes, and Steve Zhang provided technical support. Skeeter Mathurin and Luke Lee were responsible for word processing. Linda Griffin Kean of the External Relations Department edited the manuscript and coordinated the production of the publication with assistance from Lucy Scott Morales. External consultant Pavel Pimenov provided additional technical support.

The analysis has benefited from comments and suggestions by staff from other IMF departments, as well as by Executive Directors following their discussion of the report on April 1, 2013. However, both projections and policy considerations are those of the IMF staff and should not be attributed to Executive Directors or to their national authorities.

FOREWORD

What was until now a two-speed recovery, strong in emerging market and developing economies but weaker in advanced economies, is becoming a three-speed recovery. Emerging market and developing economies are still going strong, but in advanced economies, there appears to be a growing bifurcation between the United States on one hand and the euro area on the other.

This is reflected in our forecasts. Growth in emerging market and developing economies is forecast to reach 5.3 percent in 2013 and 5.7 percent in 2014. Growth in the United States is forecast to be 2 percent in 2013 and 3.0 percent in 2014. In contrast, growth in the euro area is forecast to be –0.3 percent in 2013 and 1.1 percent in 2014.

The growth figure for the United States for 2013 may not seem very high, and indeed it is insufficient to make a large dent in the still-high unemployment rate. But it will be achieved in the face of a very strong, indeed overly strong, fiscal consolidation of about 1.8 percent of GDP. Underlying private demand is actually strong, spurred in part by the anticipation of low policy rates under the Federal Reserve's "forward guidance" and by pent-up demand for housing and durables.

The forecast for negative growth in the euro area reflects not only weakness in the periphery but also some weakness in the core. Germany's growth is strengthening but is still forecast to be less than 1 percent in 2013. France's growth is forecast to be negative in 2013, reflecting a combination of fiscal consolidation, poor export performance, and low confidence. This may call into question the ability of the core to help the periphery, if and when needed. Most euro area periphery countries, notably Italy and Spain, are expected to have substantial contractions in 2013. The process of internal devaluation is slowly taking place, and most of these countries are slowly becoming more competitive. External demand, however, is just not strong enough to compensate for weak internal demand. Adverse feedback loops between weak banks, weak sovereigns, and low activity are still reinforcing each other.

Japan is forging a path of its own. After many years of deflation, and little or no growth, the new government has announced a new policy, based on aggressive quantitative easing, a positive inflation target, fiscal stimulus, and structural reforms. This policy will boost growth in the short term, and this is reflected in our forecast of 1.4 percent growth for 2013. Given the high level of public debt, however, embarking on a fiscal stimulus in the absence of a medium-term fiscal consolidation plan is risky; it increases the probability that investors will require a risk premium, and that this will lead in turn to debt unsustainability.

In contrast to this mixed picture for the advanced economies, emerging market economies are doing well. In the past, the conditions that prevail today—high commodity prices, low interest rates, large capital inflows—would often have led to credit booms and overheating. This time, however, policymakers have generally succeeded in keeping aggregate demand in line with potential. At the same time, potential growth has itself apparently declined in a number of major emerging market economies, relative to precrisis trends. Although circumstances vary across countries, the evidence suggests that some of this decline has its source in policy-induced distortions, and those should be addressed.

Turning to policies:

In the United States, the focus should be on defining the right path of consolidation. While the sequester has decreased worries about debt sustainability, it is the wrong way to proceed. There should be both less and better fiscal consolidation now and a commitment to more fiscal consolidation in the future.

In the euro area, institutional progress has been made over the past year, in particular on creating a road map for a banking union. The Outright Monetary Transactions program offered by the European Central Bank, even if not yet taken up, has reduced tail risks. Yet this is not enough. The interest rates facing borrowers in periphery countries are still too high to secure the recovery, and there is a need for further and urgent measures to strengthen banks, without weakening the sovereigns. The weakness of private demand also suggests that countries that have scope to do so should allow automatic stabilizers to operate, and some countries with fiscal space should go even beyond this.

Emerging market economies face different challenges, one of which is handling capital flows. Fundamentally attractive prospects in emerging market economies, together with low interest rates in advanced economies, are likely to lead to continuing net capital inflows and exchange rate pressure in many emerging market economies. This is a desirable process and part of the global rebalancing that must take place if the world economy is to get back to health. At the same time, as we have seen, capital flows can be volatile, making macroeconomic management more difficult. The challenge for recipient countries is to accommodate the underlying trends while reducing the volatility of the flows when they threaten macro or financial stability.

In short, recent good news about the United States has come with renewed worries about the euro area. Given the strong interconnections between countries, an uneven recovery is also a dangerous one. Some tail risks have decreased, but it is not time for policymakers to relax.

Olivier Blanchard
Economic Counsellor

EXECUTIVE SUMMARY

Global economic prospects have improved again but the road to recovery in the advanced economies will remain bumpy. World output growth is forecast to reach 3¼ percent in 2013 and 4 percent in 2014. In advanced economies, activity is expected to gradually accelerate, starting in the second half of 2013. Private demand appears increasingly robust in the United States but still very sluggish in the euro area. In emerging market and developing economies, activity has already picked up steam.

Better, but Bumpy and Divergent, Prospects for Advanced Economies

Over the past six months, advanced economy policymakers have successfully defused two of the biggest short-term threats to the global recovery, the threat of a euro area breakup and a sharp fiscal contraction in the United States caused by a plunge off the "fiscal cliff." In response, financial markets have rallied on a broad front. Moreover, financial stability has improved, as underscored in the April 2013 *Global Financial Stability Report* (GFSR).

The financial market rally has been helping economic recovery by improving funding conditions and supporting confidence, but growth prospects appear broadly unchanged. While U.S. private demand has been showing strength as credit and housing markets are healing, larger-than-expected fiscal adjustment is projected to keep real GDP growth at about 2 percent in 2013. In the euro area, better conditions for periphery sovereigns are not yet passing through to companies and households, because banks are still hobbled by poor profitability and low capital, constraining the supply of credit. Also, in many economies activity will be held back by continued fiscal adjustment, competitiveness problems, and balance sheet weaknesses. Furthermore, new political and financial risks that could put a damper on the recovery have come to the fore. Accordingly, real GDP is projected to contract relative to 2012, by about ¼

percent of GDP. Japan, by contrast, will see a fiscal- and monetary-stimulus-driven rebound, with real GDP growth reaching 1½ percent.

Overall, the annual growth forecast for advanced economies in 2013—a modest 1¼ percent—is no better than the outcome for 2012. That said, assuming that policymakers avoid setbacks and deliver on their commitments, the projections in this *World Economic Outlook* (WEO) build on continued easing of the brakes on real activity. Consequently, in 2013, after a weak first half, real GDP growth in the advanced economies is projected to rise above 2 percent for the rest of the year and to average 2¼ percent in 2014, spurred by U.S. growth of about 3 percent.

Reaccelerating Activity in Emerging Market and Developing Economies

There was a noticeable slowdown in the emerging market and developing economies during 2012, a reflection of the sharp deceleration in demand from key advanced economies, domestic policy tightening, and the end of investment booms in some of the major emerging market economies. But with consumer demand resilient, macroeconomic policy on hold, and exports reviving, most economies in Asia and sub-Saharan Africa and many economies in Latin America and the Commonwealth of Independent States are now seeing higher growth. The recovery should again gain speed in emerging Europe as demand from advanced Europe slowly picks up. However, economies in the Middle East and North Africa continue to struggle with difficult internal transitions. And a couple of economies in South America are facing high inflation and increasing exchange market pressure.

There is good news emanating from developing economies. Even as estimates of potential growth have been marked down in recent years for some of the larger emerging markets, it has been steadily improving elsewhere. In fact, Chapter 4 underscores that the prospects of many of today's dynamic low-income countries appear stronger than those of their peers during the 1960s and 1970s.

More Symmetric Risks

Notwithstanding old dangers and new turbulence, the near-term risk picture has improved as recent policy actions in Europe and the United States have addressed some of the gravest short-term risks. In the euro area, the main short-term dangers now revolve around adjustment fatigue, weak balance sheets, broken credit channels in the periphery, and insufficient progress toward stronger economic and monetary union at the euro area level. In the United States and Japan, risks relate mainly to medium-term fiscal policy. Over the short term, a failure by the U.S. Congress to replace the automatic spending cuts (budget sequester) with back-loaded measures at the end of the current fiscal year would entail somewhat lower-than-projected growth in late 2013 and beyond. Of much greater concern would be a failure to raise the debt ceiling—the risk of such self-destructive inaction, however, appears low. Over the medium term, downside risks revolve around the absence of strong fiscal consolidation plans in the United States and Japan; high private sector debt, limited policy space, and insufficient institutional progress in the euro area, which could lead to a protracted period of low growth; distortions from easy and unconventional monetary policy in many advanced economies; and overinvestment and high asset prices in many emerging market and developing economies. Unless policies address these risks, global activity is likely to suffer periodic setbacks. By the same token, a stronger-than-projected policy response could also foster a stronger recovery in activity.

Policymakers Cannot Afford to Relax Their Efforts

In advanced economies, policy should use all prudent measures to support sluggish demand. However, the risks related to high sovereign debt limit the fiscal policy room to maneuver. There is no silver bullet to address all the concerns about demand and debt. Rather, fiscal adjustment needs to progress gradually, building on measures that limit damage to demand in the short term; monetary policy needs to stay supportive of activity; financial policies need to help

improve the pass-through of monetary policy; and structural and other policies need to spur potential output and global demand rebalancing. Regarding monetary policy, one key finding of Chapter 3 is that inflation expectations have become much better anchored, affording central banks greater leeway to support activity—although they must be mindful of financial stability risks emanating from their policies, as discussed in detail in the April 2013 GFSR.

The critical fiscal policy requirements are persistent but gradual consolidation and, for the United States and Japan, the design and implementation of comprehensive medium-term deficit-reduction plans. These requirements are urgent for Japan, given the significant risks related to the renewal of stimulus in an environment of very high public debt levels. In the United States, it is worrisome that after three years of deliberations, policymakers have not agreed on a credible plan for entitlement and tax reform and that improvement in near-term prospects seems to have come with a decreased sense of urgency for progress. The specific requirements and country details are discussed in the April 2013 *Fiscal Monitor*.

The April 2013 GFSR underscores the need for further financial repair and reform, including restructuring weak banks and, in some cases, offering households and weak corporate debtors avenues other than traditional bankruptcy for dealing with debt overhang. Previous WEO reports also stressed the critical role of structural reforms in rebuilding competitiveness and boosting medium-term growth prospects in many euro area economies.

In emerging market and developing economies, some tightening of policies appears appropriate over the medium term. The tightening should begin with monetary policy and be supported with prudential measures as needed to rein in budding excesses in financial sectors. Eventually, policymakers should also return fiscal balances to levels that afford ample room for policy maneuvering. Some will need to take significant action now; others will need only limited improvements over the medium term.

Policy Spillovers

The bumpy recovery and skewed macroeconomic policy mix in advanced economies are complicating policymaking in emerging market economies. Concerns resurfaced once again recently, when looser monetary policy in Japan and other factors prompted a large depreciation of the yen. That said, complaints about competitive exchange rate depreciations appear overblown. At this juncture, there seem to be no large deviations of the major currencies from medium-term fundamentals. The U.S. dollar and the euro appear moderately overvalued and the renminbi moderately undervalued. The evidence on valuation of the yen is mixed.

The way to address currency worries is for all economies to pursue policies that foster internal and external balance. In the major advanced economies, this requires more progress with medium- and long-term fiscal adjustment plans, entitlement reform, and balance sheet repair. Short-term fiscal policies could then be less restrictive, which, together with better balance sheets, would relieve pressure from overburdened monetary policy. Emerging market and developing economies, in turn, face different challenges. Key external surplus economies should allow their exchange rates to be more market determined and should implement structural policies to rebalance the economy toward consumption-driven growth. Other economies need to deploy structural policies to foster the healthy absorption of capital inflows. When these flows threaten to destabilize their economies, they can adopt macroprudential or capital-flow-management measures to avoid the buildup of major internal imbalances.

GLOBAL PROSPECTS AND POLICIES

Global prospects have improved again but the road to recovery in the advanced economies will remain bumpy. World output growth is forecast to reach 3¼ percent in 2013 and 4 percent in 2014 (Table 1.1). In the major advanced economies, activity is expected to gradually accelerate, following a weak start to 2013, with the United States in the lead. In emerging market and developing economies, activity has already picked up steam. Advanced economy policymakers have successfully defused two of the biggest threats to the global recovery, a breakup of the euro area and a sharp fiscal contraction in the United States caused by a plunge off the "fiscal cliff." However, old dangers remain and new risks have come to the fore. In the short term, risks mainly relate to developments in the euro area, including uncertainty about the fallout from events in Cyprus and politics in Italy as well as vulnerabilities in the periphery. In the medium term, the key risks relate to adjustment fatigue, insufficient institutional reform, and prolonged stagnation in the euro area as well as high fiscal deficits and debt in the United States and Japan. In this setting, policymakers cannot afford to relax their efforts. In advanced economies, the right macroeconomic approach continues to be gradual but sustained fiscal adjustment, built on measures that limit damage to activity, and accommodative monetary policy aimed at supporting internal demand. The United States and Japan still need to devise and implement strong medium-term fiscal consolidation plans. The euro area needs to strengthen the Economic and Monetary Union (EMU). In emerging market and developing economies, some tightening of policies appears appropriate in the medium term. This tightening should begin with monetary policy and be supported with prudential measures as needed to rein in budding excesses in financial sectors. Eventually, policymakers should also return fiscal balances to their healthy pre-2008 levels, rebuilding ample room for policy maneuvering. Some will need to take significant action now; others will need only limited improvements in the medium term.

Activity Is Beginning to Recover after the Slowdown in 2012

Activity has stabilized in advanced economies and has picked up in emerging market and developing economies, supported by policies and renewed confidence. This pickup follows the slowdown in the first half of 2012, which was manifested in industrial production and global trade (Figure 1.1, panel 1). Investment in major economies also dipped, whereas consumption evolved broadly as expected—sluggishly in many advanced economies, hobbled by low employment rates (Figure 1.2, panels 3 and 4), and buoyantly in many emerging market and developing economies, where labor markets continue to perform well (Figure 1.1, panel 2).

Strong actions by European policymakers helped improve confidence and financial conditions. U.S. policymakers avoided the fiscal cliff but have failed to find durable solutions to other short-term fiscal risks. Japan adopted more expansionary macroeconomic policies in response to a larger-than-expected slowdown. In the meantime, policy easing in key emerging market economies has supported internal demand. Moreover, the production and consumption dynamics in many economies may have primed them for an inventory-led rebound (Figure 1.2, panel 5).

Financial and Monetary Conditions Have Eased

Financial markets have led the reacceleration in activity. Since mid-2012, there has been a broad market rally. Policy rates have evolved broadly as expected, with a number of central banks in advanced and emerging market economies implementing modest rate cuts in response to the latest slowdown. Although markets may have moved ahead of the real economy, the April 2013 *Global Financial Stability Report* (GFSR) underscores that near-term financial stability risks have eased.

- Equity prices in advanced and emerging markets have risen by some 15 percent, and equity price

Table 1.1. Overview of the *World Economic Outlook* Projections
(Percent change unless noted otherwise)

	2011	2012	Year over Year Projections 2013	Projections 2014	Difference from January 2013 WEO Update 2013	Difference from January 2013 WEO Update 2014	Q4 over Q4 Estimates 2012	Q4 over Q4 Projections 2013	Q4 over Q4 Projections 2014
World Output[1]	**4.0**	**3.2**	**3.3**	**4.0**	**−0.2**	**0.0**	**2.7**	**3.6**	**4.0**
Advanced Economies	**1.6**	**1.2**	**1.2**	**2.2**	**−0.1**	**0.1**	**0.8**	**2.0**	**2.3**
United States	1.8	2.2	1.9	3.0	−0.2	−0.1	1.7	2.2	3.4
Euro Area	1.4	−0.6	−0.3	1.1	−0.2	0.0	−0.9	0.6	1.1
Germany	3.1	0.9	0.6	1.5	0.1	0.0	0.4	1.5	1.1
France	1.7	0.0	−0.1	0.9	−0.4	0.0	−0.3	0.4	1.0
Italy	0.4	−2.4	−1.5	0.5	−0.4	0.0	−2.8	−0.4	0.6
Spain	0.4	−1.4	−1.6	0.7	−0.1	−0.1	−1.9	−0.7	1.1
Japan	−0.6	2.0	1.6	1.4	0.4	0.7	0.4	3.8	−0.1
United Kingdom	0.9	0.2	0.7	1.5	−0.3	−0.3	0.3	1.1	1.5
Canada	2.6	1.8	1.5	2.4	−0.3	0.1	1.1	2.0	2.5
Other Advanced Economies[2]	3.3	1.8	2.5	3.4	−0.3	0.1	2.0	3.0	3.4
Emerging Market and Developing Economies[3]	**6.4**	**5.1**	**5.3**	**5.7**	**−0.2**	**−0.1**	**5.2**	**5.7**	**5.9**
Central and Eastern Europe	5.2	1.6	2.2	2.8	−0.3	−0.4	1.4	3.1	2.4
Commonwealth of Independent States	4.8	3.4	3.4	4.0	−0.4	−0.1	1.5	4.1	3.4
Russia	4.3	3.4	3.4	3.8	−0.3	0.0	1.9	4.8	2.9
Excluding Russia	6.1	3.3	3.5	4.6	−0.8	−0.1	. . .	. . .	. . .
Developing Asia	8.1	6.6	7.1	7.3	0.0	−0.1	7.2	7.0	7.4
China	9.3	7.8	8.0	8.2	−0.1	−0.3	7.9	7.8	8.3
India	7.7	4.0	5.7	6.2	−0.2	−0.1	4.1	5.8	6.2
ASEAN-5[4]	4.5	6.1	5.9	5.5	0.3	−0.2	9.0	5.3	5.5
Latin America and the Caribbean	4.6	3.0	3.4	3.9	−0.3	0.0	2.7	3.6	3.8
Brazil	2.7	0.9	3.0	4.0	−0.5	0.1	1.4	3.8	4.1
Mexico	3.9	3.9	3.4	3.4	−0.1	−0.1	3.3	4.0	3.0
Middle East, North Africa, Afghanistan, and Pakistan	3.9	4.7	3.1	3.7	−0.3	−0.1	. . .	. . .	. . .
Sub-Saharan Africa[5]	5.3	4.8	5.6	6.1	−0.2	0.4	. . .	. . .	. . .
South Africa	3.5	2.5	2.8	3.3	0.0	−0.8	2.3	3.4	3.2
Memorandum									
European Union	1.6	−0.2	0.0	1.3	−0.2	−0.1	−0.6	0.9	1.2
Middle East and North Africa	4.0	4.8	3.1	3.7	−0.3	−0.2	. . .	. . .	. . .
World Growth Based on Market Exchange Rates	2.9	2.5	2.6	3.4	−0.2	0.0	1.9	3.0	3.3
World Trade Volume (goods and services)	**6.0**	**2.5**	**3.6**	**5.3**	**−0.2**	**−0.1**	. . .	. . .	. . .
Imports									
Advanced Economies	4.7	1.0	2.2	4.1	0.0	0.0	. . .	. . .	. . .
Emerging Market and Developing Economies	8.6	4.9	6.2	7.3	−0.3	−0.4	. . .	. . .	. . .
Exports									
Advanced Economies	5.6	1.9	2.8	4.6	0.0	0.1	. . .	. . .	. . .
Emerging Market and Developing Economies	6.4	3.7	4.8	6.5	−0.8	−0.4	. . .	. . .	. . .
Commodity Prices (U.S. dollars)									
Oil[6]	31.6	1.0	−2.3	−4.9	2.8	−2.0	−1.2	−1.3	−4.7
Nonfuel (average based on world commodity export weights)	17.8	−9.8	−0.9	−4.3	2.2	−1.3	1.2	−3.3	−2.7
Consumer Prices									
Advanced Economies	2.7	2.0	1.7	2.0	0.1	0.2	1.8	1.7	2.1
Emerging Market and Developing Economies[3]	7.2	5.9	5.9	5.6	−0.1	0.1	4.9	5.3	5.2
London Interbank Offered Rate (percent)[7]									
On U.S. Dollar Deposits	0.5	0.7	0.5	0.6	−0.1	0.0	. . .	. . .	. . .
On Euro Deposits	1.4	0.6	0.2	0.4	0.1	0.2	. . .	. . .	. . .
On Japanese Yen Deposits	0.3	0.3	0.2	0.2	0.0	0.0	. . .	. . .	. . .

Note: Real effective exchange rates are assumed to remain constant at the levels prevailing during February 11–March 11, 2013. When economies are not listed alphabetically, they are ordered on the basis of economic size. The aggregated quarterly data are seasonally adjusted.

[1]The quarterly estimates and projections account for 90 percent of the world purchasing-power-parity weights.

[2]Excludes the G7 (Canada, France, Germany, Italy, Japan, United Kingdom, United States) and euro area countries.

[3]The quarterly estimates and projections account for approximately 80 percent of the emerging market and developing economies.

[4]Indonesia, Malaysia, Philippines, Thailand, Vietnam.

[5]Regional and global aggregates include South Sudan.

[6]Simple average of prices of U.K. Brent, Dubai Fateh, and West Texas Intermediate crude oil. The average price of oil in U.S. dollars a barrel was $105.01 in 2012; the assumed price based on futures markets is $102.60 in 2013 and $97.58 in 2014.

[7]Six-month rate for the United States and Japan. Three-month rate for the euro area.

Figure 1.1. Global Indicators

The global manufacturing and trade cycle has begun to reaccelerate, particularly in the emerging market economies. Conjunctural indicators suggest that many advanced European economies are lagging behind the global upturn. Unemployment will continue to increase in Europe and the Middle East and North Africa.

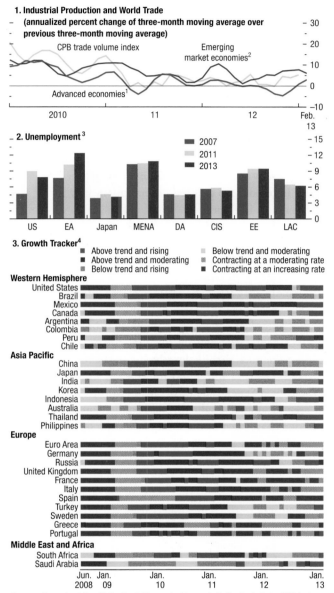

1. Industrial Production and World Trade
(annualized percent change of three-month moving average over previous three-month moving average)

2. Unemployment [3]
- 2007
- 2011
- 2013

US   EA   Japan   MENA   DA   CIS   EE   LAC

3. Growth Tracker [4]
- Above trend and rising
- Above trend and moderating
- Below trend and rising
- Below trend and moderating
- Contracting at a moderating rate
- Contracting at an increasing rate

Western Hemisphere
United States
Brazil
Mexico
Canada
Argentina
Colombia
Peru
Chile

Asia Pacific
China
Japan
India
Korea
Indonesia
Australia
Thailand
Philippines

Europe
Euro Area
Germany
Russia
United Kingdom
France
Italy
Spain
Turkey
Sweden
Greece
Portugal

Middle East and Africa
South Africa
Saudi Arabia

Jun. Jan. 2008 09   Jan. 10   Jan. 11   Jan. 12   Jan. 13

Sources: Haver Analytics; Netherlands Bureau for Economic Policy Analysis for CPB trade volume index; and IMF staff estimates.
Note: US = United States; EA = euro area; CIS = Commonwealth of Independent States; DA = developing Asia; EE = emerging Europe; LAC = Latin America and the Caribbean; MENA = Middle East and North Africa.
[1]Australia, Canada, Czech Republic, Denmark, euro area, Hong Kong SAR, Israel, Japan, Korea, New Zealand, Norway, Singapore, Sweden, Switzerland, Taiwan Province of China, United Kingdom, United States.
[2]Argentina, Brazil, Bulgaria, Chile, China, Colombia, Hungary, India, Indonesia, Latvia, Lithuania, Malaysia, Mexico, Pakistan, Peru, Philippines, Poland, Romania, Russia, South Africa, Thailand, Turkey, Ukraine, Venezuela.
[3]Sub-Saharan Africa is omitted due to data limitations.
[4]The Growth Tracker is described in Matheson (2011). Within regions, countries are listed by economic size. The colors indicate whether estimated monthly growth is positive or negative, higher or lower than estimated trend growth, and whether estimated growth has been rising or falling over the previous quarter. Trend growth is estimated using a Hodrick-Prescott filter and may differ from the IMF staff's estimates of potential growth, where these are available.

Figure 1.2. Current and Forward-Looking Growth Indicators

Indicators of manufacturing activity suggest that a reacceleration is well under way in emerging market economies but that activity in advanced economies is only beginning to stabilize, held back by major weakness in the euro area periphery and Japan. Consumption growth eased marginally during the latest slowdown. Amid contracting manufacturing output and trade, however, investment stalled. This may have come with a reduction in inventories, setting the stage for an inventory-led rebound.

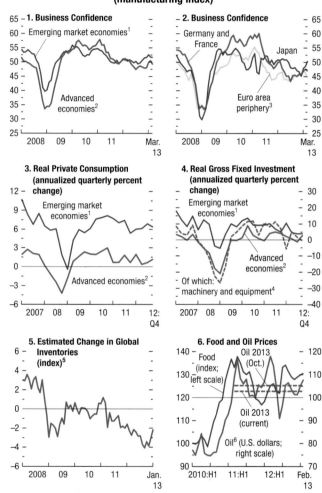

Purchasing Managers' Index
(manufacturing index)

1. Business Confidence
Emerging market economies[1]
Advanced economies[2]

2. Business Confidence
Germany and France
Japan
Euro area periphery[3]

3. Real Private Consumption
(annualized quarterly percent change)
Emerging market economies[1]
Advanced economies[2]

4. Real Gross Fixed Investment
(annualized quarterly percent change)
Emerging market economies[1]
Advanced economies[2]
Of which: machinery and equipment[4]

5. Estimated Change in Global Inventories
(index)[5]

6. Food and Oil Prices
Food (index; left scale)
Oil 2013 (Oct.)
Oil 2013 (current)
Oil[6] (U.S. dollars; right scale)

Sources: Markit/Haver Analytics; and IMF staff calculations.
Note: Not all economies are included in the regional aggregations. For some economies, monthly data are interpolated from quarterly series.
[1]Argentina, Brazil, Bulgaria, Chile, China, Colombia, Hungary, India, Indonesia, Latvia, Lithuania, Malaysia, Mexico, Peru, Philippines, Poland, Romania, Russia, South Africa, Thailand, Turkey, Ukraine, Venezuela.
[2]Australia, Canada, Czech Republic, Denmark, euro area, Hong Kong SAR, Israel, Japan, Korea, New Zealand, Norway, Singapore, Sweden, Switzerland, Taiwan Province of China, United Kingdom, United States.
[3]Greece, Ireland, Italy, Spain.
[4]Purchasing-power-parity-weighted averages of metal products and machinery for the euro area, plants and equipment for Japan, plants and machinery for the United Kingdom, and equipment and software for the United States.
[5]Based on deviations from an estimated (cointegral) relationship between global industrial production and retail sales.
[6]U.S. dollars a barrel: simple average of spot prices of U.K. Brent, Dubai Fateh, and West Texas Intermediate crude oil. The dashed lines indicate projected oil prices in the October 2012 and current WEO reports.

Figure 1.3. Financial Market Conditions

Stronger policies in the major advanced economies have triggered a broad rally in financial markets. Since summer 2012, equity prices are up some 15 percent. Euro area periphery risk spreads are down more than expected, and Target 2 liabilities of Italy and Spain have decreased. Capital flows to emerging market economies have resumed, pushing down their risk spreads.

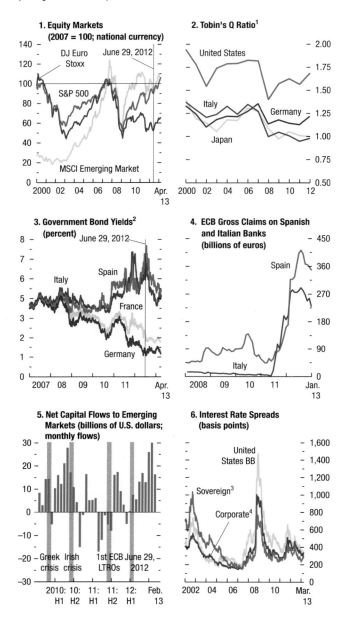

Sources: Bloomberg, L.P.; Capital Data; EPFR Global/Haver Analytics; national central banks; Worldscope; and IMF staff calculations.
Note: ECB = European Central Bank; LTROs = longer-term refinancing operations.
[1]Tobin (1969).
[2]Ten-year government bonds.
[3]JPMorgan EMBI Global Index spread.
[4]JPMorgan CEMBI Broad Index spread.

volatility has fallen to pre-2008 levels (Figure 1.3, panel 1). But proxies for Tobin's Q ratio (Tobin, 1969) are still appreciably below precrisis levels (Figure 1.3, panel 2), consistent with equity investors' subdued views of the future. High-yield bond issuance is running well above precrisis levels in the United States, buttressed by record-low yields and tight bank lending conditions. This is not, however, translating into an investment boom.

- In the euro area, periphery sovereign spreads have dropped (Figure 1.3, panel 3). For the first time in a year, selected periphery economies have successfully placed large volumes of long-term syndicated sovereign bonds. But these improvements are fragile, as suggested by the increased volatility in periphery spreads in response to political uncertainty in Italy and the events in Cyprus.

- Risk spreads on emerging market sovereigns and corporations have declined with the resumption of capital inflows (Figure 1.3, panels 5 and 6). Bond and syndicated loan issuance has been strong. Furthermore, very low U.S. dollar and euro interest rates have prompted corporations to increase their issuance of foreign-currency-denominated debt. However, bank credit remains sluggish in many advanced economies, despite the rebound in the financial markets. Demand and supply forces are at work.

- In the United States, the rate of credit growth has been picking up gradually, and bank lending conditions have been easing slowly from very tight levels (Figure 1.4, panels 2 and 3). Together with lower market risk spreads, this has noticeably eased financial conditions (Figure 1.5, panel 1). This process is supported by recovering house prices, higher household net worth, and stronger bank balance sheets and profitability (Figure 1.4, panels 4 and 5). However, many middle-income households continue to face high debt burdens.

- In the euro area, sustained, positive feedback between activity and credit still seems a distant prospect. GFSR analysis suggests that bank deleveraging is proceeding in line with the "current policies" baseline anticipated in October 2012, a reflection of continued concern about capital and liquidity. Euro area credit continues to contract and lending conditions to tighten, reflecting mainly conditions in the periphery economies but also the poor macroeconomic outlook for the region as a whole. Companies in the core face an uncertain environment and low

Figure 1.4. Monetary Conditions and Bank Lending

Monetary policy rates are forecast to remain very low over the next three years. In the euro area, credit is contracting, reflecting mainly conditions in the periphery, and lending conditions continue to tighten. By contrast, in the United States credit growth is picking up again, and lending conditions have begun to ease, and this is being helped by recovering house prices and improved household balance sheets.

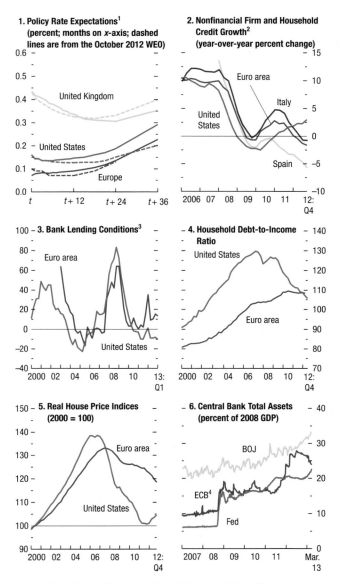

Figure 1.5. Financial Conditions Index
(Positive = tightening; standard deviations from average)

Financial conditions tightened sharply toward the end of 2011 as the economic outlook deteriorated and tensions rose in the euro area. More recently, market confidence has been bolstered by improved growth prospects and stronger policy actions. Risk spreads have narrowed as a result. Financial conditions are expected to continue easing as global growth continues to gain traction.

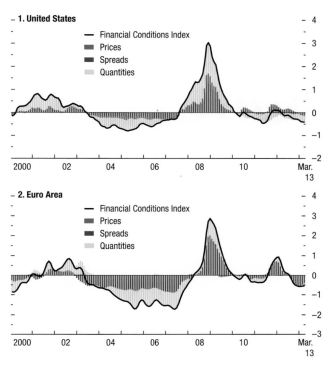

Source: IMF staff calculations.

Sources: Bank of America/Merrill Lynch; Bank of Italy; Bank of Spain; Bloomberg, L.P.; Haver Analytics; Organization for Economic Cooperation and Development; and IMF staff calculations.
Note: BOJ = Bank of Japan; ECB = European Central Bank; Fed = Federal Reserve.
[1]Expectations are based on the federal funds rate for the United States, the sterling overnight interbank average rate for the United Kingdom, and the euro interbank offered forward rates for Europe; updated April 2, 2013.
[2]Flow of funds data are used for the euro area, Spain, and the United States. Italian bank loans to Italian residents are corrected for securitizations.
[3]Percent of respondents describing lending standards as tightening "considerably" or "somewhat" minus those indicating standards as easing "considerably" or "somewhat" over the previous three months. Survey of changes to credit standards for loans or lines of credit to firms for the euro area; average of surveys on changes in credit standards for commercial and industrial and commercial real estate lending for the United States.
[4]ECB calculations are based on the Eurosystem's weekly financial statement.

Figure 1.6. Monetary Policies and Credit in Emerging Market Economies

In emerging market economies, real policy rates have fallen during the past six months. In addition, the pace of real credit growth has dropped, consistent with easing loan demand. However, in many economies it remains at a level that is generally considered high. Loan demand has been softening, except in emerging Europe, which is recovering from a credit bust. Credit standards have been in tightening territory since 2011, but less so recently.

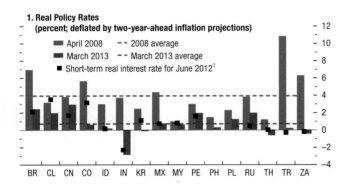

1. Real Policy Rates
(percent; deflated by two-year-ahead inflation projections)

April 2008   2008 average
March 2013   March 2013 average
Short-term real interest rate for June 2012[1]

BR CL CN CO ID IN KR MX MY PE PH PL RU TH TR ZA

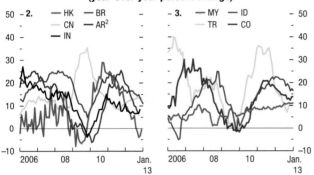

Real Credit Growth
(year-over-year percent change)

2. HK — BR — CN — AR[2] — IN
3. MY — ID — TR — CO

2006 08 10 Jan. 13
2006 08 10 Jan. 13

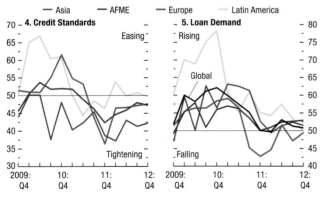

Emerging Market Bank Lending Conditions
(diffusion index; neutral = 50)

Asia   AFME   Europe   Latin America

4. Credit Standards   Easing / Tightening
5. Loan Demand   Rising / Global / Falling

2009: Q4   10: Q4   11: Q4   12: Q4
2009: Q4   10: Q4   11: Q4   12: Q4

Sources: Haver Analytics; IIF Emerging Markets Bank Lending Survey; IMF, *International Financial Statistics*; and IMF staff calculations.
Note: AR = Argentina; BR = Brazil; CL = Chile; CN = China; CO = Colombia; HK = Hong Kong SAR; ID = Indonesia; IN = India; KR = Korea; MX = Mexico; MY = Malaysia; PE = Peru; PH = Philippines; PL = Poland; RU = Russia; TH = Thailand; TR = Turkey; ZA = South Africa; AFME = Africa and Middle East.
[1]Bank of Indonesia rate for Indonesia; the Central Bank of the Republic of Turkey's effective marginal funding cost estimated by the IMF staff for Turkey.
[2]Nominal credit is deflated using the IMF staff's estimate of average provincial inflation.

demand; in the periphery, companies and households continue to struggle against weak balance sheets, or weak income prospects, or both.

Looking ahead, continued low policy interest rates are forecast for the major advanced economies (Figure 1.4, panel 1) and are expected to translate slowly into more dynamic bank lending—provided financial stability risks continue to abate. This process will take much longer in the euro area than in the United States. In Japan, the new quantitative and qualitative easing framework of monetary policy adds substantial further monetary stimulus and should help accelerate the achievement of the Bank of Japan's new 2 percent inflation target.

In many emerging market and developing economies, credit and activity are propelling each other. In some, policy rate hikes and prudential measures reduced the very high pace of credit expansion (Figure 1.6, panels 2 and 3). But in many Asian and Latin American economies, credit expansion has continued at an elevated pace and credit-to-GDP ratios have continued to move up.

With a few exceptions, central banks have held policy rates constant or cut them modestly in response to the 2012 slowdown. Real policy rates thus remain well below pre-2008 levels (Figure 1.6, panel 1). In the meantime, however, activity and capital inflows are reaccelerating, which will likely boost bank funding and ease credit conditions (Figure 1.6, panels 4 and 5). Monetary and regulatory authorities must watch for risks to financial stability that may ensue.

The Fiscal Policy Stance Will Stay Broadly Unchanged

As discussed in the April 2013 *Fiscal Monitor*, policy has evolved broadly as expected in 2012. In advanced economies, general government deficits as a percent of GDP were brought down below 6 percent in 2012, despite weak activity (Figure 1.7, panel 2). However, debt-to-GDP ratios continued to rise (Figure 1.7, panel 3). In emerging market and developing economies, deficit ratios rose modestly in response to weaker activity, while debt ratios fell.

In 2013, the fiscal withdrawal in advanced economies will be some 1 percent of GDP (Figure 1.7, panel 1). The key fiscal drivers of the *World Economic Outlook* (WEO) projections are the following:
- In Japan, fiscal policy was set to tighten as a result of the unwinding of reconstruction-related spend-

ing. However, the passage of a new stimulus equivalent to about 1½ percent of GDP during 2013–14 eases the fiscal stance moderately this year. The deficit will remain close to 10 percent of GDP for the fifth straight year, but is expected to improve markedly in 2014 with the unwinding of the stimulus and reconstruction spending and the planned consumption tax increase in April to 8 percent from 5 percent. What is worrisome is that the debt-to-GDP ratio will continue to rise, reaching 255 percent of GDP in 2018.

- U.S. fiscal policy is assumed to tighten by about 1¾ percent of GDP, which is ½ percentage point of GDP more than in 2012, largely reflecting the budget sequester. The deficit will then still exceed 5 percent of GDP in 2014, and the public debt ratio will stand at about 110 percent. The forecast assumes that the debt ceiling is raised and that the budget sequester is replaced at the end of the current fiscal year with back-loaded measures.

- In the euro area, deficits have already been reduced much more than in Japan or the United States, and the pace of consolidation will drop to ¾ percentage point of GDP in 2013, from a little less than 1½ percentage points in 2012. In particular, Germany will shift from structural tightening to slight loosening, and Italy will tighten by about 1 percent of GDP, down from 2¼ percent. Periphery economies continue to face a dangerous combination of low growth, high interest rates, high deficits, and high debt. In the United Kingdom, fiscal consolidation is now forecast to be slower than was anticipated previously.

In emerging market and developing economies, fiscal policy is expected to remain close to neutral. Elevated growth will push debt ratios farther down, to 30 percent of GDP by 2018. However, some countries continue to face significant fiscal challenges—for example, Middle Eastern oil importers with high energy subsidy spending, several emerging European economies, and India.

Global Growth Is Projected to Continue to Rise Gradually

World growth hit a trough at about 2¼ percent in the second quarter of 2012 and reached 2¾ percent in the second half of the year. Leading indicators point to accelerating activity (Figure 1.1, panel 3; Figure 1.2, panel 1). Real GDP growth is forecast to reach 3¼ percent on an annual average basis in 2013 and

Figure 1.7. Fiscal Policies

Fiscal policy will remain tight in advanced economies and broadly neutral in emerging market and developing economies. The pace of tightening will drop noticeably in the euro area during 2013–14. In advanced economies, debt ratios are forecast to stabilize soon but rise again in the medium term because of entitlement spending. In emerging market and developing economies, debt ratios are projected to continue to decline because of strong growth and low interest rates.

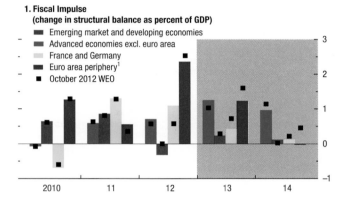

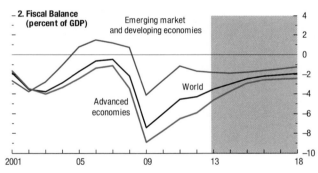

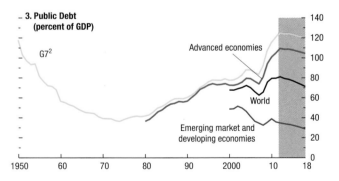

Source: IMF staff estimates.
[1]Greece, Ireland, Italy, Portugal, Spain.
[2]G7 comprises Canada, France, Germany, Italy, Japan, United Kingdom, and United States.

Figure 1.8. GDP Growth

Real GDP growth reaccelerated during 2012 and is forecast to continue to do so. Among the advanced economies, growth is projected to stay subdued in the euro area. Among emerging market and developing economies, the performance of developing Asia and Latin America depend importantly on a reacceleration of activity in India and Brazil, respectively.

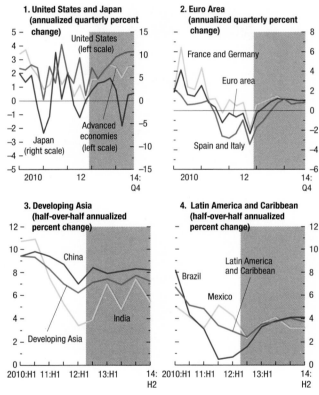

Source: IMF staff estimates.

4 percent in 2014 (see Table 1.1)—broadly unchanged from the January 2013 *WEO Update*. Chapter 2 discusses the projections for the various regions of the world in more detail.

In advanced economies, the recovery will continue to proceed at different speeds. The main revision relates to the U.S. budget sequester, which lowers the U.S. growth forecast for 2013. Following a disappointing end to 2012, easier financial conditions, accommodative monetary policies, recovering confidence, and special factors will support a reacceleration of activity, notwithstanding still-tight fiscal policy in the United States and the euro area. The reacceleration, which assumes that policymakers avoid new setbacks and deliver on their commitments, will become apparent in the second half of 2013, when real GDP growth is forecast to again surpass 2 percent.

- Thanks to increasingly robust private demand, real GDP growth in the United States is forecast to reach about 2 percent in 2013, despite a major fiscal tightening, and accelerate to 3 percent in 2014. Weak growth in the United States in the fourth quarter of 2012 reflected the unwinding of a spurt of inventory investment and defense spending during the third quarter (Figure 1.8, panel 1). Preliminary indicators suggest that private demand remained resilient this year, but across-the-board public spending cuts are expected to take a toll on the recovery going forward.

- Activity in the euro area will pick up very gradually, helped by appreciably less fiscal drag and some easing of lending conditions. However, output will remain subdued—contracting by about ¼ percent in 2013—because of continued fiscal adjustment, financial fragmentation, and ongoing balance sheet adjustments in the periphery economies (Figure 1.8, panel 2). The projection assumes that policy uncertainty does not escalate and further progress is made toward advancing national adjustment and building a strong economic and monetary union.

- Activity in Japan is expected to accelerate sharply during the first quarter of 2013, as the economy receives a lift from the recent fiscal stimulus, a weaker yen, and stronger external demand. Growth will reach 1½ percent in 2013, according to WEO projections, and will soften only slightly in 2014 as private demand continues to garner speed, helped by aggressive new monetary easing offset by the winding down of the stimulus and the consumption tax increase.

In emerging market and developing economies, the expansion of output is expected to become broad based and to accelerate steadily, from 5 percent in the first half of 2012 to close to 6 percent by 2014. The drivers are easy macroeconomic conditions and recovering demand from the advanced economies.

- In Asia, growth has already returned to a healthy pace in China. External demand, solid consumption, a better monsoon season, and policy improvements are expected to lift activity in India (Figure 1.8, panel 3).

- Growth in Latin America will strengthen this year. Activity is expected to recover in Brazil, the region's largest economy, in response to the large policy rate cuts deployed during the past year as well as to measures targeted at boosting private investment (Figure 1.8, panel 4).

- The emerging European and Commonwealth of Independent States (CIS) economies are expected to benefit from the upturn in the advanced economies as well as from easier macroeconomic policies.

- Activity in sub-Saharan Africa is forecast to remain robust, with both resource-rich and lower-income economies benefiting from robust domestic demand.

- The Middle East and North Africa (MENA) region is a notable exception: a pause in oil production growth among oil-exporting countries is expected to lead to a temporary deceleration in the region's economic growth, while ongoing political transitions and a difficult external environment are preventing a quicker recovery in some oil-importing countries.

Inflation Pressure Remains Generally under Control

There are no excess demand pressures in the major advanced economies. Inflation rates also remain generally under control in emerging market and developing economies, although unemployment rates are typically low, current account balances are falling, credit is buoyant, and asset prices are high (Figure 1.9).

Global inflation has fallen to about 3¼ percent from 3¾ percent in early 2012, and it is projected to stay around this level through 2014 (Figure 1.10, panel 1). Food and fuel supply developments will help contain upward pressure on prices of major commodities despite the expected reacceleration in global activity, according to the Commodity Market Review in this WEO report.

- In the major advanced economies, inflation will ease from about 2 percent to 1¾ percent in the United States and from 2¼ percent to 1½ percent in the euro area. Inflation will rise above zero in Japan in 2013 and will temporarily jump in 2014 and 2015 in response to increases in the consumption tax. The Bank of Japan's new quantitative and qualitative easing framework will support a steady acceleration of inflation, consistent with the Bank of Japan's policy objective (Figure 1.10, panels 2 and 3). As discussed in Chapter 3, if central bank inflation targets had not been highly credible, the years of economic slack could easily have produced deflation in many advanced economies.

- Inflation pressure is projected to remain contained in emerging market and developing economies, supported by the recent slowdown and lower food and energy prices (Figure 1.2, panel 6). IMF staff estimates point to slack in emerging Asian economies in 2013, but output is running appreciably above precrisis trends. The latter also holds for the Latin American economies, where WEO output gap estimates are projected to close. The major oil exporters also appear to be operating close to or above capacity, and some MENA economies in transition have seen large price increases in response to shocks. For these or other reasons, pressure is projected to remain fairly high in some economies and regions (Argentina, Venezuela, parts of the MENA region, various CIS and sub-Saharan African economies), spurred by food prices in some cases (India), and could surprise on the upside.

Global Current Account Balances Have Narrowed Further

The setbacks to the global recovery in 2012 were mirrored in a slowing of world trade growth, which had already cooled in 2011. Fluctuations of global trade volumes are generally more amplified than those of world GDP and, in line with earlier experience, trade volumes decelerated sharply (Figure 1.11, panel 1). This attests to the strength of spillovers via the trade channel.

In general, currencies have responded appropriately to recent changes in macroeconomic policies and falling risk aversion: there has been some appreciation of the euro and various emerging market currencies and some depreciation of the U.S. dollar. The yen has depreciated by about 20 percent in real effective terms since mid-2012, in response to expectations for easier

Figure 1.9. Overheating Indicators for the G20 Economies

Domestic overheating indicators point to ample slack in the advanced economies—most indicators flash blue, although less so in Canada. By contrast, a number of yellow and red indicators for the emerging market and developing economies point to capacity constraints. External overheating indicators flash red for Japan. Rather than raising concern, these are symptoms of an internal demand rebalancing process that has helped bring down global current account imbalances.

In Germany, which is the other major surplus economy, the rebalancing process continues to lag. Unemployment is at postunification lows, reflecting both robust economic performance and structural changes in the labor market, and does not reflect overheating. The yellow or red indicators for India, Indonesia, and Turkey point to external vulnerabilities. Credit indicators point to excesses in many emerging market economies. Other financial indicators are mostly reassuring about overheating, except for Brazil.

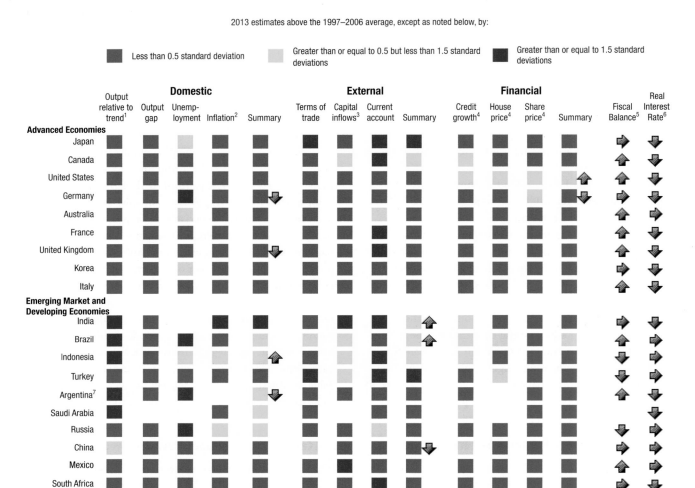

Sources: Australia Bureau of Statistics; Bank for International Settlements; CEIC; *Global Property Guide;* Haver Analytics; IMF, *Balance of Payments Statistics;* IMF, *International Financial Statistics;* National Bureau of Statistics of China; Organization for Economic Cooperation and Development; and IMF staff estimates.

Note: For each indicator, except as noted below, economies are assigned colors based on projected 2013 values relative to their precrisis (1997–2006) average. Each indicator is scored as red = 2, yellow = 1, and blue = 0; summary scores are calculated as the sum of selected component scores divided by the maximum possible sum of those scores. Summary blocks are assigned red if the summary score is greater than or equal to 0.66, yellow if greater than or equal to 0.33 but less than 0.66, and blue if less than 0.33. When data are missing, no color is assigned. Arrows up (down) indicate hotter (colder) conditions compared with the October 2012 WEO.

[1]Output more than 2.5 percent above the precrisis trend is indicated by red. Output less than 2.5 percent below the trend is indicated by blue. Output within ±2.5 percent of the precrisis trend is indicated by yellow.

[2]A new methodology is employed in the April 2013 WEO for the following inflation-targeting economies: Australia, Brazil, Canada, Indonesia, Korea, Mexico, South Africa, Turkey, and United Kingdom. End-of-period inflation above the country's target inflation band from the midpoint is assigned yellow; end-of-period inflation more than two times the inflation band from the midpoint is assigned red. For the non-inflation-targeting economies, red is assigned if end-of-period inflation is approximately 10 percent or higher, yellow if it is approximately 5 to 9 percent, and blue if it is less than 5 percent.

[3]Capital inflows refer to the latest available value relative to the 1997–2006 average of capital inflows as a percent of GDP.

[4]The indicators for credit growth, house price growth, and share price growth refer to the latest available value relative to the 1997–2006 average of output growth.

[5]Arrows in the fiscal balance column represent the forecast change in the structural balance as a percent of GDP over the period 2012–13. An improvement of more than 0.5 percent of GDP is indicated by an up arrow; a deterioration of more than 0.5 percent of GDP is indicated by a down arrow.

[6]Real policy interest rates below zero are identified by a down arrow; real interest rates above 3 percent are identified by an up arrow. Real policy interest rates are deflated by two-year-ahead inflation projections.

[7]The data for Argentina are officially reported data. The IMF has, however, issued a declaration of censure and called on Argentina to adopt remedial measures to address the quality of the official consumer price index (CPI-GBA) data. Alternative data sources have shown considerably higher inflation rates than the official data since 2007. In this context, the IMF is also using alternative estimates of CPI inflation for the surveillance of macroeconomic developments in Argentina.

Figure 1.10. Global Inflation

(Year-over-year percent change unless indicated otherwise)

Global inflation has slowed and is projected to continue to do so, helped by stabilizing commodity prices. In the major advanced economies, domestic inflation is running below medium-term inflation targets. This suggests that there is more room for easing monetary policy. In emerging market and developing economies, emerging capacity constraints mean that inflation could surprise on the upside, and policy may have to tighten again or inflation may pick up.

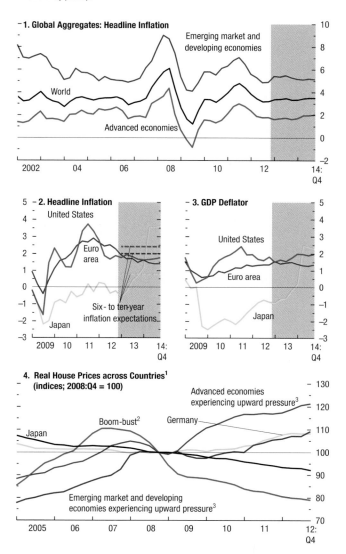

Figure 1.11. Global Imbalances

The latest slowdown in global trade is broadly consistent with the slowdown in global GDP. It has meant that global imbalances have declined modestly again. Whether imbalances stay narrow or widen again in the medium term depends on the extent to which output losses relative to precrisis trends are largely permanent: WEO projections assume they are, consistent with historical evidence. Although international capital flows have declined, persistent current account imbalances mean that economies' net international investment positions have not changed much.

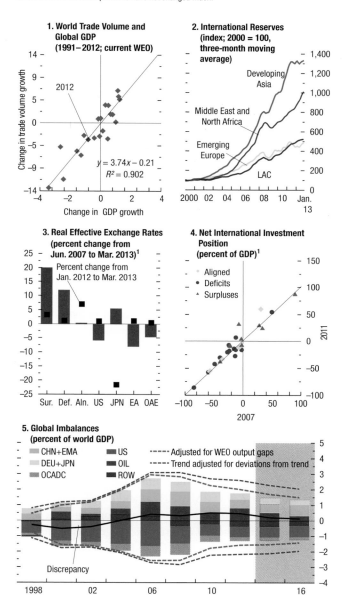

Sources: Haver Analytics; Consensus Economics; Organization for Economic Cooperation and Development, *Global Property Guide;* national sources; and IMF staff estimates.
[1]For the following countries, regional or metropolitan averages were used instead of national composites: Estonia, Hungary, India, Latvia, Lithuania, Philippines, Poland, Ukraine, and Uruguay.
[2]Boom-bust countries: Bulgaria, Croatia, Cyprus, Czech Republic, Denmark, Estonia, Finland, France, Greece, Iceland, Ireland, Italy, Latvia, Lithuania, Malta, Netherlands, New Zealand, Poland, Russia, Slovak Republic, Slovenia, South Africa, Spain, Turkey, Ukraine, United Kingdom, United States. Boom-bust countries are those in which real house prices increased by more than 10 percent in the run-up to the global financial crisis (2002–07) and have declined since then.
[3]Upward pressure countries: Australia, Austria, Belgium, Canada, Colombia, China, Hong Kong SAR, Hungary, India, Israel, Malaysia, Norway, Philippines, Switzerland, Singapore, Sweden, Uruguay.

Sources: IMF, *International Financial Statistics;* IMF, International Investment Position database; and IMF staff estimates.
Note: Aln. = aligned EM economies; CHN+EMA = China, Hong Kong SAR, Indonesia, Korea, Malaysia, Philippines, Singapore, Taiwan Province of China, Thailand; Def. = deficit EM economies; DEU+JPN = Germany and Japan; EA = euro area; EM = emerging market and developing economies; LAC = Latin America and the Caribbean; OCADC = Bulgaria, Croatia, Czech Republic, Estonia, Greece, Hungary, Ireland, Latvia, Lithuania, Poland, Portugal, Romania, Slovak Republic, Slovenia, Spain, Turkey, United Kingdom; OAE = other advanced economies; OIL = oil exporters; Sur. = surplus EM economies; ROW = rest of the world; US = United States.
[1]Classifications are based on IMF (2012a).

monetary policy and higher inflation in the future as well as a higher trade deficit and lower global risk aversion.

Taking a longer-term perspective, global current account imbalances have narrowed considerably (Figure 1.11, panel 5). Most of the adjustment took place during the Great Recession of 2008–09, when global growth was negative, and reflects lower demand in external deficit economies. This came with large declines in investment in these economies, some increase in private saving, and much lower government saving. Exchange rate adjustment played some role; policy adjustment in the key areas identified in the *Pilot External Sector Report* (IMF, 2012a) contributed disappointingly little.

The question is whether the narrowing of global imbalances will last. This depends on the future course of output and, in turn, output gaps in external deficit and surplus economies. WEO estimates do not see major differences between the output gaps in deficit and surplus economies. This may appear surprising but is consistent with widespread evidence that financial crises of the types that affected many deficit economies tend to involve permanent losses in the level of output relative to precrisis trends.[1] Accordingly, as output gaps in deficit economies close, global imbalances move broadly sideways in WEO projections (Figure 1.11, panel 5): the increase in investment in deficit economies will not be very large, and its effect on current accounts will be partly offset by rising government saving. However, what happens if output gaps in deficit economies are larger than estimated? Recovery in these economies would then come with a greater rebound in investment and a widening of current account imbalances, notwithstanding some increase in government saving.

The assessment in the summer 2012 *Pilot External Sector Report* (IMF, 2012a) and developments in exchange rates and WEO projections since then suggest that the real effective exchange rates of the major economies are not far from levels consistent with medium-term fundamentals (Figure 1.11, panel 3). The current account positions of the euro area and the United States are somewhat weaker and their real effective exchange rates are modestly stronger relative to medium-term fundamentals than they would be with more desirable policies. The evidence on valuation

of the yen is mixed, with valuation indicators based on the real effective exchange rate and current account pointing in opposite directions. As for the surplus economies—including China, Korea, Malaysia, and Singapore—current account positions remain, in most cases, moderately stronger and currencies moderately weaker than desirable, despite welcome adjustments, most notably less accumulation of reserves (Figure 1.11, panel 2). A new *External Sector Report* with a comprehensive assessment will be available in a few months.

The policies required to further reduce global imbalances remain broadly unchanged. The two major surplus economies need more consumption (China) and more investment (Germany). The major deficit economies, notably the United States, need to boost national saving through fiscal consolidation; other deficit economies also need structural reforms to rebuild competitiveness.

On the financial side, gross and net capital flows have declined relative to precrisis peaks, although there has been a noticeable shift from bank flows to debt securities flows. Overall, net capital flows have remained sizable, however, and net international asset and liability positions remain close to 2007 levels, suggesting that vulnerabilities from net external positions have not eased materially (Figure 1.11, panel 4).

Risks Are More Balanced in the Short Term

The short-term risk picture has improved considerably, mainly because policy action has lowered some major short-term risks, especially a breakup of the euro area and an economic contraction resulting from a plunge over the U.S. fiscal cliff. In addition, short-term risks for a hard landing in key emerging economies have abated. Nonetheless, near-term risks in Europe could return and other downside risks persist.

A quantitative risk assessment

The fan chart confirms that short-term risks have declined, although not significantly (Figure 1.12, panel 1). A caveat is that the fan chart does not directly assess these risks but instead draws on some market- and survey-based indicators as well as the distribution of past forecast errors to gauge uncertainty around the forecast. Overall, the fan chart suggests that the probability that global growth will fall below 2 percent in 2013 has dropped to about 2 percent, from 17 percent

---

[1]For supporting empirical evidence, see Chapter 4 of the October 2009 *World Economic Outlook*.

at the time of the October 2012 WEO.[2] For 2014, the probability is less than 8 percent. Oil prices remain an important source of downside risk, in view of elevated geopolitical tensions (Figure 1.12, panel 2).

The IMF staff's Global Projection Model (GPM) suggests that the probability that there will be recession (two successive quarters of negative growth) during 2013 in Japan has declined sharply, to about 5 percent from about 30 percent in 2012 (Figure 1.13, panel 1). For the euro area, however, the probability of recession remains about 50 percent, because activity contracted sharply during the fourth quarter and leading indicators for the first quarter of 2013 signal not growth, but stabilization at best.

A qualitative risk assessment

Short-term downside risks are lower than at the time of the October 2012 WEO. Risks related to oil supply shocks are broadly unchanged and those related to geopolitical factors feature new dimensions. Risks related to a hard landing of key emerging economies have receded. Others revolve around the following factors:

- *Adjustment fatigue or general policy backtracking in a financially fragmented euro area where financial markets remain highly vulnerable to shifts in sentiment, as evidenced by recent events:* The forecasts assume that significant progress is made in repairing bank and sovereign balance sheets as well as in implementing structural reforms. But progress could be held back by adjustment fatigue. Furthermore, efforts to strengthen the euro area architecture may stall. In such an event, periphery sovereigns could again come under intense market pressure, although the European Central Bank's (ECB's) Outright Monetary Transactions (OMTs) would presumably limit the increase in spreads. Furthermore, unless more progress is made in restructuring banks and moving to a genuine banking union, lending rates may come down less than expected even if sovereign spreads continue to decline. In this regard, it remains to be seen what repercussions the rescue package for Cyprus will have for financial market fragmentation.
- *The U.S. budget sequester and debt ceiling:* U.S. risks have abated thanks to the resolution of the

[2]This reduction reflects mainly lower baseline risk. Baseline risk is lower because April forecasts for the current year have proven more accurate than October forecasts for the year ahead, reflecting the additional information that becomes available over the ensuing six months.

Figure 1.12. Risks to the Global Outlook

Risks around WEO projections have narrowed, according to market metrics. These metrics continue to point to oil prices as the primary source of downside risks to global growth, while S&P 500 option prices point to some upside risks.

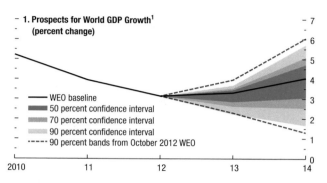

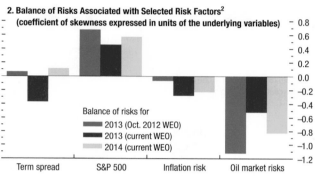

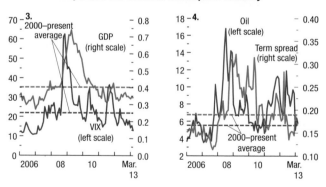

Sources: Bloomberg, L.P.; Chicago Board Options Exchange; Consensus Economics; and IMF staff estimates.
[1]The fan chart shows the uncertainty around the WEO central forecast with 50, 70, and 90 percent confidence intervals. As shown, the 70 percent confidence interval includes the 50 percent interval, and the 90 percent confidence interval includes the 50 and 70 percent intervals. See Appendix 1.2 of the April 2009 WEO for details. The 90 percent bands from the October 2012 WEO for the one-year-ahead and two-year-ahead forecasts are shown relative to the current baseline.
[2]Bars depict the coefficient of skewness expressed in units of the underlying variables. The values for inflation risks and oil market risks are entered with the opposite sign since they represent downside risks to growth. Note that the risks associated with the S&P 500 for 2014 are based on options contracts for March 2014.
[3]GDP measures the purchasing-power-parity-weighted average dispersion of GDP forecasts for the G7 economies (Canada, France, Germany, Italy, Japan, United Kingdom, United States), Brazil, China, India, and Mexico. VIX = Chicago Board Options Exchange S&P 500 Implied Volatility Index. Term spread measures the average dispersion of term spreads implicit in interest rate forecasts for Germany, Japan, United Kingdom, and United States. Oil measures the dispersion of one-year-ahead oil price forecasts for West Texas Intermediate crude oil. Forecasts are from Consensus Economics surveys.

Figure 1.13. Recession and Deflation Risks

Risks for recessions during 2013 have stayed broadly unchanged or receded. They remain relatively high in the advanced economies. The same holds for deflation risks. Deflation vulnerabilities are particularly elevated in some euro area periphery economies.

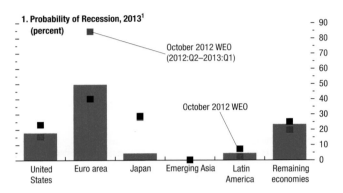

1. Probability of Recession, 2013[1]
(percent)

October 2012 WEO
(2012:Q2–2013:Q1)

October 2012 WEO

United States | Euro area | Japan | Emerging Asia | Latin America | Remaining economies

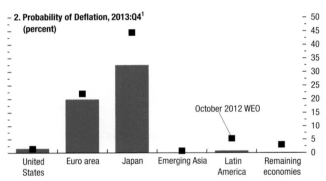

2. Probability of Deflation, 2013:Q4[1]
(percent)

October 2012 WEO

United States | Euro area | Japan | Emerging Asia | Latin America | Remaining economies

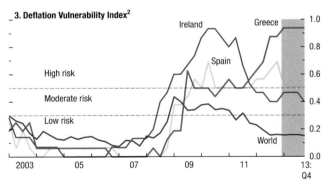

3. Deflation Vulnerability Index[2]

Ireland | Greece | Spain | World

High risk

Moderate risk

Low risk

2003 | 05 | 07 | 09 | 11 | 13: Q4

Source: IMF staff estimates.
[1]Emerging Asia: China, Hong Kong SAR, India, Indonesia, Korea, Malaysia, Philippines, Singapore, Taiwan Province of China, Thailand; Latin America: Brazil, Chile, Colombia, Mexico, Peru; remaining economies: Argentina, Australia, Bulgaria, Canada, Czech Republic, Denmark, Estonia, Israel, New Zealand, Norway, Russia, South Africa, Sweden, Switzerland, Turkey, United Kingdom, Venezuela.
[2]For details on the construction of this indicator, see Kumar (2003) and Decressin and Laxton (2009). The indicator is expanded to include house prices.

fiscal cliff. But the budget sequester has now begun and, if not reversed soon, will continue to restrain economic activity in late 2013 and beyond. Moreover, the U.S. debt ceiling will need to be raised again later this year—failure to do so would be very damaging to the global economy.

However, real GDP growth could also be higher than projected. Improvements in financial market conditions have been stronger than expected, so confidence could surprise on the upside, bringing a greater rebound of investment and durables consumption, especially in the United States. The Federal Reserve may then have to raise policy rates earlier than planned, prompting capital outflows from emerging market economies (Figure 1.14, green line). However, in this event, any commensurate increase in emerging market risk spreads would likely be limited and temporary, and the overall result would be positive. Alternatively, more rapid progress toward a comprehensive banking union in the euro area could further decrease risk aversion and boost household and business confidence, and these could spur demand and also help improve any growth dividend emanating from structural reforms (Figure 1.15, red line).

Risks Are Still High in the Medium Term

Medium-term risks fall into five categories and tilt to the downside: (1) very low growth or stagnation in the euro area; (2) fiscal trouble in the United States or Japan; (3) less slack than expected in the advanced economies or a sudden burst of inflation; (4) risks related to unconventional monetary policy; and (5) lower potential output in key emerging market economies.

Euro area risks: The forecast assumes that periphery risk spreads will gradually contract, fiscal adjustment will ease appreciably starting during 2014–15, and investment and consumption will rebound. However, in the near term, conditions in the periphery will remain strained: sovereign debt burdens are likely to increase further; banks will continue to face deleveraging pressure, elevated funding costs, deteriorating asset quality, and weak profits; and many corporations and households carry heavy debt burdens. In the face of high taxes, tight lending conditions, and weak domestic demand, investment may fail to take off, growth may disappoint, fiscal revenues may fall short, and it may not be possible to ease off on consolidation as

Figure 1.14. Interest Rate Risk Scenarios

(Percent unless noted otherwise)

The Global Integrated Monetary and Fiscal Model (GIMF) is used here to consider scenarios under which interest rates in the major advanced economies rise from their current low levels much sooner than envisaged in the WEO baseline. Three potential causes are considered: a faster-than-expected recovery in the U.S. economy; less excess capacity than expected in G3 economies; and rising concerns about fiscal sustainability. In the faster-than-expected U.S. recovery (green line), rising private demand quickly closes the output gap, putting upward pressure on inflation and thus prompting the Federal Reserve to raise the policy interest rate in 2014. Higher returns in the United States and increased optimism about advanced economy growth prospects lead to some capital flowing from emerging market economies back to advanced economies. However, the positive impact from higher advanced economy growth more than offsets the impact of capital outflows, and all regions of the world experience faster growth in 2014 and 2015. In the scenario with less excess supply than expected in the baseline (red line), the misperception starts in 2014 and is largest in the United States, roughly half the U.S. magnitude in the euro area, and a quarter of the U.S. magnitude in Japan.

With less excess supply than expected, inflation pressure starts to build in 2014 despite growth being weaker than in the baseline. Consequently, monetary policy starts to tighten in 2014, and interest rates in advanced economies are above baseline for most of the WEO horizon. Lower-than-expected supply capacity in advanced economies results in below-baseline GDP growth from 2014 onward, with negative implications for growth in all emerging market economies. In the scenario under which markets become concerned about medium-term fiscal sustainability (yellow line), sovereign risk premiums rise sharply in the United States and Japan, but more modestly elsewhere in 2015. Heightened fiscal sustainability concerns also lead to further increases in risk premiums for firms and households worldwide. With policy interest rates still very low in advanced economies in the baseline, there is only limited scope for monetary policy to offset the impact on market interest rates, and GDP growth falls sharply along with inflation in 2015. In emerging market economies, although the use of available monetary policy space helps mitigate the impact, growth also falls notably below baseline for several years.

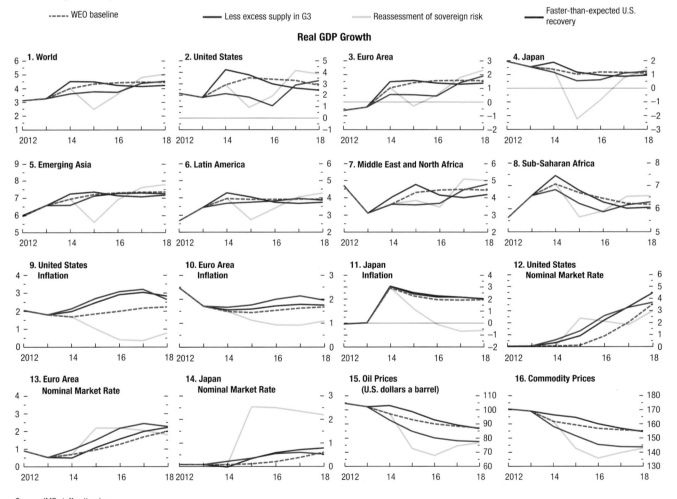

Source: IMF staff estimates.
Note: G3 = euro area, Japan, United States.

Figure 1.15. Euro Area Scenarios

(Percent unless noted otherwise)

These scenarios are simulated using EUROMOD, a new IMF model of the global economy, and consider the implications of two alternative paths for the euro area. The downside scenario (yellow line) embodies a continual process of deterioration whereby weaker-than-expected macroeconomic outcomes from a reduction in investment (as confidence wanes) heighten concerns about fiscal sustainability. This heightened concern leads to rising risk premiums and additional tightening in fiscal policy, further weakening the macroeconomic environment and confidence, notwithstanding easing by the European Central Bank (ECB). Specifically, in this scenario investment in the periphery economies falls by about 6percent each year, corporate interest rates are about 3 percent higher, and the average (of the short- and long-term) sovereign rate is 1 percent higher than in the WEO baseline by 2018. The higher sovereign rate prompts periphery economies to tighten the fiscal stance by an additional ¼ percent of GDP each year. In core economies, ECB easing eclipses a modest increase in risk premiums and interest rates end up lower than in the WEO baseline. The increase in risk premiums spills over into other regions of the world.

In the upside scenario (red line), faster-than-expected progress both on establishing the Single Supervisory Mechanism (SSM) and on giving the European Stability Mechanism (ESM) the ability to recapitalize banks sets the stage for better-than-expected macroeconomic outcomes in 2014 and beyond. Furthermore, the reforms implemented at a national level begin to pay off sooner than expected, starting in 2014, with some offsetting effects from an increase in the policy rate by the ECB. As a result, sovereign and corporate risk premiums start to decline. Declines in the average sovereign and corporate interest rates are largest in the periphery, amounting to about 0.7 and 1.5 percentage points, respectively, relative to the WEO baseline. In the core countries, the tightening of monetary policy is the dominant effect on all interest rates, so the average sovereign and corporate rates rise relative to the WEO baseline. Starting in 2014, the annual increase in productivity is roughly 0.5 percent in periphery countries and 0.1 percent in core countries, while the annual increase in investment is almost 5 percent in the periphery and 0.8 percent in the core.

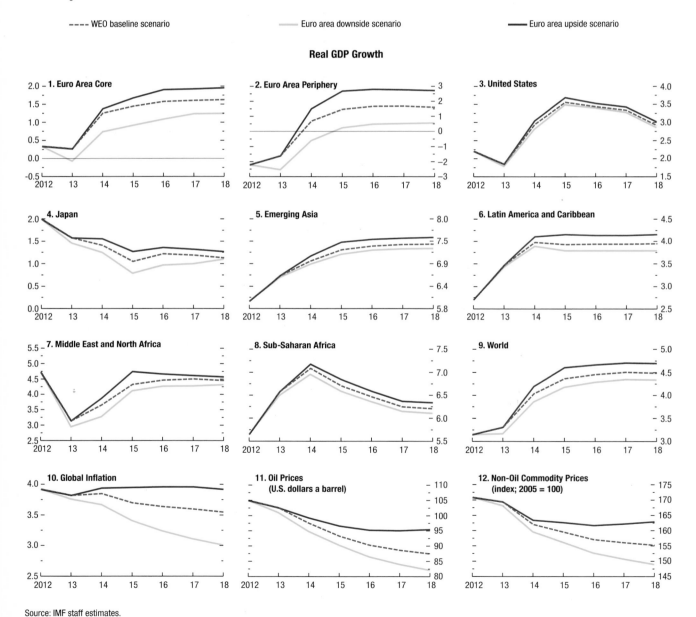

----- WEO baseline scenario — Euro area downside scenario — Euro area upside scenario

Real GDP Growth

Source: IMF staff estimates.

projected. For as long as the major periphery sovereigns maintain market access, with the support of OMT asset purchases if necessary, the damage to growth may be contained and the impact on the rest of the world limited (Figure 1.15, yellow line). However, the damage and the spillovers could be much worse if pessimism builds on pessimism and leads to a major cutoff of credit to periphery sovereigns or if stagnation raises doubts about the viability of the EMU.

Fiscal risks: The main risks relate to fiscal policies in the United States and, especially, Japan, which are not sustainable. It is therefore disconcerting that the prospects for comprehensive fiscal reform have dimmed in the United States and that policymakers in Japan have renewed fiscal stimulus before adopting a strong medium-term consolidation plan and growth strategy. The WEO projections assume that neither economy will have trouble financing its deficits and debt, because risk aversion will keep up demand for their bonds, their central banks will continue their quantitative easing programs, and deficits will continue to be reduced in the United States and will be lower in Japan starting in 2014. However, as discussed in previous WEO reports, a medium-term tail risk is the perception that these economies' political systems will be unable to deliver the required adjustments in a timely manner, which could scare off investors.[3] An increase in the sovereign risk premiums for these economies could have a large effect on global activity. Even a moderate increase in interest rates on their sovereign debt—for example, in response to a general reallocation of savings from foreign into very liquid domestic assets—would appreciably lower world growth (Figure 1.14, yellow line). Sovereign and corporate risk premiums would likely increase everywhere and confidence would suffer, setting back global investment and consumption. G3 (euro area, Japan, United States) fiscal policy may then tighten in an attempt to regain confidence among investors. With G3 monetary policy rates still low, there will be limited scope for policy rate cuts to offset the impact of higher risk premiums on the cost of borrowing. G3 exchange rates would depreciate, but with little effect, as global demand falls.

Monetary policy risks: The WEO projections assume that interest rates in the major advanced economies stay close to the zero lower bound for several years

[3]See Box 1.4 of the October 2010 *World Economic Outlook* and Box 1.2 of the October 2012 *World Economic Outlook*.

and that exit from unconventional monetary policies can proceed gradually and without unsettling financial markets. This assumption is subject to two types of risk: risk related to less-than-estimated potential output and risk related to unconventional monetary policies.

- *Problems related to less excess supply than estimated in G3 economies:* The WEO projections see appreciable slack in the advanced economies, even though inflation has been remarkably stable. Chapter 3 attributes the latter to the stability of inflation expectations and high central bank credibility as well as to nominal rigidities. However, what if inflation has been stable because there is much less slack than estimated? Expected and actual inflation would then move up sooner than projected, although a sudden inflation scare, such as in 1994—when U.S. unemployment dropped below 6 percent and markets thought the Federal Reserve was falling behind the curve—looks unlikely in the medium term. Rather, inflation expectations would likely increase gradually. Assuming such rising expectations met with timely G3 fiscal and monetary tightening, the increase in inflation would be temporary and limited and spillovers from the G3 to the rest of the world would be moderately deflationary (Figure 1.14, red line). This would contrast with the experience of the 1970s and early 1980s, when central banks were much too slow to raise interest rates and very large rate hikes became necessary to bring inflation and expectations back under control. These hikes had very damaging effects domestically and on emerging market economies.

- *Problems related to unconventional monetary policies:* Clearly, such policies are helpful in supporting confidence and activity, but they come with risks for the medium term. These risks fall into two categories: risks related to side effects from very low interest rates and the policies themselves, and risks related to the unwinding of these policies.

  o *Risks related to side effects* are broadly unchanged since the October 2012 WEO and are discussed in depth in the April 2013 GFSR. The lengthy period of very low short-term interest rates and unconventional monetary policies may encourage unduly risky lending, balance sheet mismatches, and high leverage. There are now some signs of financial engineering (such as repurchases of equities with funds raised by issuing debt securities) but not of asset price bubbles in advanced economies. However, a growing

Figure 1.16. Capacity and Credit in Emerging Market Economies

WEO output gap estimates do not point to major excess demand pressures. However, many Asian and Latin American emerging market economies operate appreciably above precrisis trends. And they have seen a large run-up in credit, even relative to unusually buoyant output. Recent shortfalls in activity from projections have prompted significant downward revisions to medium-term output levels.

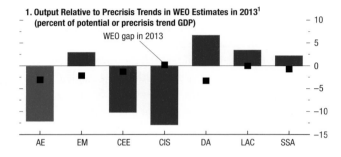

1. Output Relative to Precrisis Trends in WEO Estimates in 2013[1]
(percent of potential or precrisis trend GDP)

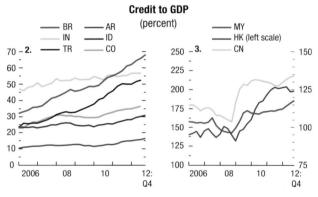

Credit to GDP
(percent)

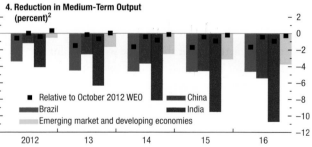

4. Reduction in Medium-Term Output
(percent)[2]

Sources: Haver Analytics; IMF, *International Financial Statistics;* and IMF staff calculations.
Note: AE = advanced economies; AR = Argentina; BR = Brazil; CEE = central and eastern Europe; CIS = Commonwealth of Independent States; CN = China; CO = Colombia; DA = developing Asia; EM = emerging market economies; HK = Hong Kong SAR; ID = Indonesia; IN = India; LAC = Latin America and the Caribbean; MY = Malaysia; SSA = sub-Saharan Africa; TR = Turkey.
[1]Precrisis trend is defined as the geometric average of real GDP level growth between 1996 and 2006.
[2]Relative to the September 2011 WEO.

concern is that corporations in emerging market economies have been leveraging up, including in foreign-currency-denominated debt. Accordingly, were capital flows to emerging market economies to reverse suddenly, they could expose vulnerabilities in these economies.

o *Risks associated with the unwinding of central bank balance sheets* reflect the extent to which central banks may face significant trade-offs between price stability and financial stability in the process of tightening monetary conditions. Such risks are particularly relevant for central banks that have been purchasing large amounts of debt securities with long maturities, such as the Federal Reserve and the Bank of Japan, which recently adopted continued monthly asset purchases, or the Bank of England.[4] In principle, central banks can tighten monetary conditions simply by raising the interest rate on excess reserves, but unpredictable variations in the transmission to broader financial conditions could make it quite difficult for policymakers to set that rate appropriately. Under such circumstances, central banks can drain some reserves from the banking system by issuing term deposits or engaging in reverse repurchase agreements, but the scope for using such tools is likely to be limited. Another approach for reabsorbing liquidity would be to issue debt obligations that can be held outside the banking system, but some central banks (including the Federal Reserve) have no legal authority to issue their own paper, and others could face opposition from a heavily indebted sovereign. Finally, the central bank can shrink the size of its balance sheet by selling its securities in the open market, but engaging in such sales at a rapid and unpredictable pace could have adverse effects on financial market functioning. In effect, central banks could face a difficult choice between exit that is associated with excessive inflation and exit that unsettles financial markets.

Emerging market risks: Activity in emerging markets has been strong but less so than projected during the past couple of years. While cyclical factors have played a role, so have permanent shocks—markdowns to medium-term output have now reached almost 4 percent since the September 2011 WEO (Figure 1.16,

[4]The ECB has declared its readiness to intervene in sovereign debt markets to stem convertibility risks but has yet to make any purchases. The expansion of its balance sheet is largely related to refinancing operations that unwind naturally.

panel 4). The WEO forecast, however, continues to see strong growth ahead, averaging about 6 percent annually during 2013–18. An important risk is that recent forecast disappointments are symptomatic of deeper, structural problems, heralding cutbacks in investment or capital outflows and lower-than-forecast growth. The risks for such an outcome are present in the short term, but they are more relevant for the medium term. Were investment to disappoint in the BRICS (Brazil, Russia, India, China, South Africa), the result would be significantly reduced global growth, inflation, and commodity prices (Figure 1.17). If this came with capital outflows, the effect on BRICS output would be appreciably larger. Also, contagion would likely raise the risk spreads of many other emerging market economies. For the advanced economies, the effect of falling external demand on output would outweigh the effect of returning capital. In such a scenario, global growth would dip to about 1½ percent, implying a decline in output per capita—the first such recession in global output per capita to originate in emerging market economies.

Policy Challenges Center on Debt in Advanced Economies and Potential Excesses in Emerging Market and Developing Economies

The global economy is on the mend again, but policies in the advanced economies are unusually tight on the fiscal front and gaining insufficient traction on the monetary front (Box 1.1). Among the risks ahead, the most insidious relate to debt overhangs and fiscal deficits in advanced economies and potential output growth and budding financial excesses in emerging market and developing economies. These risks may appear far away, but tackling them proactively would improve confidence and investment in the short term and set the global economy on a more sustainable medium-term growth trajectory.

Requirements in Advanced Economies

Fiscal tightening must continue at a pace the recovery can bear

Given still-high public debt levels and attendant risks, fiscal consolidation over the medium term needs to continue. The April 2013 *Fiscal Monitor* highlights these most pressing requirements:

- *Strong medium-term plans*: The United States and Japan need strong medium-term plans to arrest and reverse

the increase in their public debt ratios—the recent fiscal stimulus in Japan makes this even more urgent.

- *Entitlement reform:* Only limited progress has been made on entitlement reform. Almost no progress has been made in tackling health care spending, which is on an unsustainable trajectory, with projections indicating very large increases in net present value terms in many advanced economies.

- *Calibrating short-term fiscal adjustment:* Fiscal plans for 2013 are broadly appropriate in the euro area. In the United Kingdom, where recovery is weak owing to lackluster demand, consideration should be given to greater near-term flexibility in the fiscal adjustment path.[5] In Japan, the stimulus will support the new monetary policy framework but also increases fiscal vulnerabilities—the authorities plan to announce a medium-term fiscal consolidation plan this summer. In the United States, the concern is that the budget sequester will lead to excessive consolidation. Some advanced economies where private demand has been chronically disappointing should consider smoothing the pace of consolidation if they have the fiscal policy room to maneuver. By contrast, should growth surprise on the upside, policymakers should take advantage of the opportunity to reduce headline deficits faster.

Progress in putting in place medium-term fiscal plans and entitlement reforms would also help quell concerns that have been expressed about the fiscal dominance of monetary policy following the massive central bank purchases of government paper since mid-2008 (Figure 1.4, panel 6). The fear is that when the time comes to raise interest rates to forestall inflation, central banks will be hesitant to do so because of potential losses on their own balance sheets as well as pressure from overindebted governments. The more progress is made in lowering future fiscal deficits in the advanced economies, the greater is the scope to pursue supportive monetary policy without triggering concern about fiscal dominance, central bank independence, or a resurgence of inflation.

Monetary policy needs to stay easy

Monetary policy needs to stay highly accommodative to support activity as fiscal policy tightens. The challenges facing central banks are to decide what more, if anything, to do and how to prepare for the eventual exit

---

[5]On a fiscal year basis (2013/14), structural tightening, as measured by the change in the cyclically adjusted primary balance, is expected to be around 1 percentage point of potential GDP.

Figure 1.17. Emerging Market Downside Scenarios
(Percent, unless noted otherwise)

These scenarios are simulated using EUROMOD, a new IMF model of the global economy, and consider the implications of weaker private investment in emerging market economies as well as capital outflows. Given that private investment demand in emerging market economies has surprised on the downside recently, the first scenario (red line) has investment demand in the BRICS 10 percent below the WEO baseline level in 2013, but recovering fairly quickly back to baseline by 2016.

In the second scenario (yellow line), in addition to the fall in investment, capital outflows from emerging market economies lead to a sharp tightening in financial conditions. In the BRICS, sovereign and corporate risk premiums rise sharply in 2013, while the tightening in financial conditions in other emerging market economies is roughly half the magnitude of that in the BRICS. The tightening in financial conditions is short lived, with risk premiums back to baseline levels by 2016.

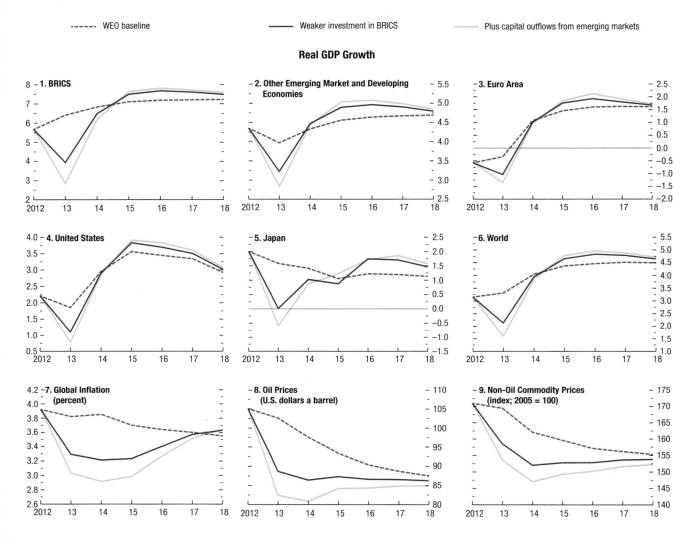

Source: IMF staff estimates.
Note: BRICS = Brazil, Russia, India, China, South Africa.

from unconventional policies. The latter may require changes to regulations or laws governing the activity of central banks, which could take time to implement. There are various options for the short term:

- *Conventional easing:* Little room is left for this option except in the euro area, where domestic (GDP) inflation has run well below the ECB's close-to-but-below 2 percent target since 2009 (Figure 1.10, panel 3), and headline inflation is projected to do so over the medium term (Figure 1.10, panel 2).

- *Better communications:* The Federal Reserve's forward policy guidance appropriately stresses that inflation will be allowed to move slightly above the 2 percent long-term target without necessarily triggering a rate hike, provided long-term inflation expectations remain well anchored and unemployment stays above 6½ percent. This may help bring down perceived real interest rates.

- *Changes to monetary policy frameworks:* Some are advocating that central banks switch to nominal income targeting. Although there are arguments in favor of such a shift, it goes against the principle of "targeting what you can hit." Furthermore, if the concern is to better anchor long-term inflation expectations so as to gain more room for short-term policy maneuvering, targeting a rising path for the price level—or, equivalently, targeting the *average* rate of inflation over a period of several years—appears superior.

- *Unconventional easing:* Purchases of assets, long-term refinancing operations, and other interventions in financial markets are helping reduce funding costs and strengthen confidence. The main problems with monetary policy transmission now are the result of weak banks in crisis economies or, in Japan, because of the zero lower bound on interest rates and continued deflation. Whereas in the United States the banking sector has been gaining strength, in the euro area, the weaknesses show few signs of abating. The best way to address continued euro area weakness is through a range of policies to strengthen bank balance sheets, including progress toward a banking union.

- *Recalibrating supervisory policy stances:* On the one hand, more bank lending is important to sustaining recovery; on the other hand, more capital and liquidity are necessary for building a safer financial system. It is very difficult to make progress on both fronts at the same time, unless public sectors stand ready to put more capital into weak but viable banks or to subsidize new lending. Examples of the latter are Japan's Loan

Support Program and the United Kingdom's Funding for Lending Scheme (FLS). Although it is still early days, so far the FLS's impact has been limited, encouraging mortgage lending more than lending to small and medium-size businesses. Within the euro area, prudential practices have contributed to financial fragmentation, with supervisors in core economies discouraging lending to periphery economies for fear of bank losses that may hit the national fiscal purse. These incentives are difficult to address, except by moving into a comprehensive banking union.

Concern that easy monetary policy may trigger high inflation appears overblown in the current situation. Chapter 3 emphasizes that Phillips curves have become flatter and inflation expectations better anchored during the past 20 years. However, central banks should have clear strategies for ensuring that long-term inflation expectations stay well anchored. This may become a challenge if the economies rebound strongly while their central banks' balance sheets remain very large. Central banks would then need all the legal and operational freedom they could get to reabsorb this liquidity—including the ability to issue their own paper.

Policymakers should consider the complications and risks associated with exceptionally easy monetary policies. More progress with medium- and long-term fiscal adjustment, including entitlement reform, would lower the need for near-term fiscal consolidation; and more progress in mending weak balance sheets would foster the transmission of low interest rates to the real economy. Progress on both fronts would be very important to lower the spillovers and risks emanating from unconventional monetary policies.

Financial policies can help improve monetary policy transmission

Financial policies need to address a variety or challenges, which are discussed in the April 2013 GFSR, including fostering better pass-through of monetary policy to the real economy. To that end, measures for building stronger banks are especially urgent in the euro area. Relative to U.S. banks, euro area banks have made less progress in rationalizing their balance sheets, cutting administrative costs, and rebuilding profitability and capital. In addition, they remain too reliant on wholesale funding. The following are needed:

- recapitalizing, restructuring, or closing weak banks not only in the periphery but also in the core economies;

- a stronger monetary union, as discussed in Chapter 2;
- scope for direct bank recapitalization through the European Stability Mechanism; and
- support for the development of new credit instruments for nonfinancial enterprises (such as securitized lending for small and medium-size businesses).

Furthermore, weak balance sheets are likely weighing on activity in periphery economies. Households and nonfinancial companies are likely to require some help in restructuring debts to banks. Compared with targeted restructuring policies, traditional bankruptcy has many drawbacks in a deep downturn. Policymakers should consider viable alternatives to default and closure, while avoiding distortions to competition from zombie enterprises. For example, alternatives could include incentives for debt-for-equity swaps or targeted interventions toward working capital support. European policymakers must also stay proactive and focused on preventing sovereign debt burdens that so discourage activity that adjustment becomes self-defeating (Box 1.2).

Structural policies are necessary to lower unemployment and rebuild competitiveness

The October 2012 WEO discussed the structural challenges and policies in detail, and progress on the various fronts is critical for stronger global growth. Rebuilding competitiveness is a particular challenge for the periphery economies in the euro area. Large external imbalances in these countries were rooted in strong import growth, changes in external funding (from transfers to debt), and deteriorating income balances (Box 1.3). Their export market shares, by contrast, held up relatively well. The challenge for them is to engineer a recovery within the new, tighter external funding constraints, and this will require policies to boost productivity growth and foster job-friendly wage setting so as to achieve sustained gains in export market shares.

The best way to address high unemployment is with macroeconomic and structural policies that foster growth. However, its magnitude and duration increasingly warrant strong complementary structural and labor market policies. Active labor market policies can help prevent further disengagement from the labor market, particularly by the young and the long-term unemployed. The Nordic countries have such programs. Some countries recently implemented youth-employment guarantees.

Trade has played an important role in pushing global growth onto a higher trajectory in recent decades. It is thus disappointing that the Doha Development Round is not gaining traction, but it is encouraging that a growing number of bilateral trade agreements are under discussion, including recently between the United States and the European Union. These discussions hold the promise of providing a new impetus to trade and global trade liberalization negotiations.

Requirements in Emerging Market and Developing Economies

With global prospects improving, the main macroeconomic policy challenge in emerging market and developing economies is to recalibrate policy settings to avoid overstimulation and rebuild macroeconomic policy buffers. The macroeconomic policy stance in many of these economies is still very accommodative, supporting domestic demand in the face of weak external demand from advanced economies. In addition, policies must address risks from recent, sustained rapid credit growth and high asset prices (Figure 1.16, panels 2 and 3). The April 2013 GFSR also flags risks from rising corporate leverage and increasing reliance on foreign currency debt.

The appropriate pace and mix of policy recalibration vary considerably—detailed policy prescriptions are in Chapter 2. In general, emerging market economies can afford to rebuild policy buffers gradually. Overheating concerns largely subsided as growth slowed during 2011–12 (Figure 1.8, panels 3 and 4). Headline and core inflation are generally declining, while IMF staff estimates suggest that some slack remains (Figure 1.16, panel 1). Real credit growth has moderated in many economies (Figure 1.6, panels 2 and 3) as a result of tighter bank credit standards (Figure 1.6, panel 4).

Policymakers must carefully consider the risks of policies falling behind the curve and becoming procyclical, which would amplify rather than modulate the cycle. The concern is that too much of the recent downturn is attributed to cyclical rather than structural factors. WEO estimates suggest that the recent downward revision of medium-term prospects in emerging market and developing economies does not reflect a reassessment of medium-term prospects in China alone (Figure 1.16, panel 4). The issue is broader and most obvious in economies where supply factors, such as infrastructure or labor market bottlenecks, and domestic policy factors, such as policy uncertainty and regulatory obstacles, have contributed to the recent stalling of investment—examples include Brazil, India, and Russia. The slowdown in capital accumulation will likely lower potential output in the medium term.

Another common challenge is to manage risks from rapid credit expansion. In many emerging market economies, credit growth has either slowed markedly over the past year or is expanding within normal bounds. Outright credit booms are currently a concern in only a few economies. These economies may need tighter prudential policies and frameworks to maintain banking sector health, and achieving a soft landing may also be helped by some macroeconomic policy tightening to moderate the feedback from activity to credit. In the other economies, policy tightening should primarily be a function of inflation pressure and slack. However, regulation and supervision should ensure that banks address potential legacy credit quality and profitability problems from a recent period of very rapid credit expansion.

With improving global economic conditions, substantial capital inflows in emerging market economies are likely to reemerge, which may require adjustments in the policy mix. Specifically, monetary policy tightening may not be as effective in forestalling overheating because it could reinforce capital inflows and boost credit. Economies with current account surpluses should consider allowing nominal appreciation, which in turn should provide room for gradual monetary tightening. In economies with current account deficits, exchange rate appreciation will not be helpful, and policymakers may need to consider tightening macroprudential measures in conjunction with monetary policy tightening. They should also consider putting greater emphasis on fiscal policy tightening, which can help keep output close to potential while avoiding unhelpful exchange rate appreciation.

The relatively strong fiscal position of most emerging market economies has allowed them to adopt a neutral stance in response to slowing growth, but when the environment allows, they should return to rebuilding room for policy maneuvering. High public debt ratios call for more immediate fiscal consolidation in some economies. Although public debt ratios in most emerging market and developing economies are lower than in advanced economies, there is a risk that the debt dynamics could become less benign. With downside risks to the medium-term growth potential and upside risks to bond yields, the interest-growth differentials could become less favorable. Debt ratios would then start increasing rapidly with primary fiscal deficits. The need for fiscal consolidation, therefore, may be more urgent in economies where debt ratios are already high or debt dynamics less favorable (Egypt, Hungary, Jordan), fiscal deficits are large (India, Pakistan), or structural impediments to growth are already present (Egypt, India, Jordan, Pakistan).

Many *low-income countries* maintained their dramatically improved growth performance of the past two decades throughout the 2011–12 global recovery. As discussed in Chapter 4, structural policies aimed at fostering favorable business and investment regimes have contributed significantly to their success. In addition, more foreign direct investment and improved fiscal positions helped achieve strong growth without major excess demand pressure. Against this backdrop, policymakers should rebuild fiscal and external buffers if these are low. In many economies, high and volatile commodity prices have led to strains on the budget, and fiscal reform is urgently needed to better target related subsidy regimes.[6] In economies where the commodity sectors are expanding rapidly, it will be critical to put in place policy frameworks that insulate the economy from the effects of commodity price volatility while using commodity revenue to meet urgent public infrastructure and social needs.

---

[6]See Appendix 1 of the April 2013 *Fiscal Monitor*.

Special Feature: Commodity Market Review

Overview

The overall IMF commodity price index fell by 9 percent since peaking in April 2011, because of generally weaker demand and an uncertain global economic outlook—a decline anticipated in the October 2012 *World Economic Outlook* (Figure 1.SF.1, panel 1). Nonetheless, prices remain elevated compared with historical levels (Figure 1.SF.1, panel 2).

Commodity prices bottomed out in June 2012 and have since risen by 12 percent as a result of supply constraints and some improvement in demand. Weather-related supply shocks helped lift cereal prices higher by 10 percent, although they have eased slightly. Energy prices climbed 15 percent on lower production by the Organization of the Petroleum Exporting Countries (OPEC) and stronger emerging market and U.S. demand. Metal prices rose 10 percent on expectations of stronger emerging market demand, but stocks remain high and most markets are in surplus.

Recent declines in commodity price volatility reflect improvements in global financial conditions, realized on the back of policy actions that lowered the acute crisis risks (Figure 1.SF.2). These improvements also affected forward-looking indicators such as purchasing managers' indices and equity prices (along with prices of other risky assets), which rose globally (Figure 1.SF.3).

The near-term outlook for commodity prices, as reflected in futures prices, shows broad declines across all main commodity groups, including oil. Overall, prices are projected to decline by 2 percent in 2013 (year over year), with improving supply prospects for all main commodity sectors. Energy prices are expected to fall by almost 3 percent on recovering oil supply from the past year's outages and strong growth in non-OPEC supply, particularly in North America, which will continue to reduce U.S. crude oil imports. Food prices are projected to fall by more than 2 percent on the assumption of normal weather and improved harvests, and beverage prices are expected to drop by about 12 percent on abundant supply. Only metal prices are projected to trend upward, by more than 3 percent, which is consistent with global economic recovery and higher demand, especially in China.

The authors of this feature are Samya Beidas-Strom, Marina Rousset, and Shane Streifel, with research assistance from Daniel Rivera Greenwood and contributions from Olivier Coibion and Akito Matsumoto.

Figure 1.SF.1. IMF Commodity Price Indices
(2005 = 100)

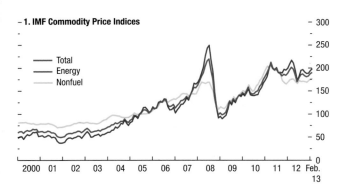

1. IMF Commodity Price Indices

Total
Energy
Nonfuel

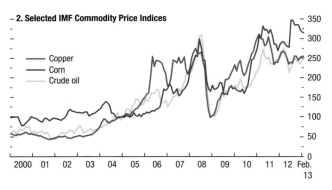

2. Selected IMF Commodity Price Indices

Copper
Corn
Crude oil

Source: IMF, Primary Commodity Price System.

Figure 1.SF.2. Equity and Commodity Market Volatility Indices

Chicago Board Options Exchange Volatility Index

——— S&P 500   ——— Oil   ········ Corn
——— Soybeans   ——— Gold

Source: Bloomberg, L.P.

Figure 1.SF.3. Commodity Prices and Economic Activity: First Principal Components
(Detrended data)

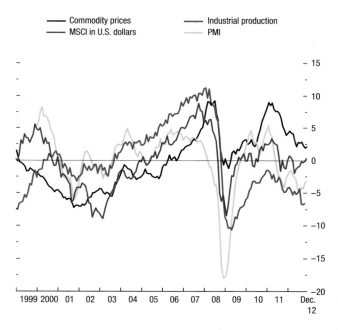

——— Commodity prices   ——— Industrial production
——— MSCI in U.S. dollars   ——— PMI

Sources: IMF, Primary Commodity Price System; Markit/Haver Analytics; and IMF staff calculations.
Note: MSCI = MSCI indices of stock prices; PMI = purchasing managers' indices.

Figure 1.SF.4. Energy Prices, Oil Price Prospects

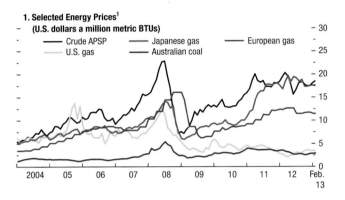

1. Selected Energy Prices[1]
(U.S. dollars a million metric BTUs)
— Crude APSP   — Japanese gas   — European gas
— U.S. gas   — Australian coal

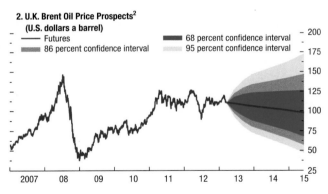

2. U.K. Brent Oil Price Prospects[2]
(U.S. dollars a barrel)
— Futures
86 percent confidence interval
68 percent confidence interval
95 percent confidence interval

Sources: Bloomberg, L.P.; IMF, Primary Commodity Price System; and IMF staff estimates.
[1]APSP = average petroleum spot price; BTU = British thermal unit.
[2]Derived from prices of futures options on March 12, 2013.

However, there are a number of risks to the outlook of falling commodity prices—beyond those of weaker or stronger growth in the global economy and, more specifically, in emerging markets. Upside risks to prices appear more pronounced than downside risks. On the supply side, a return of problems that affected metal and energy markets in the past decade (accidents, project delays, shortages of equipment and skilled labor) could again lead to supply deficits and higher prices. Much stronger Chinese demand, for both domestic consumption and restocking, is an added risk. Additional concerns include geopolitical tensions in the oil-producing regions of the Middle East and Africa and further non-OPEC supply outages or a major supply shock. For agricultural commodities, weather is the key variable, and continued adverse growing conditions could result in higher prices for grains, especially corn, whose stock levels are historically low. Downside price risks center on resurgent supplies of energy and metals, including the larger-than-expected growth in production of shale gas and tight oil in the United States and current metal supply overhangs.

Energy Market Developments and Prospects

Although energy prices rose by only 1 percent in 2012, they are up 15 percent since June 2012, led by gains in oil (19 percent) and U.S. natural gas (35 percent)—the latter on stronger demand for natural gas for power generation (which displaced coal) and depressed drilling for natural gas because of low prices (Figure 1.SF.4, panel 1). Natural gas prices continue to diverge regionally, with market segmentation driven by whether gas prices are strongly linked to long-term oil-priced contracts (yes in Japan, no in the United States) or whether this linkage has been loosened (Europe). Liquefied natural gas (LNG) prices in Japan eased as demand moderated after the surge that accompanied the shutdown of nuclear power generation in the wake of the Fukushima disaster, but prices remain high. European natural gas prices also fell on weaker demand and increasing penetration of spot-priced gas supplies.

Energy prices are expected to decline during 2013, as reflected in futures prices, led by crude oil (Figure 1.SF.4, panel 2). Falling crude oil prices reflect expected increases in non-OPEC production and declining demand in industrial countries due to improved vehicle efficiency and the effects of higher prices. However, the natural gas price index is expected to edge higher, led by a 34 percent increase in U.S. gas prices that will help sustain robust shale gas development. LNG prices in Japan are expected to continue their decline in the face of lower demand as nuclear power generation comes back on line and as oil prices fall. Coal prices are expected to decline on increasing supply and moderating demand, in part due to environmental constraints. Risks to energy prices, however, are tilted to the upside.

Oil

Spot crude prices: Crude oil prices have remained relatively stable—albeit high—since early 2011, with the average selling price near $105 a barrel during the past two years (Figure 1.SF.5, panel 1). Prices have been supported by outages due to geopolitical events in several countries in the Middle East and Africa, the European Union oil embargo and U.S. sanctions against Iran, and other unexpected outages, such as in the North Sea. The price of West Texas Intermediate (WTI) fell substantially below U.K. Brent because of a buildup in crude oil in the United States, primarily from new tight-oil production in North Dakota and Texas but also from rising Canadian oil imports. Pipeline constraints limit the movement of these supplies to refineries on the Gulf Coast and elsewhere, and producers are shipping crude oil by rail and barge, which is economical because of the large price discount. New pipeline projects and reversals of existing pipelines are under way, which will eventually lead to a narrowing of the Brent-WTI spread.

Price drivers: Weaker aggregate demand (proxied by the log change in global industrial production) and declines in other demand components (that is, inventories), along with a positive oil supply response, explain the downward pressure on the spot crude oil price during the second and third quarters of 2012 (Figure 1.SF.5, panel 2). However, the spot price began to pick up during the fourth quarter, as OPEC supply fell and geopolitical tensions rose, leading to a buildup in precautionary demand (inventories). Recent IMF staff analysis suggests that both supply and (flow and precautionary) demand shocks have been important drivers of the spot oil price (Beidas-Strom and Pescatori, forthcoming).

Demand: World oil demand grew by 1 percent, or 0.9 million barrels a day (mbd), in 2012, with a decline of 0.6 mbd in the Organization for Economic Cooperation and Development (OECD) countries and growth of 1.5 mbd in non-OECD countries (Figure 1.SF.6, panel 1). Oil demand in the OECD has fallen by 9 percent (or 4.5 mbd) since 2005 as a result of higher prices, greater

Figure 1.SF.5. Crude Oil Prices and SVAR[1] Model

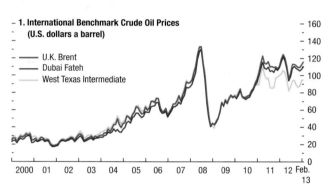

1. International Benchmark Crude Oil Prices (U.S. dollars a barrel)

2. Global SVAR of the Spot Crude Oil Market[1] (log of the real oil price, demeaned)

Sources: IMF, Primary Commodity Price System; and Beidas-Strom and Pescatori (forthcoming).
[1]SVAR = structural vector autoregression.

Figure 1.SF.6. Oil Market Developments

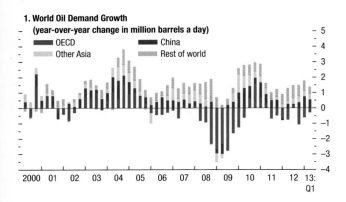

1. World Oil Demand Growth
(year-over-year change in million barrels a day)

■ OECD   ■ China
▨ Other Asia   ▨ Rest of world

2000 01 02 03 04 05 06 07 08 09 10 11 12 13:Q1

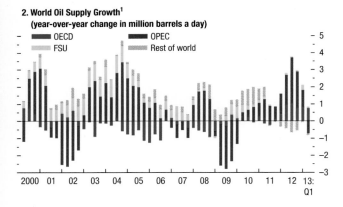

2. World Oil Supply Growth¹
(year-over-year change in million barrels a day)

■ OECD   ■ OPEC
▨ FSU   ▨ Rest of world

2000 01 02 03 04 05 06 07 08 09 10 11 12 13:Q1

Sources: International Energy Agency; and IMF staff estimates.
Note: OECD = Organization for Economic Cooperation and Development. 2013:Q1 are staff estimates.
¹OPEC = Organization of the Petroleum Exporting Countries; FSU = former Soviet Union.

efficiency, and recession—factors that are expected to affect developments into 2013 and beyond. While emerging market demand has moderated from its rapid growth in recent years, demand picked up by 1.6 mbd during the second half of 2012, led by Brazil, China, and countries in the Middle East and Asia. These emerging market economies are expected to account for all the growth in global demand in 2013, which is projected to be little more than 0.8 mbd.

Supply: World oil supply grew by 2.5 mbd in 2012, well above demand, resulting in more than 1 mbd going into inventories (Figure 1.SF.6, panel 2). The bulk of the increase was from OPEC (1.9 mbd), with the largest increments being the rebound in production from Libya, followed by rising output in Saudi Arabia and Iraq. However, OPEC supply fell during the fourth quarter, led by declines in Saudi Arabia, outages in Nigeria, and the continued impact of sanctions and embargoes on Iran. OPEC remains concerned about weak demand and rising supply and has announced its desire to keep oil prices around $100 a barrel, which generally satisfies its relatively high break-even requirements. Non-OPEC supply grew by 0.6 mbd in 2012, led by increases in the United States and Canada and by smaller increments in China and Russia, which more than offset production losses in the other regions. Non-OPEC production is expected to increase by 1 mbd in 2013, slightly exceeding the growth in demand.

Buffers: Reflecting supply and demand developments during the fourth quarter of 2012 and estimates for the first quarter of 2013, there was a seasonal drawdown of inventories among OECD countries and an increase in OPEC spare capacity, albeit still below its historical average (Figure 1.SF.7).

Food Market Developments and Prospects

Prices: Food prices have eased from recent highs on improving supply prospects, but markets remain tight due to historically low stock levels (Figure 1.SF.8). In addition, prices continue to be supported by high input prices that are transmitted through various channels, including fuel, fertilizer, and biofuel.[7] Cereal prices have edged downward from record highs in 2012 that were caused by significantly lower corn

---

[7]Fuel for agricultural machinery and transportation is a significant portion of production costs, and fertilizers also have a significant energy cost component. Biofuel production raises aggregate demand for crops and is diverted away from food supplies.

and wheat output resulting from extreme heat in the United States and drought in eastern Europe and central Asia. Oilseed and edible oil prices fell by a greater amount on better supply outlooks for South American soybean production and east Asian palm oil. Rice prices have been relatively stable during the past three years as markets remained well supplied.

Outlook: Food prices are projected to moderate but are likely to remain elevated in the first half of 2013 due to tight supplies—especially for corn, soybeans, and wheat (Figure 1.SF.9, panel 1). The probability of extreme price fluctuations over the nine-month horizon has picked up for corn and wheat since the October 2012 *World Economic Outlook*, indicating that the upside price risks have risen slightly (Figure 1.SF.9, panel 2). Contributing to these upside price risks are low inventories, adverse weather conditions, potential policy responses to tight markets (for example, export bans), and higher-than-expected oil prices. In addition, increases in biofuel production could divert crops away from food uses.[8]

Meanwhile, the upside price risks for soybeans have abated, but downside price risks have emerged.

Market balance: Amid expectations that global growth will rebound slightly in 2013, growth in food demand is expected to remain robust (Figure 1.SF.9, panel 3). Emerging market economies, especially China, are the largest source of increased demand for major crops. Although supply conditions have improved following the disruptions of 2012, inventories are not expected to be fully replenished. Overall, current global food stock-to-use ratios remain low, and they are estimated to fall below both 2012 and historical levels for most major grains and oilseeds in 2013 (Figure 1.SF.9, panel 4).

Major crops: Corn is particularly vulnerable to supply shocks because it has the lowest stock-to-use ratio among major food crops. Growing conditions in Brazil appear favorable, and, as a result, *soybean* yields are projected to rise. However, crop-producing areas of Argentina face reduced yield prospects relative to market expectations despite a significant improvement this year, because heavy rains delayed planting and dryness threatens corn and soybean harvests. Until there is more certainty about production prospects in the United States—the largest producer of both crops—prices are unlikely to ease significantly. Lending support to further corn and soybean market tightness are ethanol

---

[8]The impact of higher biofuel production on food prices is not straightforward, but depends on technological progress, policy decisions, and other factors.

Figure 1.SF.7. Oil Market Buffers[1]
(Data from January 2008–January 2013)

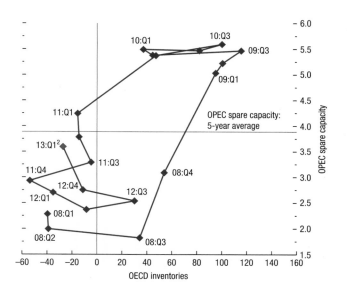

Sources: International Energy Agency; U.S. Energy Information Administration; and IMF staff estimates.
[1]Organization for Economic Cooperation and Development (OECD) stocks, deviations from five-year average (million barrels) on *x*-axis; Organization of the Petroleum Exporting Countries (OPEC) effective spare capacity (million barrels a day) on *y*-axis (excluding Iraq and Nigeria for the entire time period, Venezuela through February 2012, Libya since November 2011, and Iran since March 2012).
[2]March spare capacity and February/March stocks are estimates.

Figure 1.SF.8. IMF Food Price Indices
(2005 = 100)

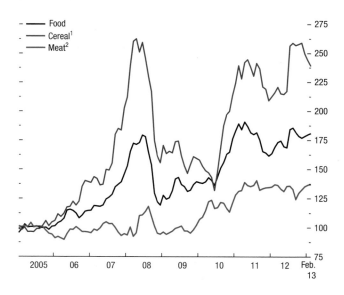

Source: IMF, Primary Commodity Price System.
[1]A weighted average of wheat, corn, rice, and barley.
[2]A weighted average of beef, lamb, pork, and poultry.

Figure 1.SF.9. Food Prices and Inventories

Agricultural Price Prospects

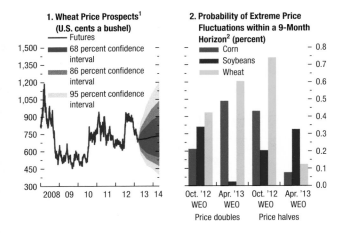

1. Wheat Price Prospects[1]
(U.S. cents a bushel)

2. Probability of Extreme Price Fluctuations within a 9-Month Horizon[2] (percent)

Global Food Market Balances

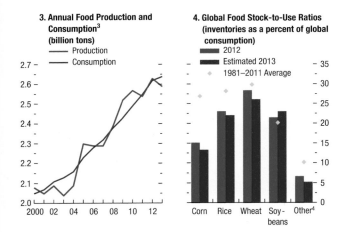

3. Annual Food Production and Consumption[3]
(billion tons)

4. Global Food Stock-to-Use Ratios
(inventories as a percent of global consumption)

Sources: Bloomberg, L.P.; United States Department of Agriculture; and IMF staff estimates.
[1]Derived from prices of futures options on March 12, 2013.
[2]Derived from prices of futures options on September 11, 2012, and March 12, 2013.
[3]Sum of major grains and oilseeds: barley, corn, millet, rice, rye, sorghum, wheat, palm kernel, rapeseed, soybean, and sunflower seed.
[4]Other = other grains and oilseeds: barley, millet, palm kernel, rapeseed, rye, sorghum, and sunflower seed.

and biodiesel production. Although their output and consumption waned in 2012, both are expected to rebound strongly by the end of this year. Among key grains, *wheat* production is expected to underperform consumption by the greatest percentage this year, which puts pressure on already declining global stocks. In contrast, the *rice* market appears adequately supplied, and 2013 production is projected to reach record-high levels and broadly align with global demand needs.

Metal Market Developments and Prospects

Prices: Metal prices have generally declined since early 2011—following large restocking in China and a sharp increase in stocks—due to slowing consumption and weak import demand in China (Figure 1.SF.10, panels 1 and 2). However, prices picked up during the fourth quarter of 2012 and into early 2013 on improving macroeconomic sentiment. For some metals (such as copper), prices remain elevated as supply continues to struggle; for other metals (such as aluminum), prices have recently moved into the upper portion of the industry cost curve, so downside price risks are much lower. Aluminum prices have remained relatively low during the past decade because of large investments in aluminum smelters (in China and the Middle East). Nonetheless, the current market remains somewhat tight: warehouse financing arrangements have kept a large portion of inventories unavailable to the market.

Outlook: The outlook for metal prices is tightly bound to developments in China, which consumes more than 40 percent of all metals. Growth in China's metal demand is expected to moderate as the economy moves more toward services. China still has plans for large infrastructure projects, which will lead to upside risks to prices (Figure 1.SF.10, panel 3). Reliance on metal futures prices, however, is not without important caveats—their predictive ability appears to have declined (Chinn and Coibion, forthcoming). For example, from 2009 to 2010, copper prices rose more than 100 percent, yet 12-month futures predicted a price increase of only 3 percent during the same period. Other metal commodities, such as lead, nickel, and tin, displayed similar patterns. In contrast, oil and natural gas futures prices were much more reliable predictors of actual price changes in these markets during the same period. Figure 1.SF.11 shows the decline in the predictive ability of futures prices and the increase in their volatility across commodity markets.

Figure 1.SF.10. Metals: Prices, Demand, and Prospects

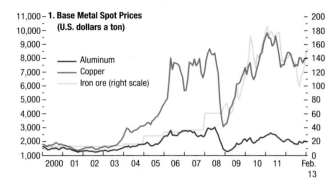

1. Base Metal Spot Prices
(U.S. dollars a ton)

Aluminum
Copper
Iron ore (right scale)

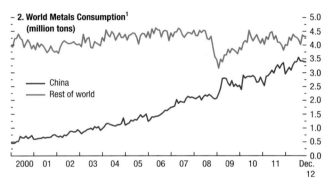

2. World Metals Consumption[1]
(million tons)

China
Rest of world

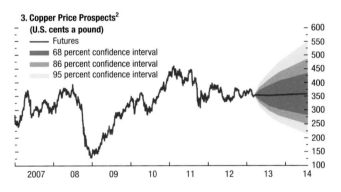

3. Copper Price Prospects[2]
(U.S. cents a pound)

Futures
68 percent confidence interval
86 percent confidence interval
95 percent confidence interval

Sources: Bloomberg, L.P.; IMF, Primary Commodity Price System; World Bureau of Metal Statistics; and IMF staff estimates.
[1]Aluminum, copper, lead, nickel, tin, zinc.
[2]Derived from prices of futures options on March 12, 2013.

Figure 1.SF.11. Predictive Content of Commodity Futures Prices
(Average deviation from unbiasedness of futures prices)

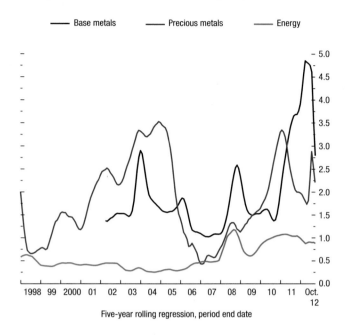

Base metals
Precious metals
Energy

Five-year rolling regression, period end date

Sources: Bloomberg, L.P.; and Chinn and Coibion (forthcoming).

Box 1.1. The Great Divergence of Policies

The current global recovery has followed an unusual path compared with the three previous global recoveries.[1] Specifically, the recovery following the Great Recession exhibits two types of divergences. The first is the sharp divergence of activity across advanced and emerging market economies, which we first noted in the April 2012 *World Economic Outlook* and that has continued since then.[2] The second is the great divergence of monetary and fiscal policies, which has become increasingly pronounced during the past two years. This box first presents a brief review of the former divergence and then provides a detailed account of the latter one.

Sharp Divergence of Activity

Overall, the ongoing global recovery has followed the pattern of recoveries in the past (Figure 1.1.1). But this global development masks a sharp divergence between the ongoing recovery paths for advanced and emerging market economies. Specifically, this recovery has been the weakest for advanced economies and the strongest for emerging markets. The advanced economies were the engine of previous global recoveries, but emerging markets account for the lion's share of the ongoing recovery. In light of the current forecasts, the sharp divergence of activity between advanced and emerging market economies is likely to persist in the coming years.

Great Divergence of Policies

The second unique feature of this recovery has been the substantially different paths of fiscal and monetary policies, mainly in advanced economies. In particular, whereas the directions of fiscal and monetary policies were aligned in previous episodes, during the current recovery these policies have marched in opposite directions. Because the focus is on the cyclical properties of fiscal and monetary policies, we use specific measures

The authors of this box are M. Ayhan Kose, Prakash Loungani, and Marco E. Terrones. Ezgi Ozturk, Bennet Voorhees, and Tingyun Chen provided research assistance.

[1]This box focuses on the recovery episodes that followed the four global recessions the world economy experienced over the past half century: 1975, 1982, 1991, and 2009. A global recession is a decline in world per capita real GDP accompanied by a broad decline in other indicators of global activity—specifically, industrial production, trade, capital flows, oil consumption, and employment. A global recovery is a rebound in worldwide activity over the three or four years following a global recession. A detailed discussion of global recessions and recoveries is presented in Kose, Loungani, and Terrones (2013).

[2]See Box 1.2 of the April 2012 *World Economic Outlook*.

Figure 1.1.1. Divergent Recoveries[1]
(Years on x-axis; indexed to 100 in the year before the global recession)

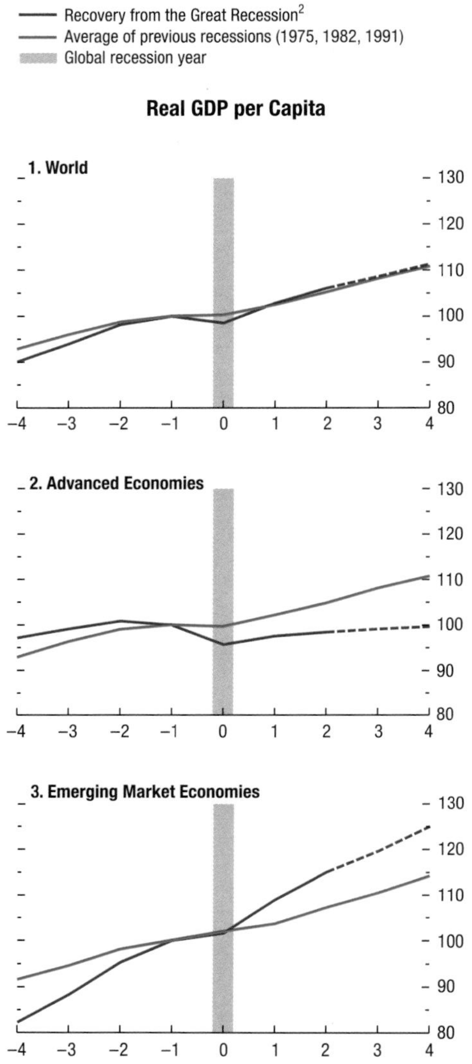

— Recovery from the Great Recession[2]
— Average of previous recessions (1975, 1982, 1991)
▨ Global recession year

Real GDP per Capita

1. World

2. Advanced Economies

3. Emerging Market Economies

Source: IMF staff estimates.
[1]Aggregates are purchasing-power-parity weighted.
[2]Dashed lines denote WEO forecasts.

for policies (that is, real primary government expenditure, short-term interest rate, and the rate of growth of central bank assets) that provide a good reading of the cyclical policy stance (Kaminsky, Reinhart, and Végh, 2005). Other indicators (such as the ratio of government deficits to GDP and real short-term interest rates) often lead to noisy signals about the stance of policies.

Box 1.1 *(continued)*

Figure 1.1.2. Government Expenditures during Global Recessions and Recoveries[1]
(Years from global recession on x-axis; indices = 100 in the year before the global recession)

—— Recovery from the Great Recession[2]
—— Average of previous recessions (1975, 1982, 1991)
▓▓▓ Global recession year

Real Primary Expenditure

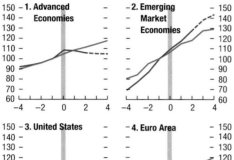

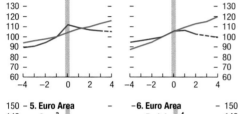

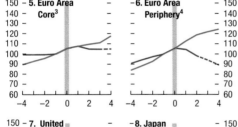

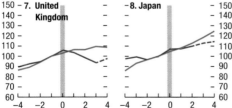

Sources: IMF, Public Finances in Modern History database; World Bank, World Development Indicators database; and IMF staff estimates.
[1]Aggregates are purchasing-power-parity weighted.
[2]Dashed lines denote WEO forecasts.
[3]France and Germany.
[4]Greece, Ireland, Italy, Portugal, Spain.

With regard to fiscal policy, the current and projected paths of government expenditures in the advanced economies are quite different than during past recoveries, when policy was decisively expansionary, with increases in real primary government expenditures. In some advanced economies, especially in the United States, the fiscal stimulus introduced at the outset of the financial crisis was far larger than during earlier recessions. However, the stimulus was unwound early in the ensuing recovery. Specifically, expenditures fell during the first two years of this global recovery and are projected to continue to decline modestly in the coming years (Figure 1.1.2).

This pattern also holds across the major advanced economies, with the euro area and the United Kingdom showing sharp departures from the typical paths of government expenditures in the past.[3] In contrast, in the emerging market economies the ongoing recovery has been accompanied by a more expansionary fiscal policy stance than during past episodes. This was possible because these economies had stronger fiscal positions this time around than in the past.

Monetary policies in the advanced economies have been exceptionally accommodative during the latest recovery compared with earlier episodes (Figure 1.1.3). In particular, policy rates have been reduced to record-low levels and central bank balance sheets in the major advanced economies have been dramatically expanded compared with earlier episodes (Figure 1.1.4). Monetary policy in emerging market economies has also been more supportive of economic activity than in the past.

What Explains the Divergence of Policies?

Caution about fiscal stimulus and the pace of consolidation in this recession and recovery are likely explained by high ratios of public debt to GDP and large deficits. Advanced economies entered the Great Recession with much higher levels of debt than in past recessions (Figure 1.1.5). The high debt levels reflect a combination of factors, including expansionary fiscal policies in the run-up to the recession, financial sector support measures, and substantial revenue losses resulting from the severity of the Great Recession. The deficit levels in some advanced economies are currently

[3]We report the average of the three previous episodes here for simplicity, but the general pattern described by the average is valid for each episode as well (Kose, Loungani, and Terrones, 2013). The findings with respect to primary expenditures do not change much when the periphery euro area countries are excluded from the sample of advanced economies.

Box 1.1 *(continued)*

Figure 1.1.3. Short-Term Interest Rates during Global Recessions and Recoveries[1]
(Percent; years from global recession on x-axis)

— Recovery from the Great Recession
— Average of previous recessions (1975, 1982, 1991)
▨ Global recession year

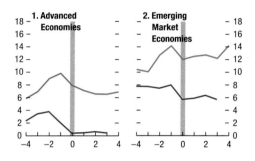

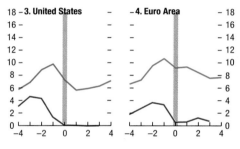

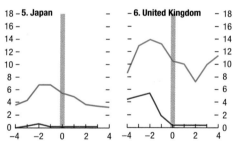

Sources: Haver Analytics; IMF, *International Financial Statistics;* and IMF staff calculations.
[1]Aggregates are market weighted by GDP in U.S. dollars; observations are dropped for countries experiencing inflation 50 percent greater than in the previous year. Policy rate used as the principal series. Three- or four-month treasury bill data used as a proxy if data series was longer.

Figure 1.1.4. Central Bank Assets in Major Advanced Economies during Global Recessions and Recoveries
(Percent of real GDP of year before global recession; years from global recession on x-axis)

— Recovery from the Great Recession
— Average of previous recessions (1975, 1982, 1991)
▨ Global recession year

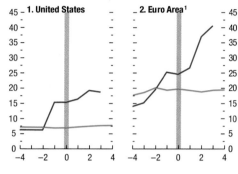

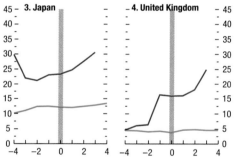

Sources: Bank of England; Eurostat; Haver Analytics; IMF, *International Financial Statistics;* World Bank, World Development Indicators database; and IMF staff calculations.
[1]Aggregate is market weighted by GDP in U.S. dollars. Data unavailable before 1975.

Box 1.1 *(continued)*

large in part because of the collapse in revenues. More-over, sovereign debt crises in some euro area periphery countries and challenges associated with market access put pressure on these economies to accelerate their fiscal consolidation plans.[4] At the same time, there was more room for monetary policy maneuvering because inflation rates were much lower at the beginning of the recession than in the past (Figure 1.1.6).

The evidence presented here does not in itself per-mit an assessment of whether the different policy mix in this recession and recovery was appropriate.[5] The response of policies may have been reasonable given the respective room available for fiscal and monetary policies in advanced economies. But there are also

[4]Structural reforms—for example, reforms of labor, goods, and product markets—for the crisis countries are also critical for regain-ing competitiveness and even for moving up in the value chain.

[5]There is extensive literature on the factors behind the slug-gish recovery in advanced economies. Some studies argue that recoveries following financial disruptions tend to be weaker and protracted; others emphasize the importance of relatively higher levels of macroeconomic and policy uncertainty (see, for details, Reinhart and Rogoff, 2009; Claessens, Kose, and Terrones, 2012; Bloom, Kose, and Terrones, 2013).

concerns. Even though monetary policy has been effective, policymakers had to resort to unconventional measures. Even with these measures, the zero bound on interest rates and the extent of financial disruption during the crisis have lowered the traction of monetary policy. This, together with the extent of slack in these economies, may have amplified the impact of contrac-tionary fiscal policies.[6] Four years into a weak recovery, policymakers may therefore need to worry about the risk of overburdening monetary policy because it is being relied on to deliver more than it traditionally has.

[6]A large amount of literature analyzes the effectiveness of fiscal and monetary policies under these circumstances. For the effectiveness of fiscal policies, see Blanchard and Leigh (2013); Christiano, Eichenbaum, and Rebelo (2011); and Auerbach and Gorodnichenko (2012). For the effectiveness of monetary policies, see Eggertsson and Woodford (2003); Krishnamurthy and Vissing-Jorgensen (2011); Carvalho, Eusipe, and Grisse (2012); and Swanson and Williams (2013), among others. Some argue that accommodative monetary policies need to be paired with expansionary fiscal policies, especially for countries with sufficient fiscal space (Corsetti, 2012; De Grauwe and Ji, 2013; Werning, 2012; Turner, 2013; McCulley and Pozsar, 2012).

Figure 1.1.5. Public-Debt-to-GDP Ratios during Global Recessions and Recoveries[1]
(Percent of real GDP in year before global recession; years from global recession on x-axis)

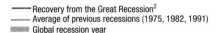

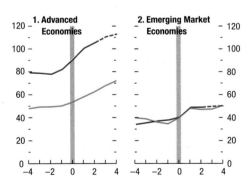

Sources: IMF, Public Finances in Modern History database; World Bank, World Development Indicators database; and IMF staff estimates.
[1]Aggregates are market weighted by GDP in U.S. dollars.
[2]Dashed lines denote WEO forecasts.

Figure 1.1.6. Inflation during Global Recessions and Recoveries[1]
(Percent; years from global recession on x-axis)

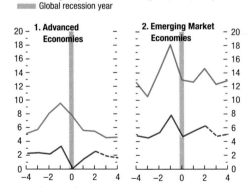

Source: IMF staff estimates.
[1]Aggregates are market weighted by GDP in U.S. dollars. Observations are dropped for countries experiencing inflation 50 percent greater than in the previous year.
[2]Dashed lines denote WEO forecasts.

Box 1.2. Public Debt Overhang and Private Sector Performance

In some advanced economies, the rapid growth of public debt along with sluggish economic performance could reflect the play of debt overhang mechanisms. The literature on debt overhang posits that larger debt stocks lead to lower activity and reduce the probability that debt will be repaid in full; beyond a particular threshold, further increases in nominal debt can actually reduce the total expected (present value of) debt payments (Myers, 1977; Krugman, 1988). Conversely, on the downward slope of this so-called debt Laffer curve—when the value of debt decreases its face value—debt restructuring can benefit both debtors and creditors.

The Effects of High Debt on Economic Activity

A debt overhang can affect economic activity in various ways. High debt payments can lead to lower public investment, which may, in turn, lead to declining private investment.[1] High debt can reduce the scope for countercyclical fiscal policies, thereby increasing volatility and constraining private sector activity. Furthermore, high debt may diminish the government's incentives to enact growth-enhancing stabilization and policy reforms, because gains will go to service foreign debt. As the risk of distortionary taxation on profit, capital income, and assets increases, high debt can generally discourage private saving and investment. This, again, adversely affects growth and worsens the debt overhang.

Much of the empirical work on debt overhangs seeks to identify the "overhang threshold," beyond which the correlation between debt and growth becomes negative. The results are broadly similar: above a threshold of about 95 percent of GDP, a 10 percentage point increase in the ratio of debt to GDP is associated with a decline in annual growth of about 0.15 to 0.20 percentage point a year (Kumar and Woo, 2010; Caner, Grennes, and Koehler-Geib, 2010; Cecchetti, Mohanty, and Zampolli, 2011; Ursua and Wilson, 2012).

But there are limits to empirical studies on the economic effects of debt overhangs. For example, countries that have high debt levels may have low

growth for other reasons that typically are not captured in the econometric models. In fact, some studies find no causal relationship between high debt and lower growth. The October 2012 *Global Financial Stability Report* finds that countries with debt above 100 percent of GDP experience lower growth, but it also finds that countries with high but falling debt ratios grew faster than countries with lower but increasing debt ratios. Estimates that define the ranges beyond which debt becomes a problem often include large confidence intervals, typically between 10 and 15 percentage points around threshold estimates. And most cross-country regression studies do not directly model the channels through which public sector debt affects economic growth.

The Effects of High Debt in Ireland and Greece

This box acknowledges that a rise in public debt does not affect all segments of the economy similarly and uses microeconomic data to obtain evidence on the channels through which a debt overhang can work. Specifically, it explores the transmission channels for the fiscal and sovereign stress risks associated with high debt levels in two euro area periphery economies, Ireland and Greece.[2] Faced with a rapid increase in public debt, firms may expect higher future taxation, lower government expenditures, and other costs, including those related to possible sovereign default. In anticipation of such costs, their market valuation falls. Conversely, debt restructuring could show up in improved firm performance and rising market valuations. In contrast with the existing literature, the objective of this analysis is not to assess the impact of changes in aggregate debt on aggregate growth, but rather to shed light on the potential distributional effects across sectors in the economy.

Large-scale financial sector bailouts by governments and sovereign debt restructuring offer a quasi-natural experiment for the study of this channel. The former typically involve large value transfers from governments to banks, including their foreign creditors, and the latter entail the opposite when banks have large holdings of restructured government securities on their books. The analysis focuses on the announcement of two such events: the financial sector bailout in Ireland on September 29, 2008, and the debt restructuring

---

The main author of this box is Romain Ranciere with research assistance from Bennet Voorhees and Tingyun Chen.

[1]Clements, Bhattacharya, and Nguyen (2003) find that for low-income countries, every percentage point of GDP increase in debt service leads to public investment declines of about 0.2 percentage point of GDP.

[2]The results are based on Imbs and Ranciere (2012), which includes findings for a larger set of European countries.

Box 1.2 *(continued)*

in Greece on February, 21, 2012. Both events marked large changes in sovereign debt.[3] For both events, we analyze cumulative abnormal stock returns of firms, as in the following model:

$$R_{i,t} = \alpha_i + \beta_i \, RM_t + \sum_{\tau=t_1}^{t_1+2} \delta_\tau \, D_{\tau,t} + \varepsilon_{i,t}, \qquad (1.2.1)$$

in which α_i is a firm-specific intercept, $R_{i,t}$ denotes the stock return of firm i at time t, RM_t is the overall stock market return at time t for either Ireland or Greece, and $D_{\tau,t}$ is an event-time indicator variable that takes value 1 at time t_1, when the bailout or restructuring is announced, and during the two days that follow. Specifically, we report the cumulative abnormal returns of the three-day period—that is, the sum of the estimates for δ_τ.[4] Notice that this approach does not consider abnormal returns in anticipation of these two events.[5]

We consider three subsets of firms to see how the events affected different segments of the economy: financial firms; domestic firms, defined as firms with no foreign assets (Greece) or with less than 20 percent foreign assets (Ireland); and firms operating in sectors for which government demand accounts for at least 10 percent of sales.[6]

Figure 1.2.1 for Ireland and Figure 1.2.2 for Greece report the point estimates for the cumulative abnormal returns, along with the 95 percent confidence intervals, for the three subsets.

In Ireland, the overall stock returns decline by 3.7 percent during the three-day window, whereas the overall world stock returns decline by only 1.7 percent in the same period. In principle, a bank bailout should be helping the economy in the short term.

---

[3]The fiscal cost associated with the Irish bailout amounts to 41 percent of GDP, and the ratio of debt to GDP increased from 24 percent in 2007 to 65 percent in 2009 (Laeven and Valencia, 2012). The Greek debt restructuring, completed in March 2012, cut about half of Greek public debt owed to private creditors. The IMF projects the Greek debt-to-GDP ratio to be reduced from 174 percent in 2012 to 120 percent in 2013.

[4]The differential impact of the bailout or restructuring announcement across different subsets of firms is captured through interaction terms.

[5]The results are virtually unchanged when the world stock market return is added as a second factor in equation 1.2.1.

[6]Reflecting the Irish economy's high degree of financial openness, foreign assets account for more than 20 percent of total assets for 75 percent of listed firms in Ireland (for which information on foreign asset holdings is available). In Greece, by contrast, 75 percent of listed firms have less than 20 percent of foreign assets, justifying a threshold of zero.

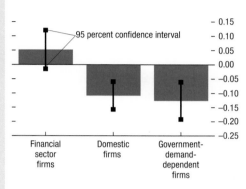

Figure 1.2.1. Cumulative Abnormal Returns of Irish Listed Firms during the 2009 Bank Bailout
(Percent; September 29–October 1, 2008)

Source: IMF staff estimates.

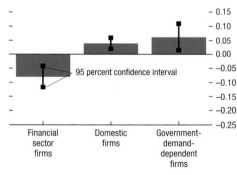

Figure 1.2.2. Cumulative Abnormal Returns of Greek Listed Firms during the 2012 Debt Restructuring
(Percent; February 23–25, 2012)

Source: IMF staff estimates.

In this case, however, the bailout involved assumption by the government of large amounts of liabilities to foreigners, and the effect differed widely across firms. Firms in the financial sector exhibit positive abnormal returns (although not significantly different from zero). For them, any expectation of future higher taxation appears to be offset by the immediate benefits of the bailout. Domestic firms and firms dependent on government demand, however, experience strongly negative abnormal returns. This suggests that the unexpected increase in public debt adversely affected the private sector in the short term through both the taxation and the demand channels.

Box 1.2 *(continued)*

In Greece, the overall stock market returns decline by 1.3 percent during the three-day window, whereas the world stock returns do not change during the period. The response likely reflects that the restructuring was widely anticipated or that a debt overhang persisted even after the restructuring. Financial firms face a large and significantly negative, cumulative, abnormal return, probably related to their large holdings of government debt. Domestic firms exhibit positive abnormal returns, which were slightly higher than for the market overall. Firms dependent on government demand show even more positive abnormal returns, suggesting that debt restructuring eases the demand channel.

Finally, although this methodology allows identification of the distributional impact of bailout and debt restructuring across sectors, it cannot identify the aggregate impact of changes in government debt on long-term economic growth.

This analysis suggests that the fiscal and sovereign default risk overhang channel may have been at play in Ireland and Greece. Transfers of future and current liabilities between the private sector and the government as well as across various sectors are central to understanding how this channel operates.

Box 1.3. The Evolution of Current Account Deficits in the Euro Area

This box reviews the various factors that led to rising external deficits and their macroeconomic implications in Greece, Ireland, Portugal, and Spain (Figure 1.3.1, panel 1).[1] Its main conclusion is that deficits widened on account of booming imports in some countries, falling transfers in others, and deteriorating income payments in all. Exports did not substantially weaken between 2000 and 2007, but, going forward, gains in export performance will be needed as these economies recover toward full employment.

A commonly held view is that the deteriorating current account deficits in the euro area periphery were caused by a deterioration in export performance. The pattern of continually worsening current account balances—from deficits that were already high with the adoption of the euro—and deterioration of conventional price competitiveness measures are superficially consistent with this view (Figure 1.3.1, panels 2 and 3). Deteriorating export performance can reflect wages that grow faster than productivity in the tradables sector, implying rising unit labor costs and appreciation of the real effective exchange rate. An alternative explanation is that these economies' export performance faded because they failed to move up the value chain while their trading partners steadily increased the quality of their exports.[2]

In fact, exports (as a share of GDP) for most periphery economies remained relatively stable or increased during the first decade of the 2000s. Moreover, market shares for merchandise exports were flat in these countries during that period (Figure 1.3.1, panels 4 and 5).[3] This occurred against the backdrop of different developments in the tradables sector, in which unit labor costs were contained, and the nontradables sectors, in which they were not. It was the increasing unit labor costs in the latter that led to the widely observed deterioration in economy-wide unit labor costs (Figure 1.3.1, panel 6). Therefore,

The authors of this box are Joong Shik Kang and Jay Shambaugh, with research assistance from Bennet Voorhees and Tingyun Chen. See Kang and Shambaugh (forthcoming) for more detailed discussion.

[1]This box focuses on these four euro area member countries, which, as of the end of 2007, had the largest precrisis current account deficits.

[2]See Chen, Milesi-Ferretti, and Tressel (2012) for a detailed discussion.

[3]Ireland's merchandise trade market share declined while that in services trade increased with its shift toward greater reliance on services in the first decade of the 2000s (Nkusu, 2013).

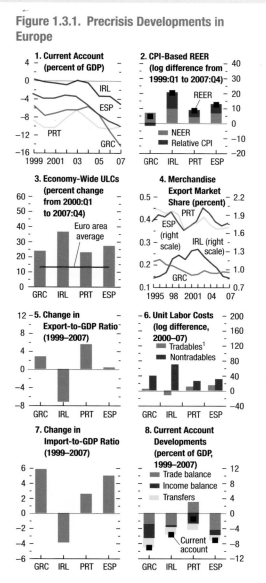

Figure 1.3.1. Precrisis Developments in Europe

Sources: Eurostat; Haver Analytics; and IMF staff calculations.
Note: CPI = consumer price index; REER = real effective exchange rate; NEER = nominal effective exchange rate; ULCs = unit labor costs; GRC = Greece; IRL = Ireland; PRT = Portugal; ESP = Spain.
[1]Tradables sectors include agriculture; forestry and fishing; industry excluding construction, trade, travel, accommodation, and food; information and communications; and financial insurance.

Box 1.3 *(continued)*

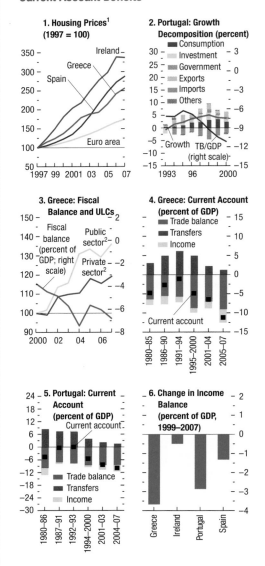

Figure 1.3.2. Different Paths to Large Current Account Deficits

Sources: Eurostat; Haver Analytics; and IMF staff calculations.
Note: ULCs = unit labor costs; TB/GDP = trade balance as percent of GDP.
[1]Free housing price index for Spain, prices of dwellings in urban areas for Greece, and prices of dwellings countrywide for Ireland and euro area.
[2]2000 = 100, left scale.

the deterioration of current account balances was more likely caused by rising imports or nontrade factors (Figure 1.3.1, panels 7 and 8).[4] Rising imports played a role in widening external imbalances in some countries, driven to varying degrees by these factors: domestic demand booms caused by capital inflows, excessive optimism about the future, or fiscal excesses. Booms driven by capital inflows and low interest rates boosted output, raised unit labor costs in the nontradables sectors, and led to housing bubbles in Ireland, Greece, and Spain (Figure 1.3.2, panel 1). Optimism about higher growth in the future led to a strong pickup in consumption and investment and contributed to higher unit labor costs and growth, particularly in Greece and Portugal in the mid-1990s (Figure 1.3.2, panel 2).[5] Large fiscal deficits contributed to a widening current account deficit in the run-up to the crisis in Greece but not in the other countries (Figure 1.3.2, panels 3 and 4).

Changes in nontrade factors also added to external imbalances. In particular, transfers declined, but rather than leading to a reduction in domestic demand and a return to balanced trade, they were replaced by loans (perhaps because of habit persistence). Accordingly, the trade deficits reflect the fact that consumption and imports did not decline with declining income. This was the case in both Greece and Portugal and was part of a persistent failure to correct imbalances that were present at the adoption the euro. (Trade deficits have been large for more than 30 years.) In addition, in all the periphery economies, deteriorating external imbalances led to rising net income payments, which further added to the imbalances. Interestingly, Portugal's trade balance actually remained relatively stable during this period (Figure 1.3.2, panel 5). Nevertheless, by running persistent current account deficits, Portugal—like the other periphery economies—faced rising net income payments to support growing external debt (Figure 1.3.2, panel 6).

Since the crisis, price-based indicators of competitiveness have improved, though not yet to pre-1999 levels, and current account deficits have shrunk. Part of this improvement is cyclical and part of it is structural, but it is not easy to disentangle the two. A large part of the improvement in current account balances

---

[4]Gaulier and Vicard (2012) also argue that weakening export performance did not generate the imbalances.
[5]Lane and Pels (2012) demonstrate that the current account balance declined in countries with rising growth forecasts.

Box 1.3 *(continued)*

has been due to import contraction (Figure 1.3.3, panels 1–4). Also, improvements in unit labor costs have been largely due to labor shedding—unemployment is very high, output stands appreciably below potential (Figure 1.3.3, panels 5 and 6). Conversely, the unwinding of unsustainable demand booms has contributed to import contraction—and thus may in part be sustainable—and, regardless of cause, unit labor costs have improved. Still, sizable gains in export performance will be needed so that deficits do not reemerge as these countries recover toward full employment. This will come with improved competitiveness, and as these countries adjust, external support will help them offset their high net income payments. Finally, even though adjustments in relative prices may help boost competitiveness, it will be important to sustain the growth of nominal GDP in these countries to avoid compromising their ability to manage their high debt levels.[6]

⁶See Shambaugh (2012) for a more detailed discussion.

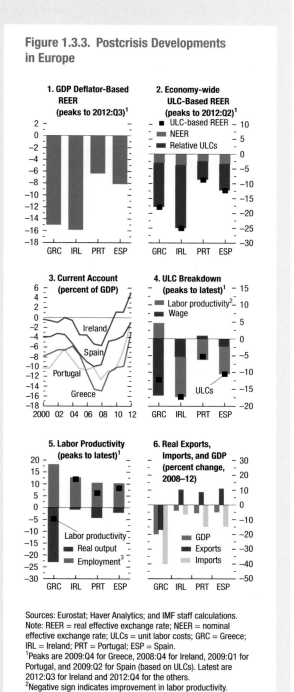

Figure 1.3.3. Postcrisis Developments in Europe

Sources: Eurostat; Haver Analytics; and IMF staff calculations.
Note: REER = real effective exchange rate; NEER = nominal effective exchange rate; ULCs = unit labor costs; GRC = Greece; IRL = Ireland; PRT = Portugal; ESP = Spain.
¹Peaks are 2009:Q4 for Greece, 2008:Q4 for Ireland, 2009:Q1 for Portugal, and 2009:Q2 for Spain (based on ULCs). Latest are 2012:Q3 for Ireland and 2012:Q4 for the others.
²Negative sign indicates improvement in labor productivity.
³Positive sign indicates decline in employment.

References

Auerbach, Alan, and Yuriy Gorodnichenko, 2012, "Measuring the Output Responses to Fiscal Policy," *American Economic Journal—Economic Policy,* Vol. 4, No. 2, pp. 1–27.

Beidas-Strom, Samya, and Andrea Pescatori, forthcoming, "Oil Price Determinants, the Role of Shocks, and Short Run Elasticities—Evidence from an Estimated Sign-Restricted VAR of the Global Oil Market," IMF Working Paper (Washington: International Monetary Fund).

Bems, Rudolfs, and Robert C. Johnson, 2012, "Value-Added Exchange Rates," NBER Working Paper No. 18498 (Cambridge, Massachusetts: National Bureau of Economic Research).

Blanchard, Olivier, and Daniel Leigh, 2013, "Growth Forecast Errors and Fiscal Multipliers," IMF Working Paper No. 13/1 (Washington: International Monetary Fund).

Bloom, Nicholas, M. Ayhan Kose, and Marco E. Terrones, 2013, "Held Back by Uncertainty," *Finance and Development,* Vol. 50, No. 1, pp. 38–41.

Caner, Mehmet, Thomas Grennes, and Fritzi Koehler-Geib, 2010, "Finding the Tipping Point—When Sovereign Debt Turns Bad," World Bank Policy Research Working Paper No. 5391 (Washington: World Bank).

Carvalho, Carlos, Stefano Eusipe, and Christian Grisse, 2012, "Policy Initiatives in the Global Recession: What Did Forecasters Expect?" *Current Issues in Economics and Finance,* Vol. 18, No. 2.

Cecchetti, Stephen, Madhusudan Mohanty, and Fabrizio Zampolli, 2011, "The Real Effects of Debt" (unpublished; Basel: Bank for International Settlements).

Chen, Ruo, Gian-Maria Milesi-Ferretti, and Thierry Tressel, 2012, "External Imbalances in the Euro Area," IMF Working Paper No. 12/236 (Washington: International Monetary Fund).

Chinn, Menzie, and Olivier Coibion, forthcoming, "The Predictive Content of Commodity Futures," *Journal of Futures Markets.*

Christiano, Lawrence, Martin Eichenbaum, and Sergio Rebelo, 2011, "When Is the Government Spending Multiplier Large?" *Journal of Political Economy,* Vol. 119, No. 1, pp. 78–121.

Claessens, Stijn, M. Ayhan Kose, and Marco E. Terrones, 2012. "How Do Business and Financial Cycles Interact?" *Journal of International Economics,* Vol. 87, No. 1, pp. 178–90.

Clements, Benedict J., Rina Bhattacharya, and Toan Quoc Nguyen, 2003, "External Debt, Public Investment, and Growth in Low-Income Countries," IMF Working Paper No. 03/249 (Washington: International Monetary Fund).

Corsetti, Giancarlo, 2012, "Has Austerity Gone Too Far?" *VoxEU.*

Decressin, Jörg, and Douglas Laxton, 2009, "Gauging Risks for Deflation," IMF Staff Position Note No. 09/01 (Washington: International Monetary Fund).

De Grauwe, Paul, and Yuemei Ji, 2013, "Panic-Driven Austerity in the Eurozone and Its Implications," *VoxEU.*

Eggerstsson, Gauti, and Michael Woodford, 2003, "The Zero Bound on Interest Rates and Optimal Monetary Policy," *Brookings Papers on Economic Activity,* Vol. 34, No. 1, pp. 139–235.

Gaulier, Guillaume, and Vincent Vicard, 2012, "Current Account Imbalances in the Euro Area: Competitiveness or Demand Shock?" *Bank of France Quarterly Selection of Articles,* No. 27.

Imbs, Jean, and Romain Ranciere, 2012, "A European Hangover," presented at Debt, Growth and Macroeconomic Policies Conference, December 6–7, Frankfurt am Main.

International Monetary Fund (IMF), 2012a, *Pilot External Sector Report* (Washington).

———, 2012b, "A Survey of Experiences with Emerging Market Sovereign Debt Restructurings" (Washington). www.imf.org/external/np/pp/eng/2012/060512.pdf.

Kaminsky, Graciela L., Carmen M. Reinhart, and Carlos A. Végh, 2005, "When It Rains, It Pours: Procyclical Capital Flows and Macroeconomic Policies," in *NBER Macroeconomics Annual 2004,* ed. by Mark Gertler and Kenneth Rogoff (Cambridge, Massachusetts: MIT Press).

Kang, Joong Shik, and Jay Shambaugh, forthcoming, "The Evolution of Current Account Deficits in the GIPS and the Baltics: Many Paths to the Same Endpoint," IMF Working Paper (Washington: International Monetary Fund).

Kose, M. Ayhan, Prakash Loungani, and Marco E. Terrones, 2013, "Global Recessions and Global Recoveries" (unpublished; Washington: International Monetary Fund).

Kose, M. Ayhan, and Eswar Prasad, 2010, *Emerging Markets: Resilience and Growth Amid Global Turmoil* (Washington: Brookings Institution Press).

Krishnamurthy, Arvind, and Annette Vissing-Jorgensen, 2011, "The Effects of Quantitative Easing on Interest Rates: Channels and Implications for Policy," *Brookings Papers on Economic Activity* (Fall), pp. 215–75.

Krugman, Paul, 1988, "Financing vs. Forgiving a Debt Overhang," *Journal of Development Economics,* Vol. 29, No. 3, pp. 253–68.

Kumar, Manmohan S., 2003, *Deflation: Determinants, Risks, and Policy Options,* IMF Occasional Paper No. 221 (Washington: International Monetary Fund).

———, and Jaejoon Woo, 2010, "Public Debt and Growth," IMF Working Paper No. 10/174 (Washington: International Monetary Fund).

Laeven, Luc, and Fabián Valencia, 2012, "Systemic Banking Crises: An Update," IMF Working Paper No. 12/163 (Washington: International Monetary Fund).

Lane, Philip, and Barbara Pels, 2012, "Current Account Imbalances in Europe," CEPR Discussion Paper No. DP8958 (London: Centre for Economic Policy Research).

Matheson, Troy, D., 2011, "New Indicators for Tracking Growth in Real Time," IMF Working Paper No. 11/43 (Washington: International Monetary Fund).

Mauro, Paolo, Rafael Romeu, Ariel Binder, and Asad Zaman, 2013, "A Modern History of Fiscal Prudence and Profligacy," IMF Working Paper No. 13/5 (Washington: International Monetary Fund).

McCulley, Paul, and Zoltan Pozsar, 2012, "Does Central Bank Independence Frustrate the Optimal Fiscal-Monetary Policy Mix in a Liquidity Trap?" (unpublished; Philadelphia, Pennsylvania: Global Society of Fellows).

Myers, Stewart, 1977, "Determinants of Corporate Borrowing," *Journal of Financial Economics*, Vol. 5, No. 2, pp. 147–75.

Nkusu, Mwanza, 2013, "Boosting Competitiveness to Grow Out of Debt—Can Ireland Find a Way Back to Its Future?" IMF Working Paper No. 13/35 (Washington: International Monetary Fund).

Reinhart, Carmen M., Vincent Reinhart, and Kenneth Rogoff, 2012, "Public Debt Overhangs: Advanced-Economy Episodes since 1800," *Journal of Economic Perspectives*, Vol. 26, No. 3, pp. 69–86.

Reinhart, Carmen M., and Kenneth S. Rogoff, 2009, *This Time Is Different: Eight Centuries of Financial Folly* (Princeton, New Jersey: Princeton University Press).

Shambaugh, Jay, 2012, "The Euro's Three Crises," *Brookings Papers on Economic Activity* (Spring), pp. 157–211.

Swanson, Eric T., and John C. Williams, 2013, "Measuring the Effect of the Zero Lower Bound on Medium- and Longer-Term Interest Rates," Working Paper No. 2012–02, (San Francisco: Federal Reserve Bank of San Francisco).

Tobin, James, 1969, "A General Equilibrium Approach to Monetary Theory," *Journal of Money Credit and Banking*, Vol. 1, No. 1, pp. 15–29. Doi:10.2307/1991374.

Turner, Adair, 2013, "Debt, Money and Mephistopheles: How Do We Get Out of this Mess?" (unpublished; London: Cass Business School).

Ursua, Jose, and Dominic Wilson, 2012, "Risks to Growth from Build-ups in Public Debt," *Global Economics Weekly*, No. 12/10.

Werning, Iván, 2012, "Managing a Liquidity Trap: Monetary and Fiscal Policy" (unpublished; Cambridge, Massachusetts: MIT Press).

The balance of risks to global growth has improved since the October 2012 World Economic Outlook (WEO), but the road to recovery remains bumpy and uneven for advanced economies. Over the past six months, policy actions have diminished risks of an acute crisis in both Europe and the United States, although the baseline outlook for these two regions diverges: in the euro area, balance sheet repair and still-tight credit conditions continue to weigh on growth prospects, whereas underlying conditions in the United States are more supportive of recovery, even with the sequester inducing a larger-than-expected fiscal consolidation. In many emerging market and developing economies, activity has already picked up following the sharper-than-expected slowdown in the middle of 2012. Policy easing in many of these economies helped arrest that slowdown, and growth in Asia, Latin America and the Caribbean (LAC), and sub-Saharan Africa is slated to strengthen further this year, while growth in the Commonwealth of Independent States (CIS) will be on par with last year (Figure 2.1). The Middle East and North Africa (MENA) region is a notable exception: a pause in oil production growth among oil-exporting countries is expected to lead to a temporary deceleration in the region's growth, while ongoing political transitions and a difficult external environment are preventing a quicker recovery in some oil-importing countries.

While tail risks to the global outlook have diminished and upside risks now exist, downside risks still predominate and could have important spillovers across regions. As noted in Chapter 1, the possibility of renewed setbacks remains in the euro area, because of either adjustment fatigue or a more general loss of

Figure 2.1. World: 2013 GDP Growth Forecasts
(Percent)

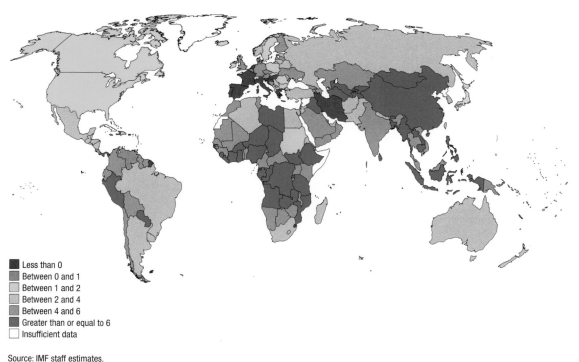

Less than 0
Between 0 and 1
Between 1 and 2
Between 2 and 4
Between 4 and 6
Greater than or equal to 6
Insufficient data

Source: IMF staff estimates.

momentum for reform. A tail risk in the medium term is that lingering fiscal problems in the United States, and especially in Japan, could result in a reassessment of sovereign risks in these economies, leading to rising interest rates and lower growth that could spill over to other regions. And the mid-2012 slowdown was just the latest in a string of downside surprises to growth in many large emerging market economies in the past two years. Combined with the fact that many of these economies have less policy room to maneuver than before the Great Recession, investors' reassessments of their growth prospects could lead to sharply lower investment and increased capital outflows. The regional effects of these risks are discussed in the sections that follow.

The Spillover Feature in this chapter assesses the extent to which policy uncertainty in the United States and Europe has affected economic activity in other regions. It finds that sharp spikes in U.S. and European policy uncertainty are associated with temporarily lower output in other regions, with the magnitude varying across regions. A reduction in policy uncertainty in the United States and Europe may thus give an added fillip to global activity.

Europe: Diminished Crisis Risks amid Prolonged Stagnation

Advanced Europe

Since the October 2012 WEO, financial stress in the euro area has moderated in response to policy actions at both the national and European levels. But economic activity remains weak, and growth projections for 2013 have been lowered because weakness has spilled over from the periphery to the core (Figure 2.2). Downside risks to the outlook include stagnation and the reemergence of stresses if policy momentum is not sustained or if events in Cyprus lead to prolonged financial market fragmentation.

Since the October 2012 WEO, acute crisis risks in the euro area have diminished. Decisive policy actions at the European level—including Outright Monetary Transactions (OMTs), the completion of the European Stability Mechanism, the deal on Greek debt relief, and the agreement on the Single Supervisory Mechanism—have increased confidence in the viability of the Economic and Monetary Union. Along with progress on economic adjustment by national governments, this

Figure 2.2. Europe: 2013 GDP Growth Forecasts
(Percent)

Less than 0
Between 0 and 1
Between 1 and 2
Between 2 and 4
Between 4 and 6
Greater than or equal to 6
Insufficient data
Covered in a different map

Source: IMF staff estimates.
Note: Projections for Cyprus are excluded due to the ongoing crisis.

has greatly improved financial conditions for sovereigns and banks (Figure 2.3).

But lower sovereign spreads and improved bank liquidity have yet to translate into either improved private sector borrowing conditions or stronger economic activity. Achieving these gains could prove even more challenging given that financial conditions remain highly vulnerable to shifts in market sentiment, as evidenced by the renewed volatility in the wake of the inconclusive outcome of Italy's elections and recent events in Cyprus. Analysis in the April 2013 *Global Financial Stability Report* (GFSR) suggests that euro area bank deleveraging is proceeding broadly in line with the baseline scenario in the October 2012 GFSR. Euro area credit has continued to contract, mainly because of conditions in the periphery economies, and lending conditions remain tight. This delayed transmission to credit conditions led euro area activity to contract by 2¼ percent in the fourth quarter of 2012, with deep recessions continuing across much of the periphery and weakness spilling over to the core, reinforcing weaker near-term growth dynamics in these economies. The need to repair public and private balance sheets, as well as continued policy uncertainty, appears to be weighing against a robust recovery in investment and consumption in both the periphery and the core, which has contributed to a steady rise in unemployment rates in many countries.

- The near-term outlook for the euro area has been revised downward, with activity now expected to contract by ¼ percent in 2013, instead of expanding by ¼ percent as projected in the October 2012 WEO (Table 2.1). This reflects declines in growth projections across all euro area countries, with notable revisions in some core members (France, Germany, Netherlands). Growth will strengthen gradually through the year, reaching 1 percent by the fourth quarter, as the pace of fiscal consolidation (at ¾ percent of GDP) is eased by almost half during 2013. But growth will generally remain subdued as improvements in private sector borrowing conditions are hampered by financial market fragmentation and ongoing balance sheet repair. Further headwinds to growth could result from a sustained appreciation of the euro that lowers competitiveness and dampens export growth.

- Activity is also subdued in the other advanced economies of the region. In the United Kingdom, the recovery is progressing slowly, notably in the context of weak external demand and ongoing fiscal

Figure 2.3. Advanced Europe: Diminished Crisis Risks amid Prolonged Stagnation

Financial stresses have moderated in response to policy actions. But economic activity remains weak because the weakness of the periphery economies has spilled over into the core. Inflation expectations remain subdued. There has been some progress toward internal rebalancing within the euro area.

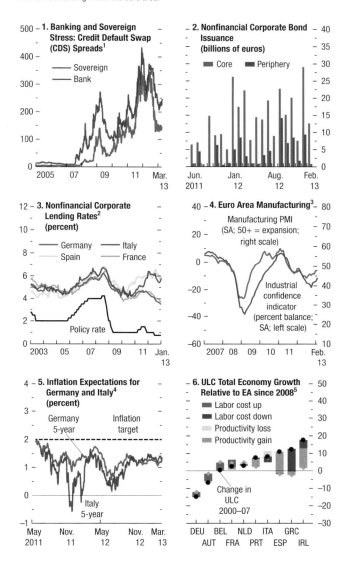

Sources: Bloomberg, L.P.; European Central Bank (ECB); European Commission; Eurostat; Markit/Haver Analytics; and IMF staff calculations.
Note: Core: Austria (AUT), Belgium (BEL), Estonia, Finland, France (FRA), Germany (DEU), Luxembourg, Netherlands (NLD); periphery: Greece (GRC), Ireland (IRL), Italy (ITA), Portugal (PRT), Spain (ESP). SA = seasonally adjusted.
[1]Five-year CDS spreads in basis points weighted by general government gross debt. All euro area countries included, except Greece.
[2]New loans with maturities of one to five years up to 1 million euros, and the ECB policy rate.
[3]Manufacturing Purchasing Managers' Index (PMI): 50+ = expansion and 50– = contraction. The euro area composite comprises eight member countries only: Austria, France, Germany, Greece, Ireland, Italy, Netherlands, and Spain. This is estimated to be 90 percent of the euro area manufacturing activity.
[4]Inflation expectations were derived from market rates for five-year-ahead inflation-linked and nominal government bonds.
[5]In percentage points. ULC = unit labor cost; EA = euro area. Change in ULC from 2008 to latest available data (mostly 2012:Q3) is represented by the distance between a circle and a diamond.

Table 2.1. Selected European Economies: Real GDP, Consumer Prices, Current Account Balance, and Unemployment

(Annual percent change unless noted otherwise)

	Real GDP			Consumer Prices[1]			Current Account Balance[2]			Unemployment[3]		
		Projections			Projections			Projections			Projections	
	2012	2013	2014	2012	2013	2014	2012	2013	2014	2012	2013	2014
Europe	**0.0**	**0.3**	**1.5**	**2.9**	**2.2**	**2.0**	**1.4**	**1.5**	**1.4**	**...**	**...**	**...**
Advanced Europe	**−0.3**	**0.0**	**1.2**	**2.4**	**1.8**	**1.7**	**2.0**	**2.2**	**2.2**	**10.3**	**11.0**	**11.0**
Euro Area[4,5]	−0.6	−0.3	1.1	2.5	1.7	1.5	1.2	2.3	2.3	11.4	12.3	12.3
Germany	0.9	0.6	1.5	2.1	1.6	1.7	7.0	6.1	5.7	5.5	5.7	5.6
France	0.0	−0.1	0.9	2.0	1.6	1.5	−2.4	−1.3	−1.4	10.2	11.2	11.6
Italy	−2.4	−1.5	0.5	3.3	2.0	1.4	−0.5	0.3	0.3	10.6	12.0	12.4
Spain	−1.4	−1.6	0.7	2.4	1.9	1.5	−1.1	1.1	2.2	25.0	27.0	26.5
Netherlands	−0.9	−0.5	1.1	2.8	2.8	1.7	8.3	8.7	9.0	5.3	6.3	6.5
Belgium	−0.2	0.2	1.2	2.6	1.7	1.4	−0.5	−0.1	0.2	7.3	8.0	8.1
Austria	0.8	0.8	1.6	2.6	2.2	1.9	2.0	2.2	2.3	4.4	4.6	4.5
Greece	−6.4	−4.2	0.6	1.0	−0.8	−0.4	−2.9	−0.3	0.4	24.2	27.0	26.0
Portugal	−3.2	−2.3	0.6	2.8	0.7	1.0	−1.5	0.1	−0.1	15.7	18.2	18.5
Finland	−0.2	0.5	1.2	3.2	2.9	2.5	−1.7	−1.7	−1.8	7.7	8.1	8.1
Ireland	0.9	1.1	2.2	1.9	1.3	1.3	4.9	3.4	3.9	14.7	14.2	13.7
Slovak Republic	2.0	1.4	2.7	3.7	1.9	2.0	2.3	2.2	2.7	14.0	14.3	14.3
Slovenia	−2.3	−2.0	1.5	2.6	1.8	1.9	2.3	2.7	2.5	9.0	9.8	9.4
Luxembourg	0.1	0.1	1.3	2.9	1.9	1.9	6.0	6.6	6.8	6.0	6.3	6.4
Estonia	3.2	3.0	3.2	4.2	3.2	2.8	−1.2	0.0	0.1	9.8	7.8	6.2
Cyprus[6]	−2.4	...	...	3.1	...	...	−4.9	...	...	12.1	...	...
Malta	0.8	1.3	1.8	3.2	2.4	2.0	0.3	0.5	0.8	6.3	6.4	6.3
United Kingdom[5]	0.2	0.7	1.5	2.8	2.7	2.5	−3.5	−4.4	−4.3	8.0	7.8	7.8
Sweden	1.2	1.0	2.2	0.9	0.3	2.3	7.1	6.0	6.8	7.9	8.1	7.8
Switzerland	1.0	1.3	1.8	−0.7	−0.2	0.2	13.4	12.6	12.3	2.9	3.2	3.2
Czech Republic	−1.2	0.3	1.6	3.3	2.3	1.9	−2.7	−2.1	−1.8	7.0	8.1	8.4
Norway	3.0	2.5	2.2	0.7	1.5	1.5	14.2	11.7	10.9	3.2	3.1	3.3
Denmark	−0.6	0.8	1.3	2.4	2.0	2.0	5.3	4.7	4.7	7.6	7.6	7.2
Iceland	1.6	1.9	2.1	5.2	4.7	4.0	−4.9	−2.8	−1.7	5.8	5.0	4.6
San Marino	−4.0	−3.5	0.0	2.8	1.6	0.9	...	...	...	6.6	6.1	5.5
Emerging Europe[7]	**1.6**	**2.2**	**2.8**	**5.8**	**4.4**	**3.6**	**−4.3**	**−4.7**	**−4.9**	**...**	**...**	**...**
Turkey	2.6	3.4	3.7	8.9	6.6	5.3	−5.9	−6.8	−7.3	9.2	9.4	9.5
Poland	2.0	1.3	2.2	3.7	1.9	2.0	−3.6	−3.6	−3.5	10.3	11.0	11.0
Romania	0.3	1.6	2.0	3.3	4.6	2.9	−3.8	−4.2	−4.5	7.0	7.0	6.9
Hungary	−1.7	0.0	1.2	5.7	3.2	3.5	1.7	2.1	1.8	11.0	10.5	10.9
Bulgaria	0.8	1.2	2.3	2.4	2.1	1.9	−0.7	−1.9	−2.1	12.4	12.4	11.4
Serbia	−1.8	2.0	2.0	7.3	9.6	5.4	−10.9	−8.7	−8.6	23.1	23.0	22.9
Croatia	−2.0	−0.2	1.5	3.4	3.2	2.3	−0.1	0.0	−0.5	15.0	15.2	14.7
Lithuania	3.6	3.0	3.3	3.2	2.1	2.5	−0.9	−1.3	−1.7	13.2	12.0	11.0
Latvia	5.6	4.2	4.2	2.3	1.8	2.1	−1.7	−1.8	−1.9	14.9	13.3	12.0

Note: Data for some countries are based on fiscal years. Please refer to the country information section of the WEO online database on the IMF website (www.imf.org) for a complete listing of the reference periods for each country.

[1]Movements in consumer prices are shown as annual averages. Year-end to year-end changes can be found in Tables A6 and A7 in the Statistical Appendix.
[2]Percent of GDP.
[3]Percent. National definitions of unemployment may differ.
[4]Current account position corrected for reporting discrepancies in intra-area transactions.
[5]Based on Eurostat's harmonized index of consumer prices.
[6]Projections for Cyprus are excluded due to the ongoing crisis.
[7]Includes Albania, Bosnia and Herzegovina, Kosovo, FYR Macedonia, and Montenegro.

consolidation. Growth is forecast at ¾ percent this year, down ¼ percentage point from the October 2012 WEO. Here too, domestic rebalancing from the public to the private sector is being held back by deleveraging, tight credit conditions, and economic uncertainty, while declining productivity growth and high unit labor costs are holding back much needed external rebalancing. Growth in other advanced economies (Sweden) has generally remained stronger, largely owing to more resilient domestic demand and relatively healthier financial systems.

Current account balances of adjusting economies have improved significantly, and this improvement is expected to continue this year. This increasingly reflects structural improvements, including falling unit labor costs, rising productivity, and trade gains outside the euro area. But cyclical factors also play a role, notably layoffs of less productive workers, and would reverse with eventual economic recovery. Both core and other advanced economies continue to benefit from trade with faster-growing emerging market economies.

Inflation pressure has moderated in the euro area and is expected to moderate further. Headline inflation declined throughout 2012 and has recently been close to target, and core inflation has been subdued, declining since mid-2012. Inflation is expected to be reduced further, to 1¾ percent from 2½ percent in 2012, because of negative growth revisions, the diminishing effects of crisis-related fiscal measures, and lower oil prices.

Amid reduced market pressure and very high unemployment, the near-term risks of incomplete policy implementation at both the national and European levels are significant, while events in Cyprus could lead to more sustained financial market fragmentation. Incomplete implementation could result in a reversal of financial market sentiment. A more medium-term risk is a scenario of prolonged stagnation in the euro area. Under such a scenario, described in more detail in Chapter 1, growth would hover around 1 percent in the medium term, gradually deepening disinflation pressure and exacerbating the challenge of reducing debt and generating negative spillovers to other regions. There are also some upside risks to the outlook, as described in Chapter 1. If euro area policymakers were to quickly implement a comprehensive banking union and if structural reforms already implemented were to deliver a larger-than-expected growth dividend, growth in the euro area could reach 2 to 2¼ percent, driven by a strong rebound in the periphery economies.

Minimizing the downside risks and bolstering the upside risks will require sustaining policy momentum. For the euro area, this means arresting the decline in demand and making further progress on banking union and fiscal integration.

- At the national level, countries should press on with needed balance sheet repair and structural reforms. Long-standing structural rigidities need to be tackled to raise long-term growth prospects. Southern Europe needs to increase competitiveness in the tradables sector, especially through labor market reforms. In the North, reforms would help generate a more vibrant services sector. These measures will help reduce unemployment and rebuild competitiveness in the periphery; as Box 1.3 notes, relative unit labor costs have fallen from their peaks in these economies. The pace of fiscal consolidation should remain credible, with targets set in structural rather than nominal terms.
- Given moderating inflation pressure, monetary policy should remain very accommodative. Room

is still available for further conventional easing, as inflation is projected to fall below the European Central Bank's target in the medium term.

- The mere existence of the OMTs may be insufficient to keep sovereign spreads low. OMTs should be made available to countries with programs that are delivering on adjustment, which may accelerate the countries' return to durable market access.
- The Single Supervisory Mechanism is a key step toward strengthening financial stability and reducing fragmentation. To ensure its timely and effective implementation at the European Central Bank, legislative agreements should be swiftly adopted, a single rulebook established, and operational details clarified.
- Tangible progress toward a single resolution authority and a deposit insurance fund—both backed by common resources—is essential to weakening sovereign-bank links and should be further supported by making direct European Stability Mechanism recapitalization available as soon as possible.
- Greater fiscal integration is needed to help address gaps in Economic and Monetary Union design and mitigate the transmission of country-level shocks across the euro area. Building political support will take time, but the priority should be to ensure a common fiscal backstop for the banking union.

Continued near-term support is important in other advanced economies while fiscal buffers are secured to guard against future risks, including from large financial sectors (Denmark, Sweden). In the United Kingdom, other forms of monetary easing could be considered, including the purchase of private sector assets and greater transparency on the likely future monetary stance. Greater near-term flexibility in the path of fiscal adjustment should be considered in the light of lackluster private demand.

Emerging Europe

Emerging Europe experienced a sharp growth slowdown in 2012, reflecting spillovers from the euro area crisis and domestic policy tightening in the largest economies in response to new capacity constraints. Only a moderate recovery lies ahead for 2013–14.

The intensification of the euro area crisis took a toll on activity in emerging Europe in 2012. Exports decelerated, confidence suffered, and beleaguered western European banks decreased funding for their subsidiaries (Figure 2.4). Compounding these effects

Figure 2.4. Emerging Europe: A Gradual Recovery from 2012 Slowdown

Emerging Europe experienced a sharp growth slowdown in 2012, reflecting spillovers from the euro area crisis and domestic policy tightening in the largest economies. The share of nonperforming loans is high in parts of the region, and cross-border bank flows have abated.

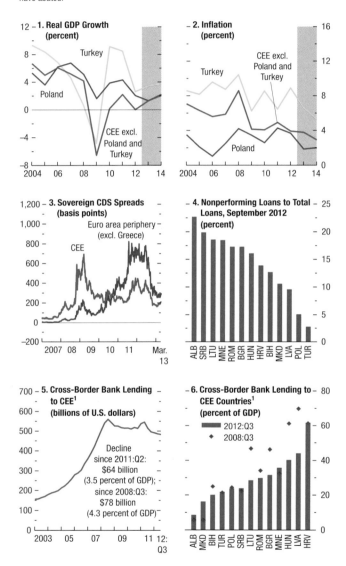

Sources: Bank for International Settlements (BIS), Locational Banking Statistics; national statistics; Thomson Reuters Datastream; and IMF staff estimates.
Note: ALB = Albania; BGR = Bulgaria; BIH = Bosnia and Herzegovina; CDS = credit default swap; CEE = central and eastern Europe; HUN = Hungary; HRV = Croatia; MKD = FYR Macedonia; MNE = Montenegro; LTU = Lithuania; LVA = Latvia; POL = Poland; ROM = Romania; SRB = Serbia; TUR = Turkey. Euro area periphery includes Greece, Ireland, Italy, Portugal, and Spain.
[1]External position of BIS-reporting banks (from 43 countries) in the CEE, vis-à-vis all sectors.

were restrictive domestic policies—in Turkey to rein in the overheated economy and in Poland to address above-target inflation and a sizable fiscal deficit. As a result, growth in the region plunged from 5¼ percent in 2011 to 1½ percent in 2012. Several economies in southeastern Europe that had yet to fully emerge from the 2008–09 crisis fell back into recession.

Growth in emerging Europe is projected to pick up to 2¼ percent in 2013 and 2¾ percent in 2014 (Table 2.1), with positive impulses from improved financial market sentiment and easing external financing conditions resulting both from recent EU-wide policy decisions and from gradual recovery in the euro area. Economic activity should also benefit from monetary easing in the second half of 2012 and smaller drag from fiscal consolidation than during 2012. Nonetheless, various factors will constrain the recovery. Emerging Europe's principal export market, the euro area, will remain lackluster, only starting to grow in the second half of 2013. And the ongoing rebalancing of funding for the region's foreign banks from parent banks to local sources will continue to weigh on credit availability. Emerging Europe is also burdened by such crisis legacies as high nonperforming loan ratios and incomplete repair of public finances.

- Growth in Turkey is projected to accelerate to 3½ percent in 2013 and 3¾ percent in 2014—helped by recovering external demand and capital flows.
- Poland's growth will slow further to 1¼ percent in 2013 before picking up to 2¼ percent in 2014, on account of lackluster private consumption, fragile export demand from key trading partners in core Europe, and a further decline in EU-funded public investment.
- Southeastern Europe will see the most tepid recovery, reflecting to various degrees entrenched structural impediments and competitiveness problems, a continued rise in nonperforming loans, and challenging public finances.
- Hungary faces a difficult outlook due to high public and external debt, along with unconventional policies that have eroded confidence and investment.

Overall, annual average inflation is expected to remain moderate this year in most of emerging Europe. Elevated rates are projected only for Turkey (6½ percent) and Serbia (9½ percent), largely reflecting inflation inertia.

The balance of risks to the outlook is tilted to the downside, though less than in the October 2012

WEO, reflecting diminished crisis tail risks from the euro area. The key downside risk is prolonged stagnation in the euro area countries, given the strong economic linkages between them and the central and eastern European countries. In addition, domestic vulnerabilities and weaknesses relating to fiscal sustainability, the banking sector, or both—particularly in some countries in southeastern Europe and in Hungary—could exacerbate the impact of external shocks.

While keeping an eye on these risks, policymakers should continue to work off crisis legacies, addressing in particular high nonperforming loans and elevated fiscal deficits or public debt in several countries. In countries with flexible exchange rates, monetary policy should support the recovery. More fundamentally, many challenges that the 2003–08 boom had obscured have now resurfaced. Depending on the country, these challenges include high structural unemployment, low labor force participation, undersized tradables sectors, and incomplete transition agendas.

The United States and Canada: Growth Still Modest, but Brighter Spots Appearing

Recovery is proceeding in the United States as the housing market recovers and financial conditions remain supportive. The threat of a "fiscal cliff" was largely averted, but durable solutions to fiscal risks are needed.

Growth in the United States remained lackluster during 2012, reflecting significant legacy effects from the financial crisis, continued fiscal consolidation, a weak external environment, and temporary shocks, including the severe drought that affected farm activity and inventories and disruptions in the northeast following Superstorm Sandy. The fiscal cliff threat may also have played some role. But the recovery is beginning to show some bright spots. Credit growth has picked up, and bank lending conditions have been easing slowly from tight levels. Construction activity rebounded in 2012, albeit from low levels; house prices began to rise; and job creation picked up in the second half of the year, bringing the unemployment rate below 8 percent (Figure 2.5). Wage growth remained subdued, helping keep inflation pressure firmly in check.

The momentum in the housing market is likely to continue for the next few years, with residential investment recovering toward trend levels and

Figure 2.5. United States and Canada: Slow but Steady Recovery

Recovery is proceeding in the United States; the housing market is recovering and the threat of the "fiscal cliff" was largely averted, but durable solutions to remaining fiscal concerns are still needed. In Canada, the U.S. recovery will support growth, but high household debt and moderation in the housing sector are likely to weigh on private consumption and residential construction.

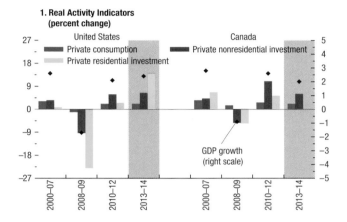

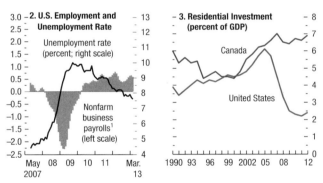

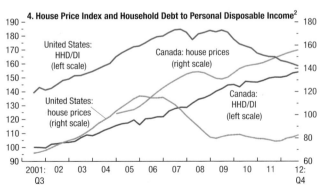

Sources: Haver Analytics; and IMF staff estimates.
[1]Moving quarterly absolute change; millions.
[2]HHD/DI = household debt to disposable income (percent)—for Canada includes only market liabilities; house prices: Case-Shiller Index (January 2005 = 100) for the United States; CREA House Price Index (2005 = 100, composite) for Canada.

Table 2.2. Selected Advanced Economies: Real GDP, Consumer Prices, Current Account Balance, and Unemployment
(Annual percent change unless noted otherwise)

	Real GDP			Consumer Prices[1]			Current Account Balance[2]			Unemployment[3]		
		Projections			Projections			Projections			Projections	
	2012	2013	2014	2012	2013	2014	2012	2013	2014	2012	2013	2014
Advanced Economies	**1.2**	**1.2**	**2.2**	**2.0**	**1.7**	**2.0**	**−0.1**	**−0.1**	**−0.1**	**8.0**	**8.2**	**8.1**
United States	2.2	1.9	3.0	2.1	1.8	1.7	−3.0	−2.9	−3.0	8.1	7.7	7.5
Euro Area[4,5]	−0.6	−0.3	1.1	2.5	1.7	1.5	1.2	2.3	2.3	11.4	12.3	12.3
Japan	2.0	1.6	1.4	0.0	0.1	3.0	1.0	1.2	1.9	4.4	4.1	4.1
United Kingdom[4]	0.2	0.7	1.5	2.8	2.7	2.5	−3.5	−4.4	−4.3	8.0	7.8	7.8
Canada	1.8	1.5	2.4	1.5	1.5	1.8	−3.7	−3.5	−3.4	7.3	7.3	7.2
Other Advanced Economies[6]	1.8	2.5	3.4	2.0	2.1	2.4	4.6	3.5	3.4	4.6	4.7	4.6

Note: Data for some countries are based on fiscal years. Please refer to the country information section of the WEO online database on the IMF website (www.imf.org) for a complete listing of the reference periods for each country.

[1]Movements in consumer prices are shown as annual averages. Year-end to year-end changes can be found in Table A6 in the Statistical Appendix.
[2]Percent of GDP.
[3]Percent. National definitions of unemployment may differ.
[4]Based on Eurostat's harmonized index of consumer prices.
[5]Current account position corrected for reporting discrepancies in intra-area transactions.
[6]Excludes the G7 (Canada, France, Germany, Italy, Japan, United Kingdom, United States) and euro area countries.

stronger house prices helping to improve household balance sheets. Personal consumption will also be supported by continued, though moderate, job gains and low borrowing rates. At the same time, business investment will be supported by favorable financial conditions and strong profitability. The strengthening of private demand will more than offset the drag on growth from fiscal consolidation (projected to be 1¾ percent of GDP in 2013), which under the baseline scenario includes the sequester only during the current fiscal year, with the automatic spending cuts replaced by more back-loaded measures beginning in the last quarter of 2013. As a result, GDP growth is expected to pick up toward the end of 2013 and to accelerate from about 2 percent in 2013 to 3 percent in 2014 (Table 2.2).

The balance of risks is still on the downside, though less so than in the October 2012 WEO. On the external front, the main risk remains a worsening of the euro area debt crisis, which would affect the United States through both trade and financial channels, including higher risk aversion and a stronger U.S. dollar amid safe haven capital inflows.

On the domestic front, passage of the American Taxpayer Relief Act resolved the immediate threat of a fiscal cliff (Figure 2.6), but offered no durable solution to looming fiscal issues, including the need to raise the debt ceiling and the deep automatic budget cuts under sequester. The budget sequester, which went into effect March 1, is projected to subtract about 0.3 percentage point from GDP growth in 2013 if maintained until the end of this fiscal year (September 30, 2013) as assumed by the IMF staff.

If the sequester continues into the next fiscal year, it could shave another 0.2 percentage point from GDP growth in 2013. Another risk is that further political entanglements over raising the debt ceiling or a lack of progress on medium-term consolidation plans could lead to a higher sovereign risk premium. Under such a scenario, also explored in Chapter 1, growth during 2015–16 would be 1½ to 2½ percentage points lower than in the baseline, with substantial negative spillovers to the rest of the world.

Developing a comprehensive medium-term deficit-reduction framework remains the top policy priority in the United States. Despite the progress made so far through discretionary spending caps and modest tax increases, a comprehensive plan is needed that includes entitlement reform and additional revenue-raising measures to put public debt on a sustainable footing. Such a comprehensive plan should place fiscal consolidation on a gradual path in the short term, in light of the fragile recovery and the limited room for monetary policy.

The output gap remains sizable, and is expected to keep inflation below 2 percent during 2013–14. Given the downside risks, the additional policy easing announced by the Federal Reserve in December 2012 is appropriate. Moreover, its conditional rate guidance further clarifies for market participants the future path of the federal funds rate. Although the IMF staff expect the first hike in policy rates to occur in early 2016, the policy tightening cycle may need to start earlier should upside risks to growth materialize.

Canadian growth slowed to about ¾ percent in the second half of 2012, with fiscal consolidation, tighter consumer credit, a cooling housing market, temporary disruptions in the energy sector, and an uncertain external environment weighing on economic activity. Economic growth is projected to be 1½ percent on average in 2013; business investment and net exports will benefit from the U.S. recovery, but high household debt and continued moderation of the housing sector will restrain domestic demand. Risks around the baseline scenario remain tilted to the downside, in particular from adverse fiscal outcomes in the United States, further turbulence in Europe, a decline in global commodity prices, and a less gradual unwinding of domestic imbalances. The main challenge for Canada's policymakers is to support growth in the short term while reducing the vulnerabilities that may arise from external shocks and domestic imbalances. Although fiscal consolidation is needed to rebuild fiscal space against future shocks, there is room to allow automatic stabilizers to operate fully if growth were to weaken further. The current monetary policy stance is appropriately accommodative, and the beginning of the monetary tightening cycle should be delayed until growth strengthens again.

Asia: Laying Foundations for Shared Prosperity

Economic performance was subdued in Asia during 2012, but growth is set to pick up gradually during 2013 on strengthening external demand and continued robust domestic demand (Figure 2.7). Private demand will be supported by accommodative monetary and, in some cases, fiscal policies; easy financial conditions; and resilient labor markets. Even as global tail risks recede, however, the risks and challenges emanating from within the region come more clearly into focus, including gradually increasing financial imbalances in some economies and the potential that any loss of confidence in regional economic policies could disrupt trade and investment. Policymakers must balance support for sustainable and more inclusive growth with the need to contain financial stability risks with adequate supervision.

Economic activity had stabilized in Asia by the start of 2013. Growth slowed across the region in the middle of 2012 following a broad-based weakening of exports both within and outside Asia and implementation by China of policies aimed at moderating and better balancing growth (Figure 2.8). Exports have recently picked up across the region, reflecting firmer demand in China and the advanced economies (notably the United States).

Figure 2.6. United States: Fiscal Developments

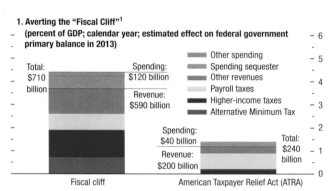

1. Averting the "Fiscal Cliff"[1]
(percent of GDP; calendar year; estimated effect on federal government primary balance in 2013)

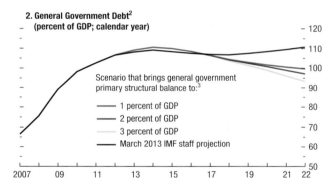

2. General Government Debt[2]
(percent of GDP; calendar year)

Scenario that brings general government primary structural balance to:[3]
— 1 percent of GDP
— 2 percent of GDP
— 3 percent of GDP
— March 2013 IMF staff projection

Sources: Congressional Budget Office; and IMF staff estimates.
[1]Fiscal cliff refers to the sizable fiscal withdrawal—a combination of tax increases and spending cuts—that was scheduled to go into effect January 1, 2013. In particular, certain income tax provisions (enacted in 2001, 2003, and 2009), certain estate and gift provisions, provisions designed to limit the reach of the Alternative Minimum Tax, and certain tax credits (including bonus depreciation) were scheduled to expire. The extension of emergency unemployment benefits and a reduction in payroll taxes were also set to expire, and automatic enforcement procedures established by the Budget Control Act of 2011 (the "sequester") and reductions in Medicare payments to physicians were also scheduled to take effect. ATRA, signed into law on January 2, 2013, averted the fiscal cliff by significantly reducing the fiscal withdrawal. Other spending includes emergency unemployment benefits and Medicare payments to physicians. Other revenues include health care reform taxes and expiration of bonus depreciation and various tax credits if the fiscal cliff materialized. ATRA expanded the bonus depreciation and most other tax credits for fiscal year 2013 but maintained the health care reform taxes, postponed the sequester for two months, and allowed the payroll tax to rise. Higher-income taxes include interactions with the Alternative Minimum Tax: ATRA permanently extended 2001 and 2003 tax cuts for incomes below $400,000/$450,000 (single/joint filers). ATRA delayed the sequester for two months. The sequester took effect on March 1, 2013, and will remain in effect until the end of fiscal year 2013 (September 30, 2013).
[2]On the basis of *Government Finance Statistics Manual 2001*.
[3]The depicted scenarios assume a structural primary withdrawal of about 1 percent of GDP annually until the target general government primary structural balance is reached.

Figure 2.7. Asia: 2013 GDP Growth Forecasts
(Percent)

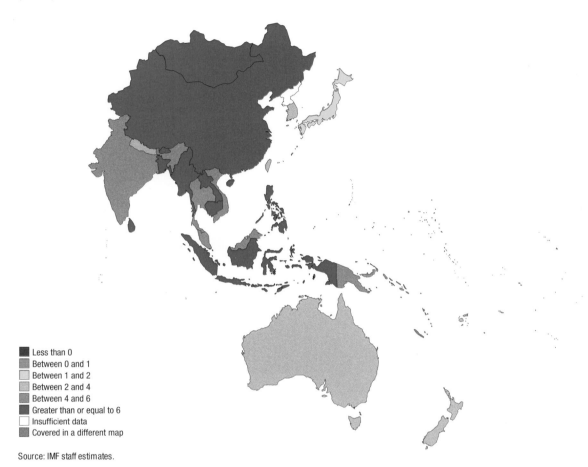

Less than 0
Between 0 and 1
Between 1 and 2
Between 2 and 4
Between 4 and 6
Greater than or equal to 6
Insufficient data
Covered in a different map

Source: IMF staff estimates.

For Asia as a whole, growth will pick up modestly to about 5¾ percent in 2013, largely as a result of recovering external demand and continued solid domestic demand (Table 2.3). Consumption and private investment will be supported by favorable labor market conditions—unemployment is at multiyear lows in several economies—and by relatively easy financial conditions. The latter reflect a combination of accommodative monetary policies; rapid credit growth, particularly in some members of the Association of Southeast Asian Nations (ASEAN); and continued robust capital inflows, which last year helped push stock prices up by 10 to 20 percent across most of the region.

Asian economies will also benefit from internal demand spillovers, particularly growing Chinese demand and the policy-led pickup in Japan. Indeed, for several economies, direct and indirect demand from China and Japan are almost as important as demand

from the United States and Europe. This dynamic may be complicated, however, by the recent yen depreciation, which may put some of the region's exporters in more direct competition with Japanese firms in world markets, while others may benefit through supply-chain linkages with Japan. The ASEAN economies have become increasingly competitive in production of final consumer goods, which will contribute favorably to intraregional demand.

Inflation is expected to remain generally within central banks' targets (explicit or implicit). Reflecting the moderate acceleration of growth and a stable outlook for global food and commodity prices, headline inflation is expected to increase slightly to 4 percent in 2013, from 3½ percent in 2012.

- In Japan, growth is projected to be 1½ percent in 2013, moderately higher than in the October 2012 WEO as a result of new fiscal and monetary stimulus, despite a sharp contraction in the second half of 2012. A sizable fiscal stimulus—about 1½ percent of GDP over two years—will boost growth by some 0.6 percentage point in 2013, and growth will be supported by a recovery in external demand and the substantial further monetary easing under the recently announced quantitative and qualitative framework in pursuit of the 2 percent inflation target.

- China's growth is set to accelerate slightly to about 8 percent in 2013, reflecting continued robust domestic demand in both consumption and investment and renewed external demand. Inflation will pick up only modestly to an average of 3 percent in 2013.
- In Korea, improved exports should help spur private investment and help growth rebound to 2¾ percent. Inflation is rising but is expected to remain close to the lower bound of the target band.
- Growth will rise in India to 5¾ percent in 2013 as a result of improved external demand and recently implemented progrowth measures. Significant structural challenges will likely lower potential output over the medium term and also keep inflation elevated by regional standards.
- Growth in the ASEAN-5 economies will remain strong at 6 percent in 2013, reflecting resilient domestic demand. A large pipeline of projects under the Economic Transformation Plan will propel strong investment in Malaysia; robust remittance flows and low interest rates should continue to support private consumption and investment in the Philippines; and Indonesia will benefit from a recovery of commodity demand in China. In Thailand, growth is expected to return to a more normal pace after a V-shaped recovery driven by public reconstruction and other flood-related investment in 2012.

The potential impact of external risks on Asia remains considerable. In the event of a severe global slowdown, falling external demand would exert a powerful drag on Asia's most open economies, including through the second-round impact of lower investment and employment in export-oriented sectors. For example, in the scenario analyzed in Chapter 1 under which a reassessment of sovereign risks in advanced economies prompts further fiscal tightening and lower growth, growth in emerging Asia would be reduced by about 1 percentage point on average in 2015–16.

As global tail risks recede somewhat, risks and challenges to growth from within the region come more clearly into focus. Financial imbalances and asset prices

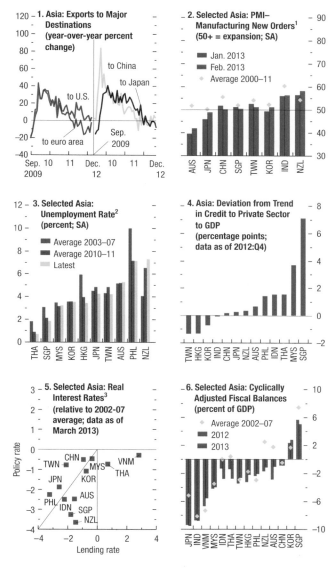

Figure 2.8. Asia: Stabilization, Recovery, and Accommodative Policies

With activity showing signs of stabilization, growth is expected to pick up gradually during 2013, as robust domestic demand is supported by favorable labor market conditions, easy financial conditions, and accommodative macroeconomic policies.

Sources: CEIC Data; Markit/Haver Analytics; and IMF staff estimates.
Note: AUS = Australia; CHN = China; HKG = Hong Kong SAR; IDN = Indonesia; IND = India; JPN = Japan; KOR = Korea; MYS = Malaysia; NZL = New Zealand; PHL = Philippines; SGP = Singapore; THA = Thailand; TWN = Taiwan Province of China; VNM = Vietnam. PMI = Purchasing Managers' Index; SA = seasonally adjusted.
[1]A reading above 50 percent indicates expansion; below 50 percent indicates contraction.
[2]Latest data as of March 2013 for the Philippines; February 2013 for Korea, Taiwan Province of China, and Hong Kong SAR; January 2013 for Japan and Thailand; 2012:Q4 for Singapore and Malaysia; and 2012:Q3 for Australia and New Zealand.
[3]A position above the 45-degree line indicates a larger lending cut, and below the line indicates a larger policy rate cut.

Table 2.3. Selected Asian Economies: Real GDP, Consumer Prices, Current Account Balance, and Unemployment
(Annual percent change unless noted otherwise)

	Real GDP			Consumer Prices[1]			Current Account Balance[2]			Unemployment[3]		
		Projections			Projections			Projections			Projections	
	2012	2013	2014	2012	2013	2014	2012	2013	2014	2012	2013	2014
Asia	**5.3**	**5.7**	**6.0**	**3.4**	**3.9**	**4.4**	**1.2**	**1.1**	**1.3**	...	...	...
Advanced Asia	**2.1**	**2.2**	**2.6**	**1.1**	**1.2**	**2.8**	**1.5**	**1.1**	**1.4**	**4.2**	**4.0**	**4.0**
Japan	2.0	1.6	1.4	0.0	0.1	3.0	1.0	1.2	1.9	4.4	4.1	4.1
Korea	2.0	2.8	3.9	2.2	2.4	2.9	3.7	2.7	2.4	3.3	3.3	3.3
Australia	3.6	3.0	3.3	1.8	2.5	2.5	–3.7	–5.5	–6.0	5.2	5.3	5.2
Taiwan Province of China	1.3	3.0	3.9	1.9	2.0	2.0	10.5	10.3	9.8	4.2	4.2	4.2
Hong Kong SAR	1.4	3.0	4.4	4.1	3.5	3.5	2.3	2.0	2.5	3.3	3.2	3.1
Singapore	1.3	2.0	5.1	4.6	4.0	3.4	18.6	16.9	17.2	2.0	2.0	2.1
New Zealand	2.5	2.7	2.6	1.1	1.4	2.2	–5.0	–5.8	–6.0	6.9	6.6	6.0
Developing Asia	**6.6**	**7.1**	**7.3**	**4.5**	**5.0**	**5.0**	**1.1**	**1.1**	**1.3**	...	...	...
China	7.8	8.0	8.2	2.6	3.0	3.0	2.6	2.6	2.9	4.1	4.1	4.1
India	4.0	5.7	6.2	9.3	10.8	10.7	–5.1	–4.9	–4.6	...	...	...
ASEAN-5	**6.1**	**5.9**	**5.5**	**3.9**	**4.5**	**4.5**	**0.8**	**0.6**	**0.4**	...	...	...
Indonesia	6.2	6.3	6.4	4.3	5.6	5.6	–2.8	–3.3	–3.3	6.2	6.1	6.0
Thailand	6.4	5.9	4.2	3.0	3.0	3.4	0.7	1.0	1.1	0.5	0.7	0.7
Malaysia	5.6	5.1	5.2	1.7	2.2	2.4	6.4	6.0	5.7	3.0	3.0	3.0
Philippines	6.6	6.0	5.5	3.1	3.1	3.2	2.9	2.4	2.0	7.0	7.0	7.0
Vietnam	5.0	5.2	5.2	9.1	8.8	8.0	7.4	7.9	6.3	4.5	4.5	4.5
Other Developing Asia[4]	**6.2**	**6.0**	**6.5**	**7.4**	**6.8**	**6.1**	**–1.6**	**–2.2**	**–2.2**	...	...	...
Memorandum												
Emerging Asia[5]	6.0	6.6	6.9	4.2	4.7	4.7	1.9	1.8	1.9	...	...	...

Note: Data for some countries are based on fiscal years. Please refer to the country information section of the WEO online database on the IMF website (www.imf.org) for a complete listing of the reference periods for each country.

[1]Movements in consumer prices are shown as annual averages. Year-end to year-end changes can be found in Tables A6 and A7 in the Statistical Appendix.
[2]Percent of GDP.
[3]Percent. National definitions of unemployment may differ.
[4]Other Developing Asia comprises Bangladesh, Bhutan, Brunei Darussalam, Cambodia, Fiji, Kiribati, Lao P.D.R., Maldives, Marshall Islands, Micronesia, Mongolia, Myanmar, Nepal, Papua New Guinea, Samoa, Solomon Islands, Sri Lanka, Timor-Leste, Tonga, Tuvalu, and Vanuatu.
[5]Emerging Asia comprises all economies in Developing Asia, Hong Kong SAR, Korea, Singapore, and Taiwan Province of China.

are building in a number of economies, fueled by rapid credit growth and easy financing conditions. In China, the use of more market-based financial instruments means that about half of financial intermediation now takes place outside traditional banking channels in less-well-supervised parts of the financial system, which leads to growing risks. In the scenario explored in Chapter 1 under which growth prospects for emerging markets are marked down and investment falls, Asia's output could be more than 2 percent below the baseline, and even lower if rising spreads lead to capital outflows. A number of other risks are more difficult to anticipate but could prove disruptive given Asia's highly integrated supply-chain network and growing dependence on regional demand and finance. These risks include disruptions to trade from territorial disputes, a loss of confidence in efforts to restore economic health in Japan, and stalled reforms and recovery in China.[1]

[1]For example, as highlighted in the IMF's *2012 Spillover Report* (IMF, 2012), a sharp rise in yields could lower growth in emerging Asia by about 2 percentage points.

Policymakers in the region must rebuild room for macroeconomic policy maneuvering while containing financial stability risks. Asian central banks have adopted an accommodative monetary policy stance, reducing policy rates or keeping them low during 2012 in the face of uncertain growth prospects and generally low and stable inflation. This stance has served them well, but the direction of future monetary policy action will diverge within the region. In emerging Asia, macroprudential measures will have to play an important role in those economies in which credit growth remains too rapid and threatens financial stability, especially if accompanied by persistently strong capital inflows. In China, financial sector reform should be accelerated to contain risks related to the rapid growth in total credit and to prevent a further buildup of excess capacity. In addition, the China Banking Regulatory Commission has recently announced steps to strengthen the supervision of banks' off-balance-sheet activities. The adoption of a new quantitative and qualitative monetary easing framework in Japan is welcome. For it to be successful and achieve 2 percent inflation within two years, easing must be accompanied by ambitious growth and fiscal reforms to ensure a sustained recovery and reduce fiscal risks.

Country circumstances will also determine the appropriate pace of fiscal consolidation, including the need for demand rebalancing and the adequacy of policy room. For some economies with large external surpluses and low public debt, it may be appropriate to use fiscal measures to support domestic demand. More generally, structural deficits are higher than before the crisis and fiscal room needs to be rebuilt. Automatic stabilizers should be the first line of defense if growth disappoints.

The key medium-term priority is to sustain economic growth and make it more inclusive. Again, the policy agenda diverges among individual countries within the region and includes economic rebalancing, strengthening private investment, reform of goods and labor markets, improving tax and spending policies, and addressing rapid demographic shifts. Asian policymakers should also undertake coordinated and collective action to deepen regional trade integration.

Latin America and the Caribbean: Higher Growth Supported by Easy Financing Conditions

Output growth moderated somewhat in Latin America and the Caribbean during 2012, but domestic demand remains strong and external current account deficits have widened further, even with high commodity prices. Growth is projected to increase to 3½ percent in 2013, supported by a pickup in external demand, favorable financing conditions, and the impact of earlier policy easing in some countries (Figure 2.9). Policymakers in Latin America need to strengthen fiscal buffers, contain the buildup of financial vulnerabilities, and move forward with growth-enhancing reforms. In the Caribbean, the policy challenges are more pressing because growth continues to be held back by high debt levels and weak competitiveness.

Real GDP growth in the LAC region declined to 3 percent in 2012, from 4½ percent in 2011, reflecting a slowdown in external demand and, in some cases, the impact of domestic factors. The deceleration was particularly pronounced in Brazil, the region's largest economy, where large policy stimulus failed to spur private investment. The slowdown in Brazil spilled over to its regional trading partners, especially Argentina, Paraguay, and Uruguay. In Argentina, widespread import and exchange controls also affected business confidence and investment. In most of the other financially integrated economies (Chile, Mexico, Peru),

growth remained strong, gradually moderating toward potential (Figure 2.10). Economic activity in Central America was also resilient, expanding by an average of 4¾ percent in 2012. However, in much of the Caribbean the recovery remained constrained by high debt levels and weak tourism receipts.

Despite the moderation in growth, domestic demand remained robust in most of Latin America, supported by easy financing conditions and high commodity prices. External current account deficits increased to 3 percent of GDP on average for the larger financially integrated economies in 2012 (from 1¼ percent in 2010).[2] Meanwhile, inflation in these economies remained generally well anchored, although it stayed above the midpoint of the inflation target in some cases (including Brazil and Uruguay). Capital inflows have been strong, and the pickup in portfolio flows in the second half of 2012 pushed up equity prices and local currencies. Bank credit growth and bond issuance remained strong in many countries, and household and corporate debt increased.

Against this backdrop, real GDP growth in the LAC region is projected to increase to 3½ percent in 2013 (Table 2.4):

- In Brazil, growth will strengthen to 3 percent, from less than 1 percent in 2012, reflecting the lagged impact of domestic policy easing and measures targeted at boosting private investment. However, supply constraints could limit the pace of growth in the near term. Activity in other commodity-exporting countries is expected to remain strong. A notable exception is Venezuela, where growth is projected to decelerate sharply as the pace of fiscal spending declines. Private consumption growth in Venezuela is also expected to decline in the near term following the recent currency devaluation and tightening of exchange controls.

- In Mexico, growth is expected to be close to potential, at 3½ percent in both 2013 and 2014, with domestic demand underpinned by sustained business and consumer confidence and resilient exports. High capacity utilization suggests that the recovery in investment will continue, and sustained employment growth and favorable credit conditions should support consumption.

- Most Central American economies are projected to expand in line with potential (by about 4½ percent), supported by strengthening in exports and remit-

---

[2]This group includes Chile, Colombia, Mexico, Peru, and Uruguay.

Figure 2.9. Latin America and the Caribbean: 2013 GDP Growth Forecasts
(Percent)

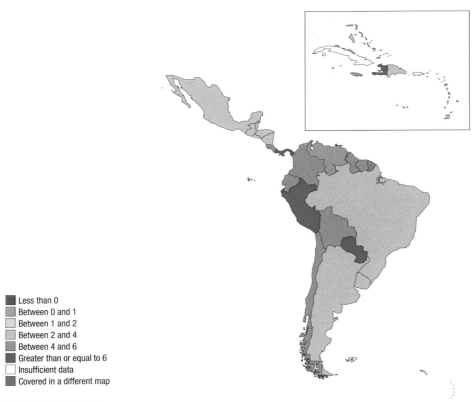

Less than 0
Between 0 and 1
Between 1 and 2
Between 2 and 4
Between 4 and 6
Greater than or equal to 6
Insufficient data
Covered in a different map

Source: IMF staff estimates.
Note: The data for Argentina are officially reported data. The IMF has, however, issued a declaration of censure and called on Argentina to adopt remedial measures to address the quality of the official GDP data. Alternative data sources have shown significantly lower real growth than the official data since 2008. In this context, the IMF is also using alternative estimates of GDP growth for the surveillance of macroeconomic developments in Argentina.

tances, although fiscal consolidation may dampen demand in some cases.

- The recovery will continue in much of the Caribbean, with a gradual pickup in tourism flows. However, high debt levels and weak competitiveness will continue to constrain growth.

The downside risks to the near-term outlook for the LAC region have diminished, as policy actions in the United States and the euro area have contained the immediate threats to global growth. However, as long as the repair of the euro area financial sector is incomplete, subsidiaries of European banks in the region remain vulnerable to potential deleveraging. Meanwhile, the reacceleration of growth in China should help support commodity prices and the region's exports. Domestic demand growth may be higher than projected, supported by strong capital inflows and easy financing conditions, particularly if slippages occur in the implementation of fiscal consolidation plans.

In the medium term, however, downside risks continue to dominate. The main risks remain the potential reversal of easy external financing conditions and favorable commodity prices. As illustrated in the risk scenarios in Chapter 1, the region would be seriously affected by a sharp slowdown in emerging market economies, particularly in China. Specifically, a 10 percent decline in private investment in the BRICS (Brazil, Russia, India, China, South Africa) could reduce output in Latin America by more than 1 percentage point during 2013–14 through its effect on demand for commodities and other exports. A combination of lower investment and capital outflows would reduce output in the region by more than 2 percentage points relative to the baseline. In addition, lingering uncertainty about the medium-term fiscal outlook for the advanced economies could result in heightened risk aversion and an increase in sovereign spreads, with negative implications for global growth.

Debt levels and fiscal deficits in many countries remain higher than before the crisis. With output gaps closed in most of the region, policymakers should take advantage of the relatively favorable economic conditions to proceed with fiscal consolidation. Fiscal prudence would also help mitigate the widening of the current accounts and the appreciation of real exchange rates. Fiscal consolidation efforts should protect much-needed public investment and education spending. If downside risks to the outlook were to materialize, monetary policy should act as the first line of defense in countries with well-anchored inflation expectations.

Large and potentially volatile capital flows continue to present a challenge for the region. Policies need to be geared toward limiting the buildup of financial and corporate sector vulnerabilities in an environment of cheap and readily available external financing. Exchange rate flexibility should continue to be used to buffer shocks and discourage speculative capital flows. Also critical will be strong prudential regulation and supervision, focused on identifying vulnerabilities and limiting systemic risks, as well as adequate capitalization and loan loss provisioning in economies that have recently experienced rapid credit growth.

The key challenge for the medium term remains boosting productivity and competitiveness. High growth rates in Latin America in recent years have been supported by an increase in labor utilization and rapid credit growth, which are likely to moderate. To maintain high rates of potential output growth, the region needs to invest more in infrastructure and human capital, improve the business and regulatory environment, and diversify exports. Increasing competitiveness is also critical for the Caribbean, where higher growth would also help alleviate the high debt burden.

Middle East and North Africa: Narrowing Differences in a Two-Speed Region

Economic performance across the Middle East and North Africa was again mixed in 2012. Although most of the region's oil-exporting countries grew at healthy rates, economic growth remained sluggish in the oil import-ers—many of which are undergoing political transitions. In 2013, these differences are expected to narrow because of a scaling back of hydrocarbon production among oil exporters and a mild economic recovery among oil importers. Many countries face the immediate challenge of reestablishing or maintaining macroeconomic stability amid political uncertainty and social unrest, but the

Figure 2.10. Latin America: Growth Supported by Easy Financing Conditions

Output growth moderated in much of the region, with Brazil observing the sharpest slowdown. Domestic demand and bank credit continue to grow at a fast pace; inflation has generally been contained, but current account deficits continue to widen. Capital flows remain buoyant, with a recent pickup in portfolio flows leading to a strengthening of both currencies and equity markets.

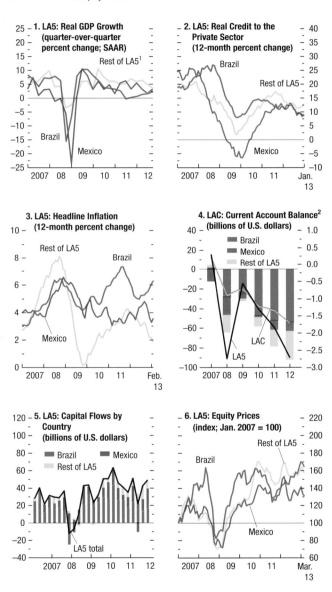

Sources: Haver Analytics; national authorities; and IMF staff calculations.
Note: LAC = Latin America and the Caribbean. LA5 includes Brazil, Chile, Colombia, Mexico, and Peru. Rest of LA5 refers to simple average for Chile, Colombia, and Peru (unless noted otherwise). SAAR = seasonally adjusted annualized rate.
[1]For Colombia, growth is averaged over four quarters.
[2]Rest of LA5: total for Chile, Colombia, Peru. LA5: simple average; percent of GDP, right scale. LAC: percent of GDP, right scale.

Table 2.4. Selected Western Hemisphere Economies: Real GDP, Consumer Prices, Current Account Balance, and Unemployment
(Annual percent change unless noted otherwise)

	Real GDP			Consumer Prices[1]			Current Account Balance[2]			Unemployment[3]		
		Projections			Projections			Projections			Projections	
	2012	2013	2014	2012	2013	2014	2012	2013	2014	2012	2013	2014
North America	**2.3**	**2.0**	**2.9**	**2.2**	**2.0**	**1.9**	**−3.0**	**−2.8**	**−2.9**	...	...	...
United States	2.2	1.9	3.0	2.1	1.8	1.7	−3.0	−2.9	−3.0	8.1	7.7	7.5
Canada	1.8	1.5	2.4	1.5	1.5	1.8	−3.7	−3.5	−3.4	7.3	7.3	7.2
Mexico	3.9	3.4	3.4	4.1	3.7	3.2	−0.8	−1.0	−1.0	4.8	4.8	4.5
South America[4]	**2.6**	**3.4**	**4.1**	**6.8**	**7.2**	**6.7**	**−1.7**	**−1.6**	**−2.1**	...	...	...
Brazil	0.9	3.0	4.0	5.4	6.1	4.7	−2.3	−2.4	−3.2	5.5	6.0	6.5
Argentina[5]	1.9	2.8	3.5	10.0	9.8	10.1	0.1	−0.1	−0.5	7.2	7.1	6.8
Colombia	4.0	4.1	4.5	3.2	2.2	3.0	−3.4	−3.4	−2.9	10.4	10.3	10.0
Venezuela	5.5	0.1	2.3	21.1	27.3	27.6	2.9	6.2	7.7	7.8	7.8	7.8
Peru	6.3	6.3	6.1	3.7	2.1	2.3	−3.6	−3.5	−3.4	6.8	6.8	6.8
Chile	5.5	4.9	4.6	3.0	2.1	3.0	−3.5	−4.0	−3.6	6.5	6.5	6.6
Ecuador	5.0	4.4	3.9	5.1	4.7	4.1	−0.5	−1.3	−1.5	5.3	5.8	6.0
Bolivia	5.2	4.8	5.0	4.5	4.6	4.3	7.5	4.8	3.5	5.4	5.4	5.3
Uruguay	3.8	3.8	4.0	8.1	7.3	7.2	−3.4	−2.9	−2.5	6.1	6.5	7.0
Paraguay	−1.2	11.0	4.6	3.8	3.6	5.0	−2.0	−2.4	−2.9	5.8	5.4	5.5
Central America[6]	**4.8**	**4.4**	**4.1**	**4.5**	**4.6**	**4.7**	**−6.6**	**−6.6**	**−6.3**	...	...	...
Caribbean[7]	**2.4**	**2.2**	**3.0**	**5.1**	**5.1**	**4.6**	**−4.5**	**−3.3**	**−2.4**	...	...	...
Memorandum												
Latin America and the Caribbean[8]	3.0	3.4	3.9	6.0	6.1	5.7	−1.7	−1.7	−2.0	...	...	...
Eastern Caribbean Currency Union[9]	0.0	1.2	2.2	3.0	3.1	2.6	−17.8	−18.3	−18.0	...	...	...

Note: Data for some countries are based on fiscal years. Please refer to the country information section of the WEO online database on the IMF website (www.imf.org) for a complete listing of the reference periods for each country.

[1]Movements in consumer prices are shown as annual averages. Year-end to year-end changes can be found in Tables A6 and A7 in the Statistical Appendix.

[2]Percent of GDP.

[3]Percent. National definitions of unemployment may differ.

[4]Includes Guyana and Suriname.

[5]The data for Argentina are officially reported data. The IMF has, however, issued a declaration of censure and called on Argentina to adopt remedial measures to address the quality of the official GDP and CPI-GBA data. Alternative data sources have shown significantly lower real growth than the official data since 2008 and considerably higher inflation rates than the official data since 2007. In this context, the IMF is also using alternative estimates of GDP growth and CPI inflation for the surveillance of macroeconomic developments in Argentina.

[6]Central America comprises Belize, Costa Rica, El Salvador, Guatemala, Honduras, Nicaragua, and Panama.

[7]The Caribbean comprises Antigua and Barbuda, The Bahamas, Barbados, Dominica, Dominican Republic, Grenada, Haiti, Jamaica, St. Kitts and Nevis, St. Lucia, St. Vincent and the Grenadines, and Trinidad and Tobago.

[8]Latin America and the Caribbean comprises Mexico and economies from the Caribbean, Central America, and South America.

[9]Eastern Caribbean Currency Union comprises Antigua and Barbuda, Dominica, Grenada, St. Kitts and Nevis, St. Lucia, and St. Vincent and the Grenadines as well as Anguilla and Montserrat, which are not IMF members.

region must not lose sight of the medium-term challenge of diversifying their economies, creating more jobs, and generating more inclusive growth.

Growth in the MENA region was relatively robust at 4¾ percent in 2012, but is expected to weaken to about 3 percent in 2013 largely because of an expected slowdown among oil exporters (Figure 2.11; Table 2.5).[3]

Oil-Exporting Economies

For MENA oil exporters, 2012 was a year of robust growth, which reached about 5¾ percent, driven largely by the almost complete restoration of Libya's oil production and strong expansions in the Gulf Cooperation Council countries. Economic growth is projected to fall

to 3¼ percent in 2013 as oil production growth pauses against a backdrop of relatively weak global oil demand. Additional oil supplies from Iraq and Libya are expected to more than offset a decline in oil exports from Iran this year, while lower net demand for Saudi Arabian exports is expected to result in slightly reduced production. As a result, aggregate oil GDP is expected to stagnate in 2013, compared with growth of 4½ percent recorded in 2012.

Sustained high government spending will continue to support buoyant non-oil GDP growth, expected at 4¼ percent this year. Overall, growth in the oil exporters of the region is projected to strengthen to about 3¾ percent in 2014 on the back of rising non-oil GDP growth and resuming oil GDP growth.[4]

[3]Syria has been excluded from regional aggregates, including projections, since 2011 because of the ongoing civil war.

[4]Saudi Arabia recently revised its GDP data, which resulted in a significantly higher level of GDP and higher estimated growth rates in 2011 and 2012.

Figure 2.11. Middle East, North Africa, Afghanistan, and Pakistan: 2013 GDP Growth Forecasts
(Percent)

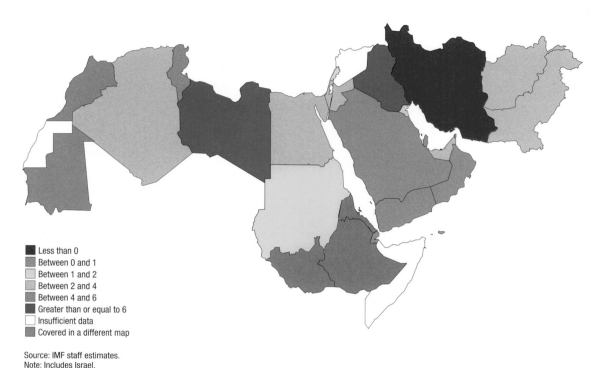

Less than 0
Between 0 and 1
Between 1 and 2
Between 2 and 4
Between 4 and 6
Greater than or equal to 6
Insufficient data
Covered in a different map

Source: IMF staff estimates.
Note: Includes Israel.

Inflation is expected to remain moderate in most oil-exporting countries because of decreasing food inflation, a benign global inflation environment, and lower increases in rents in some Gulf Cooperation Council countries. For Iran, some of these factors are envisaged to help reduce inflation in 2013. However, the macroeconomic environment is likely to remain difficult, given the sharp depreciation of the currency and adverse external conditions, which would sustain inflation at relatively high levels.

Risks to the near-term outlook for oil exporters center on the evolution of oil prices and global growth. Although fiscal and external balances are sensitive to fluctuations in oil prices, many countries have low public debt levels and would be able to draw on the reserves they have built up in the past to sustain aggregate demand in the event of a decline in oil prices. Nonetheless, a prolonged fall in oil prices brought about by lower global economic activity would result in fiscal deficits for most oil exporters. Indeed, the emerging market slowdown scenario described in Chapter 1 would place oil prices below the level required to balance the budget for most countries for many years, in the absence of a domestic policy response.

For oil exporters, increases in hard-to-reverse government expenditures such as wages should be contained to build resilience to a possible sustained decrease in the oil price. Capital expenditures can be sustained but need to be prioritized to ensure that the quality of public investment is not compromised. Fiscal consolidation is more pressing for some low-income oil exporters (particularly Yemen), which are already burdened by constrained fiscal positions. More broadly, countries need to continue their efforts to develop fiscal policy frameworks that mitigate the economic effects of oil price volatility and ensure the sustainable use of resource wealth.

To address their medium-term challenges, the oil exporters need to continue with reforms that increase the pace of economic diversification and support job creation. The former will require continued infrastructure investment and further improvements in the business climate, while the latter will require enhancing education and training, improving job placement services, and reviewing the incentives for working in the private relative to the public sector.

Oil-Importing Economies

Although growth in the MENA oil importers in 2012 was somewhat stronger than projected in the

Table 2.5. Selected Middle East and North African Economies: Real GDP, Consumer Prices, Current Account Balance, and Unemployment
(Annual percent change unless noted otherwise)

	Real GDP			Consumer Prices[1]			Current Account Balance[2]			Unemployment[3]		
		Projections			Projections			Projections			Projections	
	2012	2013	2014	2012	2013	2014	2012	2013	2014	2012	2013	2014
Middle East and North Africa	**4.8**	**3.1**	**3.7**	**10.7**	**9.6**	**9.0**	**12.5**	**10.8**	**8.9**	...	...	...
Oil Exporters[4]	**5.7**	**3.2**	**3.7**	**11.3**	**10.0**	**8.5**	**16.6**	**14.3**	**12.0**	...	...	...
Iran	−1.9	−1.3	1.1	30.6	27.2	21.1	4.9	3.6	1.9	12.5	13.4	14.7
Saudi Arabia	6.8	4.4	4.2	2.9	3.7	3.6	24.4	19.2	16.1	...	...	...
Algeria	2.5	3.3	3.4	8.9	5.0	4.5	5.9	6.1	4.5	9.7	9.3	9.0
United Arab Emirates	3.9	3.1	3.6	0.7	1.6	1.9	8.2	8.4	7.9	...	...	...
Qatar	6.6	5.2	5.0	1.9	3.0	4.0	29.5	29.3	23.7	...	...	...
Kuwait	5.1	1.1	3.1	2.9	3.3	3.8	45.0	40.8	37.6	2.1	2.1	2.1
Iraq	8.4	9.0	8.4	6.1	4.3	5.5	7.0	3.6	2.9	...	...	...
Oil Importers[5]	**1.9**	**2.7**	**3.7**	**8.7**	**8.3**	**10.6**	**−7.7**	**−5.7**	**−4.9**	...	...	...
Egypt	2.2	2.0	3.3	8.6	8.2	13.7	−3.1	−2.1	−1.6	12.3	13.5	14.3
Morocco	3.0	4.5	4.8	1.3	2.5	2.5	−9.6	−7.0	−5.8	8.8	8.7	8.6
Tunisia	3.6	4.0	4.5	5.6	6.0	4.7	−8.0	−7.3	−6.6	18.9	16.7	16.0
Sudan	−4.4	1.2	2.6	35.5	28.4	29.4	−11.2	−6.9	−5.9	10.8	9.6	8.4
Lebanon	1.5	2.0	4.0	6.6	6.7	2.4	−16.1	−16.1	−14.6	...	...	...
Jordan	2.8	3.3	3.5	4.8	5.9	3.2	−18.1	−10.0	−9.1	12.2	12.2	12.2
Memorandum												
Middle East, North Africa, Afghanistan, and Pakistan	4.7	3.1	3.7	10.7	9.4	9.0	11.5	9.9	8.2	...	...	...
Pakistan	3.7	3.5	3.3	11.0	8.2	9.5	−2.0	−0.7	−0.8	7.7	9.2	10.7
Afghanistan	10.2	3.1	4.8	4.4	6.1	5.8	4.0	1.6	0.3	...	...	...
Maghreb[6]	15.3	6.1	5.0	5.9	4.1	4.1	6.3	5.5	3.6	...	...	...
Mashreq[7]	2.2	2.1	3.3	8.2	7.9	11.8	−6.1	−4.6	−4.1	...	...	...

Note: Data for some countries are based on fiscal years. Please refer to the country information section of the WEO online database on the IMF website (www.imf.org) for a complete listing of the reference periods for each country.
[1]Movements in consumer prices are shown as annual averages. Year-end to year-end changes can be found in Table A7 in the Statistical Appendix.
[2]Percent of GDP.
[3]Percent. National definitions of unemployment may differ.
[4]Includes Bahrain, Libya, Oman, and Yemen.
[5]Includes Djibouti and Mauritania. Excludes Syria.
[6]The Maghreb comprises Algeria, Libya, Mauritania, Morocco, and Tunisia.
[7]The Mashreq comprises Egypt, Jordan, and Lebanon. Excludes Syria.

October 2012 WEO, reaching about 2 percent, growth remains weighed down by a number of factors: continued political uncertainty and bouts of social unrest across the Arab countries in transition, significant regional spillovers from the escalating conflict in Syria, soft external demand from European trading partners, and persistently high commodity prices (particularly for food and fuel).[5] As a result, exports of goods and foreign direct investment (FDI) flows have declined; tourism arrivals remain below 2010 levels (including in Egypt and Lebanon); and unemployment has risen in many countries (Figure 2.12). At the same time, inflation has generally remained muted, reflecting tepid demand. Besides these broad trends, a few prominent country-specific factors have also played a role:

- Upside surprises to growth in 2012 were driven by a favorable agricultural harvest in Afghanistan, a tour-

[5]The Arab countries in transition comprise Egypt, Jordan, Libya, Morocco, Tunisia, and Yemen.

ism rebound in Tunisia, and higher-than-expected commodity revenues in Mauritania.

- In Egypt, the uncertainty generated by a protracted political transition has held back growth and led to an increase in fiscal and external imbalances.

- In Jordan, growth has been affected by the disruption of trading routes through Syria and strikes in the mining industry.

- In Morocco, an extended period of sound economic performance has been challenged by the deterioration of the situation in Europe; high oil and food prices and, in 2012, lower-than-average agriculture production; and heightening pressure on the public and external accounts.

- In Pakistan, high fiscal deficits and a difficult business climate are contributing to a sharp fall in private investment and growth.

- In Sudan, despite a significant pickup in agricultural activity, continued military skirmishes with neighboring South Sudan and the postsecession loss of oil production and exports led to a large decline in output in 2012.

The weak domestic and external environment will continue to pose challenges for MENA oil importers during 2013–14. Growth is projected to be 2¾ percent this year, a downward revision of ½ percentage point relative to the October 2012 WEO, owing to slower progress in political transitions and the protracted recovery in European trading partners. Nonetheless, assuming progress is made in the region's political and economic transitions, growth in oil importers could accelerate to 3¾ percent in 2014. Inflation is expected to rise during 2013–14, reflecting monetization of fiscal imbalances in several countries and cutbacks in commodity price subsidies, despite moderating commodity-import prices.

Downside risks remain elevated for oil importers, largely as the result of domestic and regional political instability and social unrest. Several governments in the region are transitional, and continued political instability could further delay policy action to maintain macroeconomic stability and aid the recovery. In addition, there is a risk that the conflict in Syria could spread to neighboring countries (Iraq, Jordan, Lebanon) and the broader subregion. In addition to the political risks, an increase in global food and fuel prices could reduce output and worsen the oil importers' already large fiscal and external deficits. A protracted period of slow European growth could further affect MENA oil importers' growth through economic linkages, including trade, tourism, remittances, and FDI. However, upside risks also exist from a potential "stabilization dividend" if reform momentum continues in Europe, a scenario analyzed in Chapter 1—this upside has the potential to boost activity, especially in the Maghreb (Algeria, Libya, Mauritania, Morocco, Tunisia).[6]

Since 2010, MENA oil importers have largely relied on their policy buffers to accommodate high fiscal and external current account deficits. However, use of these buffers has led to rising public debt (as a percentage of GDP) and a drawdown of international reserves. In recent months, some macroeconomic adjustment has taken place in several countries, in the form of greater exchange rate flexibility (Egypt, Tunisia) and reduced energy subsidies (Egypt, Jordan, Mauritania, Morocco,

[6]Annex 1.2 of the November 2012 *Regional Economic Outlook: Middle East and Central Asia* provides a detailed analysis of spillovers from Europe to the Maghreb and other MENA economies.

Figure 2.12. Middle East and North Africa: Narrowing Differences in a Two-Speed Region

Growth rates will converge somewhat as oil exporters scale back oil production and oil importers recover slightly.

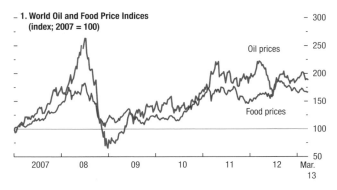

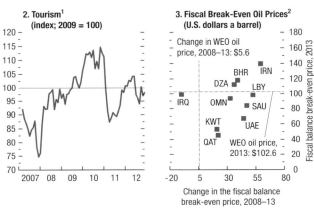

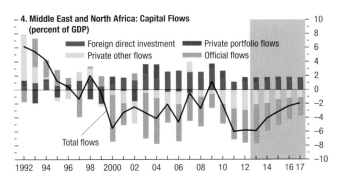

Sources: Bloomberg, L.P.; Haver Analytics; IMF, *Regional Economic Outlook: Middle East and Central Asia* (November 2012); national authorities; United Nations World Tourism Organization, World Tourism Barometer; and IMF staff estimates.
[1]Index of tourism is calculated based on the simple average of tourist arrivals of Egypt, Jordan, Lebanon, Morocco, and Tunisia. Morocco is excluded in 2007 due to data limitations.
[2]DZA = Algeria; BHR = Bahrain; IRN = Iran; IRQ = Iraq; KWT = Kuwait; LBY = Libya; OMN = Oman; QAT = Qatar, SAU = Saudi Arabia; UAE = United Arab Emirates. For Yemen, the fiscal break-even price of oil is $215 a barrel.

Tunisia).[7] Further fiscal consolidation is needed and will require reductions in inefficient spending on generalized subsidies and increased expenditures on targeted social safety nets, as well as boosts to public investment. Mobilizing external official financing can assist in smoothing the adjustment, and greater exchange rate flexibility can help protect reserves and maintain competitiveness in the face of external and domestic shocks. At the same time, action is needed to formulate and implement a credible and bold agenda of institutional and regulatory reforms, which will enhance the business environment, bolster private sector activity, and create greater and more equal access to economic and employment opportunities.

[7]See Appendix 1 of the April 2013 *Fiscal Monitor* for a more detailed discussion of energy subsidy reform.

Commonwealth of Independent States: An Improving but Vulnerable Outlook

Growth in the CIS is likely to pick up somewhat from its mediocre pace in 2012 as the external environment gradually improves and oil prices stabilize at high levels. Growth will be stronger in the Caucasus and central Asia than in the European CIS countries, underpinned by remittances and high commodity prices (Figure 2.13). Most countries in the region would benefit from structural policies to boost medium-term growth, but some, including Belarus and Ukraine, also have macroeconomic imbalances to address.

After a relatively strong start, activity decelerated in the CIS during the course of 2012, bringing growth down to 3½ percent for the year, from 4¾ percent in 2011 (Figure 2.14). The global slowdown affected exports across the region, although the impact was

Figure 2.13. Commonwealth of Independent States: 2013 GDP Growth Forecasts
(Percent)

Less than 0
Between 0 and 1
Between 1 and 2
Between 2 and 4
Between 4 and 6
Greater than or equal to 6
Insufficient data
Covered in a different map

Source: IMF staff estimates.
Note: Includes Georgia.

stronger in the European CIS countries than in the Caucasus and central Asia. Domestic demand also weakened, for varying reasons: in Russia because export prices for oil stopped rising, and in Ukraine because of higher interest rates used to defend the exchange rate. Georgia's economy slowed in the second half of the year because of uncertainties stemming from October's election and the ensuing political transition. Moldova's growth came to a halt in 2012, the result of a poor harvest, slowing trade, and stagnating remittances. Growth in the Kyrgyz Republic fell sharply, induced by shortfalls in gold production. A temporary decline in oil output accounted for the slowing of GDP growth in Kazakhstan.

Growth in the CIS is projected to remain at 3½ percent in 2013 and pick up to 4 percent in 2014, underpinned by the gradual global recovery and stable commodity prices (Table 2.6). Improved financial conditions lend further support. Since the middle of 2012, the reduction in euro area tail risks has helped reduce credit default swap spreads in the region significantly and ease access to international capital markets. In the Caucasus and central Asia, growth is projected to remain near 6 percent during 2013–14, well in excess of the CIS regional aggregate. Growth will continue to be underpinned by healthy remittance flows from Russia and high commodity (energy and minerals) prices.

- Russia's growth is projected to remain at 3½ percent this year because the output gap is essentially closed and growth is running close to potential.
- In Ukraine, after nearly zero growth in 2012 because of deteriorating terms of trade, GDP growth is likely to remain subdued in 2013 under unchanged policies.
- Growth in Armenia will moderate to about 4¼ percent during 2013–14 compared with more than 7 percent in 2012, as a return to more normal weather conditions, a slowdown in credit expansion, and a continuation of fiscal consolidation bring the economy back toward trend growth.
- In Turkmenistan, growth during 2013–14 will be close to 8 percent, led by growing gas exports to China and public investment expenditures.

Inflation is expected to remain close to current levels in 2013. In Russia, it will average about 7 percent. In Ukraine, inflation is projected to remain at ½ percent in 2013. There is concern that premature policy loosening might impede disinflation in

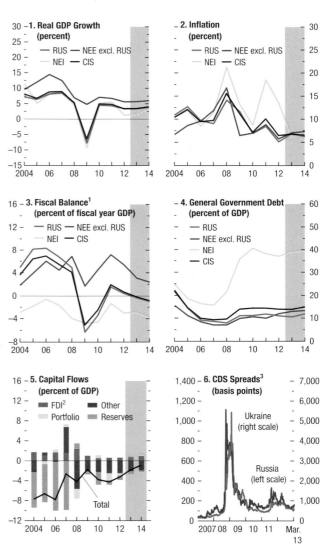

Figure 2.14. Commonwealth of Independent States: An Improving Outlook with Vulnerability to Global Slowdown

Growth in the Commonwealth of Independent States (CIS) is likely to pick up modestly as the external environment gradually improves and oil prices stabilize at high levels. Rebuilding fiscal policy buffers remains a key priority for several CIS economies. The decline in euro area tail risks has helped reduce credit default swap (CDS) spreads in the region and eased access to international capital markets.

Sources: Thomson Reuters Datastream; and IMF staff estimates.
Note: Net energy exporters (NEE): Azerbaijan, Kazakhstan, Russia (RUS), Turkmenistan, Uzbekistan. Net energy importers (NEI): Armenia, Belarus, Georgia, Kyrgyz Republic, Moldova, Tajikistan, Ukraine. NEE excl. RUS = net energy exporters excluding Russia.
[1]General government net lending/borrowing except for NEI, where it is the overall balance.
[2]FDI = foreign direct investment.
[3]Data from January 2007 through March 2013.

Table 2.6. Commonwealth of Independent States: Real GDP, Consumer Prices, Current Account Balance, and Unemployment
(Annual percent change unless noted otherwise)

	Real GDP			Consumer Prices[1]			Current Account Balance[2]			Unemployment[3]		
		Projections			Projections			Projections			Projections	
	2012	2013	2014	2012	2013	2014	2012	2013	2014	2012	2013	2014
Commonwealth of Independent States (CIS)	**3.4**	**3.4**	**4.0**	**6.5**	**6.8**	**6.5**	**3.2**	**1.9**	**0.9**	**...**	**...**	**...**
Net Energy Exporters	**3.8**	**3.8**	**4.2**	**5.2**	**6.9**	**6.4**	**4.5**	**2.9**	**1.9**	**...**	**...**	**...**
Russia	3.4	3.4	3.8	5.1	6.9	6.2	4.0	2.5	1.6	6.0	5.5	5.5
Kazakhstan	5.0	5.5	5.6	5.1	7.2	6.4	4.6	4.0	2.2	5.4	5.3	5.3
Uzbekistan	8.0	7.0	6.5	12.1	10.9	11.0	2.7	3.5	4.2	0.2	0.2	0.2
Azerbaijan	2.2	4.1	5.8	1.1	3.4	6.7	20.3	10.6	6.0	6.0	6.0	6.0
Turkmenistan	11.0	7.7	7.9	4.9	5.6	5.5	1.7	2.5	2.8	...	...	...
Net Energy Importers	**1.2**	**1.5**	**3.2**	**13.5**	**6.0**	**7.5**	**−7.3**	**−7.3**	**−7.2**	**...**	**...**	**...**
Ukraine	0.2	0.0	2.8	0.6	0.5	4.7	−8.2	−7.9	−7.8	8.0	8.2	7.9
Belarus	1.5	2.1	2.6	59.2	20.5	15.5	−2.9	−5.2	−5.5	0.6	0.6	0.6
Georgia[4]	6.5	6.0	6.0	−0.9	1.0	4.6	−12.0	−10.0	−8.4	14.6	14.0	13.3
Armenia	7.2	4.3	4.1	2.5	4.2	4.0	−10.6	−9.6	−8.2	19.0	18.5	18.0
Tajikistan	7.5	7.0	6.0	5.8	7.7	7.0	−1.9	−2.2	−2.4	...	...	...
Kyrgyz Republic	−0.9	7.4	7.5	2.8	8.6	7.2	−12.7	−7.6	−6.1	7.7	7.6	7.6
Moldova	−0.8	4.0	4.0	4.7	4.6	5.0	−9.4	−10.0	−9.7	5.5	6.2	5.7
Memorandum												
Caucasus and Central Asia[5]	5.7	5.8	6.1	5.2	6.7	7.1	5.4	3.8	2.4	...	...	...
Low-Income CIS Countries[6]	6.5	6.4	6.1	7.5	8.0	8.4	−3.3	−2.1	−1.1	...	...	...
Net Energy Exporters Excluding Russia	5.7	5.8	6.1	5.8	7.1	7.4	7.1	5.1	3.3	...	...	...

Note: Data for some countries are based on fiscal years. Please refer to the country information section of the WEO online database on the IMF website (www.imf.org) for a complete listing of the reference periods for each country.
[1]Movements in consumer prices are shown as annual averages. Year-end to year-end changes can be found in Table A7 in the Statistical Appendix.
[2]Percent of GDP.
[3]Percent. National definitions of unemployment may differ.
[4]Georgia, which is not a member of the Commonwealth of Independent States, is included in this group for reasons of geography and similarity in economic structure.
[5]Includes Armenia, Azerbaijan, Georgia, Kazakhstan, Kyrgyz Republic, Tajikistan, Turkmenistan, and Uzbekistan.
[6]Low-income CIS countries comprise Armenia, Georgia, Kyrgyz Republic, Moldova, Tajikistan, and Uzbekistan.

Belarus. Inflation in Uzbekistan will likely remain in double digits in 2013, underpinned by higher administered prices.

The regional balance of risks to the outlook remains on the downside, reflecting the balance of risks at the global level. Under a number of scenarios, such as the emerging market investment slowdown and the euro area downside scenario explored in Chapter 1, lower oil prices would transmit adverse global developments to Russia and Kazakhstan, with secondary effects from the former throughout the CIS. Trade, FDI flows, and remittance linkages are additional key spillover channels from Russia to other CIS economies—for example, remittances from immigrants working in Russia are a key driver of economic activity in Armenia, the Kyrgyz Republic, and Tajikistan. As for financial system risks, bank balance sheets remain impaired in economies with sizable nonperforming loans (Kazakhstan, Tajikistan).

Rebuilding fiscal policy buffers remains a key priority for several CIS economies. Among the energy importers, reducing fiscal deficits will help ensure public debt sustainability (Kyrgyz Republic, Tajikistan) and help narrow large current account deficits (Georgia). Fiscal consolidation is also important for Azerbaijan, whose non-oil fiscal position is well above the long-term sustainable level.

The region needs to spur structural reforms to lift its growth potential. In Russia and Kazakhstan, this means delivering on pledges to improve the business climate and diversify the economy. Gas sector reform is overdue in Ukraine. In the Kyrgyz Republic and Tajikistan, growth could be spurred by prudently financed and prioritized infrastructure investment. For Belarus, price liberalization, enterprise reform, and privatization should be priorities. In addition, European CIS countries need to maintain flexible exchange rates, and Belarus and Ukraine should address macroeconomic imbalances: Belarus needs to ensure further disinflation, and Ukraine should reduce the large current account and fiscal deficits. Further strengthening and development of institutions will help successfully implement the required policies in the region.

Sub-Saharan Africa: Strong Growth Continues

Sub-Saharan Africa is expected to continue growing at a strong pace during 2013–14, with both resource-rich and lower-income economies benefiting from robust domestic demand (Figure 2.15). The external environment is the main source of risks to growth, particularly for middle-income and mineral-exporting economies. Given the still-uncertain global environment, countries whose policy buffers are thin and where growth is strong should seek to rebuild fiscal positions without undermining productive investment.

Driven largely by domestic momentum in private consumption and investment, as well as exports, sub-Saharan Africa experienced robust growth in 2012, continuing a long trend of expansion only briefly interrupted in 2009 (Figure 2.16).[8] At 4¾ percent, regional GDP growth was slightly lower than forecast in the October 2012 WEO, reflecting mainly the impact of floods on oil and non-oil output in Nigeria and labor stoppages in South Africa.

[8]Chapter 4 has an in-depth analysis of today's dynamic low-income countries and how they differ from previous generations of fast-growing economies.

Headline growth in sub-Saharan Africa in 2012 was visibly affected by the interruption of oil exports from South Sudan. Activity in Mali and Guinea-Bissau was adversely affected by civil conflict; in Mali, 400,000 people have been displaced, half of whom fled to neighboring countries. On the positive side, Angolan oil production strengthened, and Côte d'Ivoire experienced a sharp rebound in economic activity after the election-related disruptions of 2011.

Growth is projected to reach 5½ percent in 2013, only marginally lower than forecast in the October 2012 WEO (Table 2.7). The generally strong performance is based to a significant extent on ongoing investment in infrastructure and productive capacity, continuing robust consumption, and the activation of new capacity in extractive sectors. In Nigeria, the rebound from the floods and implementation of power sector reform will boost growth in 2013. Among middle-income countries, South Africa is forecast to grow at a muted 2¾ percent, owing to sluggish mining production and the weakness of demand in the euro area, its main export market.

In 2014, regional economic growth is projected to be about 6 percent. A main driver of growth in 2014 will be the strengthening of activity in South Africa

Figure 2.15. Sub-Saharan Africa: 2013 GDP Growth Forecasts
(Percent)

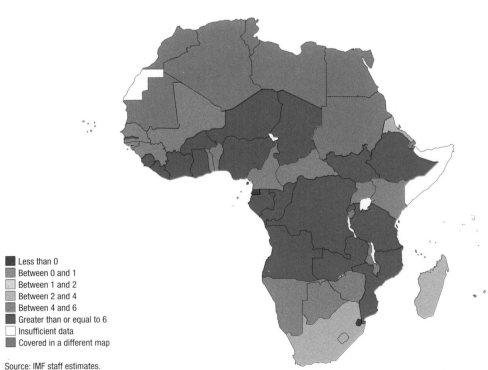

Less than 0
Between 0 and 1
Between 1 and 2
Between 2 and 4
Between 4 and 6
Greater than or equal to 6
Insufficient data
Covered in a different map

Source: IMF staff estimates.

Figure 2.16. Sub-Saharan Africa: Continued Resilience

Sub-Saharan Africa (SSA) is expected to continue growing at a strong pace during 2013–14 as a result of robust domestic demand. Some deterioration in the current account is expected resulting from projected declines in the terms of trade. Inflation has moderated. Fiscal buffers need to be strengthened in many of the region's economies.

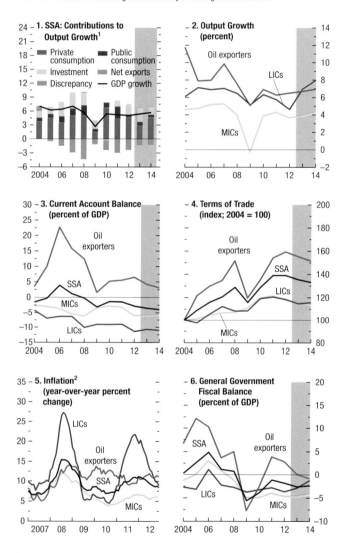

Sources: Haver Analytics; IMF, International Financial Statistics database; and IMF staff estimates.
Note: LIC = low-income country (SSA); MIC = middle-income country (SSA).
[1]Liberia, South Sudan, and Zimbabwe are excluded due to data limitations.
[2]Due to data limitations, the following are excluded: Equatorial Guinea from oil exporters; Cameroon, Côte d'Ivoire, and Zambia from MICs; Burkina Faso, Central African Republic, Comoros, Democratic Republic of the Congo, Eritrea, The Gambia, Guinea, Mozambique, São Tomé and Príncipe, South Sudan, and Zimbabwe from LICs.

and other middle-income countries, predicated on improvements in the external environment. Similarly, some low-income and fragile countries are expected to do better, including those currently experiencing internal conflict.

Some deterioration is expected in the short term in the current account balances of a number of countries, largely on account of the expected decline in the terms of trade, especially among oil exporters. Among low-income countries, some of the investment that has been raising final demand should increase capacity in tradables sectors in the medium term.

Inflation in the region moderated from 10 percent at the end of 2011 to less than 8 percent at the end of 2012, a trend expected to continue, absent new fuel and food price shocks. The improvement in 2012 was particularly marked in eastern Africa, owing to monetary policy tightening and lower food prices associated with a recovery in local food production. Some temporary headwinds to these trends have been observed in countries reforming energy subsidies, where the price level has shown one-time increases (Nigeria), and in Malawi, which has experienced some pass-through from depreciation. In sub-Saharan Africa as a whole, inflation is projected to fall further to 7 percent in 2013.

The main risks to the outlook for sub-Saharan Africa stem from the external environment, although domestic security and political risks should not be discounted. At least two of the downside scenarios discussed in Chapter 1 would pose challenges for the region—the euro area downside scenario, under which sub-Saharan Africa's middle-income countries would be especially affected, and the reduction in investment in emerging market economies (including South Africa), which would weaken key commodity prices and hit mineral exporters. Countries that regulate the prices of food and fuel products would face budgetary pressure in the event of price shocks to these commodities. Relatively few elections are scheduled for 2013, but disruptions could occur in some cases; the security difficulties in the Sahel region also pose a threat to activity in affected countries.

The setting of macroeconomic policies is largely appropriate in a majority of countries in the region. In fast-growing countries in which policy buffers still need replenishing, country authorities should consider measures to strengthen fiscal positions, including by addressing inefficient and poorly targeted price subsi-

Table 2.7. Selected Sub-Saharan African Economies: Real GDP, Consumer Prices, Current Account Balance, and Unemployment
(Annual percent change unless noted otherwise)

	Real GDP			Consumer Prices[1]			Current Account Balance[2]			Unemployment[3]		
		Projections			Projections			Projections			Projections	
	2012	2013	2014	2012	2013	2014	2012	2013	2014	2012	2013	2014
Sub-Saharan Africa	**4.8**	**5.6**	**6.1**	**9.1**	**7.2**	**6.3**	**−2.8**	**−3.5**	**−3.9**	...	...	...
Oil Exporters[4]	**6.5**	**6.7**	**6.9**	**10.9**	**9.5**	**7.6**	**6.5**	**4.2**	**3.1**	...	...	...
Nigeria	6.3	7.2	7.0	12.2	10.7	8.2	6.6	5.5	4.8	...	...	...
Angola	8.4	6.2	7.3	10.3	9.4	8.4	9.6	3.5	1.3	...	...	...
Equatorial Guinea	2.0	−2.1	−0.8	5.5	5.0	5.4	−14.7	−11.2	−11.9	...	...	...
Gabon	6.2	6.1	6.8	3.0	3.0	3.0	12.6	10.5	7.1	...	...	...
Republic of Congo	3.8	6.4	5.8	5.0	4.5	3.0	3.6	2.8	−0.1	...	...	...
Middle-Income Countries[5]	**3.6**	**3.9**	**4.3**	**5.6**	**5.7**	**5.3**	**−6.1**	**−6.1**	**−5.9**	...	...	...
South Africa	2.5	2.8	3.3	5.7	5.8	5.5	−6.3	−6.4	−6.5	25.2	25.7	25.9
Ghana	7.0	6.9	6.8	9.2	8.4	8.2	−12.6	−11.6	−10.1	...	...	...
Cameroon	4.7	5.4	5.5	3.0	3.0	2.5	−4.4	−3.5	−3.4	...	...	...
Côte d'Ivoire	9.8	8.0	8.0	1.3	3.1	2.5	−1.8	−2.7	−3.3	...	...	...
Botswana	3.8	4.1	4.2	7.5	7.2	6.9	4.9	3.9	3.3	...	...	...
Senegal	3.5	4.0	4.6	1.1	1.5	1.6	−9.8	−8.5	−7.8	...	...	...
Low-Income Countries[6]	**4.6**	**6.9**	**7.9**	**12.7**	**6.9**	**6.1**	**−11.5**	**−10.8**	**−11.2**	...	...	...
Ethiopia	7.0	6.5	6.5	22.8	8.3	9.6	−5.8	−7.5	−6.5	...	...	...
Kenya	4.7	5.8	6.2	9.4	5.2	5.0	−9.1	−7.4	−8.1	...	...	...
Tanzania	6.9	7.0	7.2	16.0	9.0	5.9	−15.8	−14.8	−13.3	...	...	...
Uganda	2.6	4.8	6.2	14.1	5.5	5.0	−10.9	−12.9	−14.8	...	...	...
Democratic Republic of the Congo	7.1	8.3	6.4	9.3	6.8	8.0	−12.4	−12.0	−13.3	...	...	...
Mozambique	7.5	8.4	8.0	2.1	5.4	5.6	−26.1	−25.4	−40.6	...	...	...
Memorandum												
Sub-Saharan Africa Excluding South Sudan	5.1	5.4	5.7	8.9	7.2	6.3	−2.8	−3.5	−4.1	...	...	...

Note: Data for some countries are based on fiscal years. Please refer to the country information section of the WEO online database on the IMF website (www.imf.org) for a complete listing of the reference periods for each country

[1]Movements in consumer prices are shown as annual averages. December–December changes can be found in Table A7 in the Statistical Appendix.

[2]Percent of GDP.

[3]Percent. National definitions of unemployment may differ.

[4]Includes Chad.

[5]Includes Cape Verde, Lesotho, Mauritius, Namibia, Seychelles, Swaziland, and Zambia.

[6]Includes Benin, Burkina Faso, Burundi, Central African Republic, Comoros, Eritrea, The Gambia, Guinea, Guinea-Bissau, Liberia, Madagascar, Malawi, Mali, Niger, Rwanda, São Tomé and Príncipe, Sierra Leone, South Sudan, Togo, and Zimbabwe.

dies. Fiscal choices are more difficult where growth is weak, given the trade-offs between supporting economic activity and containing debt accumulation. In the event of a slowdown in growth, countries should let automatic stabilizers work and avoid a procyclical fiscal contraction. The success in reducing inflation has provided room for a gradual easing of the monetary policy stance in several countries. Policymakers should also strive to make growth more inclusive, including through reforms to promote economic diversification and employment, deepen the financial sector, and tackle infrastructure gaps.

Spillover Feature: Spillovers from Policy Uncertainty in the United States and Europe

A common view is that high uncertainty in general, and high policy uncertainty more specifically, has held back global investment and output growth in the past two years. Much of the policy uncertainty emanated from the United States, with the debt ceiling dispute in August 2011 and negotiations about the "fiscal cliff" in December 2012. Policy uncertainty has also been elevated in Europe, especially in the aftermath of Greek Prime Minister George Papandreou's call for a referendum on the Greek bailout plan (and his subsequent resignation) in November 2011, and during the negotiations about a pan-European crisis response through much of 2012. Policymakers and business leaders across the globe worry about the implications of such uncertainty in the United and States and Europe—the world's two largest economies.

Spillovers from policy uncertainty can occur through several channels. Trade can be affected if increased policy uncertainty adversely affects economic activity and import demand in the United States and Europe. Policy uncertainty could also raise global risk aversion, resulting in sharp corrections in financial markets and capital outflows from emerging markets.

This Spillover Feature attempts to quantify the impact of U.S. and European policy uncertainty on other regions.[9] Specifically, it addresses the following questions: What do we mean by policy uncertainty? How well can we measure it? How has policy uncertainty in the United States and Europe evolved during the past several decades? And how large are the spillovers to economic activity in other regions?

The analysis suggests that sharp increases in U.S. and European policy uncertainty in the past have temporarily lowered investment and output in other

regions to varying degrees. It points to the possibility that a marked decrease in policy uncertainty in the United States and Europe in the near term could help boost global investment and output.

Uncertainty and Economic Activity

The idea that uncertainty can adversely affect economic activity dates back to John Maynard Keynes (1936), who argued that investment is the most volatile component of aggregate activity because it is dependent on views about the future, which are most uncertain. The idea was formalized in a number of theoretical models, ranging from Bernanke (1983) to Bloom (2009). Temporary increases in uncertainty make it worthwhile to delay investment, because investment is impossible or costly to undo or change. Investment tends to recover once uncertainty dissipates, and can overshoot as a result of pent-up demand. The same holds true for consumption of durables, which is subject to the same forces.

Two critical challenges arise in trying to estimate the spillover effects of policy uncertainty. First, it is necessary to ensure that causality is not running in the opposite direction—that policy uncertainty in the United States and Europe is not being driven by developments in economic activity elsewhere. For the most part, this is a plausible assumption—spikes in policy uncertainty are often associated with domestic economic and political events, or with global geopolitical events that can be considered exogenous to most individual countries (Figure 2.SF.1). To the extent that specific events could result in reverse causality (for example, the Russian and Long-Term Capital Management crises in 1998 resulted in a spike in policy uncertainty), the analysis verifies that the results hold even when these events are excluded.

The second challenge is to avoid attributing to policy uncertainty the effects of other factors, such as more general economic uncertainty, shifts in consumer or business confidence, or fluctuations in economic activity. This challenge is addressed by controlling for such variables, which is important because these variables tend to move together—uncertainty tends to rise and confidence tends to fall during downturns in economic activity. This means that various measures of uncertainty could be picking up actual changes in

---

The main author of this feature is Abdul Abiad, with support from Nadia Lepeshko and Katherine Pan.

[9]A number of empirical studies have analyzed the effects of uncertainty on domestic economic activity, not on activity elsewhere. These include Bloom, Bond, and van Reenen (2007); Bloom (2009); Bekaert, Hodrick, and Zhang (2010); Baker, Bloom, and Davis (2012); and Box 1.3 of the October 2012 *World Economic Outlook*. One exception is Carrière-Swallow and Céspedes (forthcoming), who look at the effects of uncertainty (as measured by implied volatility in the U.S. stock market) on economic activity in a handful of emerging market economies. The analysis in this feature is similar in spirit to that in Carrière-Swallow and Céspedes (forthcoming), but it looks specifically at policy uncertainty and investigates its impact on all the regions of the world.

economic prospects, not just the uncertainty surrounding economic prospects.

Measuring Economic Policy Uncertainty

The analysis starts with the measures of U.S. and European economic policy uncertainty constructed by Baker, Bloom, and Davis (2012). These measures use news-based indicators of policy-related economic uncertainty (the relative frequency of newspaper articles that refer to "uncertainty," "economy," and "policy"), the number of expiring tax provisions, and the dispersion in economists' forecasts about government spending and inflation levels.[10] These measures are combined to construct monthly indices of policy uncertainty dating back to 1985 for the United States and to 1997 for Europe.

This measure of economic policy uncertainty is not without issues. First, the news-based component is an indirect measure, and ascertaining whether it is measuring policy uncertainty properly is hard. Second, many expiring tax code provisions are regularly renewed and are unlikely to be a major source of uncertainty. Finally, the forecast dispersion components might rise because of other factors—inflation forecasts could become more dispersed because of uncertainty about oil or food prices, for example, and not because of uncertainty about monetary policy.

To address the first concern, Baker, Bloom, and Davis (2012) offer several "proof of concept" tests. For example, they construct a similar news-based measure for financial uncertainty by searching for news articles containing "uncertainty," "economy," and "stock market" and show that the constructed index tracks the Chicago Board Options Exchange Market Volatility Index (VIX) closely. They also note that their measure of policy uncertainty is highly correlated with other policy-uncertainty measures, such as those of Fernández-Villaverde and others (2011) and Born and Pfeifer (2011), which are constructed using very different methodologies.[11] With regard to the second and third issues, the results reported below are robust to excluding the tax-expiration and forecast-dispersion components of the

Figure 2.SF.1. Policy Uncertainty in the United States and Europe

Policy uncertainty tends to spike in response to identifiable economic, financial, and geopolitical events.

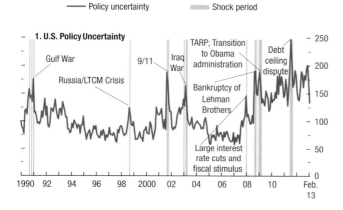

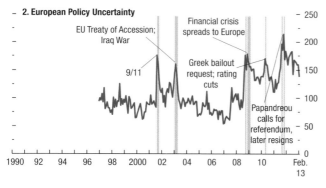

Sources: Baker, Bloom, and Davis (2012); and Haver Analytics.
Note: Uncertainty shocks are defined as periods during which detrended uncertainty is more than 1.65 standard deviations above its mean. LTCM = Long-Term Capital Management; TARP = Troubled Asset Relief Program.

[10]The European measure relies only on a news-based indicator of policy-related economic uncertainty and the dispersion in economists' forecasts because data on expiring European tax provisions are not available.

[11]Fernández-Villaverde and others (2011) and Born and Pfeifer (2011) use time series methods to estimate the time-varying volatility of taxes and government spending.

policy-uncertainty measure and relying solely on the news-based measure of policy uncertainty.

The Evolution of U.S. and European Policy Uncertainty

Policy uncertainty tends to spike in response to identifiable economic, financial, and geopolitical events (Figure 2.SF.1). Policy-uncertainty shocks, identified by vertical lines in Figure 2.SF.1, are defined as periods during which the Hodrick-Prescott detrended value of the index exceeds its mean by more than 1.65 standard deviations, following Carrière-Swallow and Céspedes (forthcoming). As noted by Baker, Bloom, and Davis (2012), many of the spikes in policy uncertainty are associated with identifiable events. For example, U.S. policy uncertainty spiked after the start of the Gulf War in August 1990, the September 11, 2001, terrorist attacks, and the run-up to the Iraq War in early 2003. More recent spikes in U.S. policy uncertainty have been associated with economic and financial events, including the recession-induced monetary and fiscal easing in January 2008, the bankruptcy of Lehman Brothers in September 2008, the debt ceiling dispute in August 2011, and the fiscal cliff negotiations in late 2012.

European policy uncertainty also spiked following the September 11 attacks and again in early 2003 with the signing of the EU Treaty of Accession (the single largest expansion of the European Union), which compounded the uncertainties from the Iraq War. Other events associated with high European policy uncertainty include the Greek bailout request in May 2010, the call in November 2011 for a Greek referendum on the terms of the bailout, and discussions on the EU-wide policy response to the expanding crisis in 2012.

These events raised uncertainty about economic policies, but they also raised general financial and economic uncertainty and caused a drop in confidence—making it critical to control for these other correlates. Policy uncertainty tends to move with general economic uncertainty—whether measured by indicators of financial uncertainty (such as implied stock market volatilities) or of economic uncertainty (such as the dispersion of economists' GDP forecasts; Figure 2.SF.2, panels 1 and 2). There are divergences, however. Most notably, general economic uncertainty has retreated from its 2008 highs, whereas policy uncertainty has remained high and has even increased. The correlation between confidence indicators (Figure 2.SF.2,

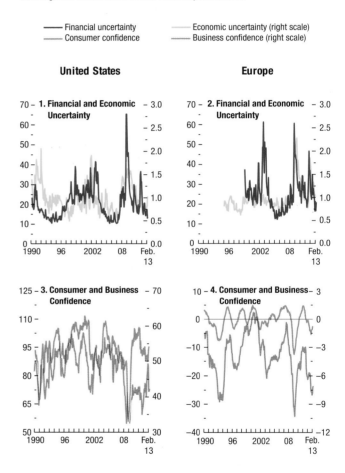

Figure 2.SF.2. General Uncertainty and Confidence in the United States and Europe

Although policy uncertainty is correlated with measures of more general financial or economic uncertainty and with indicators of business or consumer confidence, there are divergences. In particular, policy uncertainty has remained high in recent years even as general financial and economic uncertainty has declined.

——— Financial uncertainty   ——— Economic uncertainty (right scale)
——— Consumer confidence   ——— Business confidence (right scale)

Sources: Bloomberg L.P; *Consensus Forecasts;* and Haver Analytics.
Note: Financial uncertainty is measured by the implied volatility of equity markets (Chicago Board Options Exchange Volatility Index), and economic uncertainty is measured by the dispersion of economists' forecasts.

panels 3 and 4) and policy uncertainty is also evident but imperfect, making it possible to include them as control variables in the analysis.

Spillovers from Policy Uncertainty

The policy-uncertainty shocks in the United States and Europe are used as regressors to explain output and investment behavior in other regions. The methodology resembles those of Cerra and Saxena (2008) and Romer and Romer (2010), among others. Specifically, real GDP growth and real investment growth (both measured in log differences) are used as regressors to explain their lagged values to capture the normal dynamics of the growth process, as well as on contemporaneous and lagged values of a dummy variable that is equal to 1 during the policy-uncertainty shocks described above and zero otherwise.[12,13] Including lags allows for the possibility that policy-uncertainty spillovers affect other economies with a delay. The specification also includes a full set of country dummies to account for differences in normal growth rates, but the inclusion of time dummies is precluded by the fact that the variable of interest is a global variable common across all countries.

The model is estimated by region, using seasonally adjusted quarterly data for 43 economies from 1990 to 2012, although the wide variation in the availability of quarterly GDP data means the sample is highly unbalanced.[14] The effects of U.S. and European policy-uncertainty shocks are estimated separately, given their high correlation; the estimated impacts should thus be considered an upper bound because each is likely picking up the effects of the other.

[12]Using the level of the policy uncertainty variable, or of a hybrid that interacts the 0–1 dummy with the level, produces similar results. Excluding policy uncertainty shocks whose origins are outside the United States or Europe also does not materially change the findings.

[13]The regression is estimated in changes (that is, growth rates) because of nonstationarity in the log levels of real GDP and real investment. The estimated responses from the regression are cumulated to recover the response of the level of output or investment to a policy-uncertainty shock. The standard errors of the impulse responses are calculated using the delta method.

[14]The regional definitions follow those used in Chapter 2. No spillover estimates are provided for the Middle East and North Africa because of a lack of quarterly GDP data. Because the quarterly data for sub-Saharan Africa include only Botswana and South Africa, the estimates should be considered to reflect spillover effects only on the region's open middle-income economies.

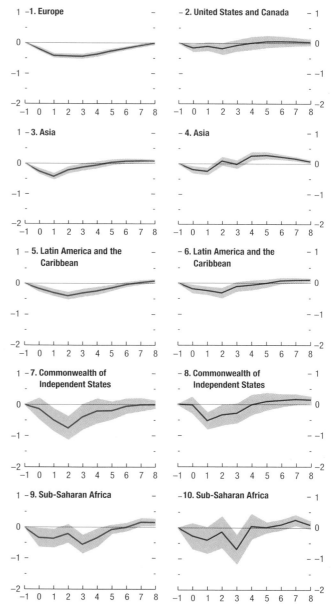

Figure 2.SF.3. Effect of a U.S. or European Policy-Uncertainty Shock on Real GDP in Other Regions
(Quarters on x-axis, percent change in real GDP on y-axis)

Policy-uncertainty shocks in the United States and Europe have a negative effect on real activity in other regions, with the magnitude, persistence, and statistical significance differing across regions. In general, the effect of U.S. policy-uncertainty shocks tends to be slightly bigger and more persistent than that of European policy-uncertainty shocks, and U.S. shocks affect Europe more than vice versa.

— Effect of a temporary U.S. policy-uncertainty shock
— Effect of a temporary European policy-uncertainty shock
▓ 90 percent confidence interval

1. Europe
2. United States and Canada
3. Asia
4. Asia
5. Latin America and the Caribbean
6. Latin America and the Caribbean
7. Commonwealth of Independent States
8. Commonwealth of Independent States
9. Sub-Saharan Africa
10. Sub-Saharan Africa

Source: IMF staff calculations.
Note: Policy-uncertainty shocks are defined as periods during which detrended uncertainty is more than 1.65 standard deviations above its mean.

Figure 2.SF.3 shows the estimated impact of a large but temporary policy-uncertainty shock—similar in magnitude to the shocks highlighted in Figure 2.SF.1—on real GDP of economies in various regions. The impulse responses are shown for an eight-quarter horizon, with the 90 percent confidence bands around the estimates shaded in gray. The impact on annual growth is significant. U.S. policy-uncertainty shocks temporarily reduce GDP growth in other regions by up to ½ percentage point in the year after the shock (Figure 2.SF.4, panel 1). European policy-uncertainty shocks temporarily reduce GDP growth in other regions by a smaller amount (Figure 2.SF.4, panel 2).[15]

One of the ways that policy uncertainty affects economic activity in other regions is by reducing investment. Figure 2.SF.5 shows the results of a similar exercise in which real investment is the dependent variable. Significant declines in investment result in all regions, except sub-Saharan Africa, with the biggest decline in the Commonwealth of Independent States (CIS).[16] The effect of European policy-uncertainty shocks tends to be similar or slightly smaller than that of U.S. shocks (Figure 2.SF.4, panels 3 and 4). In addition, European shocks tend to have a smaller effect on the United States than vice versa.

The Mechanics of Policy-Uncertainty Spillovers

The analysis addresses the possibility that the policy-uncertainty measure is picking up the effects of other variables by controlling for general uncertainty, declining confidence, or a decline in U.S. or European economic activity. Note that the results can be interpreted in two ways:

- One possibility is that the additional control variable—for example, general economic uncertainty—affects U.S. or European policy uncertainty as well as economic activity in other countries. In this case, adding the control variable improves the estimate of the spillover effects from policy uncertainty.

Figure 2.SF.4. Growth Impact of U.S. and European Policy-Uncertainty Shocks
(Percentage points)

U.S. policy-uncertainty shocks tend to reduce GDP growth in other regions by 0.2 to 0.5 percentage point. European policy-uncertainty shocks have a smaller impact. U.S. policy-uncertainty shocks affect Europe more than vice versa.

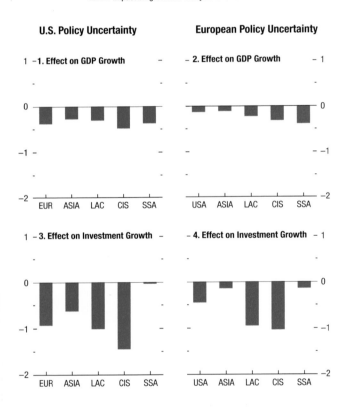

Source: IMF staff calculations.
Note: CIS = Commonwealth of Independent States; EUR = Europe; LAC = Latin America and the Caribbean; SSA = sub-Saharan Africa; USA = United States.

[15]We do not estimate the impact on domestic activity in the United States and Europe because they are much more subject to the endogeneity problem—policy uncertainty is affected by domestic activity. But for purposes of comparison, Baker, Bloom, and Davis (2012) use a vector-autoregression-based approach and find that an increase in U.S. policy uncertainty of the size that occurred between 2006 and 2011 would reduce U.S. output by up to 3.2 percent, and private investment by 16 percent.

[16]If only South Africa is used in the SSA sample (that is, if Botswana is excluded), the decline in investment is larger.

- A second possibility is that the control variable is a mediating variable through which policy uncertainty is actually conveyed—for example, higher policy uncertainty increases general uncertainty, which, in turn, affects activity elsewhere. In this case, adding the control variable nets out any effect of policy uncertainty that was conveyed through this mediating variable, resulting in an underestimation of the overall spillover effects.

The likeliest scenario is that both interpretations are valid—that is, policy uncertainty affects and is affected by the control variables (general uncertainty, confidence, and activity). As a result, the true magnitude of spillover effects from policy uncertainty is most likely somewhere between the baseline effect reported in Figures 2.SF.3 and 2.SF.5 and the effects estimated when using the control variables shown in Figure 2.SF.6.

In addition to showing the peak effect on real GDP and real investment, Figure 2.SF.6 shows the peak effect on real consumption. The dark-blue bars show the peak effect when there are no control variables other than policy uncertainty: these are the minimum values of the impulse response functions shown in Figures 2.SF.3 and 2.SF.5. The red bars show the peak effect of policy uncertainty when financial-uncertainty shocks—as measured by the VXO—are added as a control in the regression.[17] For the most part, the magnitude of the policy-uncertainty effect is broadly similar to the baseline. The same holds true in regressions that control for business confidence or the level of the stock market (Figure 2.SF.6, yellow and gray bars).

The pink bars in Figure 2.SF.6 show that controlling for import growth in the United States or Europe reduces the estimated effect of policy uncertainty in some, but not all, regions.[18] One interpretation is that U.S. or European policy uncertainty could negatively affect domestic activity, which affects activity elsewhere via lower import demand. The reduction in the impact of policy uncertainty would then indicate the strength of this particular transmission channel. For the CIS, for example, the effects of European policy uncertainty are diminished, but the effects of U.S. policy uncertainty are not. Under this interpretation, European policy uncertainty affects the CIS primarily via trade

[17]The Chicago Board Options Exchange S&P 100 Volatility Index (VXO) is a measure of implied stock market volatility similar to (and very highly correlated with) the more widely recognized VIX, but it has longer time coverage, going back to 1985.
[18]Controlling for U.S. and European GDP growth instead of import growth produces similar results.

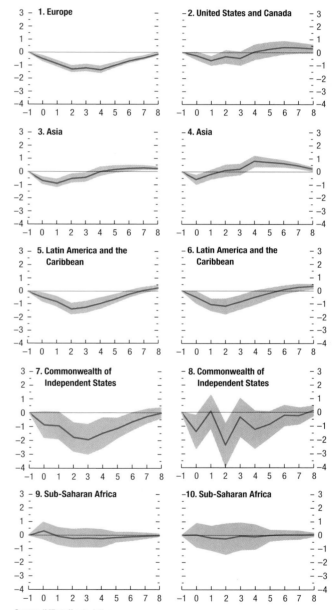

Figure 2.SF.5. Effect of a U.S. or European Policy-Uncertainty Shock on Real Investment in Other Regions
(Quarters on x-axis, percent change in real investment on y-axis)

One way policy-uncertainty shocks in the United States and Europe affect real activity in other regions is through declining investment. As with output, the magnitude, persistence, and statistical significance of the effects differ across regions. The effect of U.S. policy-uncertainty shocks tends to be slightly bigger and more persistent than that of European policy-uncertainty shocks, and U.S. shocks affect Europe more than vice versa.

—— Effect of a temporary U.S. policy-uncertainty shock
—— Effect of a temporary European policy-uncertainty shock
░░ 90 percent confidence interval

Source: IMF staff calculations.
Note: Policy-uncertainty shocks are defined as periods during which detrended uncertainty is more than 1.65 standard deviations above its mean. If only South Africa is used in the SSA sample (that is, if Botswana is excluded), the decline in investment is larger.

Figure 2.SF.6. Peak Effect of a U.S. or European Policy-Uncertainty Shock on Real GDP, Consumption, and Investment in Other Regions

The impact of policy-uncertainty shocks on economic activity tends to be attenuated, but is often still significant, when additional controls are added.

- ■ No other controls
- ■ Controlling for financial-uncertainty shock (VXO)
- ▨ Controlling for business confidence shock
- ▨ Controlling for S&P 500 shock
- ▨ Controlling for import growth in the United States or Europe
- ▨ Controlling for domestic economic uncertainty
- ◆ Statistically significant at 10 percent level

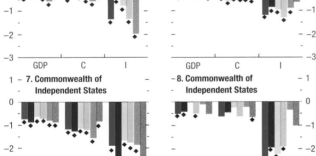
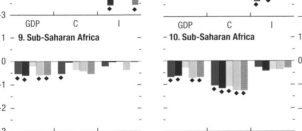

Source: IMF staff calculations.
Note: C = consumption; I = investment; VXO = Chicago Board Options Exchange S&P 100 Volatility Index.

channels, but U.S. policy uncertainty is transmitted through other channels.

A similar exercise can measure the extent to which the spillover effects of U.S. and European policy uncertainty are transmitted by raising uncertainty in other economies (measured by forecast dispersion). The spillover effects of policy uncertainty are reduced in some cases, but not in others (Figure 2.SF.6, light-blue bars), suggesting that increased uncertainty can be another channel of transmission. In most regions, policy uncertainty seems to reduce investment at least partly through its effect on higher domestic uncertainty.

Conclusion

This analysis documents significant spillover effects from policy uncertainty in the United States and Europe to other regions. It finds that sharp spikes in U.S. policy uncertainty can temporarily lower investment and output in other regions. The spillover effects from European policy uncertainty tend to be slightly smaller and less persistent and tend to have smaller effects on U.S. activity than vice versa.

Policy uncertainty has remained high in the United States and Europe since the Great Recession—even as more general uncertainty has receded and various measures of consumer and business confidence have recovered. The evidence presented here hints at the possibility that elevated policy uncertainty may have contributed to the serial disappointments and downward revisions in investment and output growth observed throughout the same period. It is futile to attempt to disentangle the effects of policy uncertainty from other variables, but suggestive evidence indicates that a reduction in policy uncertainty in the United States and Europe in the near term may give an added fillip to global investment and output.

References

Baker, Scott, Nicholas Bloom, and Steven J. Davis, 2012, "Measuring Economic Policy Uncertainty" (unpublished). Paper and indices are available at www.policyuncertainty.com.

Bekaert, Geert, Robert Hodrick, and Xiaoyan Zhang, 2010, "Aggregate Idiosyncratic Uncertainty," NBER Working Paper No. 16058 (Cambridge, Massachusetts: National Bureau of Economic Research).

Bernanke, Ben, 1983, "Irreversibility, Uncertainty, and Cyclical Investment," *Quarterly Journal of Economics,* Vol. 98, No. 1, pp. 85–106.

Bloom, Nicholas, 2009, "The Impact of Uncertainty Shocks," *Econometrica,* Vol. 77, No. 3, pp. 623–85.

———, Stephen Bond, and John van Reenen, 2007, "Uncertainty and Investment Dynamics," *Review of Economic Studies,* Vol. 74, No. 2, pp. 391–415.

Born, Benjamin, and Johannes Pfeifer, "Policy Risk and the Business Cycle," Bonn Economics Discussion Paper No. 06/2011 (Bonn: University of Bonn).

Carrière-Swallow, Yan, and Luis Felipe Céspedes, forthcoming, "The Impact of Uncertainty Shocks in Emerging Economies," *Journal of International Economics.*

Cerra, Valerie, and Sweta Saxena, 2008, "Growth Dynamics: The Myth of Economic Recovery," *American Economic Review,* Vol. 98, No. 1, pp. 439–57.

Fernández-Villaverde, Jesús, Pablo Guerrón-Quintana, Keith Kuester, and Juan Rubio-Ramírez, 2011, "Fiscal Volatility Shocks and Economic Activity," Working Paper No. 11–32 (Philadelphia: University of Pennsylvania Press).

International Monetary Fund (IMF), 2012, *2012 Spillover Report* (Washington). www.imf.org/external/np/pp/eng/2012/070912.pdf.

Keynes, John Maynard, 1936, *The General Theory of Employment, Interest, and Money* (London: MacMillan).

Romer, Christina D., and David H. Romer, 2010, "The Macroeconomic Effects of Tax Changes: Estimates Based on a New Measure of Fiscal Shocks," *American Economic Review,* Vol. 100, No. 3, pp. 763–801.

CHAPTER 3

THE DOG THAT DIDN'T BARK: HAS INFLATION BEEN MUZZLED OR WAS IT JUST SLEEPING?

"Is there any point to which you would wish to draw my attention?"
"To the curious incident of the dog in the night-time."
"The dog did nothing in the night-time."
"That was the curious incident," remarked Sherlock Holmes.
Silver Blaze, *Arthur Conan Doyle*

Inflation has been remarkably stable in the wake of the Great Recession even though unemployment has increased significantly. The analysis reported here finds that, over the past decade or so, inflation in advanced economies has become less responsive to changes in economic slack and that longer-term inflation expectations have become more firmly anchored. Thus, the recent stability of inflation is consistent with the prevalence of ongoing economic slack and a more muted response of inflation to cyclical conditions. Looking to the future, our analysis suggests that ongoing monetary accommodation is unlikely to have significant inflationary consequences, as long as inflation expectations remain anchored. In this regard, preserving central banks' independence is key. Notwithstanding this, policymakers must remain alert to possible imbalances that may not be reflected in consumer price inflation.

Introduction

Inflation has been remarkably quiet of late. While previous recessions were usually associated with marked declines in inflation, the Great Recession barely made a dent (Figure 3.1). And so, in a curious incident, we find a dog that did not bark. Some have inferred that the failure of inflation to fall is evidence that output gaps are small and that the large increases in unemployment are mostly structural. Thus, they fear that the monetary stimulus already in the pipeline may reduce unemployment, but only at the cost of overheating and a strong increase in inflation—just as during the 1970s. Others have argued that the stability of inflation reflects the success of inflation-targeting central

The authors of this chapter are John Simon (team leader), Troy Matheson, and Damiano Sandri. Gavin Asdorian and Sinem Kilic Celik provided excellent research assistance, and Andrew Levin and Douglas Laxton offered valuable comments.

Figure 3.1. The Behavior of Inflation Has Changed

Despite large rises in unemployment during the Great Recession, inflation has been remarkably stable in almost all advanced economies. This is different from the recessions in the 1970s and 1980s, when inflation fell much more when unemployment rose.

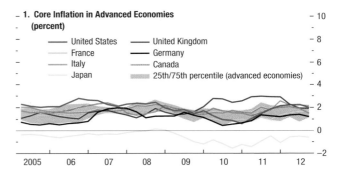

1. Core Inflation in Advanced Economies (percent)

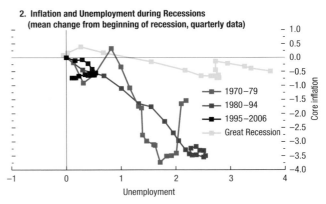

2. Inflation and Unemployment during Recessions (mean change from beginning of recession, quarterly data)

Sources: Organization for Economic Cooperation and Development; and IMF staff calculations.

banks in anchoring inflation expectations and, thus, inflation.

This chapter seeks to grasp, in Sherlock Holmes's words, "the significance of the silence of the dog, for one true inference invariably suggests others." To do this, we use a simple economic framework to interpret some basic summary data on recent developments. This provides some suggestive hints about what may have been going on. We then put the data together in an econometric model that more formally tests the alternative views of what drove inflation in the past and what is driving it now. These tests suggest that inflation has been quiescent recently because expectations have become more anchored and the relationship between cyclical unemployment and inflation has become more muted. We then look to the future and ask what other inferences these findings suggest for inflation. We first assess the implications for the risks, alluded to above, that ongoing monetary stimulus may lead to a strong cyclical increase in inflation. We then consider the possibility that current conditions may be a prelude to stagflation, facilitated by a disanchoring of expectations as occurred during the 1970s. To do this, we consider lessons from the contrasting experiences of the United States and Germany in the 1970s. We conclude by considering the policy implications of our findings.

The Missing Disinflation: Why Didn't Inflation Fall More?

Two broad explanations have been offered for the recent stability of inflation. The first suggests that much of the rise in unemployment during the Great Recession was structural and, consequently, current high levels of unemployment exert less of an influence on wages and prices than in the past.[1] The second suggests that the behavior of inflation has changed and it is now much less volatile and less responsive to changes in economic slack than in the past. We discuss these two hypotheses informally, introduce an economic framework that helps organize the competing explanations, and look at what the data suggest.

The first explanation focuses on the behavior of the labor market. In normal recessions, when many unemployed workers are looking for jobs, inflation tends to be lower since wage pressures are more moderate and

people have less money to spend. If, however, many of those who are unemployed cannot effectively compete for jobs, they may have much less influence on the wages of those who are employed. This can translate into less influence on the prices firms charge for their goods and services. Such unemployment is termed "structural."

There are certainly reasons for suspecting that many currently unemployed workers could be structurally unemployed. For example, the length of the Great Recession has put long-term unemployment near record levels. And the longer people are out of work, the more likely it is that their skills have faded or become less applicable to the available jobs. Thus, the high levels of long-term unemployment may suggest high levels of structural unemployment.

The second explanation for the stability of inflation focuses on the behavior of inflation more directly. For example, it is argued that the strengthening of central banks' credibility and their success in delivering stable inflation over the past decade have affected the way people think about future inflation. And people's expectations about the future affect inflation today. For example, if prices are expected to increase in the future, workers will demand increased wages today, and those increases will be passed on in the form of higher prices today. Thus, more stable inflation expectations resulting from credible central banks may have contributed to more stable inflation.

The behavior of inflation may also have been affected by central banks' low inflation targets. It has been suggested that at low levels, inflation may become stickier and less responsive to economic fluctuations. For example, workers are very resistant to wage cuts, and this may prevent producers from cutting prices when aggregate demand falls. It has also been suggested that the presence of costs to adjustment in nominal prices (menu costs) leads firms to change prices less frequently when inflation is lower. Similarly, globalization may have made inflation more responsive to global demand developments and less responsive to domestic demand developments.

Framework

Each of these explanations is reflected in the conceptual framework known as the New Keynesian Phillips curve, which focuses on the core issue of interest here—the relationship between inflation and unemployment. Under this framework, inflation, π_t, is

---

[1]Kocherlakota (2010), for example, expresses this view in the case of the United States.

determined by inflation expectations, π_t^e, and the level of cyclical unemployment, $\tilde{u}_t$, according to the following simple equation:

$$\pi_t = \pi_t^e - \kappa \tilde{u}_t, \qquad (3.1)$$

in which κ is a parameter commonly referred to as the slope of the Phillips curve.[2] It captures the strength of the relationship between cyclical unemployment and inflation. Viewed through the lens of this framework, we can then summarize the ideas above as follows. First, inflation may not have fallen much because the increased unemployment was structural and there was minimal change in cyclical unemployment, $\tilde{u}_t$. Second, improved central bank credibility may have made inflation expectations more stable. Finally, the lower level of inflation at the beginning of the Great Recession, or other changes, may account for the reduced inflationary response to cyclical developments—that is, the Phillips curve is flatter than in the past and κ is smaller.

A Look at the Data

Critical elements in thinking about these possibilities are the amount of economic slack in economies today, the anchoring of inflation expectations, and the responsiveness of inflation to economic slack. We begin with the available estimates of economic slack. As shown in Figure 3.2, current estimates from the IMF, Organization for Economic Cooperation and Development (OECD), and national authorities indicate the presence of significant output gaps, suggesting considerable economic slack. A similar picture emerges from a comparison of current and precrisis capacity utilization and unemployment (see Figure 3.2). The OECD and national authorities estimate that capacity utilization decreased by about 5 to 6 percent since the beginning of the Great Recession. The picture is similar in the labor market.[3] Unemployment gaps average about 2 percent, judging by changes in short-term

Figure 3.2. Measures of Current Economic Slack

A wide range of indicators prepared by various institutions suggest that advanced economies are confronting considerable economic slack. This condition is particularly acute in a few countries, as seen in the fact that the cross-country means tend to be above the medians.

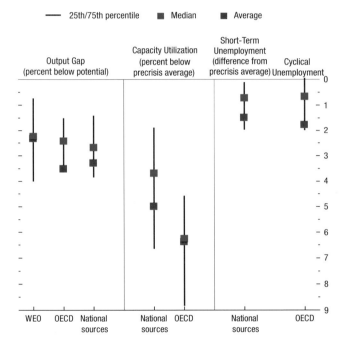

Sources: Haver Analytics; Organization for Economic Cooperation and Development; and IMF staff calculations.
Note: OECD = Organization for Economic Cooperation and Development; WEO = *World Economic Outlook*.

---

[2]Despite its apparent simplicity, this framework is surprisingly rich and is the workhorse for most work in this area. It can incorporate additional influences, such as import price effects and asset price effects. A number of these elements are introduced in the econometrics below. For a fuller treatment of the New Keynesian theory, see Woodford (2003) and Galí (2008).

[3]The magnitude of the estimates cannot be directly compared across these measures. For example, as documented in Abel and Bernanke (2005), it is fairly standard to assume that output gaps are approximately twice the size of unemployment gaps based on Okun's law.

unemployment from its precrisis average and OECD estimates of cyclical unemployment, defined as the gap between current unemployment and the nonaccelerating inflation rate of unemployment (NAIRU). This suggests that a considerable share of the increase in unemployment during the Great Recession was cyclical.

A second critical element in exploring recent inflation dynamics is the anchoring of inflation expectations. Figure 3.3 compares long-term inflation expectations with 2012 inflation rates in advanced economies as deviations from central banks' inflation targets.[4] Although current and expected inflation are positively correlated, the low regression slope suggests that expectations are strongly anchored to the central banks' inflation targets rather than being particularly affected by current inflation levels. Indeed, despite wide variations in actual inflation, long-term inflation expectations remain close to targets. This was the case even for Japan, where expectations remained close to the 1 percent target announced in February 2012 despite a prolonged period of deflation.

To further explore the extent to which institutional and behavioral changes in central banks have helped anchor inflation expectations, we estimate the degree of anchoring over time using the following simple regression:

$$\bar{\pi}_t^e - \pi^* = \alpha + \beta(\pi_t - \pi^*) + \varepsilon_t, \tag{3.2}$$

in which $\bar{\pi}_t^e$ is the long-term inflation expectation at a given time, π_t is the inflation rate when inflation expectations are collected, and π^* is the central bank's target level of inflation.

Inflation expectations that are strongly anchored to the inflation target should result in estimates for both α and β that are close to zero. A zero β coefficient implies that expectations are not influenced by the contemporaneous level of inflation, and a zero α means that the inflation expectations are centered at the target level. We ran the regression for 12 advanced economies over five-year rolling windows since 1990, reflecting the available data. The cross-country average

Figure 3.3. Current Headline Inflation Compared with Expectations

Long-term inflation expectations have remained very close to central banks' targets. This is true even in countries where 2012 inflation was significantly above or below target.

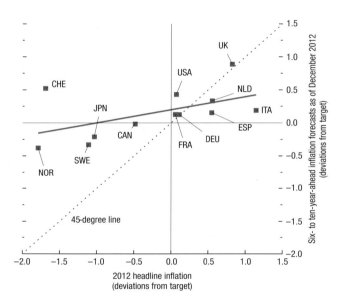

Sources: *Consensus Forecasts;* Organization for Economic Cooperation and Development; and IMF staff calculations.
Note: CAN = Canada; CHE = Switzerland; DEU = Germany; ESP = Spain; FRA = France; ITA = Italy; JPN = Japan; NLD = Netherlands; NOR = Norway; SWE = Sweden; UK = United Kingdom; USA = United States.

[4]The target is the rate announced by the central bank or the simple average of the announced range (Canada 2 percent, Norway 2.5 percent, Sweden 2 percent, Switzerland 1 percent, and United Kingdom 2 percent). A target of 1.9 percent is used for the countries in the euro area, given that the European Central Bank (ECB) defines price stability as an increase in inflation below, but close to, 2 percent. We use 1 percent for Japan, consistent with the announcement by the Bank of Japan on February 14, 2012. A target of 2 percent was introduced on January 22, 2013. Finally, we use 2 percent for the United States, the rate announced by the Federal Reserve on January 25, 2012.

of the estimates for α and β and the cross-country range of estimated coefficients are plotted in Figure 3.4. The estimates for both coefficients are clearly declining and are currently very close to zero. Inflation expectations have become much more anchored around targets during the past two decades.

Finally, we consider the evidence on the relationship between the level of inflation and the responsiveness of inflation to economic slack. Figure 3.5 shows the relationship between cyclical unemployment and the level of inflation. The figure shows the cross-country means of inflation and cyclical unemployment at quarterly frequencies since 1975, with fitted regression lines during several periods.[5] Broadly speaking, inflation was high in the late 1970s and early 1980s, when the relationship between inflation and unemployment appears relatively steep; it was more muted between 1985 and 1994, when many economies experienced disinflation as central banks started establishing the current targeting regimes; and it was particularly flat after 1995, a period of stable inflation around 2 percent.

This preliminary evidence suggests that economic slack persists and that the recent stability of inflation is indicative of greater anchoring of expectations and a more muted relationship between economic slack and inflation. This, however, is only a tentative observation. To test the robustness and plausibility of this possibility we make use of a formal econometric model.

Econometric Results

Although an initial look at the data suggested some possible explanations for the recent experience—a muted relationship between inflation and unemployment and better anchoring of expectations—they are only tentative and partial. This section examines these explanations to see whether they continue to hold within a formal econometric framework. This approach allows us to find the interpretation of the data that is both internally consistent and statistically most likely.

Based on the framework set out in equation (3.1), we estimate the following unemployment-based Phillips curve:

$$\pi_t = (1 - \vartheta)\pi_{t-1} + \vartheta\pi_t^e - \kappa\bar{u}_t + \gamma\pi_t^m + \varepsilon_t, \qquad (3.3)$$

[5] Cyclical unemployment is computed by subtracting the OECD estimates of the NAIRU from the unemployment rate. The NAIRU is the rate of structural unemployment consistent with no inflation pressure. Because the NAIRU estimates are available only at annual frequencies, we use linear interpolation to generate quarterly values.

Figure 3.4. Rolling Regressions of Inflation Expectations over Actual Inflation
(Net of inflation target)

Inflation expectations are now better anchored to targets and respond less to actual changes in inflation. This is shown below in rolling regressions of inflation expectations over actual inflation in deviations from central banks' targets, which reveal that both the intercept α and the slope β have moved closer to zero.

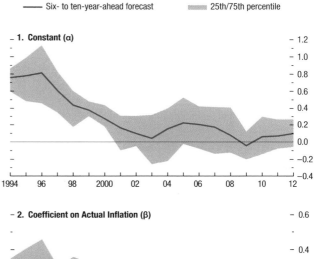

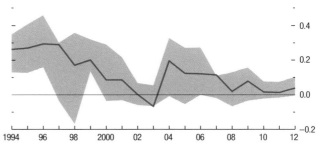

Sources: *Consensus Forecasts;* Organization for Economic Cooperation and Development; and IMF staff calculations.

in which π_t is headline consumer price index inflation, π_t^e is long-term inflation expectations, $\bar{u}_t$ is cyclical unemployment, and π_t^m is inflation in the relative price of imports. Relative to the basic specification in equation (3.1), the estimated equation incorporates two new features that allow for a better characterization of the inflation process. First, we introduce lagged inflation, π_{t-1}, to allow for some inflation persistence. The idea is that when people set wages and prices, they may be incorporating both their expectations about future inflation and the latest actual inflation rate. The parameter ϑ determines the balance between these two factors. Second, we introduce the import price inflation term, π_t^m, for two reasons. First, headline inflation is used to estimate the regression because historical core inflation data are generally not available. But because headline inflation includes many short-term fluctuations caused by commodity price volatility and because commodities are traded internationally, the import price term allows us to capture many of these fluctuations. Second, incorporating import price effects allows us to investigate the contention that globalization makes inflation more dependent on global factors (captured through the import price term) than on domestic factors. The regression equation also allows for transitory shocks; ε_t, which captures fluctuations in inflation that may be driven by temporary supply factors. Furthermore, supply shocks, for example linked to swings in oil prices, are captured by the import inflation term, π_t^m, as well as by changes in the NAIRU that the model internally estimates given constraints we impose on how volatile this term can be. Cyclical unemployment, $\bar{u}_t$, is then derived by subtracting from the unemployment data the estimates of the NAIRU. Asset price effects on inflation are also captured by this term to the extent that they affect aggregate demand. Appendix 3.1 provides technical details of the model.

An important feature of the estimation is that we allow for time variation in all the parameters: ϑ, γ, and κ.[6] This is essential for assessing whether the economy of today differs from the economy of the past. An increase in ϑ implies that current inflation has become more anchored to long-term expectations and is less influenced by past inflation. Given that long-term

Figure 3.5. Inflation and Cyclical Unemployment
(Percent; average across advanced economies)

From its peak in the 1970s, the average level of inflation has fallen as a result of central banks' disinflationary policies. What is also noticeable is that the relationship between cyclical unemployment and inflation appears to have moderated as the level has fallen.

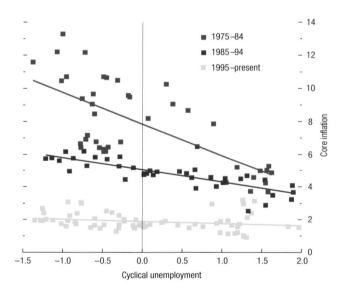

Sources: Organization for Economic Cooperation and Development; and IMF staff calculations.
Note: Each square represents the average across advanced economies of inflation and cyclical unemployment in one quarter.

---

[6]In the past, most work has assumed either that the slope of the Phillips curve was constant over the estimation period or that it was nonlinear in ways that linked the slope to the level of inflation. Our approach encompasses both possibilities without imposing them.

inflation expectations are now more stable than in the past (see Figure 3.4), a higher ϑ would also imply that inflation has become less persistent. Time variation in γ allows for the possibility that inflation is now more dependent on global developments, perhaps because of globalization. Finally, time variation in the parameter κ makes it possible to directly test the hypothesis suggested in Figure 3.5 that the relationship between inflation and unemployment may have become more muted—that is, that the Phillips curve is flatter.

We estimate the model for all advanced economies for which data are available, which produces estimates for 21 countries, usually starting in the 1960s. The results are remarkably consistent across countries (Figure 3.6) and tell a story that confirms the preliminary results:

- *Unemployment gaps have opened in many countries.* Figure 3.6, panel 1, confirms the findings reported in Figure 3.2 that there are unemployment gaps in almost all the countries in the data set. Furthermore, because a number of countries have very large unemployment gaps, the distribution is skewed and the average is above the median.

- *The responsiveness of inflation to unemployment has been gradually declining over the past several decades.* Figure 3.6, panel 2, shows that κ has decreased (that is, the average slope of the Phillips curve has flattened). The interquartile range also demonstrates that this decline occurred throughout the advanced economies in the data set. Furthermore, in results not reported here, there is a correlation between the level of inflation and the slope, as suggested by Figure 3.5. However, the degree of potential nonlinearity is very modest at the rates of inflation observed over the past few decades. We consider some of the implications of a flatter Phillips curve for policy in Box 3.1.

- *The relationship between current and past inflation has weakened over time.* Figure 3.6, panel 3, shows that θ has increased since the 1970s, which means that the persistence of inflation has declined such that deviations of inflation expectations from its long-term trend are more short lived relative to the 1970s—in short, inflation has become more "anchored." Once again, this is a change that has occurred throughout advanced economies.

- *At the aggregate level, the contribution of global inflation to country-specific inflation shows no clear trend.* While we find that, for a number of individual countries, the imported inflation parameter has

Figure 3.6. Changes in the Inflation Process

The recent rise in cyclical unemployment is similar to that in previous recessions, although the starting position was lower and there is a significant dispersion across countries. There has been a decline in the responsiveness of inflation to unemployment —that is, the slope of the Phillips curve—and a rise in the anchoring to long-term inflation expectations since the 1970s. There is no clear trend in the importance of import price inflation.

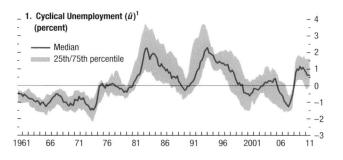

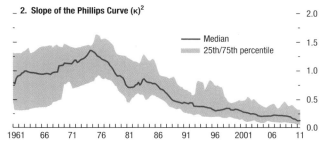

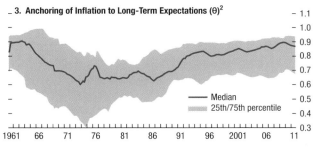

Sources: Board of Governors of the Federal Reserve System; *Consensus Forecasts;* Organization for Economic Cooperation and Development; and IMF staff calculations.
Note: Country sample includes Australia, Austria, Belgium, Canada, Denmark, Finland, France, Germany, Greece, Ireland, Italy, Japan, Netherlands, New Zealand, Norway, Portugal, Spain, Sweden, Switzerland, United Kingdom, and United States.
[1]Unemployment rate minus model-generated estimates of the nonaccelerating inflation rate of unemployment.
[2]See equation (3.3) in the text.

Figure 3.7. Robustness to Alternative Estimates of the NAIRU

Changes to the assumption about the flexibility of the NAIRU leave the core findings unchanged—inflation expectations are more anchored and the Phillips curve is flatter.

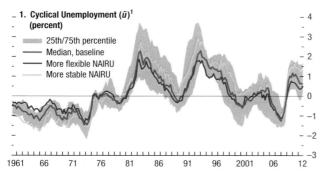

1. Cyclical Unemployment ($\bar{u}$)[1]
(percent)

25th/75th percentile
Median, baseline
More flexible NAIRU
More stable NAIRU

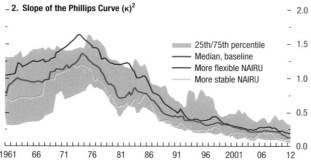

2. Slope of the Phillips Curve (κ)[2]

25th/75th percentile
Median, baseline
More flexible NAIRU
More stable NAIRU

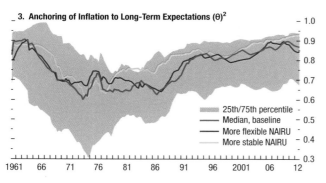

3. Anchoring of Inflation to Long-Term Expectations (θ)[2]

25th/75th percentile
Median, baseline
More flexible NAIRU
More stable NAIRU

Sources: Board of Governors of the Federal Reserve System; *Consensus Forecasts;* Organization for Economic Cooperation and Development; and IMF staff calculations.
Note: NAIRU = nonaccelerating inflation rate of unemployment. Country sample includes Australia, Austria, Belgium, Canada, Denmark, Finland, France, Germany, Greece, Ireland, Italy, Japan, Netherlands, New Zealand, Norway, Portugal, Spain, Sweden, Switzerland, United Kingdom, and United States.
[1]Unemployment rate minus model-generated estimates of the NAIRU.
[2]See equation (3.3) in the text.

increased over time, which is consistent with greater import penetration associated with globalization, there is no clear trend in the median (Figure 3.6, panel 4).

These findings are also consistent with much of the earlier research. First, many researchers find evidence that, since the mid-1990s, inflation has become better anchored around long-term expectations, which themselves have become more stable.[7] It is natural to associate this with the simultaneous trends toward more central bank independence and the adoption of inflation-targeting regimes across advanced economies. Second, the observed flattening of the Phillips curve as inflation rates declined is consistent with evidence that there is downward nominal wage rigidity—that is, people are very resistant to nominal wage reductions (Yellen, 2012).

The flattening of the Phillips curve at low levels of inflation may also reflect the fact that there are costs associated with adjusting nominal prices that lead firms to change prices less frequently when inflation is lower (Ball, Mankiw, and Romer, 1988). Cross-country evidence compiled by Klenow and Malin (2010) confirms that firms do change prices less frequently when inflation is lower. As to whether globalization has affected the slope of the Phillips curve, consonant with our findings on the import price parameter, the evidence so far is either inconclusive or negative (Ball, 2006; Gaiotti, 2010).

Importantly, the flattening of the Phillips curves is robust to alternative specifications of the NAIRU. In the estimation procedure, we assume a certain flexibility in the NAIRU, which affects the size of unemployment gaps over time. It is possible that the implied estimates of the unemployment gap are wrong even though they match well with the alternative measures presented in Figure 3.2. To allow for this possibility we test specifications in which the NAIRU is more flexible and more stable than in the baseline. Figure 3.7 shows that this assumption does not materially affect the key findings. Regardless of one's view of the flexibility of the NAIRU and thus the current size of the output gap, the slope of the Phillips curve has fallen over time, and the slope is currently very flat.

These results are, of course, subject to the usual caveats that accompany any econometric work. It is possible that particular variations in the framework,

[7]See, for example, Stock and Watson (2007) and Kuttner and Robinson (2010).

data, or estimation technique could affect the results. Tests of a number of variations in the framework, data, and estimation method yielded results that were broadly unchanged. Nevertheless, the more compelling argument in favor of these results is that they agree both with the descriptive data and with earlier results on individual aspects of the model. That is, the accumulation of evidence points in the same direction—namely, that inflation has been more stable than in the past both because it has become better anchored to stable long-term expectations and because the relationship between inflation and unemployment is much more muted.

To illustrate this finding, Figure 3.8 shows actual inflation in the United States during the Great Recession compared with two predictions. The first prediction (yellow line) uses the latest parameter estimates of the econometric model with a flat Phillips curve and well-anchored inflation. The second path (red line) uses the parameters from the 1970s, when the slope of the Phillips curve was higher and expectations were less well anchored, which predicts deflation following the Great Recession. The absence of deflation can be explained by the changes in the economy and in institutions since the 1970s.

How Much Should We Worry about Inflation?

If the inflation stability during the Great Recession reflects a flat Phillips curve and the anchoring of inflation expectations, there seems little risk of strong inflation pressure during the ongoing recovery. However, there is a risk that inflation could become much more sensitive to output gaps during future periods of expansion. For example, there could be nonlinearities in the Phillips curve: the slope of the curve could be flat when the economy faces cyclical unemployment but steep if unemployment falls below the NAIRU. This concern becomes particularly salient if estimates that suggest there are now large output gaps and high cyclical unemployment (see Figure 3.2) turn out to be wrong. For example, it may be that slower productivity growth and yet-unrecognized structural changes have lowered potential output and raised the NAIRU—just as during the 1970s.

In this respect, there are useful lessons from the experiences of several countries during the early 2000s, when unemployment was below the NAIRU for an extended period but inflation and inflation expectations remained remarkably stable (Figure 3.9). These phenomena were particularly evident in several euro

Figure 3.8. Actual and Predicted Inflation in the United States
(Percent, year over year)

If inflation in the U.S. economy behaved as it did during the 1970s, the United States would have experienced significant deflation starting in 2010. The fact that it did not is evidence that the behavior of inflation and its reaction to economic slack have changed. Inflation is now much more stable than in the past. (The large fall in inflation in 2009 reflects the commodity price swing that affected headline inflation in most economies at that time. The contribution from economic slack was relatively minor.)

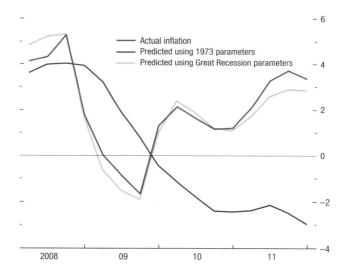

Sources: Board of Governors of the Federal Reserve System; Organization for Economic Cooperation and Development; and IMF staff calculations.

Figure 3.9. Unemployment and Inflation in Selected Economies
(Percent)

Despite unemployment below the NAIRU for about a decade, inflation and inflation expectations remained remarkably stable and well anchored in Ireland, Spain, and the United Kingdom.

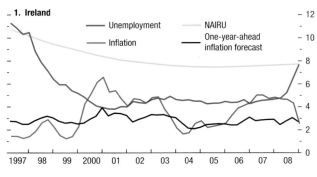

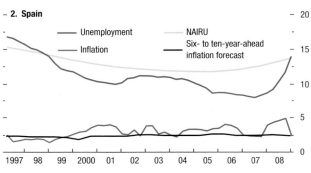

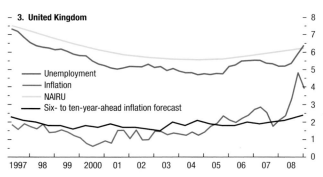

Sources: *Consensus Forecasts;* Organization for Economic Cooperation and Development; and IMF staff calculations.
Note: NAIRU = nonaccelerating inflation rate of unemployment (from Organization for Economic Cooperation and Development).

area countries that entered the monetary union and became subject to ECB monetary policies that were too loose for their particular circumstances. Emblematic cases are Ireland and Spain (Figure 3.9, panels 1 and 2). Despite large reductions in unemployment fueled by inappropriately loose monetary policies, inflation did not rise nearly as much as the experience of the 1970s would suggest.[8] This pattern was not confined to the euro area. The United Kingdom had a similar experience during this period (Figure 3.9, panel 3). Although there was less overheating, there was the same combination of modest inflation pressure and a sustained period of tight capacity. These cases clearly demonstrate that flat Phillips curves are just as applicable to periods of strong growth as to recessions and are readily observable in the economic experiences of the past decade.[9]

An important implication of a flat Phillips curve under both positive and negative unemployment gaps is that the precise determination of the current degree of economic slack is not that important in terms of the consequences for inflation. It is notoriously difficult to estimate potential output and employment in real time. Therefore, even though the indicators presented in Figure 3.2 and our own econometric estimates all suggest continuing slack, we cannot rule out the possibility that advanced economies are much closer to potential. But even in this case, the experiences of the early 2000s suggest that the monetary stimulus in the pipeline is unlikely to generate high inflation because the Phillips curve is likely to remain flat.

Given that the risks from movement along a flat Phillips curve seem modest—and that most economies are still operating with significant output gaps—the greatest risk for inflation, just as in the 1970s, is the possibility that expectations will become disanchored. Even though long-term expectations are currently close to targets and well anchored, our estimates show that

[8]For example, contemporary analysis of the Spanish economy acknowledged that the monetary policies, set as they were for the whole of the euro area, were inappropriate for Spain. This can be seen, for example, in the IMF Article IV report from 2001: "Even before the November 8 cut in interest rates, monetary conditions were easier than justified from a purely Spanish perspective, the authorities noted." (IMF, 2002)

[9]As mentioned in the discussion of the results, we find some evidence that the slope of the Phillips curve is higher at higher levels of inflation. If we restrict the model such that the slope of the Phillips curve is related to the level of inflation, we find that the nonlinearity is very modest—that is, the slope does not rise appreciably at moderate inflation levels.

the behavior of inflation has changed in the past and may change again in the future.

To assess the risk that inflation expectations will disanchor, we look back to the 1970s—the last time they did. In particular, we contrast the experiences of the United States and Germany. In the 1970s both countries experienced rising unemployment as the rapid growth of the immediate postwar period slowed and the world economy suffered from oil shocks. However, even though inflation kept increasing in the United States, it remained remarkably well anchored in Germany (Figure 3.10). Comparing these two cases yields valuable insights about the factors that can guard against a possible disanchoring today.

Anchoring and Disanchoring in the 1970s

United States: Disanchoring of inflation expectations

U.S. economic policy after World War II was shaped against the vivid memory of the Great Depression. High unemployment and deflation were more feared than inflation. In this climate, inflation pressure built up gradually as policy targeted a "natural rate" of unemployment of about 4 percent—a level achieved only briefly in the late 1960s and today recognized as too low.[10]

This gradual buildup in inflation has been linked to several factors. First, there was limited understanding of how to effectively control inflation. The economic approach was initially shaped by simple Keynesian models and the idea of a stable trade-off between unemployment and inflation. Furthermore, some believed that inflation could be managed through wage and price controls, and these were, in fact, used sporadically during the 1970s, including two complete wage and price freezes under President Richard Nixon.[11] One consequence was that there was less use of more effective monetary tools. Second, as Orphanides (2002) argues, there was a misperception about the sustainable rate of unemployment

Figure 3.10. Headline Inflation in the United States and Germany
(Percent)

Despite facing similar shocks during the 1970s, Germany ended the decade with much lower inflation than the United States. This largely reflects the countries' differing approaches to monetary policy.

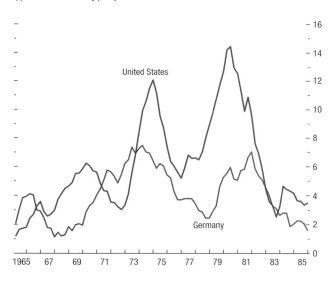

Source: Organization for Economic Cooperation and Development.

[10]Meltzer (2009, p. 2) summarizes it thus: "The principal monetary and financial legacies of the Great Depression were a highly regulated financial system and the Employment Act of 1946, which evolved into a commitment by the government and the Federal Reserve to maintain economic conditions consistent with full employment. The Employment Act was not explicit about full employment and even less explicit about inflation. For much too long, the Federal Reserve and the administration considered a 4 percent unemployment rate to be the equilibrium rate. The Great Inflation changed that."

[11]See, for example, Nelson (2005), who discusses the cases of Australia, Canada, and New Zealand.

and, more generally, the size of the output gap. These errors spurred policies that, in hindsight, were too stimulative.

Another important contributor to the disanchoring of inflation expectations in the United States during the 1970s was the lack of independence of the Federal Reserve (Fed), which stemmed from the lack of social consensus on the appropriate objectives for monetary policy. The Fed's lack of independence and its deference to political interests are evident in Arthur Burns's 1979 Per Jacobsson lecture in which he looked back over his experiences as chairman of the Fed:

> Viewed in the abstract, the Federal Reserve System had the power to abort the inflation at its incipient stage fifteen years ago or at any later point, and it has the power to end it today… It did not do so because the Federal Reserve was itself caught up in the philosophic and political currents that were transforming American life and culture… If the Federal Reserve then sought to create a monetary environment that fell seriously short of accommodating the upward pressures on prices that were being released or reinforced by government action, severe difficulties could be quickly produced in the economy. Not only that, the Federal Reserve would be frustrating the will of Congress to which it was responsible. (Burns, 1979, pp. 15–16)

Throughout this period, increases in inflation and inflation expectations were not reversed and were effectively condoned.[12] Indeed, there was a sense of fatalism about increased inflation. This is expressed by President Jimmy Carter in 1978:

> The human tragedy and waste of resources associated with policies of slow growth are intolerable, and the impact of such policies on the current inflation is very small. (*Economic Report of the President*, 1978, p. 17)[13]

Inflation was finally brought down only when the de facto independence of the Fed was established with the appointment of Paul Volcker in 1979, who made it clear to President Carter that he was "mainly concerned that the president not be under any misunderstanding about my own concern about the importance of an independent central bank and the need for the tighter money…" (Volcker and Gyohten, 1992, p. 164). This development reflected a social and political evolution that ranked inflation as a more important

problem than unemployment only toward the end of the 1970s and not at the beginning of the decade.

Germany: Institutional independence and anchoring

German economic policy in the post–World War II era was shaped against the vivid memory of the hyperinflation of the 1920s and the monetary reform of 1948 that wiped out savings. Inflation was feared more than anything else. The Bundesbank, set up as an independent institution by the war powers, fought to maintain this independence in the mid-1950s, when the governing law was rewritten. As reported in 1957:

> President Vocke had incurred the Chancellor's wrath because he pursued a monetary policy that paid scant attention to Konrad Adenauer's amateurish ideas and politically dictated wishes… On such occasions Vocke demonstrated that the Chancellor's power ceased to apply at the gates of the central bank. (*Der Spiegel*, July 17, 1957, pp. 18–20)

Public support for an independent, inflation-fighting central bank ensured that the Bundesbank emerged from this political fight with legal and, more important, practical independence. It wasn't until the end of the 1970s that the United States developed a social aversion to high inflation; Germans required no such persuasion.

However, the Bretton Woods fixed exchange rate system meant that the Bundesbank was constrained in its implementation of monetary policy. The upshot was that Germany ended up importing inflation from the United States throughout the late 1960s and early 1970s (see Figure 3.10). When it regained its independence in 1973 with the abandonment of the Bretton Woods system, the Bundesbank strengthened its reputation for independence and anti-inflation credibility. Its first step was to quickly raise interest rates to about 7 percent. It also looked for ways to anchor expectations. In 1974 it introduced a system of monetary targeting. Moreover, the Bundesbank made pronouncements about the level of "unavoidable inflation," which were gradually ratcheted down, as an additional way to communicate its objectives and manage expectations. Bundesbank Chief Economist Helmut Schlesinger explained the purpose of the targets in 1979:

> But as the monetary target tends to act as a signpost the pressure to exercise cost and price discipline is likely to grow. Indeed, experience even permits the conclusion that the formulation of this target helped bring about a "social consensus" among all groups… (Schlesinger, 1979, p. 308)

---

[12]See Levin and Taylor (2010) for a more extensive discussion of this point.

[13]Available at www.presidency.ucsb.edu/economic_reports/1978.pdf.

This framework was, in many ways, the precursor to the "flexible inflation targeting" practiced today by central banks. The ECB's current 2 percent target for inflation descends from the Bundesbank's concept of "unavoidable inflation."

The Bundesbank's success, however, was not based on it being infallible. Its success in hitting the monetary targets was limited—the authorities overshot their point target before moving to a target range in 1979, which it still struggled to hit. Moreover, as demonstrated by Gerberding, Seitz, and Worms (2005), the Bundesbank overestimated the output gap—just as U.S. authorities did. In 1975, the bank calculated the output gap at about 9 percent, whereas ex post estimates put it closer to 1 percent. These overestimations were persistent from 1974 until the mid-1980s.

Nor was the Bundesbank's success based on its being, in the words of Bank of England Governor Mervyn King, an "inflation nutter." The bank did not behave as if it had an inflation-only target but also placed weight on the output gap and cyclical developments.[14] For example, a recession in 1975 led the Bundesbank to so fear weak growth and undershooting its newly introduced monetary targets that it engaged in what is now known as quantitative easing. In a move that stirred considerable controversy, the bank bought government bonds on the secondary market totaling about 4 percent of the outstanding stock, or 1 percent of GDP. More explicitly, in its 1976 and 1977 annual reports the Bundesbank indicated that its goal was "strong economic growth and a further containment of inflation."

During this period, and in common with the Fed, the Bundesbank was also pressured to place greater weight on reducing unemployment. Helmut Schmidt, the minister for economics and finance, famously declared in 1972 that "5 percent inflation is easier to bear than 5 percent unemployment." In addition, as in the United States, government concerns over rising unemployment meant that fiscal policy was relatively loose in the 1970s, with the government running a deficit from 1974 on. The pressure can be seen, for example, in a *Der Spiegel* cover in 1975 that asked, "1.3 million unemployed: Is the Bundesbank to blame?"

Given these "errors" and concerns about unemployment, it may seem surprising that the Bundesbank managed to bring down inflation in the challenging environment of the 1970s. But it did. Through the use of explicit monetary and inflation targets, the authorities managed to anchor expectations. As a truly independent central bank with the flexibility to do what it judged best to achieve its mandate, the Bundesbank outstripped its peers.

Case Study Analysis

The large increase in inflation and the disanchoring of inflation expectations in the United States have been attributed to a variety of factors. Although we cannot rule out the possibility that other factors, including some not mentioned above—such as labor and product market differences—may have contributed to the different inflation dynamics in Germany and the United States, we focus on two that are particularly relevant today. First, the increase in unemployment was for some time erroneously interpreted as cyclical, thus requiring fiscal and monetary support. Second, the Fed was strongly influenced by political pressures to address increasing unemployment. As a result the Fed was reluctant to tighten policies enough to reduce inflation both because it overestimated the amount of economic slack and because such tightening would have involved "unacceptably" high unemployment. As a consequence, inflation expectations were gradually but inexorably disanchored, which eventually led to the stagflation that is a lasting symbol of those times.

The relative importance of these two elements in explaining the disanchoring of expectations is illuminated by a comparison with Germany. The Bundesbank shared many similarities with the Fed: both overestimated the size of the output gap, interpreting the increase in unemployment as mostly cyclical, and both operated within a political context that placed great weight on unemployment. What set them apart was their degree of actual independence. Unlike the Fed, the Bundesbank enjoyed a broad social consensus regarding its primary task of ensuring the stability of the currency.

This independence was reflected in the framework adopted by the Bundesbank, which allowed it to preserve its independence and keep expectations stable without excess tightening. As the case reveals, the Bundesbank's success was not linked to meticulously meeting the monetary targets, which it actually missed

---

[14]Both Clarida and Gertler (1997) and Gerberding, Seitz, and Worms (2005) estimate policy reaction functions for the Bundesbank and conclude that it placed significant weight on short-term objectives such as output stabilization.

throughout the 1970s, or to focusing on inflation with no regard for output developments. Rather the Bundesbank's success was a reflection of the robust framework it developed, which allowed it to keep longer-term inflation expectations anchored while flexibly responding to shorter-term output shocks.[15] The importance of operational independence has been emphasized in a large body of literature (such as Alesina and Summers, 1993) and is also underscored by the experience of the Fed: once the Fed was free to focus on inflation under chairman Volcker, it also achieved lower inflation and, after a painful recession, lower unemployment.

These experiences offer several valuable lessons for today. First, the similarities between the Bundesbank's approach then and the "flexible inflation targeting" framework used by many central banks today suggest that mistaken estimates of current economic slack seem unlikely, by themselves, to generate a sharp rise in inflation or in inflation expectations. Both the Fed and the Bundesbank overestimated the output gap, but inflation remained under control in Germany while it rose dramatically in the United States. Although it is hard to be definitive, a crucial difference was that the Bundesbank had the operational independence to credibly commit to taking action if inflation was projected to drift away from target. In the United States, the Fed effectively condoned increases in inflation and inflation expectations and thereby ratified them.

Conclusions

The data and case studies presented here suggest some important conclusions. First, the Phillips curve is considerably flatter today than in the past, and the inflation consequences of changes in economic slack are therefore much smaller. Second, inflation expectations are much better anchored now than in the past. Together, these two factors largely explain why the declines in inflation during the Great Recession were small. It also follows that these small declines are consistent with continued economic slack in most advanced economies.

An important policy conclusion is that, as long as inflation expectations remain firmly anchored, fears about high inflation should not prevent monetary authorities from pursuing highly accommodative monetary policy. Indeed the combination of a relatively flat

Phillips curve and strongly anchored inflation expectations implies that any temporary overstimulation of the economy—perhaps stemming from misperception about the size of output gaps—is likely to have only small effects on inflation.

There are two important caveats. First, moderate inflation could induce complacency—and complacency would be a mistake. Although consumer price inflation was well contained in the first decade of the 2000s, many economies experienced rampant asset price inflation, most notably in residential housing. These housing bubbles helped destabilize the global financial system and contributed to the subsequent recession. Therefore, low consumer price inflation does not necessarily equate with a lack of economic imbalances. Policymakers must be alert to signs of growing imbalances and respond with appropriate policies. Furthermore, as discussed in Box 3.1, the muted relationship between inflation and output raises particular challenges for monetary policymaking for which there are no clear solutions.

Second, the comparison of the U.S. and German experiences in the 1970s should serve as an important reminder about the inflation risks arising from political pressure and limited central bank independence. Although a flatter Phillips curve can mitigate the inflationary effects of expansion, history clearly demonstrates the risks associated with curtailing appropriate monetary tightening in response to persistently rising inflation. The end result can be the disanchoring of inflation expectations and stagflation.

In the wake of the Great Recession, there is political urgency to reduce unemployment, as during the 1970s. In addition, the unprecedented growth in central bank balance sheets has been suggested as a possible vector through which central bank independence could be undermined during the recovery.[16] For example, capital losses on large bond holdings could expose central banks to political pressure. Similarly, there are concerns that the stimulative effects of unconventional monetary policies may gather momentum as the recovery strengthens, and these policies may be hard to reverse. We do not analyze these issues here (see Chapter 1). Instead, what our analysis underscores is that, whatever the source, limits on central banks' independence and operational restrictions that limit their flexibility in

---

[15]This conclusion is very much in line with the findings of Beyer and others (2009).

[16]See the April 2013 *Global Financial Stability Report* for a discussion of the potential financial stability risks of such actions, which are not addressed here.

responding to evolving challenges can cause problems and must be avoided.

In short, the dog did not bark because the combination of anchored expectations and credible central banks has made inflation move much more slowly than caricatures from the 1970s might suggest—inflation has been muzzled. And, provided central banks remain free to respond appropriately, the dog is likely to remain so.

Appendix 3.1. Econometric Model

An unemployment-based Phillips curve is estimated that allows for time-varying parameters. The Phillips curve is:

$$\pi_t = \theta_t \, \bar{\pi}_t + (1 - \theta_t)\pi_{t-1}^4 - \kappa_t(u_t - u_t^*)$$
$$+ \, \gamma_t \, \hat{\pi}_t^m + \varepsilon_t^\pi, \tag{3.4}$$

in which π_t is headline consumer price index (CPI) inflation, $\bar{\pi}_t$ is long-term inflation expectations, π_{t-1}^4 is year-over-year headline CPI inflation (lagged one quarter), θ_t is a time-varying parameter, u_t is the unemployment rate, u_t^* is the nonaccelerating inflation rate of unemployment (NAIRU), $\hat{\pi}_t^m$ is inflation in the relative price of imports (deviation from average), and ε_t^π is a cost-push shock. The unemployment gap and the NAIRU are assumed to evolve as follows:

$$(u_t - u_t^*) = \rho(u_{t-1} - u_{t-1}^*) + \varepsilon_t^{(u-u^*)},$$

with

$$u_t^* = u_{t-1}^* + \varepsilon_t^{u^*}. \tag{3.5}$$

The parameters $(\kappa_t, \gamma_t, \theta_t)$ are assumed to be constrained random walks (κ_t and $\gamma_t \geq 0$ and $0 \leq \theta_t \leq 1$), and ρ is assumed to be constant ($0 \leq \rho \leq 1$).

The data are measured at a quarterly frequency and are seasonally adjusted. The relative price of imports is the import-price deflator relative to the GDP deflator. All inflation rates are annualized. Where possible, inflation data have been adjusted for changes in indirect taxes. Sample periods vary across countries, depending on data availability, with most data beginning in the early 1960s. Long-term inflation expectations are six- to ten-year-ahead inflation forecasts from Consensus Economics.[17]

The parameters and shock variances are estimated with maximum likelihood using a constrained, nonlinear Kalman filter. The parameters are initialized using estimates from 10-year rolling regressions using nonlinear least squares, subject to the same constraints described above and with the NAIRU assumed to be fixed in each rolling window. For each country, the variance of demand shocks $\varepsilon_t^{(u-u^*)}$ relative to NAIRU shocks $\varepsilon_t^{u^*}$ is calibrated.

In addition to the robustness check discussed in the main text, the baseline results were found to be qualitatively similar if different estimation methods are used. Various approaches were examined, including rolling regressions (with a variety of rolling-window sizes) and regressions with deterministic trends in the parameters. Likewise, the results are robust to changing the assumptions relating to the stability of long-term inflation expectations.

---

[17]Long-term inflation expectations for the United States are sourced from the Federal Reserve Board. If data are missing, long-term inflation expectations are estimated using a model similar to that used by Stock and Watson (2007).

Box 3.1. Does Inflation Targeting Still Make Sense with a Flatter Phillips Curve?

This box considers some of the possible implications of a flatter Phillips curve for the conduct of monetary policy. It does not, however, suggest particular solutions—its purpose is merely to review some of the issues currently under debate.

Over the past couple of decades, many central banks have adopted inflation targeting or similar frameworks. These decades, at least until the Great Recession, were also some of the least troubled from a macro-economic point of view, with stable economic growth and lengthy expansions. Indeed, some have linked the Great Moderation with improvements to monetary policymaking over this period.[1] And the acceptability of these frameworks by the public was certainly helped by their seeming ability to deliver stable inflation, low unemployment, and stable output growth. The Great Recession changed all that.

There are suggestions that, particularly in the current economic circumstances, inflation-targeting frameworks may be less than optimal. Wren-Lewis (2013) suggests that the combination of a flatter Phillips curve and persistent shocks to inflation that are unrelated to domestic cyclical conditions means that central banks may end up stabilizing inflation at the cost of economic growth. For example, central banks may cease providing stimulus to an economy that is experiencing high inflation due to exchange rate effects or commodity price cycles, even though unemployment remains high and there are large amounts of economic slack. Analogously, stabilizing inflation may involve much larger swings in economic activity than in the past because the flatter Phillips curve means central banks must effect larger changes in economic slack to obtain a given change in inflation. These considerations suggest a need to reconsider how monetary policy can best contribute to general economic welfare under the circumstances now facing advanced economies.

Any such reconsideration should, however, clearly recognize that the stability of inflation and the anchoring of expectations are essential in order to avoid repeating the experiences of the 1970s. The key issue is whether there is a need to modify the monetary policy framework to ensure that stabilizing inflation is more consistent with stabilizing output.

Various central banks have already adopted "flexible inflation-targeting" regimes that give weight to output stabilization if it is not in conflict with their inflation targets. For example, inflation is allowed to deviate from the target for extended periods if it results from external or tax shocks. To the extent that such shocks are now more important relative to domestic cyclical conditions, extra flexibility may be appropriate. For example, in countries with considerable economic slack, the central bank can react less aggressively than in the past when inflation fluctuates above the target, provided expectations remain anchored.

Another approach is to focus on inflation measures other than the consumer price index that respond more closely to domestic cyclical conditions. For example, targets could be defined in terms of the rate of increase in labor earnings net of productivity gains. Monetary policy would thus be tightened when abnormal increases in wages signal bottlenecks in the labor market. Another suggestion is to give asset price inflation more prominence in monetary policymaking, given the large asset price rises that occurred during the first decade of the 2000s and their role in the financial crisis. However, Bernanke and Gertler (2000) point out the unintended consequences that can attend such an approach.

A more far-reaching approach would complement the inflation target with an explicit mandate to stabilize output. In this dual-mandate framework, central banks' decisions would be based not only on their views about inflation, but also on direct measures of output and unemployment gaps. Central banks would thus have more discretion to allow inflation fluctuations if addressing them would exacerbate cyclical downturns. There is some debate about whether such a dual mandate is compatible with inflation targeting. Bullard (2012) argues that the two are compatible and that differences amount only to the relative weight that is placed on inflation and output fluctuations.

Central banks are already making use of whatever flexibility they have in responding to the unprecedented circumstances following the Great Recession. However, changes in the behavior of inflation and profound challenges in the aftermath of the Great Recession may mean there is need for even greater flexibility. As such, it is worth thinking about whether improvements can be made to frameworks in light of the changed circumstances.

The authors of this box are Damiano Sandri and John Simon.
[1] See Bernanke (2004) or Blanchard and Simon (2001).

References

Abel, Andrew B., and Ben Bernanke, 2005, *Macroeconomics* (Upper Saddle River, New Jersey: Pearson Addison Wesley, 5th ed.).

Alesina, Alberto, and Lawrence H. Summers, 1993, "Central Bank Independence and Macroeconomic Performance: Some Comparative Evidence," *Journal of Money, Credit and Banking*, Vol. 25, No. 2, pp. 151–62.

Ball, Laurence M., 2006, "Has Globalization Changed Inflation?" NBER Working Paper No. 12687 (Cambridge, Massachusetts: National Bureau of Economic Research).

———, N. Gregory Mankiw, and David Romer, 1988, "The New Keynesian Economics and the Output-Inflation Trade-off," *Brookings Papers on Economic Activity: 1*, pp. 1–82.

Bernanke, Ben S., 2004, "The Great Moderation," speech at the meetings of the Eastern Economic Association, Washington, February 20.

———, and Mark Gertler, 2000, "Monetary Policy and Asset Price Volatility," NBER Working Paper No. 7559 (Cambridge, Massachusetts: National Bureau of Economic Research).

Beyer, Andreas, Vítor Gaspar, Christina Gerberding, and Otmar Issing, 2009, "Opting out of the Great Inflation: German Monetary Policy after the Breakdown of Bretton Woods," ECB Working Paper No. 1020 (Frankfurt: European Central Bank).

Blanchard, Olivier, and John Simon, 2001, "The Long and Large Decline in U.S. Output Volatility," *Brookings Papers on Economic Activity: 1*, pp. 135–64.

Bullard, James, 2012, "Hawks, Doves, Bubbles and Inflation Targets," George S. Eccles Distinguished Lecture at Utah State University, Logan, Utah, April 16.

Burns, Arthur, 1979, "The Anguish of Central Banking," Per Jacobsson Lecture, Belgrade, September 30.

Clarida, Richard H., and Mark Gertler, 1997, "How the Bundesbank Conducts Monetary Policy," in *Reducing Inflation: Motivation and Strategy*, ed. by Christina D. Romer and David H. Romer (Chicago: University of Chicago Press), pp. 363–412.

Gaiotti, Eugenio, 2010, "Has Globalization Changed the Phillips Curve? Firm-Level Evidence on the Effect of Activity on Prices," *International Journal of Central Banking*, Vol. 6, No. 1, pp. 51–84.

Galí, Jordi, 2008, *Monetary Policy, Inflation, and the Business Cycle: An Introduction to the New Keynesian Framework* (Princeton, New Jersey: Princeton University Press).

Gerberding, Christina, Franz Seitz, and Andreas Worms, 2005, "How the Bundesbank Really Conducted Monetary Policy," *North American Journal of Economics and Finance*, Vol. 16, No. 3, pp. 277–92.

International Monetary Fund (IMF), 2002, "Spain: 2001 Article IV Consultation," Country Report No. 02/53 (Washington).

Klenow, Peter J., and Benjamin A. Malin, 2010, "Microeconomic Evidence on Price-Setting," NBER Working Paper No. 15826 (Cambridge, Massachusetts: National Bureau of Economic Research).

Kocherlakota, Narayana, 2010, "Inside the FOMC," speech delivered in Marquette, Michigan, August 17.

Kuttner, Ken, and Tim Robinson, 2010, "Understanding the Flattening Phillips Curve," *The North American Journal of Economics and Finance*, Vol. 21, No. 2, pp. 110–25.

Levin, Andrew, and John B. Taylor, 2010, "Falling Behind the Curve: A Positive Analysis of Stop-Start Monetary Policies and the Great Inflation," NBER Working Paper No. 15630 (Cambridge, Massachusetts: National Bureau of Economic Research).

Meltzer, Allan H., 2009, *A History of the Federal Reserve*, Vol. 2 (Chicago: University of Chicago Press). http://press.uchicago.edu/Misc/Chicago/520018.html.

Nelson, Edward, 2005, "Monetary Policy Neglect and the Great Inflation in Canada, Australia, and New Zealand," *International Journal of Central Banking*, Vol. 1, pp. 133–79.

Orphanides, Athanasios, 2002, "Monetary-Policy Rules and the Great Inflation," *American Economic Review*, Vol. 92, No. 2, pp. 115–20.

Schlesinger, Helmut, 1979, "Recent Experiences with Monetary Policy in the Federal Republic of Germany," in *Inflation, Unemployment, and Monetary Control*, ed. by K. Brunner and M.J.M. Neumann, supplement to *Kredit und Kapital Vol. 5* (Berlin: Duncker and Humblot).

Stock, James H., and Mark W. Watson, 2007, "Why Has U.S. Inflation Become Harder to Forecast?" *Journal of Money Credit and Banking*, supplement to Vol. 39, No. 1, pp. 3–33.

Volcker, Paul A., and Toyoo Gyohten, 1992, *Changing Fortunes: The World's Money and the Threat to American Leadership* (New York: Times Books).

Woodford, Michael, 2003, *Interest and Prices: Foundations of a Theory of Monetary Policy* (Princeton, New Jersey: Princeton University Press).

Wren-Lewis, Simon, 2013, "Written Evidence on the Appointment of Dr. Mark Carney as Governor of the Bank of England," House of Commons Treasury Committee, pp. 3–6. www.parliament.uk/documents/commons-committees/treasury/MarkCarneyEvidence%20(2).pdf.

Yellen, Janet L., 2012, "Perspectives on Monetary Policy," speech at the Boston Economic Club, June 6.

CHAPTER 4

BREAKING THROUGH THE FRONTIER: CAN TODAY'S DYNAMIC LOW-INCOME COUNTRIES MAKE IT?

The frequency of growth takeoffs in low-income countries (LICs) has risen markedly during the past two decades, and these takeoffs have lasted longer than those that took place before the 1990s. Economic structure has not mattered much in sparking takeoffs—takeoffs have been achieved by LICs rich in resources and by those oriented toward manufacturing. A striking similarity between recent takeoffs and those before the 1990s is that they have been associated with higher investment and national saving rates and with stronger export growth, which sets them apart from LICs that were unable to take off and confirms the key role of capital accumulation and trade integration in development. However, recent takeoffs stand out from earlier takeoffs in two important aspects. First, today's dynamic LICs have achieved strong growth without building macroeconomic imbalances—as reflected in declining inflation, more competitive exchange rates, and appreciably lower public and external debt accumulation. For resource-rich LICs, this has been due to a much greater reliance on foreign direct investment (FDI). For other LICs, strong growth was achieved despite lower investment levels than in the previous generation. Second, recent takeoffs are associated with a faster pace of implementing productivity-enhancing structural reforms and strengthening institutions. For example, these LICs have a lower regulatory burden, better infrastructure, higher education levels, and greater political stability. Looking forward, there remain many challenges to maintaining strong growth performance in today's dynamic LICs, including the concentration of their growth in only a few sectors and the need to diversify their economies, and ensuring that growth leads to broad-based improvements in living standards. Still, if these countries succeed in preserving their improved policy foundation and maintaining their momentum in structural reform, they seem more likely to stay on course and avoid the reversals in economic fortunes that afflicted many dynamic LICs in the past.

The authors of this chapter are John Bluedorn, Rupa Duttagupta (team leader), Jaime Guajardo, Nkunde Mwase, Shan Chen, and Angela Espiritu. Many helpful suggestions were provided by Andrew Berg, Romain Duval, Andrew Levin, Chris Papageorgiou, and Catherine Pattillo.

Introduction

LICs have made a comeback during the past two decades (Figure 4.1). Growth in their output per capita rebounded beginning in the 1990s. Furthermore, they have grown at a faster pace than advanced economies since the turn of the 21st century and have even outpaced other emerging market and developing economies since the Great Recession.[1] Could this be the beginning of a new era for LIC growth and convergence?

For skeptics, however, this comeback evokes the 1960s and early 1970s, when LIC growth looked promising, only to disappoint when global economic conditions turned sour in the 1980s. LICs' subsequent economic deceleration induced deep pessimism about their prospects, and many wondered if they could escape poverty and economic divergence given their weak institutions, unimpressive economic reform, and resource-curse issues.[2] Is the recent comeback just déjà vu?

This chapter sheds light on the above debate by analyzing growth takeoffs in LICs during the past 60 years and comparing takeoffs beginning in the 1990s with those in earlier decades. It assesses whether recent takeoffs are less vulnerable than in the past, improving LICs' ability to take off and rise out of poverty even in a sluggish world economy. Specifically, the chapter addresses the following questions:

- How do recent growth takeoffs in LICs compare with those of the past? Are they stronger? Have they lasted longer?
- What has changed in the economic and structural conditions and policies of LICs that have taken off since the 1990s compared with those that took off in the past? For both eras, what separated LICs that launched a takeoff from those that did not?

[1]Some studies have also noted the recent increased persistence of LIC growth. See Chapters 2 and 3, respectively, of the October 2008 and April 2011 *Regional Economic Outlook: Sub-Saharan Africa* reports.

[2]See Pritchett (1997), Sachs and Warner (1997, 2001), Easterly and Levine (1997), and Rodrik (1999).

- Can historical experience shed further light on specific policies that can help LICs ignite and sustain growth takeoffs?
- What are the key policy lessons for today's LICs?

This chapter addresses these questions by examining the nature of growth takeoffs in more than 60 LICs since the 1950s. It first defines and identifies LIC growth takeoffs and compares the strength of these takeoffs from a historical perspective. It then uses statistical associations and multivariate estimations to gauge the differences in the economic conditions and policies in LICs that experienced growth takeoffs since the 1990s compared with LICs that took off in earlier periods, and between today's dynamic LICs and their counterparts that could not take off. The analysis then zooms in on country-specific experiences to draw lessons for today's LICs. The chapter concludes by assessing the economic prospects for LICs.

LIC Takeoffs in Historical Perspective

This section identifies growth takeoffs in LICs during the past two decades and compares them with earlier takeoffs.[3] A growth takeoff is identified as an upswing in LIC output per capita that lasts at least five years, with average annual growth in real output per capita during the upswing of at least 3.5 percent. The Harding and Pagan (2002) methodology is used to pick turning points in each LIC's annual level of purchasing-power-parity (PPP)-adjusted real GDP per capita from 1950 to 2011 and then to identify the upswings.[4] The threshold of 3.5 percent growth is the 60th percentile of growth in output per capita in all emerging market and developing economies over the past two decades and is the standard threshold used in

Figure 4.1. Economic Performance of Low-Income Countries and Others

Low-income countries (LICs) have seen a major improvement in their economic performance since the 1990s. Growth in output per capita for the median LIC has increased since the 1990s. It is now higher than median growth in other economy groups.

- LICs
- Other emerging market and developing economies
- Advanced economies

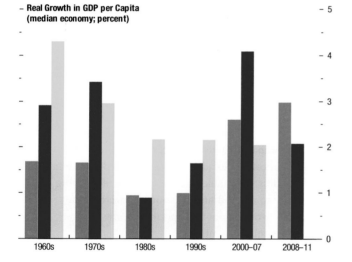

Sources: IMF, World Economic Outlook database (October 2012); Penn World Table 7.1; World Bank, World Development Indicators database; and IMF staff calculations.
Note: Economy groups and indicators are defined in Appendix 4.1. Real GDP per capita is in purchasing-power-parity terms. The 2008–11 median of real GDP per capita growth of advanced economies is near zero (0.02 percentage point).

[3]Throughout the chapter, growth is expressed in terms of growth in PPP-adjusted real GDP per capita. Advanced economies correspond to the member economies of the Organization for Economic Cooperation and Development as of 1990, with the exception of Turkey. All other economies are classified as emerging market and developing economies (EMDEs). At any given time, an LIC is defined as an economy whose average real output per capita over the previous five years is lower than a time-varying low-income threshold. The low-income threshold in 1990 is set at the bottom 45th percentile of average EMDE output per capita (about $2,600 in PPP-adjusted constant 2005 U.S. dollars). This threshold is extrapolated backward and forward using the average growth rate of global output per capita during 1950–2011 (about 2.3 percent per year) to get a low-income threshold for each year. To ensure that the results are unaffected by very small economies, the sample excludes economies whose average 1950–2011 population was less than 1 million. China and India are included in EMDEs, but not LICs.

[4]See Appendix 4.1 for a description of the methodology.

Table 4.1. Takeoffs in Low-Income Countries, 1990–2011

Economic Structure	Country	Start	End[1]	Duration (years)[2]	Average Annual Real GDP per Capita Growth (percent)[3]
Predominantly Agricultural	Sudan	1994		18	4.62
	Rwanda	1995		17	6.93
	Kyrgyz Republic	1996	2008	13	3.65
	Liberia	1996	2002	7	17.54
	Nigeria[4]	1996	2008	13	4.70
	Lao P.D.R.[4]	1999		13	6.10
	Sierra Leone	2000		12	5.87
	Ethiopia	2004		8	7.09
	Liberia	2006		6	4.12
Predominantly Manufacturing	Sri Lanka	1992	2000	9	4.39
	Yemen[4]	1992	1998	7	5.12
	Cambodia	1996		16	5.63
	Bangladesh	1997		15	3.93
	Tajikistan	1997	2007	11	6.20
	Indonesia[4]	2000		12	3.76
	Moldova	2000	2008	9	6.00
	Sri Lanka	2002		10	4.88
Predominantly Nonrenewable Resource and Forestry	Azerbaijan	1997	2010	14	11.97
	Chad	1997	2005	9	6.55
	Zambia	2000	2008	9	4.70
	Angola	2002	2009	8	10.72
	Georgia	2002		10	6.28
	Ghana	2002		10	4.59
	Mongolia	2002	2008	7	6.22
	Uzbekistan	2002		10	6.04
Other (no specialized economic structure)	Mozambique	1996		16	5.78
	Tanzania	1997		15	4.10
	Afghanistan	2002	2007	6	13.15
	Malawi	2002		10	4.32

Source: IMF staff calculations.

Note: The table lists emerging market and developing economies that started with real output per capita (purchasing-power-parity-adjusted constant 2005 U.S. dollars) below the time-varying threshold at the beginning of the episode and grew at an average rate of 3.5 percent or higher for at least five years at any time since 1990. See Appendix 4.1 for details on how the economic structure classifications are derived. Countries in red were experiencing or recovering from a serious external or internal conflict at the start of their takeoffs. See Appendix 4.1 for the definition of conflict and the source of the conflict data.

[1]Ongoing takeoffs as of 2011 are left blank.
[2]Ongoing takeoffs as of 2011 use duration as of 2011.
[3]Ongoing takeoffs as of 2011 use average growth as of 2011.
[4]Countries are also validly classified as predominantly nonrenewable resource and forestry producers.

other studies.[5] The window of five years is long enough to rule out one-time increases in growth in output per capita within shorter periods. Together, these criteria identify 29 growth takeoffs during 1990–2011 (Table 4.1) and 41 episodes in earlier decades (Table 4.2).[6]

The frequency of LICs starting or sustaining a takeoff has increased since 1990. Figure 4.2, panel 1, shows the number and share of LICs that embarked

on a takeoff each year and confirms an increase in this frequency since the late 1990s.

Panel 2 shows the total number and share of LICs that either took off or sustained an ongoing takeoff. It suggests that there were two waves of takeoffs, one from the mid-1960s to the early 1970s and one beginning in the 1990s. The frequency of growth takeoffs declined after 2008, in part because of data censoring, but also because of a drop in the share of LICs that had sustained their takeoffs.[7] Nevertheless, despite the Great Recession, one-third of LICs still sustained their takeoffs as of 2011 compared with an average of 20 percent during the 1980s.

Takeoffs since the 1990s have lasted longer than those in the previous generation (Figure 4.2, panel 3). Over the past two decades, the median duration was 9 years for growth episodes that were already completed and 12 years for episodes that were still ongoing as of

[5]See Hausmann, Pritchett, and Rodrik (2005) and Johnson, Ostry, and Subramanian (2007). The empirical results hold for modifications to the definition for low-income (for instance, a fixed low-income threshold) or to the criteria for identifying takeoffs (for example, a higher growth threshold or a longer-lived upswing). See Appendices 4.2 and 4.3 for details.
[6]Some of these episodes followed serious internal or external conflicts and were excluded from the analysis (see Appendix 4.1 for the definition of a postconflict takeoff). However, the results hold even with the inclusion of postconflict cases. Note also that some of the episodes in Tables 4.1 and 4.2 would be considered to be of longer duration if short-lived breaks between episodes for the same country were excluded. The empirical results of the chapter are broadly unchanged with an alternative definition of growth takeoffs that allows for such breaks. See Appendices 4.2 and 4.3 for details.

[7]Given the criterion that a takeoff must last at least five years, it is not possible to identify new takeoffs that began after 2007.

Table 4.2. Takeoffs in Low-Income Countries before 1990

Economic Structure	Country	Start	End[1]	Duration (years)[2]	Average Annual Real GDP per Capita Growth (percent)[3]
Predominantly Agricultural	Mauritania[4]	1962	1976	15	7.95
	Nigeria[4]	1969	1974	6	8.93
	Mali	1975	1986	12	4.00
	Lao P.D.R.	1980	1986	7	5.43
	Lao P.D.R.	1989	1997	9	4.28
Predominantly Manufacturing	Sri Lanka	1966	1970	5	4.87
	Morocco[4]	1967	1971	5	5.32
	Malawi	1968	1978	11	5.24
	Zimbabwe[4]	1969	1974	6	9.09
	Morocco[4]	1973	1977	5	7.33
	Thailand	1973	1982	10	4.95
	Zimbabwe[4]	1978	1983	6	5.72
	Vietnam	1981		31	4.89
	Egypt[4]	1982	2010	29	4.19
	Indonesia[4]	1983	1997	15	4.81
Predominantly Nonrenewable Resource and Forestry	Zambia	1963	1968	6	6.69
	Indonesia	1964	1981	18	4.87
	Botswana	1966	1973	8	15.48
	Republic of Congo	1978	1984	7	9.10
	Uganda	1988	1994	7	4.70
Other (no specialized economic structure)	Thailand	1959	1971	13	5.43
	Togo	1963	1972	10	4.38
	Republic of Congo	1964	1973	10	6.41
	Cameroon	1968	1979	12	4.38
	Sierra Leone	1968	1972	5	5.49
	Lesotho	1972	1978	7	9.97
	Sri Lanka	1972	1982	11	4.82
	Sierra Leone	1981	1987	7	4.65
	Lesotho	1985	1990	6	3.71
	Tanzania	1985	1991	7	4.33
	Mozambique	1987	1991	5	4.19
Missing Data	Bulgaria	1953	1988	36	5.28
	Cambodia	1954	1963	10	3.58
	Morocco	1958	1964	7	8.69
	Malawi	1960	1966	7	5.97
	Burundi	1962	1973	12	3.81
	Tanzania	1962	1975	14	3.76
	Ghana	1968	1974	7	5.01
	Haiti	1973	1980	8	3.91
	Vietnam	1975	1979	5	4.55
	Cambodia	1983	1988	6	6.32

Source: IMF staff calculations.
Note: The table lists emerging market and developing economies that started with real output per capita (purchasing-power-parity-adjusted constant 2005 U.S. dollars) below the time-varying threshold at the beginning of the episode and grew at an average rate of 3.5 percent or higher for at least five years at any time before 1990. See Appendix 4.1 for details on how the economic structure classifications are derived. Countries in red were experiencing or recovering from a serious external or internal conflict at the start of their takeoffs. See Appendix 4.1 for the definition of conflict and the source of the conflict data.
[1]Ongoing takeoffs as of 2011 are left blank.
[2]Ongoing takeoffs as of 2011 use duration as of 2011.
[3]Ongoing takeoffs as of 2011 use average growth as of 2011.
[4]Countries are also validly classified as predominantly nonrenewable resource and forestry producers.

2011. Before 1990, the median duration of a takeoff was seven years. Median growth in output per capita was 6¼ percent and 5¼ percent, respectively, in ended and ongoing takeoffs over the past two decades, compared with about 5 percent for takeoffs before 1990.

Global conditions helped spur LIC takeoffs, but there was obviously more at play. Figure 4.3 documents the behavior of global growth, the U.S. real interest rate as a proxy for global interest rates, and terms-of-trade growth underlying LIC takeoffs before and after the 1990s. Each global indicator is presented in three snapshots: its average level during the five years before

takeoff, five years after takeoff, and during years six to ten after takeoff.[8] Compared with pre-1990 takeoffs, recent takeoffs started under weaker global growth and higher global interest rates. However, global growth and interest rate conditions tended to improve after takeoff for the current generation, whereas they deteriorated for the previous generation. Terms-of-trade growth before takeoff was more favorable for the former than the latter, although terms-of-trade growth rose for both

[8]Global growth and interest rates are expressed as deviations from their average value during the entire sample period (1950–2011).

Figure 4.2. Frequency of New and Ongoing Takeoffs in Low-Income Countries

The share of low-income countries (LICs) starting and sustaining growth takeoffs increased sharply beginning in the 1990s. Nearly one-third of LICs were still sustaining a takeoff in 2011 despite the Great Recession. On average, takeoffs during the past two decades have been stronger and longer than those before the 1990s.

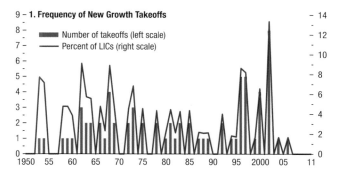

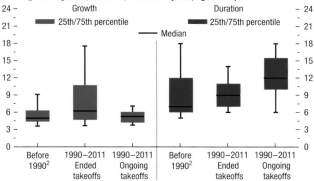

Sources: IMF, World Economic Outlook database (October 2012); Penn World Table 7.1; World Bank, World Development Indicators database; and IMF staff calculations.
Note: Economy groups and indicators are defined in Appendix 4.1. See the text for definitions of new and ongoing growth takeoffs.
[1]The horizontal line inside each box is the median within the group; the upper and lower edges of each box show the top and bottom quartiles. The distance between the black lines (adjacent values) above and below the box indicates the range of the distribution within that generation, excluding outliers.
[2]The episodes before 1990 include one ongoing takeoff (Vietnam since 1981).

Figure 4.3. The Global Environment behind Low-Income Countries' Growth Takeoffs
(Median economy; t *= 1 in the first year of a strong or weak growth episode)*

Global growth and interest rate conditions tended to improve after takeoff for the current generation, whereas they deteriorated for the previous generation. Terms-of-trade growth tended to improve during takeoffs for both generations.

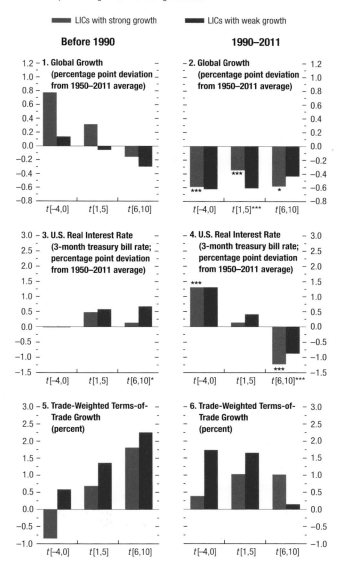

Sources: Haver Analytics; IMF, World Economic Outlook database (October 2012); Penn World Table 7.1; World Bank, World Development Indicators database (2012); and IMF staff calculations.
Note: LICs = low-income countries. Economy groups and indicators are defined in Appendix 4.1. LICs exclude countries experiencing or recovering from a serious external or internal conflict at the start of their takeoffs. See the text for definitions of strong and weak growth episodes (takeoffs are strong growth episodes). See Appendix 4.1 for the definition of conflict and the source of the conflict data. *, **, and *** denote statistically significant difference in distributions (based on the Kolmogorov-Smirnov test) at the 10 percent, 5 percent, and 1 percent levels, respectively. Significance tests on the x-axis are for the difference in the distributions between the groups of strong and weak growth episodes. Significance tests on the blue bars are for the difference in the distributions across 1990–2011 and before 1990 (not shown for red bars). A constant composition sample underlies each of the panels to ensure comparability within the group of strong and weak growth episodes across time for that panel.

**Figure 4.4. Real Output per Capita after Takeoff in
Low-Income Countries**
(Median economy; normalized to 100 at t = 0, *the year before the start of a
strong or weak growth episode; years on x-axis)*

Output per capita tended to stay on a higher trajectory for low-income countries (LICs)
that succeeded in taking off, compared with those that did not. It typically increased by 60
percent during the 10 years after takeoff for the current generation of dynamic LICs and
by 50 percent for the previous generation. This compares with an increase of less than 15
percent for the LICs that were unable to take off for the current generation and less than
5 percent for the previous generation. However, some dynamic LICs in the previous
generation experienced reversals in output per capita growth within 20 years of takeoff.

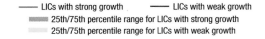

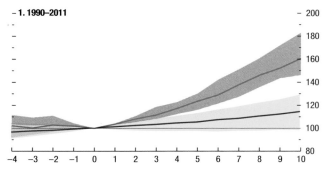

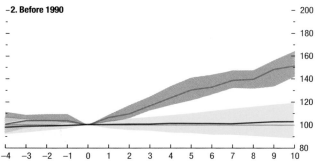

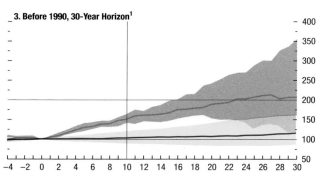

Source: IMF staff calculations.
Note: Economy groups and indicators are defined in Appendix 4.1. LICs exclude countries
experiencing or recovering from a serious external or internal conflict at the start of their
takeoffs. See the text for definitions of strong and weak growth episodes (takeoffs are
strong growth episodes). See Appendix 4.1 for the definition of conflict and the source of
the conflict data.
[1]The vertical line indicates the 10-year horizon.

generations after takeoff. That said, LICs that were
unable to take off faced similar global conditions as
those that did, suggesting that domestic conditions and
policies also affect whether or not an LIC takes off.

Igniting takeoffs pays off in long-term gains in
output per capita. Figure 4.4 shows that LICs that
succeeded in taking off tended to remain on a stronger trajectory for output per capita in the years after
takeoff.[9] For the current generation, output per capita
increased by 60 percent over the 10 years following
takeoff, compared with about 15 percent for LICs with
weaker growth (Figure 4.4, panel 1). For the previous-
generation dynamic LICs, output per capita typically
increased by 50 percent 10 years after takeoff and
doubled within 25 years (Figure 4.4, panels 2 and 3).

LICs that took off had a variety of economic structures, with some rich in resources and others focused
on manufacturing. The same holds for their peers that
did not take off. Among the current generation of
takeoffs, the resource-rich LICs performed particularly
well—their GDP per capita typically rose by 80 percent in 10 years—but many of their resource-rich peers
could not jump-start growth (Figure 4.5, panels 1 and
2). Among dynamic LICs prior to 1990, resource-rich
LICs tended to perform strongly in the first 10 years
after takeoff but were overtaken after 10 years by other
LICs (Figure 4.5, panel 3). Among past weak performers, resource-rich LICs in fact experienced the slowest
growth (Figure 4.5, panel 4).[10] Manufacturing-oriented
dynamic LICs among both the current and previous
generation of takeoffs saw a 50 percent rise in GDP
per capita after 10 years. But many of their manufacturing-oriented peers were unable to take off.

History tells a cautionary tale for LICs today. First,
many currently dynamic LICs also belonged to the
previous cohort of dynamic LICs, which raises questions about whether the vulnerabilities of these LICs
have changed fundamentally. Second, close to one-
third of previous takeoffs ended with a currency, debt,
or banking crisis (Table 4.3). Although fewer of the
recent takeoffs have ended with crises thus far (less than

[9]In Figure 4.4, the year before the start of each growth takeoff is
centered at zero. The control group includes country-year pairs of
LICs that did not experience a new or ongoing growth takeoff in the
years in which the dynamic LICs took off.
[10]The poor performance of resource-rich economies in earlier
decades confirms the conventional wisdom about the unintended consequences of resource abundance—the so-called resource curse manifested in Dutch disease, rent seeking, and extractive political regimes
(IMF, 2012b; Iimi, 2007). What is most striking is that a group of
resource-rich LICs was able to overcome the curse and take off.

Table 4.3. Crises and the Ends of Growth Takeoffs in Low-Income Countries, 1970–2011

Country	Takeoff Start	Takeoff End	Crisis[1]
Indonesia	1964	1981	1979 (currency)
Thailand	1973	1982	1983 (banking)
Mali	1975	1986	1987 (banking)
Vietnam	1975	1979	1981 (currency)
Republic of Congo	1978	1984	1986 (debt)
Zimbabwe	1978	1983	1983 (currency)
Lao P.D.R.	1980	1986	1997 (currency)
Sierra Leone	1981	1987	1989 (currency)
Indonesia	1983	1997	1997 (banking)
			1998 (currency)
			1999 (debt)
Tanzania	1985	1991	1990 (currency)
Uganda	1988	1994	1994 (banking)
Lao P.D.R.	1989	1997	1986 (currency)
Yemen	1992	1998	1996 (banking)
Nigeria	1996	2008	2009 (banking)
Zambia	2000	2008	2009 (currency)
Mongolia	2002	2008	2008 (banking)

Sources: Laeven and Valencia (2012); and IMF staff calculations.

Note: Countries shown in red were experiencing or recovering from a serious external or internal conflict at the start of their takeoffs. See Appendix 4.1 for the definition of conflict and the source of the conflict data.

[1]Growth takeoffs are shown if their end year is coincident with a financial crisis, a financial crisis occurred in the previous two years, or a financial crisis occurred in the following two years. A financial crisis is a banking, currency, or sovereign debt crisis, taken from Laeven and Valencia (2012). Over the period 1970–89, 32 percent of growth takeoffs (either ended or ongoing) were associated with a financial crisis near their end. Over the period 1990–2011, the corresponding incidence was only 14 percent.

15 percent), their future prospects remain uncertain. Finally, Figure 4.4, panel 3, shows that the pace of growth in the previous generation of takeoffs slowed after 10 years, and that the output per capita of dynamic LICs in the bottom quartile of the distribution began to reverse its gains within 20 years after takeoff. Is the current generation of takeoffs vulnerable to similar reversals? The next section addresses this question.

What Lies within: The Role of Economic and Structural Policies and Institutions

This section draws on the growth and development literature to address two key questions about the nature of LIC growth takeoffs. First, is takeoff associated with strong investment growth? The idea that investment is crucial to fostering growth in developing economies has a long history.[11] Second, is the growth strategy likely to endure? Even if investment were strong, growth could still fizzle if investment is not financed by sustainable means—giving rise to macroeconomic imbalances—or if it is not productive. Thus, to catalyze a takeoff and sustain it, strong investment

[11]See, for instance, Rostow (1956) and Rosenstein-Rodan (1943), among others.

Figure 4.5. Economic Structure and Real Output per Capita after Takeoff in Low-Income Countries

(Median economy; normalized to 100 at t = 0, the year before the start of a strong or weak growth episode; years on x-axis)

Among the current generation of dynamic low-income countries (LICs) resource-rich LICs have typically grown faster than others. For the previous generation, although resource-rich economies were also among the strongest performers during the first 10 years after takeoff, they were eventually overtaken by other LICs. Among the weak performers, resource-rich LICs experienced the slowest growth.

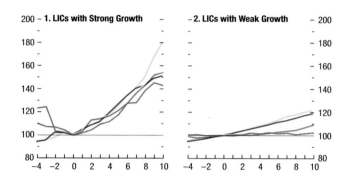

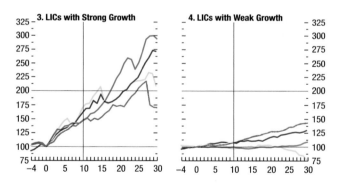

Source: IMF staff calculations.

Note: Economy groups and indicators are defined in Appendix 4.1. LICs exclude countries experiencing or recovering from a serious external or internal conflict at the start of their takeoffs. See the text for definitions of strong and weak growth episodes (takeoffs are strong growth episodes). See Appendix 4.1 for the definition of conflict and the source of the conflict data.

[1]The vertical line indicates the 10-year horizon.

Figure 4.6. Investment and Financing in Low-Income Countries

(Median economy; t *= 1 in the first year of a strong or weak growth episode)*

Dynamic low-income countries (LICs) from both generations tended to experience sharp increases in investment and saving rates during and after takeoffs. However, the current generation of dynamic LICs has tended to finance its current account deficits with a significantly higher share of foreign direct investment (FDI) flows than the weaker LICs and the previous generation of dynamic LICs.

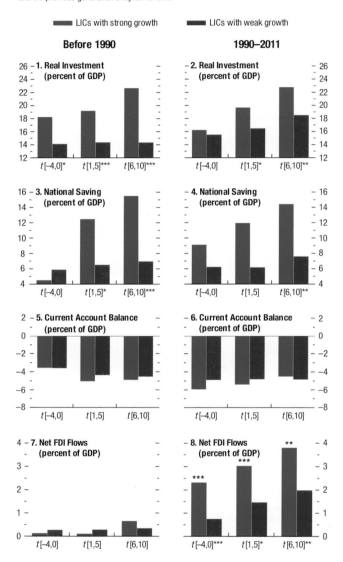

Sources: IMF, Balance of Payments Statistics database; IMF, World Economic Outlook database (October 2012); Penn World Table 7.1; World Bank, World Development Indicators database (2012); and IMF staff calculations.

Note: Economy groups and indicators are defined in Appendix 4.1. LICs exclude countries experiencing or recovering from a serious external or internal conflict at the start of their takeoffs. See the text for definitions of strong and weak growth episodes (takeoffs are strong growth episodes). See Appendix 4.1 for the definition of conflict and the source of the conflict data. *, **, and *** denote statistically significant difference in distributions (based on the Kolmogorov-Smirnov test) at the 10 percent, 5 percent, and 1 percent levels, respectively. Significance tests on the x-axis are for the difference in the distributions between the groups of strong and weak growth. Significance tests on the blue bars are for the difference in the distributions across 1990–2011 and before 1990 (not shown for red bars). A constant composition sample underlies each of the panels to ensure comparability within the group of strong and weak growth episodes across time for that panel.

growth should be supported by policies that do not induce macroeconomic vulnerability and by reforms and institutions that foster productivity and competitiveness.[12] Against this premise, this section documents the differences in economic conditions in recent LIC growth takeoffs compared with those that occurred prior to the 1990s. However, all stylized facts are based on correlations and should be interpreted as associations with takeoffs rather than drivers of takeoffs.

Although both the current and previous generation of takeoffs coincided with strong investment growth, they differed significantly in how the saving-investment gaps were financed. Takeoffs in both generations were correlated with higher levels of investment and national saving rates compared with LICs that could not launch a growth takeoff (Figure 4.6, panels 1–4). In addition, current account deficits were broadly similar in both generations (Figure 4.6, panels 5 and 6). However, a larger share of the current account deficits was financed by FDI flows for the current generation of takeoffs compared with the previous generation. FDI flows also rose sharply after takeoff for the current generation of dynamic LICs compared with both the LICs with weak growth and the previous generation of dynamic LICs (Figure 4.6, panels 7 and 8).[13]

Recent LIC takeoffs were supported by sharp declines in public and external debt levels, in part as a result of their greater reliance on FDI, as well as by policy adjustments undertaken to qualify for debt relief (Figure 4.7, panels 1–4). Among the current-generation dynamic LICs, within 10 years after takeoff public debt decreased from more than 90 percent of GDP to 44 percent of GDP, and external debt fell from more than 70 percent of GDP to about 44 percent. Even if economies that received debt relief are excluded from the sample, the pattern of lower external and public debt within 10 years of takeoff still holds.[14]

More reliance on FDI and greater macroeconomic policy discipline have fostered similarly strong growth but lower inflation after takeoff relative to dynamic LICs in the previous generation (Figure 4.7, panels 5

[12]See Commission on Growth and Development (2008), Spence (2011), Lin (2012), and Rodrik (2003).

[13]The remarkable increase in FDI inflows to LICs has also been noted by others (Dabla-Norris and others, 2010). However, as shown below, for the manufacturing-oriented LICs, although FDI levels for the current generation exceeded those in previous generations, they did not increase sharply following takeoff. The share of foreign aid in GDP was also higher for the current generation of dynamic LICs than for the previous generation.

[14]See Appendix 4.2.

and 6). For the latter, public and external debt stood at 40 and 33 percent of GDP, respectively, before takeoff, but more than doubled within 10 to 20 years after takeoff, and inflation tended to increase as well.

There is no compelling evidence that recent takeoffs are accompanied by rising financial imbalances. The ratio of credit to GDP tended to increase gradually in recent takeoffs, corroborating the symbiotic relationship between financial intermediation and growth (Figure 4.7, panels 7 and 8). Still, credit-to-GDP ratios in current-generation dynamic LICs were lower than in LICs with weaker growth and in LICs that took off in the previous generation.[15]

Competitiveness and export growth are important for LIC takeoffs. Both today and in the previous generation, LICs with takeoffs experienced stronger export growth than LICs with weaker growth (Figure 4.8, panels 1 and 2). Today's LIC takeoffs tended to have more geographically diversified exports, which may be one reason they were able to sustain strong export growth—along with the fast growth in EMDEs such as China and India—despite anemic growth in advanced economies (Figure 4.8, panels 3 and 4).[16] However, greater trade exposure to other EMDEs also implies greater exposure to risks to growth in the latter and the related risks to commodity prices.

Related to the above, export structures were also more diversified in the dynamic LICs of both generations than in those with weak growth, but diversification reversed in the 10 years after takeoff for the current generation (Figure 4.8, panels 5 and 6). The greater concentration of exports after takeoff is partly related to increased specialization in commodity-related activity in LICs that discover natural resources. Given the potential risks from such product concentration, including increased exposure to adverse external shocks and limited scope for quality upgrading, continued economic and export diversification will be needed to improve the resilience of today's LIC takeoffs.[17]

---

[15]Owing to data constraints, we were unable to assess other dimensions of financial stability related to prudential supervision and regulation or the use of macroprudential policies.

[16]Dabla-Norris, Espinoza, and Jahan (2012) find a sharp increase in LIC exports to emerging markets during the past three decades. They find that China and India have become significant destinations for LIC exports from all regions, whereas other emerging market economies, such as Brazil, Mexico, Russia, Saudi Arabia, South Africa, and Turkey, account for a large share of regional LIC exports.

[17]See, for example, Hausmann, Rodriguez, and Wagner (2006) and Papageorgiou and Spatafora (2012) for the benefits of economic diversification.

Figure 4.7. Macroeconomic Conditions in Low-Income Countries

(Median economy; t = 1 in the first year of a strong or weak growth episode)

Recent takeoffs were characterized by sharp reductions in public and external debt levels and inflation. In contrast, previous-generation takeoffs were characterized by generally worsening macroeconomic conditions.

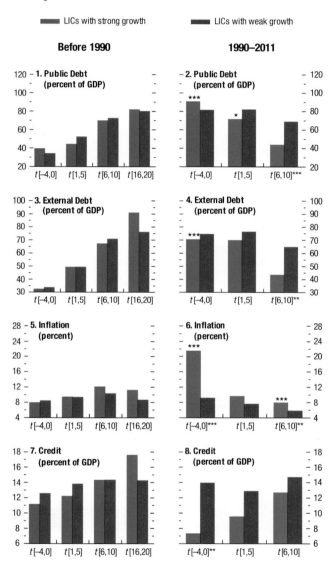

Sources: Abbas and others (2010); IMF, International Financial Statistics database; IMF, World Economic Outlook database (October 2012); Lane and Milesi-Ferretti (2007) updated to 2011; World Bank, World Development Indicators database (2012); and IMF staff calculations.

Note: LICs = low-income countries. Economy groups and indicators are defined in Appendix 4.1. LICs exclude countries experiencing or recovering from a serious external or internal conflict at the start of their takeoffs. See the text for definitions of strong and weak growth episodes (takeoffs are strong growth episodes). See Appendix 4.1 for the definition of conflict and the source of the conflict data. *, **, and *** denote statistically significant difference in distributions (based on the Kolmogorov-Smirnov test) at the 10 percent, 5 percent, and 1 percent levels, respectively. Significance tests on the x-axis are for the difference in the distributions between the groups of strong and weak growth. Significance tests on the blue bars are for the difference in the distributions across 1990–2011 and before 1990 (not shown for red bars). A constant composition sample underlies each of the panels to ensure comparability within the group of strong and weak growth episodes across time for that panel.

Figure 4.8. External Competitiveness, Export Growth, and Diversification in Low-Income Countries
(Median economy; t = 1 *in the first year of a strong or weak growth episode)*

In the current and previous generations of takeoffs, dynamic low-income countries (LICs) experienced stronger export growth than weakly performing LICs. Today's dynamic LICs tended to have deeper trade linkages with emerging market and developing economies (EMDEs) and took off with more diversified exports, although diversification tended to reverse later. Today's dynamic LICs also have more competitive real exchange rates and a greater accumulation of foreign reserves.

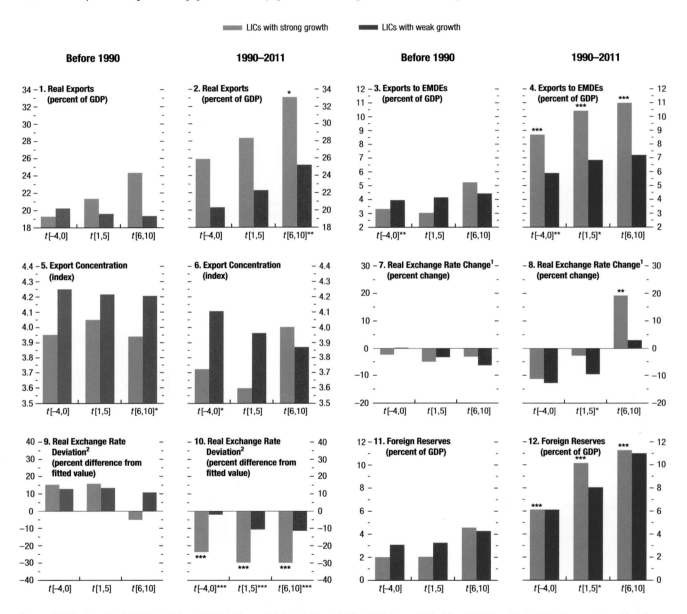

Sources: IMF, Direction of Trade Statistics database; IMF, World Economic Outlook database (October 2012); Lane and Milesi-Ferretti (2007) updated to 2011; Papageorgiou and Spatafora (2012); Penn World Table 7.1; World Bank, World Development Indicators database (2012); and IMF staff calculations.
Note: Economy groups and indicators are defined in Appendix 4.1. LICs exclude countries experiencing or recovering from a serious external or internal conflict at the start of their takeoffs. See the text for definitions of strong and weak growth episodes (takeoffs are strong growth episodes). See Appendix 4.1 for the definition of conflict and the source of the conflict data. *, **, and *** denote statistically significant difference in distributions (based on the Kolmogorov-Smirnov test) at the 10 percent, 5 percent, and 1 percent levels, respectively. Significance tests on the x-axis are for the difference in the distributions between the groups of strong and weak growth. Significance tests on the blue bars are for the difference in the distributions across 1990–2011 and before 1990 (not shown for red bars). A constant composition sample underlies each of the panels to ensure comparability within the group of strong and weak growth episodes across time for that panel.
[1]The real exchange rate change is the percent change in the five-year average real exchange rate versus the United States over a five-year period.
[2]The real exchange rate deviation is the residual from a linear regression of the log real exchange rate versus the United States on the productivity differential of a country and the United States, as proxied by the income per capita differential.

The real exchange rate also seemed to help boost export performance for recent LIC takeoffs. Their real exchange rates versus the U.S. dollar typically depreciated during the five-year periods before and at the start of a takeoff, but there was appreciation pressure during the 6 to10 years after takeoff (Figure 4.8, panels 7 and 8).[18] However, the real exchange rate was typically some 25 to 30 percent weaker than its productivity-adjusted long-term level (Figure 4.8, panels 9 and 10), implying that these dynamic LICs were able to maintain price competitiveness.[19] A greater accumulation of foreign reserves (Figure 4.8, panels 11 and 12) may have helped in this regard. For takeoffs before 1990, the behavior of the real exchange rate was not that different during the periods before and after takeoff, but it was as much as 10 to 15 percent stronger than its productivity-adjusted long-term level until five years after takeoff. This may have been associated with weaker macroeconomic conditions combined with exchange rate pegs.[20]

LIC takeoffs tend to be complemented by improvements in the business climate and with productivity growth, but the record for the recent generation of takeoffs is much stronger than for the previous generation. Dynamic LICs in both generations tend to have smaller governments, lower regulatory barriers (proxied by the level of regulation in business, labor, and credit markets), better infrastructure, and higher human capital levels (proxied by the number of years of schooling) than LICs with weaker growth (Figure 4.9, panels 1–8). For recent takeoffs, the size of government and the level of regulatory barriers continued to decline after takeoff, and infrastructure and education continued to improve, whereas with the exception

of education, these conditions remained the same or deteriorated for the previous generation.[21]

Turning to the role of social and political institutions in underpinning growth takeoffs, the findings suggest that today's dynamic LICs performed better on these institutional measures compared with both LICs with weak growth and dynamic LICs before the 1990s. The recent literature underscores the central role of economic and political institutions in determining why some economies are able to escape poverty and sustain strong growth, whereas others are not.[22] We analyze the evolution of economic and political inclusiveness, as proxied by the degree of income inequality and the degree of control over the executive, respectively (Figure 4.9, panels 9–12). Recent takeoffs display less income inequality, whereas income inequality was typically high in the previous generation of takeoffs. Political institutions are also stronger in the current generation of takeoffs—possibly reflecting the end of conflicts or greater democratization in many dynamic LICs in recent years.

Although the nature of takeoffs is broadly similar for dynamic LICs regardless of their economic structure, a few differences emerge in patterns of investment and its financing (Figure 4.10).[23] For resource-rich dynamic LICs, investment rates increased sharply around the time of takeoff for both generations (Figure 4.10, panels 1 and 2). Although saving rates rose as well, they fell short of investment rates, resulting in current account deficits for both generations (Figure 4.10, panels 3 and 4). This deficit was somewhat larger for the current generation, but it was more than fully offset by net FDI inflows (Figure 4.10, panels 5 and 6). FDI flows accounted for less than 50 percent of the current account deficit after takeoff for the previous generation. The current generation also received a sizably higher share of foreign aid (Figure 4.10, panels 7 and 8). Thus, these LICs were able to resist building

---

[18]The real effective exchange rate is not shown because fewer LICs have these data. For those that do, the observed pattern is similar to that based on the real exchange rate versus the U.S. dollar.

[19]The measure for the long-term real exchange rate level follows Rodrik (2008). It involves the regression of an economy's real exchange rate—measured by the price level relative to that of the United States—on its real GDP per capita relative to that of the United States. The predicted value of the real exchange rate from this regression provides the long-term level of the real exchange rate, whereas the difference between the predicted and actual real exchange rate is the degree of overvaluation. See also Johnson, Ostry, and Subramanian (2007).

[20]We also find a much lower share of fixed and hard pegs among dynamic LICs of the current generation relative both to LICs with weak growth and to dynamic LICs of the previous generation. For the latter it is possible that fixed exchange rate regimes, combined with other macroeconomic vulnerabilities, including rising inflation pressure, resulted in the observed overvaluation.

[21]Aiyar and others (2013) discuss the positive association between deterioration in these measures and economic deceleration in middle-income countries, suggesting that productivity-enhancing structural reforms are not just important for LICs.

[22]See Acemoglu and Robinson (2012) and Johnson, Ostry, and Subramanian (2007) on the role of political institutions. See Berg, Ostry, and Zettelmeyer (2012); Hausmann, Pritchett, and Rodrik (2005); and Abiad and others (2012) on economic institutions as proxied by income inequality. Although not shown here, we found that recent takeoffs were positively correlated with greater life expectancy as well.

[23]It was not possible to conduct tests for statistical significance across the groups owing to the small number of countries in each group.

Figure 4.9. Structural Reforms, Infrastructure, and Political Conditions in Low-Income Countries

(Median economy; t = 1 in the first year of a strong or weak growth episode)

Today's dynamic low-income countries (LICs) tend to have smaller governments, lower regulatory barriers, and better infrastructure than their weaker counterparts from the current generation and dynamic LICs of previous generations. In addition, growth takeoffs tended to occur in economies with higher human capital levels and, for the current generation, more equal income distributions. The current generation of LICs also tends to have better checks and balances on the executive branch of the government.

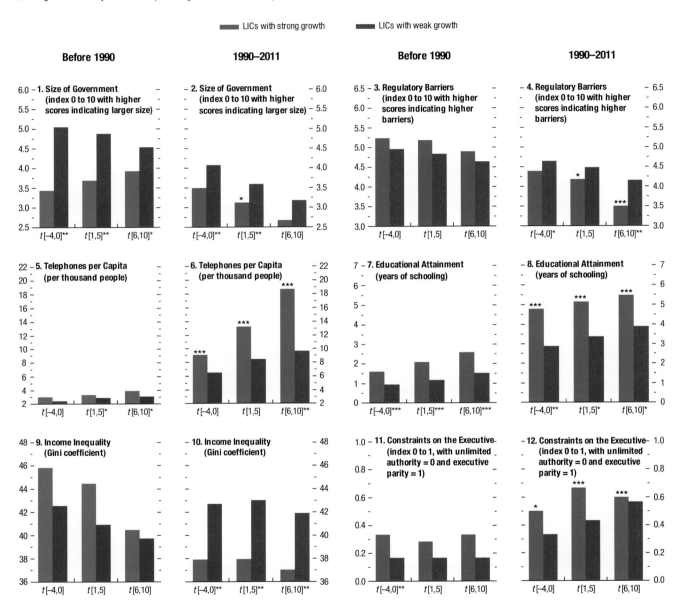

Sources: Banks and Wilson (2012); Barro and Lee (2010); Gwartney, Lawson, and Hall (2012); Political Regime Characteristics and Transitions database (2011); Solt (2009); World Bank, World Development Indicators database (2012); and IMF staff calculations.

Note: Economy groups and indicators are defined in Appendix 4.1. LICs exclude countries experiencing or recovering from a serious external or internal conflict at the start of their takeoffs. See the text for definitions of strong and weak growth episodes (takeoffs are strong growth episodes). See Appendix 4.1 for the definition of conflict and the source of the conflict data. *, **, and *** denote statistically significant difference in distributions (based on the Kolmogorov-Smirnov test) at the 10 percent, 5 percent, and 1 percent levels, respectively. Significance tests on the x-axis are for the difference in the distributions between the groups of strong and weak growth. Significance tests on the blue bars are for the difference in the distributions across 1990–2011 and before 1990 (not shown for red bars). A constant composition sample underlies each of the panels to ensure comparability within the group of strong and weak growth episodes across time for that panel.

Figure 4.10. Investment and Financing across the Spectrum of Today's Dynamic Low-Income Countries

(Median economy; t = 1 in the first year of a strong growth episode)

Investment rates were relatively high for both generations of dynamic low-income countries (LICs). However, external financing of this investment differed across groups. In the current generation, resource-oriented economies benefited most from foreign direct investment (FDI), while agriculture- and other-oriented economies benefited most from aid. Partly because of shifts in external financing, external debt eventually fell for all groups of today's dynamic LICs. Moreover, today's manufacturing- and resource-oriented economies helped to fuel their growth by reducing regulatory barriers while strengthening political institutions. At the same time, educational attainment improved for all groups.

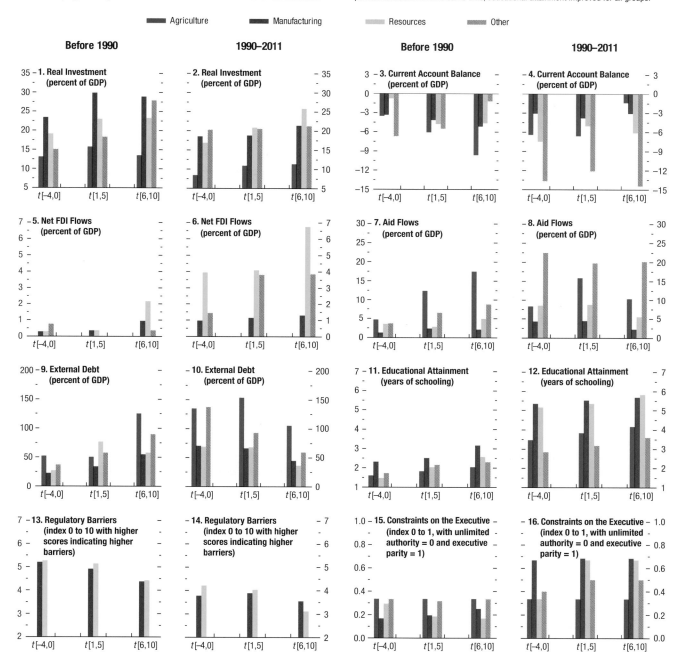

Sources: Barro and Lee (2010); Gwartney, Lawson, and Hall (2012); IMF, Balance of Payments Statistics database; IMF, International Financial Statistics database; IMF, World Economic Outlook database (October 2012); Lane and Milesi-Ferretti (2007) updated to 2011; Penn World Table 7.1; Political Regime Characteristics and Transitions database (2011); World Bank, World Development Indicators database; and IMF staff calculations.
Note: Economy groups and indicators are defined in Appendix 4.1. LICs exclude countries experiencing or recovering from a serious external or internal conflict at the start of their takeoffs. See the text for the definition of strong growth episodes (takeoffs). See Appendix 4.1 for the definition of conflict and the source of the conflict data. A constant composition sample underlies each of the panels to ensure comparability within the group of strong growth episodes across time for that panel. Bars are plotted only if there are at least three takeoffs.

up external debt after takeoff (Figure 4.10, panels 9 and 10). Resource-rich dynamic LICs from the current generation also outperformed their resource-rich peers of the previous generation in terms of stronger human capital levels, lower regulatory barriers, and stronger political institutions (Figure 4.10, panels 11–16). Such reforms, if sustained, will help these LICs engineer more broad-based growth over time (see the example of Indonesia below).

Takeoffs in today's manufacturing-oriented dynamic LICs were associated with lower investment than in the past (see Figure 4.10). However, this did not compromise their growth rates, GDP per capita increased 50 percent after 10 years for both generations (see Figure 4.5). This suggests that the current generation likely enjoyed greater productivity gains. Indeed, proxies for productivity-inducing structural conditions and institutions were much stronger for the current generation of LIC compared with their peers of the past. However, these LICs may still need to raise the rate of productive investment over time: manufacturing-oriented dynamic LICs in the past had stronger investment rates than did their resource-rich counterparts and eventually had stronger output per capita gains. Finally, the current generation of manufacturing-oriented LICs also had lower current account deficits than did the previous generation, and their net FDI and aid inflows were marginally higher. Some manufacturing-oriented dynamic LICs have recently experienced sharp increases in FDI, intended to raise investment and spur export growth and diversification (see the example of Cambodia below).

These stylized facts inspire more confidence in the strength of recent LIC growth takeoffs compared with those in the past. The correlations cannot answer whether there are one or more key drivers of these takeoffs, and in all likelihood the recent takeoffs were the result of a combination of several factors and their interplay with global conditions. Moreover, the policy improvements thus far may not be enough for sustained improvements in growth and income convergence. That said, the overall picture is promising. The strong investment-oriented and externally oriented growth in recent takeoffs relied less on foreign borrowing, which likely gave dynamic LICs more room for policy maneuver. Growth was also helped by a broad range of productivity-enhancing structural reforms, although further export diversification will be essential to improve their economic resilience. Finally, recent

takeoffs have also occurred under more inclusive institutions. Many of these indicators are regarded as key determinants of sustained growth and bode well for today's dynamic LICs, particularly if they can maintain their policy momentum.[24]

Putting It All Together

To assess which conditions and policies are most strongly associated with growth takeoffs, the conditional probability of an LIC growth takeoff is estimated at an annual frequency. A logistic regression (logit) model allows the analysis to jointly consider a number of indicators identified as important in the stylized facts, depending on their data availability over the sample period. However, as in most statistical investigations, all estimated relationships should be interpreted solely as associational, rather than causal. Moreover, given the limited availability of data for many variables and the relative rarity of a takeoff, the model's results should be taken with a grain of salt.[25]

The overall picture suggests that a country's chances of a new growth takeoff are related both to the global economic environment and to the initial levels and changes in the LIC's domestic macroeconomic conditions and structural characteristics (Table 4.4). Some of these relationships have changed since 1990 (highlighted in bold in the table). In particular, the following have become more important: a more competitive exchange rate, deeper export links with other EMDEs, higher human capital levels, initial levels of income per capita, and overall economic size. Indeed, as global trade and competition increase, greater external competitiveness, export diversification, and productivity improvements may raise LICs' chances of takeoff relatively more than when the global economy is less integrated.

The baseline results suggest that the chances of takeoff more than tripled during the 2000s compared with the period before 1990 (Figure 4.11). The predicted

---

[24]See Berg, Ostry, and Zettelmeyer (2012); Hausmann, Pritchett, and Rodrik (2005); Jones and Olken (2008); and Abiad and others (2012).

[25]A number of variables that stood out as significantly different for the current generation of takeoffs could not be incorporated into the logit model because of limited data coverage. These include net FDI flows, external debt, foreign reserves, and income inequality, among others. For the robustness of the findings to the rare-events problem and alternative definitions of low income, criteria for identifying takeoff, and estimation methods, see Appendix 4.3.

annual probability of a new takeoff in any given year increased from less than 1 percent before 1990 to close to 3 percent during the 2000s. Improved structural conditions (particularly, more years of schooling) contributed most to this increase. Better macroeconomic conditions (higher investment growth, falling debt) are the next most important. Finally, stronger global conditions and more outward-oriented policies (a more competitive real exchange rate, more exports to EMDEs) equally boosted the chance of a new takeoff. Higher initial income per capita in the 2000s lowered the chance of a takeoff, reflecting convergence, whereas larger economic size raised it, suggesting gains from economies of scale. However, as noted, the results should be treated with caution because these are only associations and because data issues preclude a deeper analysis of some channels.

Lessons from History

This section looks at five individual experiences with growth takeoffs to provide more details on the specific policies and conditions that affected these countries' macroeconomic outcomes after takeoff. The cases include two economies that pursued industrial development with very different growth strategies (Brazil and Korea, 1960–80),[26] a resource-rich economy that diversified into manufacturing (Indonesia since the mid-1960s), an economy that is shifting into commodities (Mozambique since the mid-1990s), and an economy driven by manufacturing activity (Cambodia since the mid-1990s). Rather than a detailed discussion of the country experiences, which is already available for some of these cases in the development literature (see the references for each case study), the focus here is on drawing out differences in these countries' growth and investment strategies, the financing of their saving-investment gaps, and policy measures that affected productivity and competitiveness.

Figure 4.11. Contributors to the Changing Likelihood of a Growth Takeoff in Low-Income Countries
(Percent change in odds ratio; 2000s versus before 1990)

The predicted annual chance of a strong growth takeoff for an average low-income country was larger in the 2000s than it was before 1990. More favorable global conditions, greater economic size, a larger share of exports going to emerging market and developing economies, a more competitive real exchange rate, more years of schooling, higher investment, lower inflation, and lower public debt all contributed to this rise; higher initial income per capita lowered the chances.

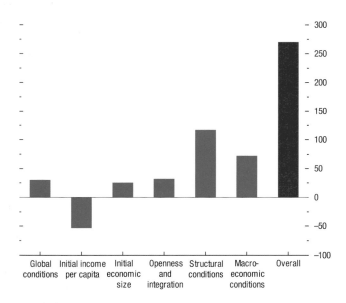

Source: IMF staff calculations.
Note: The odds ratio is the probability of starting a takeoff divided by the probability of not starting one. The estimated contribution of the variables to the percent change in the predicted odds ratio is based on the logistic regression coefficient estimates in Table 4.4, for the full sample. The variable groups shown correspond to those in Table 4.4. The average values of the variables over either the period before 1990 or 2000–11 are used to calculate the predicted odds ratio. The associated predicted probabilities at these average values are 0.8 percent for the subsample before 1990 and 2.8 percent for the 2000–11 subsample. To calculate the overall change, the product of the contributions is used. See Appendix 4.3 for additional details on the model specification and estimation.

---

[26]Note that Brazil and Korea were not LICs at the time of their takeoffs, as determined by the chapter's baseline definition of a time-varying low-income threshold. However, their initial income levels were low in absolute terms, and their experiences portray efforts in structural transformation and development.

Table 4.4. Explaining Growth Takeoffs in Dynamic Developing Economies

Explanatory Variable	Full Sample		Before 1990		1990–2011	
	Logit Coef.	Aver. Marg. Eff.	Logit Coef.	Aver. Marg. Eff.	Logit Coef.	Aver. Marg. Eff.
Global Conditions						
Contemporaneous World Real GDP Growth	0.800**	2.250**	0.859**	2.450**	1.866***	4.200***
	(0.323)	(1.060)	(0.420)	(1.210)	(0.567)	(1.480)
Contemporaneous U.S. Three-Month Treasury Bill Real Rate	0.032	0.091	0.110	0.313	0.433	0.973
	(0.220)	(0.621)	(0.381)	(1.110)	(0.330)	(0.764)
Contemporaneous Terms-of-Trade Growth	0.008	0.024	0.031	0.088	0.002	0.005
	(0.018)	(0.052)	(0.019)	(0.063)	(0.028)	(0.062)
Income per Capita and Size						
Initial Log Real GDP per Capita	−2.439***	−6.880***	**−1.543**	−4.400	**−7.095***	−16.000***
	(0.724)	(2.160)	(1.361)	(3.900)	(2.073)	(4.820)
Initial Log Real GDP Level	0.538*	1.520*	**0.363**	1.030	**1.707***	3.840***
	(0.290)	(0.903)	(0.566)	(1.630)	(0.417)	(1.160)
Openness and Integration						
Initial Real Exchange Rate vs. U.S. Deviation	−0.013*	−0.038*	**0.005**	0.015	**−0.069***	−0.154***
	(0.007)	(0.020)	(0.010)	(0.029)	(0.015)	(0.040)
Change in Real Exchange Rate vs. U.S.	−0.021*	−0.058*	**−0.004**	−0.010	**−0.087***	−0.195***
	(0.011)	(0.032)	(0.017)	(0.050)	(0.025)	(0.063)
Initial Trade Openness	0.001	0.003	−0.005	−0.015	0.036	0.080
	(0.013)	(0.035)	(0.022)	(0.063)	(0.042)	(0.092)
Initial Exports to EMDEs[1] Divided by GDP	0.027	0.075	**−0.298**	−0.851*	**0.012**	0.026
	(0.016)	(0.046)	(0.137)	(0.435)	(0.058)	(0.131)
Structural Conditions						
Initial Indicator for Constraint on Executive	0.063	0.176	1.470	4.190	−2.472	−5.560
	(0.820)	(2.310)	(1.663)	(5.030)	(1.833)	(4.560)
Initial Life Expectancy	0.012	0.033	0.059	0.170	0.044	0.099
	(0.046)	(0.129)	(0.071)	(0.188)	(0.065)	(0.147)
Initial Educational Attainment	0.301*	0.848*	**0.048**	0.137	**0.903**	2.030*
	(0.163)	(0.484)	(0.270)	(0.773)	(0.422)	(1.060)
Initial Real Investment Divided by GDP	0.066	0.186	0.160***	0.456***	0.010	0.023
	(0.041)	(0.123)	(0.045)	(0.126)	(0.132)	(0.299)
Macroeconomic Conditions						
Change in Real Investment Divided by GDP	0.149***	0.420***	0.234***	0.668***	0.177***	0.397***
	(0.045)	(0.148)	(0.082)	(0.245)	(0.053)	(0.125)
Change in Inflation	−0.002	−0.006	−0.004	−0.012	0.019	0.043
	(0.006)	(0.018)	(0.071)	(0.202)	(0.013)	(0.029)
Change in Public Debt Divided by GDP	−0.003	−0.009	−0.019	−0.055	−0.014***	−0.031**
	(0.004)	(0.012)	(0.030)	(0.088)	(0.005)	(0.012)
Observations	892		383		509	
Pseudo *R* Squared	0.171		0.259		0.386	
Number of Cases	28		13		15	
Log Likelihood	−103.2		−42.1		−41.5	
AUC[2]	0.818		0.845		0.940	
90% Lower Bound for AUC[2]	0.750		0.752		0.906	
90% Upper Bound for AUC[2]	0.886		0.938		0.973	
Optimal Youden Cutoff	0.025		0.125		0.045	
True Positive Rate (%)	89		62		87	
False Positive Rate (%)	35		5		13	

Source: IMF staff calculations.

Note: The dependent variable is a dummy variable for the start of a new growth takeoff. Indicators (variables) are defined in Appendix 4.1. Heteroscedasticity and autocorrelation within country robust standard errors are in parentheses under the logistic (logit) regression coefficient estimates. *, **, and *** denote significance at the 10 percent, 5 percent, and 1 percent levels, respectively. Statistically significantly different coefficient estimates across the subsamples before 1990 and for 1990–2011 are shown in bold (at the 10 percent level or lower). The average marginal effects by variable on the chances of a new growth takeoff are shown in the column next to the corresponding sample's logit coefficients. The marginal effect shows the average impact of a one-unit change in the explanatory variable on the probability of a growth takeoff (scaled to range from zero to 100).

[1]EMDEs = emerging market and developing economies.

[2]AUC = area under the receiver operating characteristic curve.

Brazil and Korea, 1960–80: Strong Takeoffs but Diverging Trajectories[27]

These two experiences emphasize the importance of mobilizing sustainable finances for an investment-driven growth strategy. Although both these economies focused on industrialization, Brazil increasingly relied on external debt to finance its saving-investment gap, with the situation exacerbated by large public dissaving. Korea started with a much worse current account position than Brazil, but strengthened its external balances with greater fiscal discipline, higher domestic saving rates, and strong export growth.

Both Brazil and Korea experienced strong growth between 1960 and 1980, but their post-1980 experiences were diametrically opposite (Figure 4.12, panel 1). In Brazil, output per capita stagnated for more than two decades after a debt crisis in the early 1980s. In Korea, after a recession in 1980, the economy regained momentum.

Although both economies pursued industrial development policies, they had markedly different growth strategies. Brazil's growth model was oriented inward, with production geared toward its large domestic market. Import substitution—which discouraged imports and subsidized domestic producers—was the cornerstone of the strategy. Growth was driven mainly by domestic demand, and export growth was slow (Figure 4.12, panels 2 and 3). In contrast, Korea began to shift away from import-substitution policies beginning in the 1960s and became increasingly export oriented. Initially, the government promoted labor-intensive industrial exports, but in the face of increased protectionism for labor-intensive industries in advanced economies, the focus shifted to promoting higher-value-added industries. Large-scale investment in shipbuilding, steel, and petrochemicals helped Korea become a leading producer and exporter in these sectors.

The ways in which Brazil and Korea financed investment, particularly after the first oil price shock in the early 1970s, also help explain the differences in their macroeconomic outcomes. Although Brazil's national saving rate was high, it did not keep pace with investment. The rising current account deficit was increasingly financed by external borrowing. Public debt also rose beginning in the 1970s (Figure 4.12, panels 4–6).

[27]The Brazil case study draws on Baer (2001), Coes (1995), Pinheiro and others (2004), and World Bank (1983). The Korea case draws on Collins (1991), Dornbusch and Park (1987), Kim (2008), Kwon (1990), and Song (2003).

Figure 4.12. Brazil's and Korea's Growth Experiences during 1960–90

These two experiences emphasize the importance of mobilizing sustainable finance for an investment-driven growth strategy. Although both economies focused on industrialization, Brazil increasingly relied on external debt to finance its saving-investment gap, and the situation was exacerbated by growing public debt. Korea started out with a much worse current account position than Brazil, but strengthened its external balances with greater fiscal discipline, higher domestic saving rates, and strong export growth.

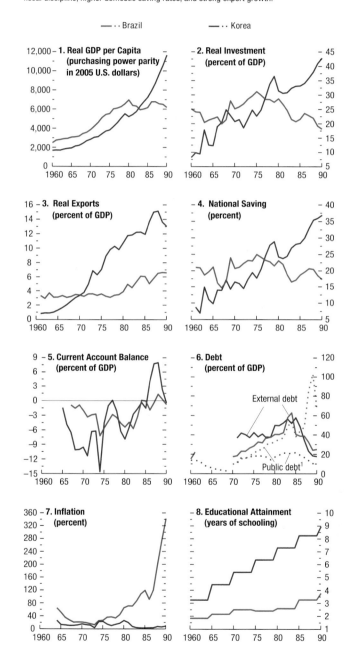

Sources: Abbas and others (2010); Barro and Lee (2010); IMF, World Economic Outlook database (October 2012); Lane and Milesi-Ferretti (2007) updated to 2011; Penn World Table 7.1; World Bank, World Development Indicators database (2012); and IMF staff calculations.
Note: Indicators are defined in Appendix 4.1.
[1]Public debt data for Brazil are missing from 1962 to 1969, and for Korea for 1970.

Figure 4.13. Indonesia's Growth Experience since the 1960s

Indonesia's experience stands out not only because growth was remarkably strong over a long period, but also because the economy was able to achieve a structural shift from commodities into the manufacturing sector. The use of oil windfalls to develop infrastructure, and strengthen health and education, and the continued focus on rural development and agricultural productivity, also allowed growth to be more inclusive.

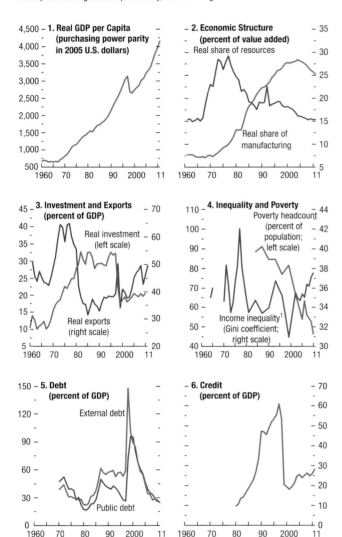

Sources: Abbas and others (2010); IMF, International Financial Statistics database; IMF, World Economic Outlook database (October 2012); Lane and Milesi-Ferretti (2007) updated to 2011; Penn World Table 7.1; Solt (2009); World Bank, World Development Indicators database (2012); and IMF staff calculations.
Note: Indicators are defined in Appendix 4.1.
[1]Income inequality data are missing from 1966 to 1969.

Overheating pressure intensified when policies to push growth were not adjusted after the first oil shock (Figure 4.12, panel 7). Debt became unsustainable after the economy was hit by the second oil price shock, combined with significantly higher world interest rates, culminating in the debt crisis. Korea also had a large current account deficit until the early 1970s, which was financed with foreign aid and external borrowing. However, the saving rate grew rapidly over time: the budget deficit stayed relatively low and the government encouraged both personal saving, through mandatory long-term saving for civil servants and other employees, and corporate saving, through a policy mandating low dividends. This helped narrow the current account deficit in the 1970s. Although it rose again after the second oil shock, it fell soon thereafter on the back of strong export growth. Fiscal discipline and strict monetary targeting helped keep inflation under control.

Policies in Korea were better aligned with maintaining external competitiveness and sustaining investment productivity, and these in turn were helped by macroeconomic policies to contain internal imbalances. The real exchange rate was maintained at a relatively depreciated level (using step devaluations within an implicit crawling peg), exporters received a variety of incentives, and labor skills in key sectors were upgraded via vocational and in-plant training. The government put a high priority on increasing overall education levels (Figure 4.12, panel 8). In the 1960s, when policy promoted labor-intensive industries, the emphasis was on general education. Later, when high-value-added industries were targeted, the emphasis was on strengthening engineering education and establishing specialized research institutes. Income inequality remained relatively low in Korea even after takeoff, whereas Brazil experienced persistently high income inequality and slow educational advancements.

Indonesia, Mid-1960s to Present: Growth with Shared Prosperity[28]

Indonesia's experience stands out not only because growth remained remarkably strong over a long period but also because the structure of the economy successfully shifted from commodities to manufacturing (Figure 4.13). The development strategy put a priority on rural and agricultural development, and oil windfalls were used to develop infrastructure and strengthen health and

[28]This case study draws on Temple (2003), Timmer (2007), and World Bank (2005).

education. Thus, growth was both strong and relatively inclusive.

Indonesia's takeoff started out with commodities and became more broad based over time. Growth was led by the energy sector until the early 1980s and increasingly by the manufacturing sector afterward (Figure 4.13, panels 1 and 2). In the 1960s and 1970s, a large share of the government's revenue from commodity windfall gains was directed toward public investment in rural infrastructure, agriculture, health, and education.[29] When the oil boom ended in the early 1980s, the government supported a shift toward manufacturing. Private investment and export growth were encouraged through industrial deregulation and through trade, capital account, and financial liberalization (Figure 4.13, panel 3). At the same time, growth in the agricultural sector was supported by efforts to improve agricultural productivity, including through the adoption of high-yield seeds and increased use of fertilizers and irrigation—so-called Green Revolution technologies. Strong growth during this period was accompanied by sharp declines in poverty levels and relatively low income inequality (Figure 4.13, panel 4).

Growth was also accompanied by macroeconomic policy discipline. The government used strict monetary targets to reduce inflation from triple digits in the mid-1960s to less than 15 percent by the end of that decade. Fiscal targets adopted in the late 1970s kept public debt relatively low (Figure 4.13, panel 5). However, strong growth and macroeconomic stability masked some latent financial and corporate sector imbalances, whereby financial deregulation in the absence of adequate prudential regulation and supervision fueled a credit boom centered in the property sector beginning in the 1980s (Figure 4.13, panel 6). The boom was financed by short-term capital flows in the context of a pegged exchange rate regime. In 1998, after the economy was hit by contagion from Thailand, Indonesia experienced a banking and balance of payments crisis. The economy rebounded again in 2000, based on stronger macroeconomic policies and structural reforms. Annual growth in per capita real GDP averaged 3¾ percent in the 2000s, and Indonesia remained resilient through the Great Recession.

Mozambique, 1990s to Present: How Will History See It?[30]

Mozambique's experience highlights the benefits of undertaking policies and measures that attract FDI to finance private investment. It also reveals the challenges arising from commodity-based growth, specifically the need for durable structural reforms that support broad-based improvements in productivity, growth, and living standards.

Peace and political stability have supported vibrant growth in Mozambique for nearly two decades. By the end of the civil war in 1992, Mozambique had endured nearly 30 years of conflict and was the second poorest country in our sample of LICs.[31] However, the economy rebounded in 1996, and annual growth in per capita real GDP averaged 5¾ percent over the next 16 years (Figure 4.14, panel 1).

Growth was driven by a surge in investment, supported by improvements in the business climate. Investment before the takeoff largely reflected aid-financed reconstruction (Figure 4.14, panels 2 and 3). After takeoff, investment included public-private initiatives for infrastructure building to develop the resource sector. The government took several steps to make the economy more investment friendly, including establishing a one-stop investment center, improving investor property rights and contract enforcement, and providing generous tax incentives.[32] Although investment declined after the completion of major infrastructure projects, growth was sustained with a commensurate rise in resource exports, particularly aluminum. Investment in the resource sector accelerated again in recent years, particularly in coal mining and

[29]The contribution of the oil boom to economic development in other sectors also reduced the risk of Dutch disease effects. Moreover, the pro-poor growth focus contrasts sharply with the behavior often associated with resource-rich economies—namely, risky investment of resource windfalls.

[30]This study draws on: African Development Bank (2012); Banco Português de Investimento (2012); Batley (2005); Brück (1997, 2006); Brück, FitzGerald, and Grigsby (2000); Canning (1998); Clément and Peiris (2008); Economic Commission for Africa (2004); Hall and Young (1997); Hoeffler (2000); Lledó and Garcia-Verdu (2011); Pretorius (2000); Schwartz, Hahn, and Bannon (2004); United Nations (2012); United Nations Development Program (2011); Vitek (2009); and Wiles, Selvester, and Fidalgo (2005).

[31]Mozambique's war of independence against Portugal started in 1964 and came to an unexpected end with the military coup in Portugal in April 1974. The civil war began in 1977 and lasted until 1992.

[32]Specifically, the government supported establishment of "development corridors," which created industrial clusters along major highways and connected these clusters to a port. A key project focused on processing imported bauxite into aluminum for export. Note that although we highlight the role of domestic policies, other factors also played a role in investment growth, including the country's vast natural resources, favorable global commodity prices, and continued donor support, as well as proximity to South Africa and recent alliances with other EMDEs.

Figure 4.14. Mozambique's Growth Experience since the 1990s

Mozambique's experience highlights the benefits of undertaking policies and measures that attract private investment financed by foreign direct investment (FDI). It also reveals the challenges arising from commodity-based growth, whereby lasting structural reforms will be needed for broad-based improvements in productivity, growth, and living standards.

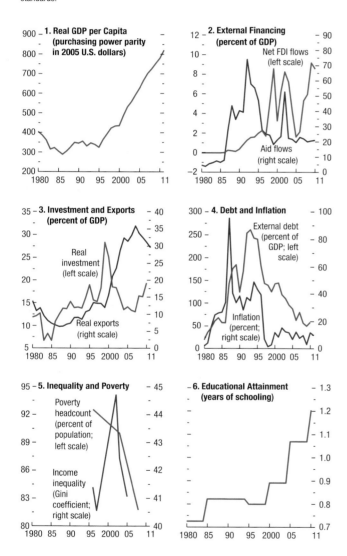

Sources: Barro and Lee (2010); IMF, Balance of Payments Statistics database; IMF, World Economic Outlook database (October 2012); Lane and Milesi-Ferretti (2007) updated to 2011; Penn World Table 7.1; Solt (2009); World Bank, World Development Indicators database (2012); and IMF staff calculations.
Note: Indicators are defined in Appendix 4.1.

natural gas exploration (the existence of vast offshore gas fields was confirmed in 2011).

Given its own limited savings, the government sought to attract FDI to fund its public-private investment projects. Improved macroeconomic policies—relatively low inflation and reduction in fiscal deficits—helped provide a stable economic environment for such FDI (Figure 4.14, panel 4). Mozambique qualified for debt relief under the Heavily Indebted Poor Country Initiative and Multilateral Debt Relief Initiative, which freed up fiscal space for the government's contributions for the infrastructure projects.

Nonetheless, Mozambique's growth experience has been capital intensive and focused on resources. As such, its investment projects have generated employment only to a limited extent. It has also allowed only limited fiscal gains, given the tax exemptions for these projects. Furthermore, there have been only modest declines in poverty and income inequality, and slow improvement in health and education, despite donor support (Figure 4.14, panels 5 and 6). The country ranks among the poorest performers in the United Nations Development Program's *Human Development Report*. Moreover, although the FDI- and aid-financed growth strategy has reduced vulnerabilities related to external borrowing, it has raised the risks of Dutch disease effects that will need to be addressed.

Thus, the economy faces an unfinished policy agenda. In this context, the experience of Indonesia in the 1960s and 1970s in reorienting investment toward rural and agricultural development is illuminating. Key policy priorities for Mozambique include developing transport and energy infrastructures, continuing to enhance human capital, ensuring access to financing more broadly to attract domestic private investment, and expanding the use of agricultural land to enhance agricultural productivity.

Cambodia, 1990s to Present: Remarkable Strides, but Far to Go[33]

Cambodia's experience underscores the importance of peace and stability as well as that of recent government efforts toward investment and development. It also illustrates the benefits of tapping into a vibrant regional production chain. However, Cambodia still needs to make

[33]This study draws on Coe (2006), IMF (2011, 2012a, 2013, forthcoming), and Rungcharoenkitkul (2012).

significant improvements to its infrastructure and business climate to attract private investment and further diversify its economy.

Real GDP per capita gained momentum in the mid-1990s when reconstruction, macroeconomic adjustments, and structural reform bore fruit after years of conflict and political tension. Rapid growth has continued for nearly two decades, and output per capita has grown at an average annual rate of 6 percent over the past decade (Figure 4.15, panel 1). This suggests that Cambodia's takeoff is more than a postconflict recovery story.

Growth has been supported by a steady rise in investment related to the export-oriented textile industry, although more recently also to investment in infrastructure (Figure 4.15, panels 2 and 3). The growth takeoff was catalyzed by Cambodia's preferential access to the United States under the Multi-Fiber Arrangement (MFA).[34] Investment growth decelerated in the early 2000s in part because of concerns about a burdensome regulatory environment, but it picked up again recently, after a concerted government effort to improve the business climate.[35] Recent public-private initiatives have focused on power generation and rural development. Rice exports have increased sharply since 2010, largely as the result of measures to boost yields, storage capacity, and trade.

Cambodia has relied heavily on FDI to finance its saving-investment gap (Figure 4.15, panel 4). Recent FDI flows have been harnessed into public-private initiatives to improve power generation. The economy's relatively open trade and investment regimes, combined with Cambodia's proximity to some of the most dynamic economies in the world, have also attracted FDI in the manufacturing sector recently. In fact, there have been promising signs of diversification in the manufacturing sector, particularly through outsourcing efforts by multinational companies that are responding to rising wages elsewhere in Asia, and these will likely increase with improved power generation. Thus far, the textile sector continues to dominate the economy—accounting for three-quarters of total exports of goods—followed by tourism and agricultural products.

[34]Although the MFA ended in 2005, Cambodia has continued to enjoy preferential access to markets in the European Union.

[35]Cambodia's rank in the World Bank's *Doing Business* indicators moved up by eight places in 2012, to 133rd out of 185 countries, for several measures to reduce the regulatory burden and improve the business climate. The government also strengthened enforcement of the anticorruption law in 2011.

Figure 4.15. Cambodia's Growth Experience since the 1990s

Cambodia's experience underscores the importance of peace and stability and recent government efforts for investment and development. It also illustrates the benefits of proximity to dynamic economies and joining the regional production chain. However, efforts are needed to improve the economy's infrastructure and business climate to attract private investment and accomplish further diversification.

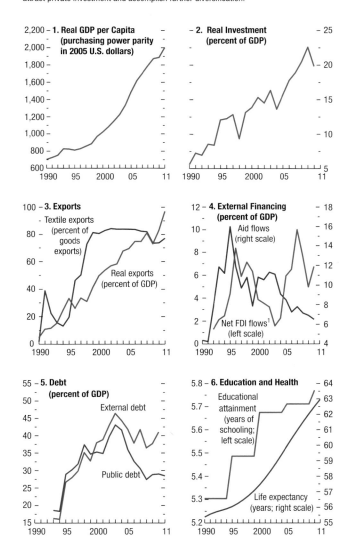

Sources: Abbas and others (2010); Barro and Lee (2010); IMF, Balance of Payments Statistics database; IMF, World Economic Outlook database (October 2012); Lane and Milesi-Ferretti (2007) updated to 2011; Penn World Table 7.1; UN Comtrade Statistics; World Bank, World Development Indicators database (2012); and IMF staff calculations.
Note: Indicators are defined in Appendix 4.1.
[1]FDI = foreign direct investment.

Sustaining strong growth in Cambodia will require further economic diversification and strengthened macroeconomic policies. Removing infrastructure bottlenecks and improving the business climate will remain critical for attracting private investment and for further diversification. Financial intermediation must continue to deepen, and financial stability must be maintained through strong prudential supervision and regulation—the credit-to-GDP ratio has quadrupled to 35 percent in less than 10 years and continues to rise unabated. Improved public debt management will lower risks arising from the potentially large contingent fiscal liabilities inherent in substantial public-private initiatives. Mobilizing fiscal revenue will help build fiscal buffers to meet the country's development needs, including human capital development through improved health and education (Figure 4.15, panels 5 and 6).

Takeaways from the Case Studies

The case studies echo the development literature in emphasizing that growth takeoffs are feasible under a variety of development strategies. Growth was strong in all five of these economies despite their different economic structures and strategies. Cambodia, Indonesia, Korea, and Mozambique took the standard route of promoting growth through investment and exports; in Brazil, investment was geared toward the domestic market. The degree of government involvement also varied among these countries. In Mozambique and Cambodia in the 1990s, the government focused on maintaining political stability in the postwar era—the key prerequisite for growth—and developing an investment-friendly environment. There was much heavier public sector involvement in Brazil and Korea in the 1960s, with varying macroeconomic effects.

However, a key lesson from these countries' experiences is that sustaining strong growth requires continued effort to reduce external and internal imbalances. For all five economies, the growth takeoff was accompanied by some narrowing of fiscal and external current account deficits, but not all were able to sustain this momentum. Where imbalances grew or where growth was excessively reliant on foreign borrowing, the takeoffs ended disruptively or were interrupted even after decades of strong growth (Brazil in 1982, Indonesia in 1997). These experiences suggest that today's dynamic LICs, now only 9 to 12 years into

their takeoffs, should avoid financing investment by excessive debt. Further reductions in their debt levels—which are still relatively high at more than 40 percent of GDP—are needed to build the fiscal space required for higher public investment.

A second lesson is that structural reforms can be instrumental in raising productivity and ensuring broad-based growth. In Korea, labor training in the export-oriented sectors helped sustain growth by moving the manufacturing sector up the value chain. In both Korea and Indonesia in the 1960s, measures were taken to upgrade agricultural productivity, infrastructure, and human capital, and these raised living standards on a broad scale. In contrast, growth from infrastructure projects and import substitution in Brazil in the 1960s did not alleviate income inequality. Similarly, the capital-intensive growth under way in Mozambique, with limited employment generation, may increase social vulnerabilities unless emphasis continues on improving productivity, education, and health. In addition, although Mozambique's FDI-financed growth strategy produces less debt, it could produce Dutch disease challenges as the economy broadens its growth strategy.

Finally, these countries' experiences demonstrate that policies need to adjust to changing global conditions. Strong global growth, low interest rates, and terms-of-trade gains or preferential access to larger markets benefited all five economies at different times. Indonesia's timely shift from natural resources helped it maintain strong growth even after the end of the oil price boom in the 1980s and underscores the significance of further economic diversification for many of today's dynamic LICs. Brazil's struggle to adjust domestic demand to the oil price shocks of the 1970s exacerbated its external imbalances. The important lesson for today's LICs is to avoid procyclical policies despite the prevalence of ultralow global interest rates.

Policy Conclusions

The turn of the 21st century has brought new hope for many LICs. This chapter finds that growth in a significant number of LICs has taken off—defined as an expansion in income per capita for at least five years averaging at least 3½ percent—since the 1990s. These takeoffs have already lasted 9 to 12 years on average, and more than half of these dynamic LICs continued to expand at strong rates through the Great Recession. Compared with major LIC growth takeoffs during the 1960s and early 1970s, the post-1990 period has seen more and longer-lasting takeoffs.

The post-1990 LIC growth takeoffs resemble those in previous decades in important ways. A striking similarity is that both recent and earlier takeoffs were based on higher investment and national saving rates and greater trade integration, which sets apart dynamic LICs of both generations from LICs that failed to take off. This is consistent with the literature, which has long emphasized the key role of capital accumulation and trade integration in economic development. Export growth rose faster in dynamic LICs than in LICs that were unable to take off, and it was higher in recent takeoffs than in earlier ones.

However, the current generation of takeoffs stands apart from those in the previous generation in two key dimensions. First, today's dynamic LICs achieved strong growth without building obvious macroeconomic imbalances. For the resource-rich dynamic LICs, this was due to a much greater reliance on FDI than in the previous generation. For the others, strong growth was achieved despite lower levels of investment than in the previous generation. The more sustainable nature of recent takeoffs is reflected in lower inflation, more competitive exchange rates, and appreciably lower public and external debt accumulation. Second, the post-1990 takeoffs were also associated with faster-paced implementation of productivity-enhancing structural reforms and institution building. These include lower regulatory burdens, stronger infrastructure, higher education levels, and greater political stability. The greater effort toward lowering macroeconomic imbalances and implementing structural reforms bodes well for the future of today's dynamic LICs and highlights priorities for LICs that have yet to jump-start growth.

Despite their achievements, today's dynamic LICs have much left to accomplish. With their per capita income level still a fraction of that in advanced economies, they face a long journey toward income convergence. Moreover, these economies' greater reliance on FDI flows could lead to familiar Dutch disease challenges, which would need to be addressed. A related challenge for LICs that have relied on resource-intensive growth is to diversify their economies to raise growth, employment, and living standards on a broader scale. In sum, dynamic LICs cannot afford to

lose sight of the need to sustain the pace of reforms, avoid major macroeconomic imbalances, and maintain external competitiveness.

Appendix 4.1. Data Definitions, Sources, and Country Groupings

Data Definitions and Sources

The primary data sources for this chapter are the IMF's World Economic Outlook (WEO), Penn World Table version 7.1 (PWT; Heston, Summers, and Aten, 2012), and the World Bank's World Development Indicators (WDI) databases. All the data sources used in the analysis are listed in Table 4.5. For indicators with multiple sources, the sources are listed in the order in which they are spliced (which entails extending the level of a primary series using the growth rate of a secondary series). For example, aggregate real GDP and real GDP per capita in constant 2005 purchasing-power-parity-adjusted U.S. dollars are from the PWT, and where missing, are extended with data from the WEO and WDI.

Domestic Shocks

Bank, currency, and debt crises are from Laeven and Valencia (2012). *Conflict* indicates whether a country is involved in a serious internal or external conflict in a given year in which the country's output per capita falls by more than 3 percent. This measure is derived from information on external and internal state conflicts from the Correlates of War (COW) database (The New COW War Data, 1816–2007 v. 4.0) and the measure of real output per capita detailed earlier. In the analysis, low-income country (LIC) episodes of strong or weak growth are excluded if they occur in the year after a conflict to avoid confounding a growth takeoff with a bounce back from a war.

Economic Structure

Export concentration is from Papageorgiou and Spatafora (2012) and corresponds to the Theil index on an updated version of the UN-NBER data set, which harmonizes Comtrade bilateral trade flow data at the four-digit Standard International Trade Classification (Rev. 1) level. *Exports to emerging and developing economies* are from the IMF's Direction of Trade Statistics database. It is calculated by taking the sum of the bilateral merchandise exports data across all EMDEs (see Table 4.6 for country groupings) for a given coun-

Table 4.5. Data Sources

Indicator	Source
Global Conditions	
Global Growth (percent)	IMF, World Economic Outlook Database (2012); Penn World Table 7.1 (2012)
U.S. Real Interest Rate (three-month treasury bill rate minus realized inflation rate; annualized percent)	Haver Analytics
Country-Specific Variables	
Aid Flows (millions of current U.S. dollars)	World Bank, World Development Indicators Database (2012)
Bank Crises	Laeven and Valencia (2012)
Conflict	The New COW War Data, 1816–2007 v. 4.0 (2011)
Currency Crises	Laeven and Valencia (2012)
Current Account Balance (percent of GDP)	World Bank, World Development Indicators Database (2012); IMF, World Economic Outlook Database (2012)
Credit (percent of GDP)	IMF, International Financial Statistics Database
Debt Crises	Laeven and Valencia (2012)
Educational Attainment (years of schooling)	Barro and Lee (2010)
Constraints on the Executive (index 0 to 1; unlimited authority = 0 and executive parity = 1)	Political Regime Characteristics and Transitions Database (2011)
Export Concentration	Papageorgiou and Spatafora (2012)
Exports to EMDEs (percent of GDP)	IMF, Direction of Trade Statistics Database
External Debt (percent of GDP)	Lane and Milesi-Ferretti (2007) updated to 2011
Foreign Reserves (percent of GDP)	Lane and Milesi-Ferretti (2007) updated to 2011
Income Inequality (Gini coefficient)	Standardized World Income Inequality Database v. 3.1 (Solt, 2009)
Inflation (percent)	World Bank, World Development Indicators Database (2012); IMF, World Economic Outlook Database (2012)
Life Expectancy (years)	World Bank, World Development Indicators Database (2012)
National Saving (percent of GDP)	Penn World Table 7.1 (2012); IMF, World Development Indicators Database (2012)
Net FDI Flows (percent of GDP)	IMF, Balance of Payments Statistics Database; IMF, World Economic Outlook Database (2012)
Poverty Headcount (percent of population)	World Bank, World Development Indicators Database (2012)
Public Debt (percent of GDP)	Abbas and others (2010); Lane and Milesi-Ferretti (2007) updated to 2011
Real Exchange Rate Change (percent change)	Penn World Table 7.1 (2012)
Real Exchange Rate Deviation (percent difference from fitted value)	Penn World Table 7.1 (2012)
Real Exports (percent of GDP)	World Bank, World Development Indicators Database (2012); IMF, World Economic Outlook Database (2012)
Real GDP (billions of purchasing-power-parity-adjusted 2005 U.S. dollars)	Penn World Table 7.1 (2012); IMF, World Economic Outlook Database (2012); World Bank, World Development Indicators Database (2012)
Real GDP per Capita (purchasing-power-parity-adjusted 2005 U.S. dollars)	Penn World Table 7.1 (2012); IMF, World Economic Outlook Database (2012); World Bank, World Development Indicators Database (2012)
Real Investment (percent of GDP)	Penn World Table 7.1 (2012)
Real Share of Manufacturing (percent of value added)	World Bank, World Development Indicators Database (2012)
Real Share of Resources (percent of value added)	World Bank, World Development Indicators Database (2012)
Regulatory Barriers (index 0 to 10 with higher scores indicating higher barriers)	Gwartney, Lawson, and Hall (2012)
Size of Government (index 0 to 10 with higher scores indicating larger size)	Gwartney, Lawson, and Hall (2012)
Telephones per Capita (per thousand people)	Banks and Wilson (2012)
Textile Exports (percent of goods exports)	United Nations, Comtrade Statistics
Trade Openness	World Bank, World Development Indicators Database (2012); IMF, World Economic Outlook Database (2012)
Trade-Weighted Terms-of-Trade Growth (percent)	World Bank, World Development Indicators Database (2012); IMF, World Economic Outlook Database (2012)

Note: EMDEs = emerging market and developing economies; FDI = foreign direct investment.

try. It is expressed as a percent of nominal GDP in U.S. dollars from the WDI, extended with the WEO. *National saving* to GDP is derived as the share of real gross national product in real GDP from the WDI minus the share of private and public consumption in real GDP from the PWT. *Real exports* to GDP is real exports of goods and services as a percent of GDP, from the WDI, extended with the WEO. *Real investment* in percent of GDP is from the PWT. *Real share of manufacturing* and *real share of resources in value added* are from the WDI. Resources are calculated as the contribution of industry in value added minus the contribution of manufacturing in value added. Total value added is the sum of value added from agriculture, industry, and services. *Textile exports* as a percent

of goods exports is from the United Nations Comtrade Statistics database.

External policies

Aid flows is from the WDI and is deflated by the U.S. consumer price index to obtain *real aid flows*. The *current account balance* in percent of GDP is from the WDI, extended with the WEO. *Foreign reserves* to GDP is from the External Wealth of Nations Mark II Database (Lane and Milesi-Ferretti, 2007). *Net FDI Flows* as a percent of GDP is from the IMF Balance of Payments Statistics database (line 4500), extended with the WEO. *Trade openness* is measured as the sum of imports and exports of goods and services divided by GDP. The individual components are from the WDI, extended with the WEO.

Table 4.6. Economy Groups

Advanced Economies (AEs)	Emerging Market and Developing Economies (EMDEs)		
Australia	Afghanistan*+	Guinea*+	Pakistan*
Austria	Albania*	Haiti*+	Panama
Belgium	Algeria	Honduras*+	Papua New Guinea*
Canada	Angola*	Hong Kong SAR	Paraguay*
Denmark	Argentina	Hungary	Peru
Finland	Armenia*	India	Philippines*
France	Azerbaijan*	Indonesia*	Poland
Germany	Bangladesh*	Iran	Republic of Congo*+
Greece	Belarus	Iraq*	Romania
Ireland	Benin*+	Israel	Russia
Italy	Bolivia*+	Jamaica	Rwanda*+
Japan	Bosnia and Herzegovina*	Jordan	Saudi Arabia
Netherlands	Botswana	Kazakhstan	Senegal*+
New Zealand	Brazil	Kenya*	Serbia
Norway	Bulgaria	Korea	Sierra Leone*+
Portugal	Burkina Faso*+	Kuwait	Singapore
Spain	Burundi*+	Kyrgyz Republic*	Slovak Republic
Sweden	Cambodia*	Lao P.D.R.*	Slovenia
Switzerland	Cameroon*+	Latvia	Somalia*+
United Kingdom	Central African Republic*+	Lebanon	South Africa
United States	Chad*+	Lesotho*	Sri Lanka*
	Chile	Liberia*+	Sudan*+
	China	Libya	Syrian Arab Republic*
	Colombia	Lithuania	Taiwan Province of China
	Costa Rica	Madagascar*+	Tajikistan*
	Côte d'Ivoire*+	Malawi*+	Tanzania*+
	Croatia	Malaysia	Thailand
	Czech Republic	Mali*+	Togo*+
	Democratic Republic	Mauritania*+	Tunisia
	of the Congo*+	Mexico	Turkey
	Dominican Republic	Moldova*	Turkmenistan
	Ecuador	Mongolia*	Uganda*+
	Egypt*	Morocco*	Ukraine
	El Salvador	Mozambique*+	United Arab Emirates
	Eritrea*+	Namibia	Uruguay
	Estonia	Nepal*	Uzbekistan*
	Ethiopia*+	Nicaragua*+	Venezuela
	FYR Macedonia	Niger*+	Vietnam*
	Georgia*	Nigeria*	Yemen*
	Ghana*+	Oman	Zambia*+
	Guatemala		Zimbabwe*

Note: * denotes low-income countries (LICs) anytime from 1990 onward based on a time-varying threshold for low-income output per capita. The definition of LICs is given in Appendix 4.1. The sample of countries excludes economies that had an average population less than 1 million. The group of LICs also excludes China and India. + denotes countries eligible for the Heavily Indebted Poor Countries (HIPC) Initiative.

Global environment

Global growth is the world GDP growth aggregate from the WEO, weighted by purchasing-power-parity (PPP) GDP. It is then extended by the growth of the aggregate PPP GDP levels from the PWT. The *U.S. real interest rate* is the U.S. three-month treasury bill rate (secondary market, annual average) minus the realized U.S. inflation rate, expressed in annualized percent. Both the interest rate and the inflation rate are from Haver Analytics.

International relative prices

The *real exchange rate* comes from the PWT and is the price level of GDP versus that of the United States. The *real exchange rate deviation* is the residual from a linear regression of the log real exchange rate on the productivity differential of the country with the United States, as proxied by the difference in log real GDP per capita with the United States. The *real exchange rate change* is the percent change over a five-year period in the five-year average of the real exchange rate. The *trade-weighted terms of trade* is the percent change of the terms-of-trade index constructed using the deflators of exports and imports of goods and services and the series of GDP, exports, and imports of goods and services in nominal terms—all from the WDI and WEO. In particular, the terms-of-trade index is calculated as the ratio of the export price deflator exponentiated by the share of exports in GDP to the import price deflator exponentiated by the share of imports in GDP.

Monetary and fiscal policies

Credit as a percent of GDP is from the IMF's *International Financial Statistics* publication and refers to bank credit to the private sector (line 22D). *External debt* to GDP is from the External Wealth of Nations

Mark II database (Lane and Milesi-Ferretti, 2007). *Inflation* is calculated as the log difference of the consumer price index (CPI). CPI data are from the WDI, extended with WEO data. *Public debt* is from Abbas and others (2010) taken as a ratio to GDP; the GDP data are from the WDI, extended with WEO data. The public-debt-to-GDP ratio is then extended using the change in external debt to GDP.

Structural and political conditions

Constraints on the executive is from the Political Regime Characteristics and Transitions database (2011) but rescaled to zero to 1(from 1 to 7): unlimited authority equals zero and executive parity equals 1. *Educational attainment* is measured by years of schooling from Barro and Lee (2010). *Income inequality* is the Gini coefficient of household disposable income from Solt (2009). *Life expectancy* is from the WDI and refers to life expectancy at birth, in years. *Poverty headcount* is also from the WDI and is the percent of the population living on $2 a day in PPP terms. *Regulatory barriers* and *size of government* are from the Economic Freedom Network's *Economic Freedom of the World 2012 Annual Report* (Gwartney, Lawson, and Hall, 2012). These indices are from zero to 10 with 10 indicating the most freedom (lower barriers and smaller government size, respectively) but are positively transformed (10 minus the original values) so that higher scores indicate more restraints and larger size, respectively. For poverty headcount, regulatory restraints, and size of government, missing data in intervening years are linearly interpolated to obtain a time series. *Telephones per capita* is from the Banks and Wilson Cross-National Time-Series Data Archive (2012). The data are expressed in units of telephones per thousand people.

Methodology to identify upswings in per capita real GDP

Following Chapter 4 of the October 2012 *World Economic Outlook,* we use the Harding and Pagan (2002) algorithm to identify turning points in LIC real GDP per capita. The algorithm searches for local maximums (peaks) and minimums (troughs) that meet specified conditions for the length of cycles and their phases (upswings and downswings). The only condition we impose is that the cycle (comprising a contiguous upswing and downswing) be at least five years long.

Transformations for the logistic regression

Variables used in the logistic regression appear in one of three forms: (1) initial—the once-lagged, backward-looking five-year average, which captures the average behavior of the variable in the five years before a potential takeoff; (2) contemporaneous—the current year, forward-looking five-year average, which captures the average behavior of the variable in the first five years of a potential takeoff; and (3) change—the difference between the contemporaneous and initial values of a variable as defined here, capturing the average trajectory of the variable from before the takeoff during the first years of a potential takeoff. The moving average in each case is calculated only if there are at least two nonmissing observations for the indicated variable during the window.

Country Groups

Advanced economies comprise the member economies of the Organization for Economic Cooperation and Development before 1990, with the exception of Turkey. The other economies are classified as EMDEs. At any given time, LICs are defined as economies in which output per capita, averaged over the previous five years, is lower than the corresponding low-income threshold, which is time varying. The low-income output per capita threshold represents the bottom 45th percentile of EMDEs' output per capita in 1990 ($2,600 in 2005 U.S. dollar PPP terms). This threshold is then spliced back for the pre-1990 period and forward for the post-1990 period using the average growth rate of global output per capita during 1950–2011 (about 2.3 percent a year) to obtain the low-income thresholds for the whole sample period. The group of other EMDEs corresponds to the group of EMDEs excluding LICs. To ensure that the results are unaffected by very small economies, the analysis excludes economies whose average 1950–2011 population was less than 1 million. Also, China and India are included in the group of EMDEs but not LICs. See Table 4.6 for the country composition of each of these analytical groupings. For each of the bar charts comparing cases and referents from Figure 4.3 onward, a constant composition sample underlies each of the panels to ensure comparability within the group of cases or referents across time.

The sample of country episodes is divided into four nonexclusive groups according to their economic structure. In particular, the analysis uses data from the WDI on sectoral value added in local currency at constant prices to classify the country episodes as predominantly agricultural, manufacturing oriented, resource rich, or "other." The exercise starts by constructing the shares of each sector—agriculture, manufacturing, resources, and other—in total value added and considers nonmanufacturing industry to be resources.[36] The 10-year average of these shares is then calculated from the start of a growth episode or from the first year for which a country episode is considered a valid LIC. A country episode is classified as predominantly agricultural if its 10-year average agriculture share is in the 70th percentile for the whole sample of country episodes between 1960 and 2011. Similarly, a country episode is classified as manufacturing oriented (or resource rich) if its 10-year average share of manufacturing (or resources) value added is higher than the 70th percentile for the whole sample of country episodes between 1960 and 2011. The group "other" includes all country episodes that were not classified either as predominantly agricultural, manufacturing oriented, or resource rich.

For country episodes with insufficient data, the grouping is complemented with WDI data on rents from resources. There were a few cases for which data for an industry were available but not their decomposition between manufacturing and nonmanufacturing. In these cases, a country episode was classified as resource rich if its 10-year average resource rents as a percent of GDP were in the 70th percentile for all country episodes between 1960 and 2011.[37] A country episode was classified as manufacturing oriented if the 10-year average of its industry sector value-added share was in the 70th percentile of all country episodes between 1960 and 2011 and the 10-year average of its resource rents as a percent of GDP was not in the 70th percentile of all country episodes between 1960 and 2011. Tables 4.1 and 4.2 present the list of LIC takeoffs grouped according to their underlying economic structure.

Appendix 4.2. Additional Results and Alternative Measures of Takeoffs

Investment Financing and Macroeconomic Policy in Non-HIPC-Eligible Countries

Two key findings in this chapter are that today's dynamic low-income countries (LICs) achieve sharp reductions in inflation and public and external debt and that they finance their investment growth with a higher share of external non-debt-creating flows. This behavior is in sharp contrast to the previous generation of dynamic LICs, in which inflation and debt levels increased after takeoff, suggesting that the means to finance investment raised macroeconomic vulnerabilities. This section of the appendix assesses whether the improvements in macroeconomic outcomes and investment financing in today's dynamic LICs are broad-based—that is, not limited to the dynamic LICs benefiting from the Heavily Indebted Poor Country (HIPC) Initiative.[38]

Figure 4.16 suggests that the sharp decrease in inflation and debt levels in today's dynamic LICs is broad-based. The dynamic LICs that did not receive HIPC assistance also experienced sharp drops in inflation and debt within 10 years after takeoff. The higher level of foreign direct investment (FDI) flows for dynamic LICs relative to LICs with weaker growth is also seen for LICs that did not receive HIPC assistance (Figure 4.17). Moreover, recent takeoffs are associated with higher FDI flows compared with takeoffs before the 1990s and relative to LICs that did not take off. Recent takeoffs are also associated with higher aid flows than takeoffs in previous generations, but not relative to the LICs that did not take off.

Alternative Samples of LICs

This appendix also explores whether the chapter's findings are robust to alternative samples of LICs. The baseline sample considers a time-varying income threshold, in which a country is defined as an LIC if its average real output per capita during the previous five years is below that threshold. In addition, the baseline sample excludes LICs experiencing or recovering

---

[36]Nonmanufacturing industry value added is a proxy for resource-related value added, because this sector includes not only mining and quarrying but also construction and utilities.

[37]The WDI resource rents are defined as the difference between the value of production at world prices and total costs of production for oil, natural gas, coal, minerals, and forestry. These series are calculated at current prices and are thus affected by changes in international resource prices.

[38]The HIPC Initiative was launched in 1996 by the IMF and the World Bank, with the aim of ensuring that no poor country faces a debt burden it cannot manage. To be considered for HIPC assistance, a country must be facing an unsustainable debt burden that cannot be addressed through traditional debt-relief mechanisms and must have established a track record of reform and sound policies through IMF- and World Bank–supported programs. In this chapter, the sample of non-HIPC-eligible countries excludes LICs that were eligible for HIPC assistance at any time.

Figure 4.16. Macroeconomic Conditions for Non-HIPC-Eligible Low-Income Countries

(Median economy; t = 1 in the first year of a strong or weak growth episode)

The improvements in macroeconomic stability in today's low-income countries (LICs) are not limited to countries benefiting from the Heavily Indebted Poor Countries (HIPC) Initiative.

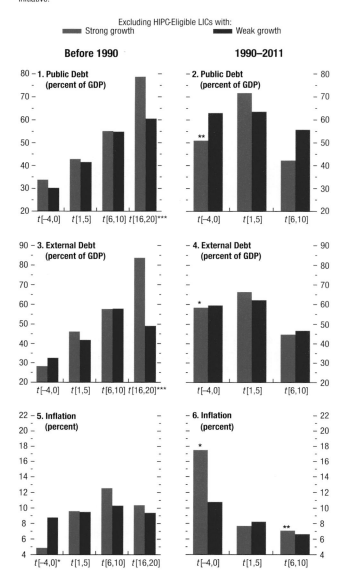

Figure 4.17. Aid and FDI Flows to Non-HIPC-Eligible Low-Income Countries

(Median economy; t = 1 in the first year of a strong or weak growth episode)

Financing by foreign direct investment (FDI) and aid has also increased for low-income countries (LICs) that were not eligible for debt relief under the Heavily Indebted Poor Countries (HIPC) Initiative.

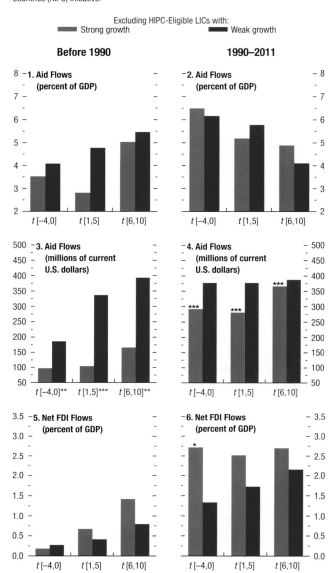

Sources: Abbas and others (2010); IMF, World Economic Outlook database (October 2012); Lane and Milesi-Ferretti (2007) updated to 2011; World Bank, World Development Indicators database (2012); and IMF staff calculations.
Note: Economy groups and indicators are defined in Appendix 4.1. LICs exclude countries experiencing or recovering from a serious external or internal conflict at the start of their takeoffs. See the text for definitions of strong and weak growth episodes (takeoffs are strong growth episodes). See Appendix 4.1 for the definition of conflict and the source of the conflict data. *, **, and *** denote statistically significant difference in distributions (based on the Kolmogorov-Smirnov test) at the 10 percent, 5 percent, and 1 percent levels, respectively. Significance tests on the x-axis are for the difference in the distributions between the groups of strong and weak growth. Significance tests on the blue bars are for the difference in the distributions across 1990–2011 and before 1990 (not shown for red bars). A constant composition sample underlies each of the panels to ensure comparability within the group of strong and weak growth episodes across time for that panel.

Sources: IMF, Balance of Payments Statistics database; IMF, World Economic Outlook database (October 2012); World Bank, World Development Indicators database (2012); and IMF staff calculations.
Note: Economy groups and indicators are defined in Appendix 4.1. LICs exclude countries experiencing or recovering from a serious external or internal conflict at the start of their takeoffs. See the text for definitions of strong and weak growth episodes (takeoffs are strong growth episodes). See Appendix 4.1 for the definition of conflict and the source of the conflict data. *, **, and *** denote statistically significant difference in distributions (based on the Kolmogorov-Smirnov test) at the 10 percent, 5 percent, and 1 percent levels, respectively. Significance tests on the x-axis are for the difference in the distributions between the groups of strong and weak growth. Significance tests on the blue bars are for the difference in the distributions across 1990–2011 and before 1990 (not shown for red bars). A constant composition sample underlies each of the panels to ensure comparability within the group of strong and weak growth episodes across time for that panel.

from a serious external or internal conflict at the start of their takeoffs. This section considers two alternative samples: (1) the baseline sample including LICs experiencing or recovering from a serious conflict; and (2) an alternative sample built with a time-invariant income threshold, in which a country is considered an LIC if its average real output per capita over the previous five years is below $2,600 in purchasing-power-parity-adjusted constant 2005 U.S. dollars. This threshold corresponds to the 45th percentile of per capita real GDP output for the entire sample of emerging market and developing economies as of 1990. This sample excludes LICs experiencing or recovering from conflict. The chapter's key stylized facts broadly hold for these alternative samples of LICs.

Alternative Measures of Takeoffs

As a robustness check for the baseline results, three alternative measures of takeoffs are considered. First, a growth acceleration, as measured by Hausmann, Pritchett, and Rodrik (2005), is defined as a growth episode that is at least eight years long, during which GDP per capita growth averages at least 3.5 percent, average growth during the episode is at least 2 percentage points higher than during the eight years before the takeoff, and output at the end of the episode exceeds its peak before the takeoff. Second, exclusion of temporary delays corresponds to the baseline sample excluding all growth episodes that start within five years of the end of a previous episode for the same country. Instead of considering those as new episodes, they are considered to be a continuation of the previous episode. Third, a faster growth episode is defined as a cyclical upswing in LIC output per capita that lasts at least five years, with average annual output per capita growth during the upswing of at least 5 percent.

Applying the Hausmann, Pritchett, and Rodrik (2005) algorithm to the sample of LICs results in 55 growth accelerations (31 during 1990–2011 and 24 prior to the 1990s), with a significant overlap with the baseline sample. Excluding temporary delays from the baseline sample reduces the number of episodes from 29 to 24 during 1990–2011 and from 41 to 31 during the period prior to the 1990s. If the cutoff for qualification as a takeoff is raised to 5 percent, the number of takeoffs falls to 17 from 29 during 1990–2011 and to 20 from 41 during 1950–89.

The chapter's findings generally hold for these alternative definitions of growth takeoffs. As in the baseline, both current- and previous-generation dynamic LICs experienced high investment and national saving rates compared with other LICs. The current account deficits were broadly similar for both generations of dynamic LICs, but a larger share of the deficit was financed by FDI flows for the current generation. Recent LIC takeoffs were also supported by sharp decreases in inflation and public and external debt, which contrasts with the increases in these indicators in the previous generation. Moreover, both current- and previous-generation takeoffs involved stronger export growth, although today's LIC takeoffs have more geographically diversified exports and more competitive exchange rates. Finally, dynamic LICs, especially the current generation, have smaller governments, better infrastructure, and higher human capital levels than LICs with weaker growth.

However, there are two differences between the results using the baseline criteria and those with the alternative criteria using the Hausmann, Pritchett, and Rodrik (2005) methodology. Although income inequality is still lower in dynamic LICs than in LICs with lower growth, current-generation dynamic LICs do not have lower income inequality than those before 1990. Second, the current-generation dynamic LICs do not have stronger political institutions, as measured by the constraints on the executive, than the previous-generation dynamic LICs or the LICs with low growth. There are also two differences between the baseline results and the ones using a higher threshold for takeoff (at 5 percent growth in GDP per capita). We found that recent takeoffs have lower income inequality and stronger political institutions than takeoffs prior to the 1990s, but not relative to the LICs that did not take off. All other stylized facts are broadly similar to those with the baseline criteria.

Appendix 4.3. Logistic Regression and Robustness of the Baseline Results

To simultaneously investigate multiple covariates of the start of strong growth takeoffs in low-income countries (LICs), a logistic regression (logit) model is used. The binary dependent variable is an indicator for a strong growth takeoff:

$$g_{i,t} = \left\{ \begin{array}{l} 1, \text{ if economy } i \text{ starts a strong growth takeoff at time } t \\ 0, \text{ if not starting or not in a strong growth takeoff at time } t \end{array} \right\},$$

in which $i = 1,\ldots,N$ indexes countries and $t = 1,\ldots,T$ indexes time (years). The logit model assumes that the conditional probability of an event ($g_{i,t} = 1$) takes the form

$$P(g_{i,t} = 1 \mid x_{j,i,t} \ \forall j \in \{1, \ldots K\})$$

$$= \frac{1}{exp[-(\alpha + \sum_{j=1}^{K} \beta_j x_{j,i,t})] + 1},$$

in which j indexes the set of K potential covariates, β_j is the coefficient on variable x_j, and α is a constant term (the constant is not reported in results tables to save space). The models are estimated by maximum likelihood.

To help assess the performance of the logit models, statistics from the receiver operating characteristic (ROC) curve defined by the estimates are shown. The ROC curve summarizes how well the model is able to explain the occurrence of a success (takeoff) and a failure (no takeoff). See Berge and Jordà (2011) for an in-depth discussion of the interpretation of ROC statistics. In brief, the ROC captures the relationship between the true positive rate, $TPR(\pi)$, or share of correctly classified takeoffs for the threshold probability π, and the false positive rate, $FPR(\pi)$, or share of incorrectly classified nontakeoffs. The area under the ROC curve (AUC) is a global measure of the performance of different logit models—the most accurate model shows the largest AUC and the least accurate shows an AUC close to one-half. To make the classification using the model practicable, an optimal threshold probability needs to be selected from the large set of possible thresholds characterized by the ROC curve. Because of its simplicity, the so-called Youden index and its associated cutoff threshold, π^*, are used. The Youden index (J) is the difference between the true positive rate and the false positive rate. Then π^* is the value of π that maximizes $J = \{TPR(\pi) - FPR(\pi)\}$.

Robustness to Alternative Specification and Definition of Takeoff

The analysis considers a specification that adds decadal dummies to the baseline and two alternative definitions of takeoff, one drawing on the Hausmann, Pritchett, and Rodrik (HPR) definition of growth acceleration (2005) and the second using a fixed income per capita threshold below which a country is classified as an LIC set at $2,600 purchasing-power-parity-adjusted 2005 constant U.S. dollars, which is roughly the 45th percentile of income per capita in 1990 among emerging market and developing economies (see Appendix 4.2 for further details). As shown in Table 4.7, the baseline findings are robust to the alternative specification and definition. When the HPR-derived definition of takeoff is used, the same general pattern of coefficient signs is seen, although they are statistically insignificant for the structural conditions. This insignificance may reflect the lower incidence of HPR growth accelerations in the full sample and their greater concentration in the sample since 1990. The model based on the HPR definition is not estimable before 1990 because of the paucity of growth accelerations among LICs during that period.

In other checks (not shown), we also found our baseline results to be robust to including serious conflict cases and to merging takeoff episodes that are within five years of each other. The latter check reduced the number of takeoffs in the logit sample to 17 from 28, so the results should be interpreted with caution.

Robustness to Alternative Estimation Methods

Because growth takeoffs are comparatively rare events (with a less than 5 percent unconditional probability of occurrence in a year), alternative estimators that are more robust to the problems associated with rare events in the logit model (for example, attenuation bias in small samples) were also tried. In particular, the baseline model was also estimated using: (1) Firth's (1993) bias-reducing transformation of the log likelihood; (2) King and Zeng's (2001) procedure for the generation of approximately unbiased coefficients in logit modeling; (3) the complementary log-log transformation, which helps account for skew in the distribution of the dependent variable; and (4) the random effects logit model. As seen in Table 4.8, the signs and magnitudes of the logit coefficients are similar across estimation methods (full sample shown).

Table 4.7. Logistic Regression Robustness to Alternative Specifications and Definition

Explanatory Variable	Decadal Dummies			HPR Growth Acceleration		Fixed Income—LIC Threshold		
	Full Sample	Before 1990	1990–2011	Full Sample	1990–2011	Full Sample	Before 1990	1990–2011
Global Conditions								
Contemporaneous World Real	0.640*	0.561	1.392*	0.788**	1.896***	0.509*	0.403	2.191*
GDP Growth	(0.346)	(0.463)	(0.727)	(0.360)	(0.567)	(0.285)	(0.429)	(1.247)
Contemporaneous U.S. Three-Month Treasury	0.099	−0.081	1.124	−0.277*	−0.592	−0.002	−0.086	0.585
Bill Real Rate	(0.289)	(0.531)	(0.859)	(0.158)	(0.415)	(0.195)	(0.328)	(0.364)
Contemporaneous Terms-of-Trade Growth	0.011	0.033*	0.001	0.007	−0.013	−0.003	0.011	0.024
	(0.018)	(0.019)	(0.028)	(0.010)	(0.018)	(0.016)	(0.018)	(0.031)
Income per Capita and Size								
Initial Log Real GDP per Capita	−2.691***	−1.642	−7.016***	−0.010	−0.382	−1.551**	−1.445	−9.854***
	(0.786)	(1.413)	(2.014)	(0.623)	(0.944)	(0.656)	(1.052)	(2.698)
Initial Log Real GDP Level	0.582**	0.391	1.687***	0.301	0.612*	0.128	−0.005	1.966**
	(0.286)	(0.636)	(0.406)	(0.240)	(0.316)	(0.313)	(0.512)	(0.872)
Openness and Integration								
Initial Real Exchange Rate vs. U.S. Deviation	−0.017**	0.006	−0.072***	−0.014*	−0.033***	−0.012*	−0.003	−0.088***
	(0.007)	(0.012)	(0.016)	(0.007)	(0.013)	(0.006)	(0.009)	(0.027)
Change in Real Exchange Rate vs. U.S.	−0.027**	−0.004	−0.091***	−0.022**	−0.046***	−0.016	−0.017	−0.099**
	(0.012)	(0.019)	(0.025)	(0.010)	(0.015)	(0.011)	(0.015)	(0.040)
Initial Trade Openness	0.008	−0.006	0.036	0.007	0.000	−0.009	0.003	0.077
	(0.011)	(0.024)	(0.044)	(0.011)	(0.020)	(0.012)	(0.020)	(0.065)
Initial Exports to EMDEs[1]	0.025	−0.321**	0.014	−0.027	−0.031	0.040**	−0.030	−0.054
Divided by GDP	(0.017)	(0.163)	(0.061)	(0.023)	(0.042)	(0.017)	(0.100)	(0.063)
Structural Conditions								
Initial Indicator for	−0.371	1.615	−2.454	−0.471	−1.517	0.510	1.155	−0.984
Constraint on Executive	(1.095)	(1.685)	(1.811)	(0.802)	(1.604)	(0.739)	(1.189)	(1.886)
Initial Life Expectancy	0.019	0.062	0.041	−0.019	−0.039	0.022	0.117	0.057
	(0.046)	(0.078)	(0.065)	(0.037)	(0.057)	(0.041)	(0.077)	(0.069)
Initial Educational Attainment	0.417***	0.017	0.882**	0.212	0.330	0.144	−0.335	0.975***
	(0.159)	(0.251)	(0.420)	(0.168)	(0.250)	(0.158)	(0.233)	(0.348)
Initial Real Investment	0.044	0.170***	0.016	0.001	0.050	0.096***	0.128***	−0.131
Divided by GDP	(0.036)	(0.052)	(0.138)	(0.030)	(0.064)	(0.037)	(0.037)	(0.166)
Macroeconomic Conditions								
Change in Real Investment	0.145***	0.241***	0.181***	0.054	0.151**	0.152***	0.190***	0.217***
Divided by GDP	(0.042)	(0.082)	(0.055)	(0.043)	(0.069)	(0.046)	(0.068)	(0.061)
Change in Inflation	0.000	−0.001	0.021	−0.006	−0.015	−0.004	−0.004	0.029**
	(0.007)	(0.071)	(0.013)	(0.009)	(0.012)	(0.007)	(0.077)	(0.013)
Change in Public Debt	−0.006	−0.018	−0.013**	−0.006**	−0.008**	−0.001	−0.017	−0.019***
Divided by GDP	(0.004)	(0.032)	(0.005)	(0.003)	(0.004)	(0.004)	(0.018)	(0.007)
Observations	892	383	509	1,008	560	926	452	474
Pseudo *R* Squared	0.202	0.262	0.394	0.139	0.305	0.155	0.248	0.458
Number of Cases	28	13	15	25	18	30	17	13
Log Likelihood	−99.3	−41.9	−41.0	−100.8	−55.3	−111.9	−54.5	−32.3
AUC[2]	0.845	0.847	0.939	0.785	0.904	0.797	0.819	0.958
90% Lower Bound for AUC[2]	0.784	0.751	0.909	0.689	0.859	0.724	0.714	0.928
90% Upper Bound for AUC[2]	0.907	0.942	0.968	0.880	0.949	0.870	0.923	0.989
Optimal Youden Cutoff	0.050	0.170	0.034	0.032	0.014	0.054	0.089	0.057
True Positive Rate (%)	79	62	93	76	94	60	65	85
False Positive Rate (%)	16	3	15	22	32	15	8	9

Source: IMF staff calculations.

Note: The dependent variable is the indicator for a new takeoff in growth. Heteroscedasticity and autocorrelation within country robust standard errors are in parentheses under the logistic (logit) regression coefficient estimates. *, **, and *** denote significance at the 10 percent, 5 percent, and 1 percent levels, respectively. The last two columns show results using the Hausmann, Pritchett, and Rodrik (HPR, 2005) definition of growth accelerations as the binary dependent variable. The subsample before 1990 is not shown because of the exceedingly low incidence of takeoffs as defined by HPR during the period.

[1]EMDEs = emerging market and developing economies.

[2]AUC = area under the receiver operating characteristic curve.

Table 4.8. Logistic Regression Robustness to Alternative Estimation Methods, Full Sample

Explanatory Variable	Baseline	Firth (1993) Correction	King and Zeng (2001) Correction	Complementary Log-Log Transformation	Random Effects
Global Conditions					
Contemporaneous World Real GDP Growth	0.800**	0.760**	0.765**	0.754**	0.927**
	(0.323)	(0.349)	(0.334)	(0.301)	(0.415)
Contemporaneous U.S. Three-Month Treasury Bill Real Rate	0.032	0.034	0.034	0.017	−0.006
	(0.220)	(0.166)	(0.221)	(0.219)	(0.186)
Contemporaneous Terms-of-Trade Growth	0.008	0.010	0.009	0.005	0.019
	(0.018)	(0.016)	(0.016)	(0.017)	(0.020)
Income per Capita and Size					
Initial Log Real GDP per Capita	−2.439***	−2.252***	−2.258***	−2.441***	−2.989***
	(0.724)	(0.679)	(0.775)	(0.720)	(0.988)
Initial Log Real GDP Level	0.538*	0.499**	0.498**	0.533*	0.766**
	(0.290)	(0.224)	(0.227)	(0.280)	(0.338)
Openness and Integration					
Initial Real Exchange Rate vs. U.S. Deviation	−0.013*	−0.011	−0.010	−0.013*	−0.018**
	(0.007)	(0.007)	(0.007)	(0.007)	(0.009)
Change in Real Exchange Rate vs. U.S.	−0.021*	−0.019*	−0.019	−0.020*	−0.027**
	(0.011)	(0.010)	(0.012)	(0.011)	(0.012)
Initial Trade Openness	0.001	0.002	0.002	0.001	0.011
	(0.013)	(0.011)	(0.012)	(0.012)	(0.016)
Initial Exports to EMDEs[1] Divided by GDP	0.027	0.026	0.025	0.026*	0.007
	(0.016)	(0.022)	(0.022)	(0.015)	(0.034)
Structural Conditions					
Initial Indicator for Constraint on Executive	0.063	0.024	0.001	0.102	−0.003
	(0.820)	(0.795)	(0.799)	(0.769)	(1.020)
Initial Life Expectancy	0.012	0.010	0.011	0.013	0.013
	(0.046)	(0.048)	(0.047)	(0.045)	(0.062)
Initial Educational Attainment	0.301*	0.291**	0.293**	0.295*	0.255
	(0.163)	(0.148)	(0.140)	(0.163)	(0.197)
Initial Real Investment Divided by GDP	0.066	0.063**	0.063	0.063	0.047
	(0.041)	(0.031)	(0.038)	(0.041)	(0.041)
Macroeconomic Conditions					
Change in Real Investment Divided by GDP	0.149***	0.138***	0.138***	0.139***	0.171***
	(0.045)	(0.039)	(0.042)	(0.037)	(0.050)
Change in Inflation	−0.002	−0.005	−0.005	−0.002	−0.003
	(0.006)	(0.006)	(0.006)	(0.006)	(0.009)
Change in Public Debt Divided by GDP	−0.003	−0.004	−0.004	−0.003	−0.005
	(0.004)	(0.003)	(0.004)	(0.004)	(0.004)
Observations	892	892	892	892	892
Number of Cases	28	28	28	28	28
AUC[2]	0.818	0.818	0.818	0.814	0.817
90% Lower Bound for AUC[2]	0.750	0.749	0.750	0.743	0.752
90% Upper Bound for AUC[2]	0.886	0.886	0.887	0.884	0.882

Source: IMF staff calculations.

Note: The dependent variable is a dummy variable for the start of a new growth takeoff. Indicators (variables) are defined in Appendix 4.1. Heteroscedasticity and autocorrelation within country robust standard errors are in parentheses under the logistic regression coefficient estimates. *, **, and *** denote significance at the 10 percent, 5 percent, and 1 percent levels, respectively.

[1]EMDEs = emerging market and developing economies.
[2]AUC = area under the receiver operating characteristic curve.

References

Abbas, S. Ali, Nazim Belhocine, Asmaa El Ganainy, and Mark Horton, 2010, "A Historical Public Debt Database," IMF Working Paper No. 10/245 (Washington: International Monetary Fund).

Abiad, Abdul, John Bluedorn, Jaime Guajardo, and Petia Topalova, 2012, "The Rising Resilience of Emerging Market and Developing Economies," IMF Working Paper No. 12/300 (Washington: International Monetary Fund).

Acemoglu, Daron, and James Robinson, 2012, *Why Nations Fail—The Origins of Power, Prosperity, and Poverty* (New York: Crown Publishers).

African Development Bank, 2012, "African Economic Outlook: Mozambique" (Paris: African Development Bank/Organization for Economic Cooperation and Development).

Aiyar, Shekhar, Romain Duval, Damien Puy, Yiqun Wu, and Longmei Zhang, 2013, "Growth Slowdowns and the Middle-Income Trap," IMF Working Paper No. 13/71 (Washington: International Monetary Fund).

Baer, Werner, 2001, *The Brazilian Economy: Growth and Development* (Westport, Connecticut: Praeger Publishers, 5th ed.).

Banco Português de Investimento, 2012, "Mozambique Repositioning in the International Arena," BPI Research Department paper (Lisbon).

Banks, Arthur S, and Kenneth A. Wilson, 2012, Cross-National Time-Series Data Archive. www.databanksinternational.com.

Barro, Robert J., and Jong-Wha Lee, 2010, "A New Data Set of Educational Attainment in the World, 1950–2010," NBER Working Paper No. 15902 (Cambridge, Massachusetts: National Bureau of Economic Research).

Batley, Richard, 2005, "Mozambique: The Cost of 'Owning' Aid," *Public Administration and Development, Special Issue: Reforming Aid Management,* Vol. 25, No. 5, pp. 415–24.

Berg, Andrew, Jonathan Ostry, and Jeromin Zettelmeyer, 2012, "What Makes Growth Sustained?" *Journal of Development Economics,* Vol. 98, No. 2, pp. 149–66.

Berge, Travis J., and Óscar Jordà, 2011, "Evaluating the Classification of Economic Activity into Recessions and Expansions," *American Economic Journal Macroeconomics,* Vol. 3, No. 2, pp. 246–77.

Brück, Tilman, 1997, "Macroeconomic Effects of the War in Mozambique," Working Paper No. 11 (Oxford: Oxford University).

———, 2006, "War and Reconstruction in Northern Mozambique," *The Economics of Peace and Security Journal,* Vol. 1, No. 1, pp. 29–39.

———, Valpy FitzGerald, and Arturo Grigsby, 2000, "Enhancing the Private Sector Contribution to Post-War Recovery in Poor Countries," QEH Working Paper No. 45(1) (Oxford: Queen Elizabeth House, University of Oxford International Development Center).

Canning, David, 1998, "A Database of World Infrastructure Stocks, 1950–95," Policy Research Working Paper No. 1929 (Washington: World Bank).

Clément, Jean A.P., and Shanaka J. Peiris, eds., 2008, *Post-Stabilization Economics in Sub-Saharan Africa: Lessons from Mozambique* (Washington: International Monetary Fund).

Coe, David, ed., 2006, *Cambodia: Rebuilding for a Challenging Future* (Washington: International Monetary Fund).

Coes, Donald, 1995, *Macroeconomic Crises, Policies, and Growth in Brazil, 1964–90,* World Bank Comparative Macroeconomic Studies (Washington: World Bank).

Collins, Susan, M., 1991, "Saving Behavior in Ten Developing Countries," in *National Saving and Economic Performance,* ed. by B. Douglas Bernheim and John B. Shoven (Chicago: National Bureau of Economic Research, University of Chicago Press), pp. 349–76.

Commission on Growth and Development, 2008, *The Growth Report: Strategies for Sustained Growth and Inclusive Development* (Washington: International Monetary Fund on behalf of the Commission on Growth and Development).

Dabla-Norris, Era, Raphael Espinoza, and Sarwat Jahan, 2012, "Spillovers to Low-Income Countries: Importance of Systemic Emerging Markets," IMF Working Paper No. 12/49 (Washington: International Monetary Fund).

Dabla-Norris, Era, Jiro Honda, Amina Lahreche, and Geneviève Verdier, 2010, "FDI Flows to Low-Income Countries: Global Drivers and Growth Implications," IMF Working Paper No. 10/132 (Washington: International Monetary Fund).

Dornbusch, Rudiger, and Yung Chul Park, 1987, "Korean Growth Policy," *Brookings Papers on Economic Activity: 2* (Washington: Brookings Institution), pp. 389–454.

Easterly, William, Michael Kremer, Lant Pritchett, and Lawrence H. Summers, 1993, "Good Policy or Good Luck? Country Growth Performance and Temporary Shocks," *Journal of Monetary Economics,* Vol. 32, No. 3, pp. 459–83.

Easterly, William, and Ross Levine, 1997, "Africa's Growth Tragedy: Policies and Ethnic Divisions," *Quarterly Journal of Economics,* Vol. 112, No. 4, pp. 1203–50.

Economic Commission for Africa, 2004, "Minerals Cluster Policy Study in Africa: Pilot Studies of South Africa and Mozambique," ECA Report No. SDD/05/08 (Addis Ababa).

Firth, David, 1993, "Bias Reduction of Maximum Likelihood Estimates," *Biometrika,* Vol. 80, No. 1, pp. 27–38.

Gwartney, James, Robert Lawson, and Joshua Hall, 2012, *Economic Freedom of the World 2012 Annual Report* (Vancouver, British Columbia: Fraser Institute).

Hall, Margaret, and Tom Young, 1997, *Confronting Leviathan: Mozambique Since Independence* (London: Hurst).

Harding, Don, and Adrian Pagan, 2002, "Dissecting the Cycle: A Methodological Investigation," *Journal of Monetary Economics,* Vol. 49, No. 2, pp. 365–81.

Hausmann, Ricardo, Lant Pritchett, and Dani Rodrik, 2005, "Growth Accelerations," *Journal of Economic Growth*, Vol. 10, No. 4, pp. 303–29.

Hausmann, Ricardo, Francisco R. Rodriguez, and Rodrigo Andres Wagner, 2006, *Growth Collapses,* Center for International Development Working Paper No. 136 (Cambridge, Massachusetts: Harvard University).

Heston, Alan, Robert Summers, and Bettina Aten, 2012, Penn World Table Version 7.1 (Philadelphia, Pennsylvania: Center for International Comparison of Production, Income and Prices at the University of Pennsylvania).

Hoeffler, Anke E., 2000, "The Augmented Solow Model and the African Growth Debate," CID Working Paper No. 36. (Cambridge, Massachusetts: Center for International Development, Harvard University).

Iimi, Atsushi, 2007, "Escaping the Resource Curse: Evidence from Botswana and the Rest of the World," *IMF Staff Papers*, Vol. 54, No. 4, pp. 665–99.

International Monetary Fund (IMF), 2011, "Cambodia: 2010 Article IV Consultation," Country Report No. 11/45 (Washington).

———, 2012a, "Cambodia: 2011 Article IV Consultation," Country Report No. 12/46 (Washington).

———, 2012b, "Macroeconomic Policy Frameworks for Resource-Rich Developing Countries," IMF Policy Paper (Washington). www.imf.org/external/np/pp/eng/2012/082412.pdf.

———, 2013, "Cambodia: 2012 Article IV Consultation Report," Country Report No. 13/2 (Washington).

———, forthcoming, *Cambodia: Entering a New Phase of Growth* (Washington).

Johnson, Simon, Jonathan Ostry, and Arvind Subramanian, 2007, "The Prospects for Sustained Growth in Africa: Benchmarking the Constraints," NBER Working Paper No. 13120 (Cambridge, Massachusetts: National Bureau of Economic Research).

Jones, Benjamin F., and Benjamin A. Olken, 2008, "The Anatomy of Start-Stop Growth," *Review of Economics and Statistics*, Vol. 90, No. 3, pp. 582–87.

Kim, Chuk Kyo, 2008, "Korea's Development Policy: Experience and Implications for Developing Countries" (Seoul: Korea Institute for International Economic Policy).

King, Gary, and Langche Zeng, 2001, "Logistic Regression in Rare Events Data," *Political Analysis*, Vol. 9, pp. 137–63.

Kwon, Jene K., 1990, *Korean Economic Development: Contributions in Economics and Economic History* (New York: Praeger).

Laeven, Luc, and Fabián Valencia, 2012, "Systemic Banking Crises Database: An Update," IMF Working Paper No. 12/163 (Washington: International Monetary Fund).

Lane, Philip R., and Gian Maria Milesi-Ferretti, 2007, "Europe and Global Imbalances," IMF Working Paper No. 07/144 (Washington: International Monetary Fund).

Lin, Justin Yifu, 2012, *The Quest for Prosperity: How Developing Economies Can Take Off* (Princeton, New Jersey: Princeton University Press).

Lledó, Victor D., and Rodrigo Garcia-Verdu, 2011, "Macroeconomics of Inclusive Growth," IMF presentation at seminar on "Growth, Economic Transformation, and Job Creation," Mozambique, February.

Papageorgiou, Chris, and Nikola Spatafora, 2012, "Economic Diversification in LICs: Stylized Facts and Macroeconomic Implications," IMF Staff Discussion Note No. 12/13 (Washington: International Monetary Fund).

Pinheiro, Armando Castelar, Indermit S. Gill, Luis Serven, and Mark Roland Thomas, 2004, "Brazilian Economic Growth, 1900–2000: Lessons and Policy Implications," Economic and Social Study Series RE1-04-011 (Washington: Inter-American Development Bank).

Pretorius, Leon, 2000, "Regional Integration and Development in Southern Africa: A Case Study of the MOZAL Project and its Implications for Workers," International Labour Resource and Information Group paper (Cape Town: International Labour Resource and Information Group).

Pritchett, Lant, 1997, "Divergence, Big Time," *Journal of Economic Perspectives,* Vol. 11, No. 3, pp. 3–17.

Rodrik, Dani, 1999, "Where Did All the Growth Go? External Shocks, Social Conflict and Growth Collapses," *Journal of Economic Growth*, Vol. 4, No. 4, pp. 385–412.

———, 2003, "Growth Strategies," NBER Working Paper No. 100050 (Cambridge, Massachusetts: National Bureau of Economic Research).

———, 2008, "The Real Exchange Rate and Economic Growth," *Brookings Papers on Economic Activity* (Fall), pp. 365–412.

Rosenstein-Rodan, Paul, 1943, "Problems of Industrialization of Eastern and South-Eastern Europe," *Economic Journal,* Vol. 53, No. 210/211, pp. 202–11.

Rostow, Walt Whitman, 1956, "The Take-Off into Self-Sustained Growth," *Economic Journal*, Vol. 66, pp. 25–48.

Rungcharoenkitkul, Phurichai, 2012, "Modeling with Limited Data: Estimating Potential Growth in Cambodia," IMF Working Paper No. 12/96 (Washington: International Monetary Fund).

Sachs, Jeffrey D., and Andrew M. Warner, 1997, "Sources of Slow Growth in African Economies," *Journal of African Economies,* Vol. 6, No. 3, pp. 335–76.

———, 2001,"The Curse of Natural Resources," *European Economic Review,* Vol. 45, No. 4, pp. 827–38.

Schwartz, Jordan, Shelly Hahn, and Ian Bannon, 2004, "The Private Sector's Role in the Provision of Infrastructure in Post-Conflict Countries: Patterns and Policy Options," Social Development Papers, Conflict Prevention and Reconstruction Paper No. 16 (Washington: United States Institute of Peace).

Solt, Frederick, 2009, "Standardizing the World Income Inequality Database," *Social Science Quarterly*, Vol. 90, No. 2, pp. 231–42.

Song, Byung-Nak, 2003, *The Rise of the Korean Economy* (New York: Oxford University Press, 3rd ed.).

Spence, A. Michael, 2011, *The Next Convergence: The Future of Economic Growth in a Multispeed World* (New York: Farrar, Straus and Giroux).

Temple, Jonathan, 2003, "Growing into Trouble—Indonesia after 1966," in *In Search of Prosperity*, ed. by Dani Rodrik (Princeton, New Jersey: Princeton University Press), pp. 152–83.

Timmer, Peter C., 2007, "A Historical Perspective on Pro-Poor Growth in Indonesia," in *Determinants of Pro-Poor Growth: Analytical Issues and Findings from Country Cases*, ed. by Michael Grimm, Stephan Klasen, and Andrew McKay (New York: Palgrave Macmillan), pp. 164–88.

United Nations, 2012, *United Nations Development Assistance Framework for Mozambique, 2012–15* (New York).

United Nations Development Program, 2011, "Sustainability and Equity: A Better Future for All," *Human Development Report* (New York).

Vitek, Francis, 2009, "An Assessment of External Price Competitiveness for Mozambique," IMF Working Paper No. 09/165 (Washington: International Monetary Fund).

Wiles, Peter, Kerry Selvester, and Lourdes Fidalgo, 2005, *Learning Lessons from Disaster Recovery: The Case of Mozambique*, Disaster Risk Management Working Paper Series No. 12 (Washington: World Bank).

World Bank, 1983, *Brazil: Industrial Policies and Manufactured Exports*, World Bank Country Study (Washington).

———, 2005, *Economic Growth in the 1990s: Learning from a Decade of Reform* (Washington).

IMF EXECUTIVE BOARD DISCUSSION OF THE OUTLOOK, APRIL 2013

The following remarks were made by the Chair at the conclusion of the Executive Board's discussion of the World Economic Outlook, Global Financial Stability Report, *and* Fiscal Monitor *on April 1, 2013.*

Executive Directors welcomed recent signs of improved global economic prospects and financial conditions. They noted that strong policy actions had averted the risks of a euro area breakup and a sharp fiscal contraction in the United States. Meanwhile, financial stability has generally strengthened, with a decline in market and liquidity risks. Activity in emerging market and developing economies has picked up and is expected to strengthen further this year, while low-income countries have achieved more robust growth with macroeconomic stability.

Directors stressed, however, that there is no room for complacency. They observed that the near-term outlook for key advanced economies remains clouded by lingering risks. In the euro area, the main downside risks include persistent financial fragmentation, balance-sheet weaknesses, and adjustment fatigue, as well as renewed financial strain in the periphery. In addition, uncertainties about fiscal policy in the United States and high and rising debt ratios in Japan continue to pose risks. These daunting challenges require further decisive actions to boost confidence.

Directors noted the continued presence of medium-term risks. These relate to high private sector debt and limited policy space in the euro area, the absence of strong fiscal consolidation plans in the United States and Japan, complications from easy and unconventional monetary policy in many advanced economies, and overinvestment and high asset prices in several emerging market and developing economies.

Against this background, Directors underscored that policies need to remain proactive. They generally agreed that, in advanced economies, policymakers should prudently use all available measures to stimulate demand and growth, complemented with structural policies to boost employment and competitiveness. In emerging market and developing economies, strengthening policy buffers and guarding against financial excesses are key objectives.

Directors welcomed the many important actions taken by the euro area authorities to restore market confidence and underscored the need to fully implement the measures recently announced. They highlighted that rapid progress toward a stronger and deeper economic and monetary union, including a banking union, is critical for financial stability. Directors also noted that growth prospects in the euro area would benefit from internal rebalancing within the union, including through reforms of labor and product markets.

Directors concurred that, for most advanced economies, fiscal consolidation should be gradual but sustained toward credible medium-term objectives, in the context of growth-friendly strategies that are suitable for each country. They underlined the urgency of formulating clear and credible plans in Japan and the United States to bring debt ratios down over the medium term. Directors considered it important that fiscal policies avoid procyclicality. In this regard, they generally supported focusing on structural balances and, if financing allows, letting automatic fiscal stabilizers operate fully, although a few Directors pointed to the practical difficulties of estimating structural balances. Most Directors noted that where private demand has been chronically disappointing and room for policy maneuvering exists, consideration should be given to smoothing the pace of consolidation. Directors urged faster progress on entitlement reforms in many advanced economies to tackle spending pressures related to pensions and health care expenditures.

Directors broadly agreed that monetary policy in advanced economies should remain accommodative to support activity as fiscal policy tightens, provided that long-term inflation expectations stay well anchored. In this context, it is important that central banks maintain operational independence and communicate monetary policy in a clear and transparent manner. In addition, progress in repairing the financial sector is crucial, especially in light of the currently impaired credit transmission. Noting financial stability risks that could arise from prolonged use of easy and unconventional monetary policies, including excessive risk taking and misallocation of resources, Directors encouraged authorities to take appropriate measures to mitigate these risks and to pay due attention to spillover effects on emerging market economies. In addition, they encouraged central banks to prepare well in advance for a smooth and appropriately timed exit from these extraordinary policies.

Directors noted that considerable progress has been made to improve financial regulation at both the national and global levels, but that important work still lies ahead. An immediate priority is to complete the regulatory reform agenda, particularly with regard to the too-big-to-fail problem, nonbank financial institutions, and shadow banking. Prompt and consistent implementation of the reform agenda, including Basel III requirements—though challenging in the current environment—is necessary to underpin future financial stability.

Directors emphasized that the main macroeconomic policy challenges for emerging market and developing economies are to manage financial risks and buttress policy buffers. They shared the view that some tightening of policies would be warranted in many of these economies over the medium term, beginning with monetary policy. Where financial stability is at risk, macroeconomic policy adjustment could be supported by prudential measures, and in certain circumstances, capital flow management measures may also be useful. Specifically, policymakers must remain vigilant to potential risks from sustained rapid credit growth, high asset prices, rising corporate leverage, and increasing foreign currency debt. Directors also considered it prudent to return fiscal balances, as soon as conditions permit, to levels that provide ample room to handle future shocks. Moreover, strengthened fiscal institutions would enhance the prospects for fiscal sustainability. In many economies, especially low-income countries, efforts must also continue to improve the targeting of subsidy regimes, diversify the economy, and enhance social policies.

Directors cautioned that the bumpy recovery and the macroeconomic policy mix in advanced economies could complicate policymaking elsewhere. They considered that the pursuit in all economies of policies that foster internal and external balance would help dispel concerns about competitive devaluations. In addition, concerted efforts continue to be required to further reduce global imbalances—notably and where applicable, stronger domestic demand and exchange rate flexibility in surplus economies and increased public saving and structural reforms to boost competitiveness in deficit economies.

The Statistical Appendix presents historical data as well as projections. It comprises five sections: Assumptions, What's New, Data and Conventions, Classification of Countries, and Statistical Tables.

The assumptions underlying the estimates and projections for 2013–14 and the medium-term scenario for 2015–18 are summarized in the first section. The second section presents a brief description of the changes to the database and statistical tables since the October 2012 issue of the *World Economic Outlook*. The third section provides a general description of the data and the conventions used for calculating country group composites. The classification of countries in the various groups presented in the *World Economic Outlook* is summarized in the fourth section.

The last, and main, section comprises the statistical tables. (Statistical Appendix A is included here; Statistical Appendix B is available online.) Data in these tables have been compiled on the basis of information available through early April 2013. The figures for 2013 and beyond are shown with the same degree of precision as the historical figures solely for convenience; because they are projections, the same degree of accuracy is not to be inferred.

Assumptions

Real effective *exchange rates* for the advanced economies are assumed to remain constant at their average levels during the period February 11–March 11, 2013. For 2013 and 2014, these assumptions imply average U.S. dollar/SDR conversion rates of 1.519 and 1.513, U.S. dollar/euro conversion rates of 1.329 and 1.318, and yen/U.S. dollar conversion rates of 93.3 and 93.8, respectively.

It is assumed that the *price of oil* will average $102.60 a barrel in 2013 and $97.58 a barrel in 2014.

Established *policies* of national authorities are assumed to be maintained. The more specific policy assumptions underlying the projections for selected economies are described in Box A1.

With regard to *interest rates,* it is assumed that the London interbank offered rate (LIBOR) on six-month U.S. dollar deposits will average 0.5 percent in 2013 and 0.6 percent in 2014, that three-month euro deposits will average 0.2 percent in 2013 and 0.4 percent in 2014, and that six-month yen deposits will average 0.2 percent in 2013 and 2014.

With respect to *introduction of the euro,* on December 31, 1998, the Council of the European Union decided that, effective January 1, 1999, the irrevocably fixed conversion rates between the euro and currencies of the member countries adopting the euro are as follows.

1 euro	=	13.7603	Austrian schillings
	=	40.3399	Belgian francs
	=	0.585274	Cyprus pound[1]
	=	1.95583	Deutsche mark
	=	15.6466	Estonian krooni[2]
	=	5.94573	Finnish markkaa
	=	6.55957	French francs
	=	340.750	Greek drachma[3]
	=	0.787564	Irish pound
	=	1,936.27	Italian lire
	=	40.3399	Luxembourg francs
	=	0.42930	Maltese lira[1]
	=	2.20371	Netherlands guilders
	=	200.482	Portuguese escudos
	=	30.1260	Slovak koruna[4]
	=	239.640	Slovenian tolars[5]
	=	166.386	Spanish pesetas

[1]Established on January 1, 2008.
[2]Established on January 1, 2011.
[3]Established on January 1, 2001.
[4]Established on January 1, 2009.
[5]Established on January 1, 2007.

See Box 5.4 of the October 1998 *World Economic Outlook* for details on how the conversion rates were established.

What's New

- Projections for Cyprus are excluded due to the ongoing crisis.
- Mongolia is classified as Developing Asia (previously classified as a member of the Commonwealth of Independent States).
- Afghanistan and Pakistan, previously classified as Developing Asia, have been added to the Middle East and North Africa (MENA) to create the Middle East, North Africa, Afghanistan, and Pakistan (MENAP) region. The MENA aggregate (excluding Afghanistan and Pakistan) will be maintained.
- Data for the Marshall Islands and Micronesia are now included in the Developing Asia region.
- As in the October 2012 *World Economic Outlook,* data for Syria are excluded for 2011 onward due to the uncertain political situation.
- Starting with the April 2013 *World Economic Outlook,* the Newly Industrialized Asian Economies (NIEs) grouping has been eliminated.

Data and Conventions

Data and projections for 188 economies form the statistical basis of the *World Economic Outlook* (the WEO database). The data are maintained jointly by the IMF's Research Department and regional departments, with the latter regularly updating country projections based on consistent global assumptions.

Although national statistical agencies are the ultimate providers of historical data and definitions, international organizations are also involved in statistical issues, with the objective of harmonizing methodologies for the compilation of national statistics, including analytical frameworks, concepts, definitions, classifications, and valuation procedures used in the production of economic statistics. The WEO database reflects information from both national source agencies and international organizations.

Most countries' macroeconomic data presented in the *World Economic Outlook* conform broadly to the 1993 version of the *System of National Accounts* (SNA). The IMF's sector statistical standards—the *Balance of Payments and International Investment Position Manual, Sixth Edition* (BPM6), the *Monetary and Financial Statistics Manual* (MFSM 2000), and the *Government Finance Statistics Manual 2001* (GFSM 2001)—have been or are being aligned with the 2008 SNA.[1] These

standards reflect the IMF's special interest in countries' external positions, financial sector stability, and public sector fiscal positions. The process of adapting country data to the new standards begins in earnest when the manuals are released. However, full concordance with the manuals is ultimately dependent on the provision by national statistical compilers of revised country data; hence, the *World Economic Outlook* estimates are only partially adapted to these manuals. Nonetheless, for many countries the impact of conversion to the updated standards will be small on major balances and aggregates. Many other countries have partially adopted the latest standards and will continue implementation over a period of years.

Consistent with the recommendations of the *1993 SNA,* several countries have phased out their traditional *fixed-base-year* method of calculating real macroeconomic variable levels and growth by switching to a *chain-weighted* method of computing aggregate growth. The chain-weighted method frequently updates the weights of price and volume indicators. It allows countries to measure GDP growth more accurately by reducing or eliminating the downward biases in volume series built on index numbers that average volume components using weights from a year in the moderately distant past.

Composite data for country groups in the *World Economic Outlook* are either sums or weighted averages of data for individual countries. Unless noted otherwise, multiyear averages of growth rates are expressed as compound annual rates of change.[2] Arithmetically weighted averages are used for all data for the emerging market and developing economies group except inflation and money growth, for which geometric averages are used. The following conventions apply.

- Country group composites for exchange rates, interest rates, and growth rates of monetary aggregates are weighted by GDP converted to U.S. dollars at market exchange rates (averaged over the preceding three years) as a share of group GDP.

---

[1]Many other countries are implementing the 2008 SNA and will release national accounts data based on the new standard in 2014.

A few countries use versions of the SNA older than 1993. A similar adoption pattern is expected for the BPM6. Although the conceptual standards use the BPM6, the *World Economic Outlook* will continue to use the BPM5 presentation until a representative number of countries have moved their balance of payments accounts into the BPM6 framework.

[2]Averages for real GDP and its components, employment, per capita GDP, inflation, factor productivity, trade, and commodity prices, are calculated based on the compound annual rate of change, except for the unemployment rate, which is based on the simple arithmetic average.

- Composites for other data relating to the domestic economy, whether growth rates or ratios, are weighted by GDP valued at purchasing power parity (PPP) as a share of total world or group GDP.[3]
- Composites for data relating to the domestic economy for the euro area (17 member countries throughout the entire period unless noted otherwise) are aggregates of national source data using GDP weights. Annual data are not adjusted for calendar-day effects. For data prior to 1999, data aggregations apply 1995 European currency unit exchange rates.
- Composites for fiscal data are sums of individual country data after conversion to U.S. dollars at the average market exchange rates in the years indicated.
- Composite unemployment rates and employment growth are weighted by labor force as a share of group labor force.
- Composites relating to external sector statistics are sums of individual country data after conversion to U.S. dollars at the average market exchange rates in the years indicated for balance of payments data and at end-of-year market exchange rates for debt denominated in currencies other than U.S. dollars.
- Composites of changes in foreign trade volumes and prices, however, are arithmetic averages of percent changes for individual countries weighted by the U.S. dollar value of exports or imports as a share of total world or group exports or imports (in the preceding year).
- Unless noted otherwise, group composites are computed if 90 percent or more of the share of group weights is represented.

Data refer to calendar years, except for a few countries that use fiscal years. Please refer to the *country information* section of the WEO online database on the IMF website (www.imf.org) for a complete listing of the reference periods for each country.

Classification of Countries

Summary of the Country Classification

The country classification in the *World Economic Outlook* divides the world into two major groups:

advanced economies and emerging market and developing economies.[4] This classification is not based on strict criteria, economic or otherwise, and it has evolved over time. The objective is to facilitate analysis by providing a reasonably meaningful method of organizing data. Table A provides an overview of the country classification, showing the number of countries in each group by region and summarizing some key indicators of their relative size (GDP valued by PPP, total exports of goods and services, and population).

Some countries remain outside the country classification and therefore are not included in the analysis. Anguilla, Cuba, the Democratic People's Republic of Korea, and Montserrat are examples of countries that are not IMF members, and their economies therefore are not monitored by the IMF. Palau and Somalia are omitted from the emerging market and developing economies group composites because of data limitations.

General Features and Composition of Groups in the *World Economic Outlook* Classification

Advanced Economies

The 35 advanced economies are listed in Table B. The seven largest in terms of GDP—the United States, Japan, Germany, France, Italy, the United Kingdom, and Canada—constitute the subgroup of *major advanced economies* often referred to as the Group of Seven (G7). The members of the *euro area* are also distinguished as subgroups. Composite data shown in the tables for the euro area cover the current members for all years, even though the membership has increased over time.

Table C lists the member countries of the European Union, not all of which are classified as advanced economies in the *World Economic Outlook*.

Emerging Market and Developing Economies

The group of emerging market and developing economies (153) includes all those that are not classified as advanced economies.

The *regional breakdowns* of emerging market and developing economies are *central and eastern Europe*

---

[3]See Box A2 of the April 2004 *World Economic Outlook* for a summary of the revised PPP-based weights and Annex IV of the May 1993 *World Economic Outlook*. See also Anne-Marie Gulde and Marianne Schulze-Ghattas, "Purchasing Power Parity Based Weights for the *World Economic Outlook*," in *Staff Studies for the World Economic Outlook* (International Monetary Fund, December 1993), pp. 106–23.

[4]As used here, the terms "country" and "economy" do not always refer to a territorial entity that is a state as understood by international law and practice. Some territorial entities included here are not states, although their statistical data are maintained on a separate and independent basis.

(CEE, sometimes also referred to as emerging Europe*), Commonwealth of Independent States (CIS), developing Asia, Latin America and the Caribbean (LAC), Middle East and North Africa, Afghanistan, and Pakistan (MENAP),* and *sub-Saharan Africa (SSA).*

Emerging market and developing economies are also classified according to *analytical criteria.* The analytical criteria reflect the composition of export earnings and other income from abroad; a distinction between net creditor and net debtor economies; and, for the net debtors, financial criteria based on external financing sources and experience with external debt servicing. The detailed composition of emerging market and developing economies in the regional and analytical groups is shown in Tables D and E.

The analytical criterion by *source of export earnings* distinguishes between categories: *fuel* (Standard International Trade Classification—SITC 3) and *nonfuel* and then focuses on *nonfuel primary products* (SITCs 0, 1, 2, 4, and 68). Economies are categorized into one of these groups when their main source of export earnings exceeds 50 percent of total exports on average between 2007 and 2011.

The financial criteria focus on *net creditor economies, net debtor economies,* and *heavily indebted poor countries*

(HIPCs). Economies are categorized as net debtors when their current account balance accumulations from 1972 (or earliest data available) to 2011 are negative. Net debtor economies are further differentiated on the basis of two additional financial criteria: *official external financing* and *experience with debt servicing.*[5] Net debtors are placed in the official external financing category when 66 percent or more of their total debt, on average between 2007 and 2011, was financed by official creditors.

The HIPC group comprises the countries that are or have been considered by the IMF and the World Bank for participation in their debt initiative known as the HIPC Initiative, which aims to reduce the external debt burdens of all the eligible HIPCs to a "sustainable" level in a reasonably short period of time.[6] Many of these countries have already benefited from debt relief and have graduated from the initiative.

---

[5]During 2007–11, 39 economies incurred external payments arrears or entered into official or commercial bank debt-rescheduling agreements. This group is referred to as *economies with arrears and/or rescheduling during 2007–11.*

[6]See David Andrews, Anthony R. Boote, Syed S. Rizavi, and Sukwinder Singh, *Debt Relief for Low-Income Countries: The Enhanced HIPC Initiative,* IMF Pamphlet Series No. 51 (Washington: International Monetary Fund, November 1999).

Table A. Classification by *World Economic Outlook* Groups and Their Shares in Aggregate GDP, Exports of Goods and Services, and Population, 2012[1]

(Percent of total for group or world)

	Number of Economies	GDP Advanced Economies	GDP World	Exports of Goods and Services Advanced Economies	Exports of Goods and Services World	Population Advanced Economies	Population World
Advanced Economies	**35**	**100.0**	**50.1**	**100.0**	**61.2**	**100.0**	**14.9**
United States		37.7	18.9	16.0	9.8	30.5	4.5
Euro Area	17	27.4	13.7	40.7	24.9	32.1	4.8
Germany		7.7	3.8	12.9	7.9	7.9	1.2
France		5.4	2.7	5.7	3.5	6.2	0.9
Italy		4.4	2.2	4.4	2.7	5.9	0.9
Spain		3.4	1.7	3.2	1.9	4.5	0.7
Japan		11.1	5.6	6.6	4.1	12.4	1.8
United Kingdom		5.6	2.8	5.6	3.4	6.1	0.9
Canada		3.6	1.8	4.0	2.4	3.4	0.5
Other Advanced Economies	14	14.7	7.3	27.1	16.6	15.5	2.3
Memorandum							
Major Advanced Economies	7	75.5	37.8	55.3	33.9	72.4	10.7

	Number of Economies	GDP Emerging Market and Developing Economies	GDP World	Exports of Goods and Services Emerging Market and Developing Economies	Exports of Goods and Services World	Population Emerging Market and Developing Economies	Population World
Emerging Market and Developing Economies	**153**	**100.0**	**49.9**	**100.0**	**38.8**	**100.0**	**85.1**
Regional Groups							
Central and Eastern Europe	14	6.9	3.4	8.8	3.4	3.0	2.6
Commonwealth of Independent States[2]	12	8.6	4.3	10.4	4.0	4.8	4.1
Russia		6.1	3.0	6.7	2.6	2.4	2.0
Developing Asia	28	50.4	25.1	42.9	16.7	57.6	49.0
China		29.9	14.9	25.8	10.0	22.9	19.5
India		11.3	5.6	5.1	2.0	20.7	17.6
Excluding China and India	26	9.2	4.6	12.0	4.7	14.0	11.9
Latin America and the Caribbean	32	17.4	8.7	14.3	5.6	9.9	8.4
Brazil		5.7	2.8	3.2	1.3	3.4	2.9
Mexico		4.2	2.1	4.4	1.7	1.9	1.7
Middle East, North Africa, Afghanistan, and Pakistan	22	11.7	5.8	18.2	7.1	10.3	8.8
Middle East and North Africa	20	10.4	5.2	17.8	6.9	6.7	5.7
Sub-Saharan Africa	45	5.1	2.5	5.4	2.1	14.4	12.3
Excluding Nigeria and South Africa	43	2.6	1.3	3.0	1.2	10.7	9.1
Analytical Groups[3]							
By Source of Export Earnings							
Fuel	26	18.0	9.0	28.8	11.2	10.9	9.3
Nonfuel	126	82.0	40.9	71.2	27.6	88.9	75.7
Of Which, Primary Products	27	3.0	1.5	3.1	1.2	6.5	5.6
By External Financing Source							
Net Debtor Economies	123	46.1	23.0	37.4	14.5	59.1	50.3
Of Which, Official Financing	32	4.1	2.1	3.2	1.2	12.1	10.3
Net Debtor Economies by Debt-Servicing Experience							
Economies with Arrears and/or Rescheduling during 2007–11	39	4.7	2.3	4.0	1.6	9.2	7.8
Other Net Debtor Economies	84	41.4	20.7	33.4	12.9	49.9	42.5
Other Groups							
Heavily Indebted Poor Countries	38	2.4	1.2	1.9	0.7	10.9	9.3

[1]The GDP shares are based on the purchasing-power-parity valuation of economies' GDP. The number of economies comprising each group reflects those for which data are included in the group aggregates.

[2]Georgia, which is not a member of the Commonwealth of Independent States, is included in this group for reasons of geography and similarity in economic structure.

[3]South Sudan is omitted from the analytical groups composite for lack of a fully developed database.

Table B. Advanced Economies by Subgroup

Major Currency Areas

United States
Euro Area
Japan

Euro Area

Austria	Germany	Netherlands
Belgium	Greece	Portugal
Cyprus	Ireland	Slovak Republic
Estonia	Italy	Slovenia
Finland	Luxembourg	Spain
France	Malta	

Major Advanced Economies

Canada	Italy	United States
France	Japan	
Germany	United Kingdom	

Other Advanced Economies

Australia	Israel	Singapore
Czech Republic	Korea	Sweden
Denmark	New Zealand	Switzerland
Hong Kong SAR[1]	Norway	Taiwan Province of China
Iceland	San Marino	

[1]On July 1, 1997, Hong Kong was returned to the People's Republic of China and became a Special Administrative Region of China.

Table C. European Union

Austria	Germany	Netherlands
Belgium	Greece	Poland
Bulgaria	Hungary	Portugal
Cyprus	Ireland	Romania
Czech Republic	Italy	Slovak Republic
Denmark	Latvia	Slovenia
Estonia	Lithuania	Spain
Finland	Luxembourg	Sweden
France	Malta	United Kingdom

Table D. Emerging Market and Developing Economies by Region and Main Source of Export Earnings

	Fuel	Nonfuel Primary Products
Commonwealth of Independent States		
	Azerbaijan	Uzbekistan
	Kazakhstan	
	Russia	
	Turkmenistan	
Developing Asia		
	Brunei Darussalam	Marshall Islands
	Timor-Leste	Micronesia
		Mongolia
Latin America and the Caribbean		
	Ecuador	Bolivia
	Trinidad and Tobago	Chile
	Venezuela	Guyana
		Peru
		Suriname
		Uruguay
Middle East, North Africa, Afghanistan, and Pakistan		
	Algeria	Mauritania
	Bahrain	Sudan
	Iran	
	Iraq	
	Kuwait	
	Libya	
	Oman	
	Qatar	
	Saudi Arabia	
	United Arab Emirates	
	Yemen	
Sub-Saharan Africa		
	Angola	Burkina Faso
	Chad	Burundi
	Republic of Congo	Central African Republic
	Equatorial Guinea	Democratic Republic of the Congo
	Gabon	Côte d'Ivoire
	Nigeria	Guinea
		Guinea-Bissau
		Malawi
		Mali
		Mozambique
		Niger
		Sierra Leone
		Zambia
		Zimbabwe

Table E. Emerging Market and Developing Economies by Region, Net External Position, and Status as Heavily Indebted Poor Countries

	Net External Position		Heavily Indebted Poor Countries[2]		Net External Position		Heavily Indebted Poor Countries[2]
	Net Creditor	Net Debtor[1]			Net Creditor	Net Debtor[1]	
Central and Eastern Europe				Mongolia		•	
Albania		*		Myanmar		*	
Bosnia and Herzegovina		*		Nepal		*	
Bulgaria		*		Papua New Guinea		*	
Croatia		*		Philippines	*		
Hungary		•		Samoa		*	
Kosovo		*		Solomon Islands		*	
Latvia		*		Sri Lanka		•	
Lithuania		*		Thailand	*		
FYR Macedonia		*		Timor-Leste	*		
Montenegro		*		Tonga		*	
Poland		*		Tuvalu		•	
Romania		*		Vanuatu		*	
Serbia		*		Vietnam		*	
Turkey		*		**Latin America and the Caribbean**			
Commonwealth of Independent States[3]				Antigua and Barbuda		*	
Armenia		*		Argentina		*	
Azerbaijan	*			The Bahamas		*	
Belarus		*		Barbados		*	
Georgia		*		Belize		*	
Kazakhstan		*		Bolivia	*		•
Kyrgyz Republic		•		Brazil		*	
Moldova		*		Chile		*	
Russia	*			Colombia		*	
Tajikistan		•		Costa Rica		*	
Turkmenistan	*			Dominica		*	
Ukraine		*		Dominican Republic		*	
Uzbekistan	*			Ecuador		•	
Developing Asia				El Salvador		*	
Bangladesh		•		Grenada		*	
Bhutan		•		Guatemala		*	
Brunei Darussalam	*			Guyana		*	•
Cambodia		*		Haiti		•	•
China	*			Honduras		*	•
Fiji		*		Jamaica		*	
India		*		Mexico		*	
Indonesia	*			Nicaragua		*	•
Kiribati		•		Panama		*	
Lao P.D.R.		*		Paraguay		*	
Malaysia	*			Peru		*	
Maldives		*		St. Kitts and Nevis		*	
Marshall Islands		•		St. Lucia		*	
Micronesia		•		St. Vincent and the Grenadines		•	

Table E. *(concluded)*

	Net External Position — Net Creditor	Net Debtor[1]	Heavily Indebted Poor Countries[2]		Net External Position — Net Creditor	Net Debtor[1]	Heavily Indebted Poor Countries[2]
Suriname		•		Chad		*	*
Trinidad and Tobago	*			Comoros		•	•
Uruguay		*		Democratic Republic of the Congo		•	•
Venezuela	*			Republic of Congo		•	•
Middle East, North Africa, Afghanistan, and Pakistan				Côte d'Ivoire		*	•
Afghanistan		•	•	Equatorial Guinea		*	
Algeria	*			Eritrea		•	*
Bahrain	*			Ethiopia		•	•
Djibouti		*		Gabon	*		
Egypt		*		The Gambia		*	•
Iran	*			Ghana		*	•
Iraq	*			Guinea		*	•
Jordan		*		Guinea-Bissau		•	•
Kuwait	*			Kenya		*	
Lebanon		*		Lesotho		*	
Libya	*			Liberia		*	•
Mauritania		*	•	Madagascar		*	•
Morocco		*		Malawi		•	•
Oman	*			Mali		•	•
Pakistan		•		Mauritius		*	
Qatar	*			Mozambique		*	•
Saudi Arabia	*			Namibia	*		
Sudan		•	*	Niger		*	•
Syria		•		Nigeria	*		
Tunisia		*		Rwanda		*	•
United Arab Emirates	*			São Tomé and Príncipe		•	•
Yemen		*		Senegal		*	•
Sub-Saharan Africa				Seychelles		*	
Angola	*			Sierra Leone		*	•
Benin		*	•	South Africa		*	
Botswana	*			South Sudan[4]		...	
Burkina Faso		•	•	Swaziland		*	
Burundi		•	•	Tanzania		*	•
Cameroon		*	•	Togo		•	•
Cape Verde		*		Uganda		*	•
Central African Republic		•	•	Zambia		*	•
				Zimbabwe		*	

[1]Dot instead of star indicates that the net debtor's main external finance source is official financing.

[2]Dot instead of star indicates that the country has reached the completion point.

[3]Georgia, which is not a member of the Commonwealth of Independent States, is included in this group for reasons of geography and similarity in economic structure.

[4]South Sudan is omitted from the external financing group composites for lack of a fully developed database.

Box A1. Economic Policy Assumptions Underlying the Projections for Selected Economies

Fiscal Policy Assumptions

The short-term fiscal policy assumptions used in the *World Economic Outlook* (WEO) are based on officially announced budgets, adjusted for differences between the national authorities and the IMF staff regarding macroeconomic assumptions and projected fiscal out- turns. The medium-term fiscal projections incorporate policy measures that are judged likely to be imple- mented. In cases where the IMF staff has insufficient information to assess the authorities' budget inten- tions and prospects for policy implementation, an unchanged structural primary balance is assumed unless indicated otherwise. Specific assumptions used in some of the advanced economies follow. (See also Tables B5 to B9 in the online section of the Statistical Appendix for data on fiscal net lending/borrowing and structural balances.[1])

Argentina: The 2012 estimates are based on actual data on outturns and IMF staff estimates. For the outer years, the assumed improvement in the fis- cal balance is predicated on an assumed growth of revenues in the context of a pickup in economic activity combined with a decline in the growth of expenditures.

Australia: Fiscal projections are based on the 2012/13 Mid-Year Economic and Fiscal Out- look, Australian Bureau of Statistics, and IMF staff projections.

Austria: Projections take into account the 2013–16 federal financial framework as well as associated fur- ther implementation needs and risks.

Belgium: IMF staff projections for 2013 and beyond are based on unchanged policies.

---

[1] The output gap is actual minus potential output, as a percent of potential output. Structural balances are expressed as a percent of potential output. The structural balance is the actual net lending/borrowing minus the effects of cyclical output from potential output, corrected for one-time and other factors, such as asset and commodity prices and output composition effects. Changes in the structural balance consequently include effects of temporary fiscal measures, the impact of fluctuations in interest rates and debt-service costs, and other noncyclical fluctuations in net lending/borrowing. The computations of structural balances are based on IMF staff estimates of potential GDP and revenue and expenditure elasticities. (See the October 1993 *World Eco- nomic Outlook*, Annex I.) Net debt is defined as gross debt minus financial assets of the general government, which include assets held by the social security insurance system. Estimates of the output gap and of the structural balance are subject to significant margins of uncertainty.

Brazil: For 2012, the estimates are based on actual data concerning (1) outturns for the central govern- ment and (2) financing needs of subcentral govern- ments and public enterprises. For 2013, the projection is based on the budget approved in March 2013. In outer years, the IMF staff assumes adherence to the announced primary target.

Canada: Projections use the baseline forecasts in Jobs, Growth, and Long-Term Prosperity, March 21, 2013 (the fiscal year 2013/14 budget). The IMF staff makes some adjustments to this forecast for differ- ences in macroeconomic projections. The IMF staff forecast also incorporates the most recent data releases from Statistics Canada's Canadian System of National Economic Accounts, including federal, provincial, and territorial budgetary outturns through the end of the fourth quarter of 2012.

China: For 2013, the fiscal impulse is assumed to be neutral.

Denmark: Projections for 2012–14 are aligned with the latest official budget estimates and the underly- ing economic projections, adjusted where appropriate for the IMF staff's macroeconomic assumptions. For 2015–18, the projections incorporate key features of the medium-term fiscal plan as embodied in the authorities' 2012 Convergence Program submitted to the European Union.

France: Projections for 2012 and beyond reflect the authorities' 2012–17 multiyear budget, adjusted for fiscal packages and differences in assumptions on macro and financial variables, and revenue projec- tions. The fiscal deficit remains unchanged for 2013 compared with the October 2012 figure. For 2012 it was revised from 4.7 percent of GDP to 4.6 percent because of preliminary data provided by the authori- ties during the 2012 Article IV Consultation. The underlying assumptions remain unchanged: the 2013 budget was available at the time of the October 2012 submission. The 2013 budget contains fiscal measures equivalent to 1.2 percent of GDP. Combined with the measures already taken in July 2012, total structural adjustment in 2013 is estimated by the IMF staff to be 1.3 percent of (potential) GDP (three-quarters of this adjustment as a result of revenue measures), following a 2012 structural adjustment expected to be close to 1 percent of potential GDP. The difference in the 2013 fiscal deficit between IMF staff figures (3.7 percent of GDP) and those of the authorities (3.0 percent of GDP) can be attributed to different growth

Box A1. *(continued)*

projection (0.8 percent by the government and –0.1 percent by the IMF staff).

Germany: The estimates for 2012 are preliminary estimates from the Federal Statistical Office of Germany. The IMF staff's projections for 2013 and beyond reflect the authorities' adopted core federal government budget plan adjusted for the differences in the IMF staff's macroeconomic framework and staff assumptions about fiscal developments in state and local governments, the social insurance system, and special funds. The estimate of gross debt includes portfolios of impaired assets and noncore business transferred to institutions that are winding up as well as other financial sector and EU support operations.

Greece: Fiscal projections for 2012 and the medium term are consistent with the policies discussed between the IMF staff and the authorities in the context of the Extended Fund Facility. Public debt projections assume an additional haircut (official sector involvement) to bring the debt ratio to 124 percent of GDP by 2020.

Hong Kong SAR: Projections are based on the authorities' medium-term fiscal projections.

Hungary: Fiscal projections include IMF staff projections of the macroeconomic framework and of the impact of recent legislative measures as well as fiscal policy plans announced at the end of January 2013.

India: Historical data are based on budgetary execution data. Projections are based on available information on the authorities' fiscal plans, with adjustments for IMF staff assumptions. Subnational data are incorporated with a lag of up to two years; general government data are thus finalized well after central government data. IMF and Indian presentations differ, particularly regarding divestment and license auction proceeds, net versus gross recording of revenues in certain minor categories, and some public sector lending.

Indonesia: The 2011 central government deficit was lower than expected (1.1 percent of GDP), reflecting underspending, particularly on public investment. The central government 2012 deficit is estimated at 1.8 percent of GDP, slightly lower than the revised budget estimate of 2.2 percent of GDP. Budget execution remains a problem and is reflected in the low budget deficit. Fiscal projections for 2013–18 are built around key policy reforms needed to support economic growth—namely, enhancing budget implementation to ensure fiscal policy effectiveness, reducing energy subsidies through gradual administrative price

increases, and continuous revenue mobilization efforts to increase space for infrastructure development.

Ireland: Fiscal projections are based on the 2013 budget and the Medium-Term Fiscal Statement (published in November 2012), which commits to a €8.6 billion consolidation during 2013–15. It also includes the estimated fiscal impact of the February 2013 promissory note transaction. The fiscal projections are adjusted for differences between the macroeconomic projections of the IMF staff and those of the Irish authorities.

Italy: Fiscal projections incorporate the impact of the government's announced fiscal adjustment package, as outlined in the September 2012 update to the Documento di Economia e Finanza and the 2013 Budget. The estimates for the 2012 outturn are preliminary. The IMF staff projections are based on the authorities' estimates of the policy scenario and are adjusted mainly for differences in macroeconomic assumptions—they do not include the impact of the government's proposal to clear payment arrears. After 2015, projections are made on the basis of unchanged policies, assuming a constant structural primary balance.

Japan: The projections include fiscal measures already announced by the government, including consumption tax increases, earthquake reconstruction spending, and the stimulus package. The medium-term projections assume that expenditure and revenue of the general government are adjusted in line with current underlying demographic and economic trends and recent fiscal stimulus.

Korea: Fiscal projections assume that fiscal policies will be implemented in 2013 as announced by the government. Projections of expenditure for 2013 are in line with the budget. Revenue projections reflect the IMF staff's macroeconomic assumptions, adjusted for discretionary revenue-raising measures already announced by the government. The medium-term projections assume that the government will continue with its consolidation plans and balance the budget (excluding social security funds) by 2014, consistent with the government's medium-term goal.

Mexico: Fiscal projections for 2012 are broadly in line with the approved budget; projections for 2013 onward assume compliance with the balanced budget rule.

Netherlands: Fiscal projections for the period 2012–18 are based on the authorities' Bureau for Economic Policy Analysis budget projections, after adjusting for differences in macroeconomic assumptions.

Box A1. *(continued)*

New Zealand: Fiscal projections are based on the authorities' 2012 Half Year Economic and Financial Update and IMF staff estimates.

Portugal: Projections reflect the authorities' commitments under the EU- and IMF-supported program for 2013–14 and IMF staff projections thereafter.

Russia: Projections for 2013–18 are based on the oil-price-based fiscal price rule introduced in December 2012, with adjustments for the IMF staff's revenue forecast and for public spending already budgeted for 2013–15.

Saudi Arabia: The authorities base their budget on a conservative assumption for oil prices with adjustments to expenditure allocations considered in the event that revenues exceed budgeted amounts. IMF staff projections of oil revenues are based on *World Economic Outlook* baseline oil prices. On the expenditure side, wage bill estimates incorporate 13th-month pay awards every three years in accordance with the lunar calendar; capital spending estimates over the medium term are in line with the authorities' priorities established in the National Development Plans.

Singapore: For fiscal year 2012/13, projections are based on budget numbers. For the remainder of the projection period, the IMF staff assumes unchanged policies.

South Africa: Fiscal projections are based on the authorities' 2013 Budget Review released on February 27, 2013.

Spain: For 2013 and beyond, fiscal projections are based on the measures specified in the Stability Program Update 2012–15, the revised fiscal policy recommendations by the European Council in July 2012, the subsequent fiscal package, the biannual budget plan for 2013–14 announced in August 2012, and the 2013 budget approved in December 2012.

Sweden: Fiscal projections for 2012 are broadly in line with the authorities' projections. The impact of cyclical developments on the fiscal accounts is calculated using the Organization for Economic Cooperation and Development's latest semi-elasticity.

Switzerland: Projections for 2012–18 are based on IMF staff calculations, which incorporate measures to restore balance in the federal accounts and strengthen social security finances.

Turkey: Fiscal projections assume that current expenditures will be in line with the authorities' 2012–14 Medium-Term Program but that capital expenditures will be exceeded, given projects initiated in 2011.

United Kingdom: Fiscal projections are based on the U.K. Treasury's 2013 budget, published in March 2013. However, on the revenue side, the authorities' projections are adjusted for differences between IMF staff forecasts of macroeconomic variables (such as GDP growth) and the forecasts of these variables assumed in the authorities' fiscal projections. In addition, IMF staff projections exclude the temporary effects of financial sector interventions and the effect on public sector net investment during 2012–13 of transferring assets from the Royal Mail Pension Plan to the public sector. Real government consumption and investment are part of the real GDP path, which, according to the IMF staff, may or may not be the same as projected by the U.K. Office for Budget Responsibility. Subsequent to the finalization of these projections, previously unpublished data were provided on the timing of transfers of profits from the Bank of England's Asset Purchases Facility. Such transfers affect general government net interest payments. Consequently, the overall balance is unchanged, but calendar year primary balances are affected. The new information on timing arithmetically reduces primary deficits in calendar year 2012 and increases them in calendar year 2013. The numbers do not change fiscal year projections.

United States: Fiscal projections are based on the February 2013 Congressional Budget Office baseline adjusted according to the IMF staff's policy and macroeconomic assumptions. This baseline incorporates the provisions of the American Taxpayer Relief Act, signed into law on January 2, 2013. The key near-term policy assumptions include replacement of automatic spending cuts ("sequester") with back-loaded consolidation measures in fiscal year 2014 and onward. (The sequester is assumed to be in full effect from March 1, 2013, to September 30, 2013.) Over the medium term, the IMF staff assumes that Congress will continue to make regular adjustments to Medicare payments ("DocFix") and extend certain traditional programs (such as the research and development tax credit). The fiscal projections are adjusted to reflect the IMF staff's forecasts of key macroeconomic and financial variables and different accounting treatment of the financial sector support and are converted to the general government basis.

Monetary Policy Assumptions

Monetary policy assumptions are based on the established policy framework in each country. In most cases, this implies a nonaccommodative stance over the busi-

Box A1. *(concluded)*

ness cycle: official interest rates will increase when economic indicators suggest that inflation will rise above its acceptable rate or range; they will decrease when indicators suggest that inflation will not exceed the acceptable rate or range, that output growth is below its potential rate, and that the margin of slack in the economy is significant. On this basis, the London interbank offered rate (LIBOR) on six-month U.S. dollar deposits is assumed to average 0.5 percent in 2013 and 0.6 percent in 2014 (see Table 1.1). The rate on three-month euro deposits is assumed to average 0.2 percent in 2013 and 0.4 percent in 2014. The interest rate on six-month Japanese yen deposits is assumed to average 0.2 percent in 2013 and 2014.

Australia: Monetary policy assumptions are in line with market expectations.

Brazil: Monetary policy assumptions are based on current policy settings and are consistent with gradual convergence of inflation toward the middle of the target over the relevant horizon.

Canada: Monetary policy assumptions are in line with market expectations.

China: Monetary tightening built into the baseline is consistent with projected GDP growth.

Denmark: The monetary policy is to maintain the peg to the euro.

Euro area: Monetary policy assumptions for euro area member countries are in line with market expectations.

Hong Kong SAR: The IMF staff assumes that the Currency Board system remains intact and projects broad money growth based on the past relationship with nominal GDP.

India: The policy (interest) rate assumption is based on the average of market forecasts.

Indonesia: Bank Indonesia is expected to use a combination of macroprudential measures and policy rate increases.

Japan: The current monetary policy conditions are maintained for the projection period, and no further tightening or loosening is assumed.

Korea: Monetary policy assumptions incorporate maintenance of the current accommodative stance over the course of 2013.

Mexico: Monetary assumptions are consistent with attaining the inflation target.

Russia: Monetary projections assume unchanged policies, as indicated in recent statements by the Central Bank of Russia. Specifically, policy rates are assumed to remain at the current levels, with limited interventions in the foreign exchange markets.

Saudi Arabia: Monetary policy projections are based on the continuation of the exchange rate peg to the U.S. dollar.

Singapore: Broad money is projected to grow in line with the projected growth in nominal GDP.

South Africa: Monetary projections are consistent with South Africa's 3 to 6 percent inflation target range.

Sweden: Monetary projections are in line with Riksbank projections.

Switzerland: Monetary policy variables reflect historical data from the national authorities and the market.

Turkey: Broad money and the long-term bond yield are based on IMF staff projections. The short-term deposit rate is projected to evolve with a constant spread against the interest rate of a similar U.S. instrument.

United Kingdom: On monetary policy, the projections assume no changes to the policy rate or the level of asset purchases through 2014.

United States: Given the outlook for sluggish growth and inflation, the IMF staff expects the federal funds target to remain near zero until late 2014. This assumption is consistent with the Federal Open Market Committee's statement following its January meeting (and reaffirmed in subsequent meetings) that economic conditions are likely to warrant an exceptionally low federal funds rate at least through late 2014.

List of Tables

Table A1. Summary of World Output[1]

(Annual percent change)

	Average 1995–2004	2005	2006	2007	2008	2009	2010	2011	2012	Projections 2013	2014	2018
World	**3.6**	**4.6**	**5.3**	**5.4**	**2.8**	**−0.6**	**5.2**	**4.0**	**3.2**	**3.3**	**4.0**	**4.5**
Advanced Economies	**2.8**	**2.6**	**3.0**	**2.8**	**0.1**	**−3.5**	**3.0**	**1.6**	**1.2**	**1.2**	**2.2**	**2.5**
United States	3.3	3.1	2.7	1.9	−0.3	−3.1	2.4	1.8	2.2	1.9	3.0	2.9
Euro Area	2.2	1.7	3.2	3.0	0.4	−4.4	2.0	1.4	−0.6	−0.3	1.1	1.6
Japan	1.1	1.3	1.7	2.2	−1.0	−5.5	4.7	−0.6	2.0	1.6	1.4	1.1
Other Advanced Economies[2]	3.7	3.6	3.9	4.2	0.9	−2.1	4.5	2.6	1.4	1.9	2.8	3.1
Emerging Market and Developing Economies	**4.9**	**7.3**	**8.3**	**8.8**	**6.1**	**2.7**	**7.6**	**6.4**	**5.1**	**5.3**	**5.7**	**6.2**
Regional Groups												
Central and Eastern Europe	4.1	5.9	6.4	5.4	3.1	−3.6	4.6	5.2	1.6	2.2	2.8	3.8
Commonwealth of Independent States[3]	2.9	6.7	8.8	8.9	5.3	−6.4	4.9	4.8	3.4	3.4	4.0	4.0
Developing Asia	7.1	9.5	10.4	11.6	7.9	6.9	9.9	8.1	6.6	7.1	7.3	7.7
Latin America and the Caribbean	2.6	4.7	5.7	5.8	4.2	−1.5	6.1	4.6	3.0	3.4	3.9	3.9
Middle East, North Africa, Afghanistan, and Pakistan	4.6	6.1	6.7	6.3	5.0	2.9	5.3	3.9	4.7	3.1	3.7	4.5
Middle East and North Africa	4.6	5.8	6.8	6.2	5.2	3.0	5.5	4.0	4.8	3.1	3.7	4.6
Sub-Saharan Africa	4.5	6.2	6.4	7.0	5.6	2.7	5.4	5.3	4.8	5.6	6.1	5.5
Memorandum												
European Union	2.6	2.3	3.6	3.4	0.5	−4.2	2.0	1.6	−0.2	0.0	1.3	2.0
Analytical Groups												
By Source of Export Earnings												
Fuel	3.8	7.0	7.9	7.7	5.3	−1.2	5.1	4.8	4.9	3.6	4.1	4.2
Nonfuel	5.1	7.4	8.4	9.1	6.3	3.6	8.2	6.7	5.1	5.7	6.0	6.5
Of Which, Primary Products	4.3	5.5	6.2	6.6	6.0	1.9	6.8	5.4	5.3	5.9	5.7	5.6
By External Financing Source												
Net Debtor Economies	3.9	6.0	6.7	6.9	4.7	0.6	7.0	5.4	3.2	4.0	4.5	5.1
Of Which, Official Financing	4.4	6.6	5.9	5.6	4.5	2.9	4.3	4.7	3.9	4.3	4.6	4.7
Net Debtor Economies by Debt-Servicing Experience												
Economies with Arrears and/or Rescheduling during 2007–11	3.3	7.5	7.7	7.5	5.9	2.0	6.8	6.4	3.2	4.0	4.3	4.4
Memorandum												
Median Growth Rate												
Advanced Economies	3.3	3.1	3.9	3.9	0.8	−3.7	2.4	1.8	0.9	1.0	1.7	2.2
Emerging Market and Developing Economies	4.3	5.4	5.7	6.2	5.1	1.7	4.7	4.4	3.9	4.2	4.3	4.4
Output per Capita												
Advanced Economies	2.1	1.9	2.3	2.0	−0.7	−4.1	2.4	1.1	0.7	0.7	1.7	1.9
Emerging Market and Developing Economies	3.6	6.1	7.1	7.6	4.9	1.5	6.5	5.3	4.0	4.3	4.7	5.2
World Growth Rate Based on Market Exchange	**2.9**	**3.4**	**4.0**	**4.0**	**1.5**	**−2.2**	**4.1**	**2.9**	**2.5**	**2.6**	**3.4**	**3.9**
Value of World Output (billions of U.S. dollars)												
At Market Exchange Rates	32,999	45,679	49,452	55,827	61,364	57,983	63,468	70,221	71,707	74,172	77,805	97,599
At Purchasing Power Parities	41,505	56,955	61,825	66,983	70,300	70,306	74,879	79,286	83,140	87,210	92,483	119,344

[1]Real GDP.
[2]In this table, Other Advanced Economies means advanced economies excluding the United States, Euro Area countries, and Japan.
[3]Georgia, which is not a member of the Commonwealth of Independent States, is included in this group for reasons of geography and similarity in economic structure.

Table A2. Advanced Economies: Real GDP and Total Domestic Demand[1]

(Annual percent change)

	Average 1995–2004	2005	2006	2007	2008	2009	2010	2011	2012	Projections 2013	Projections 2014	Projections 2018	Fourth Quarter[2] 2012:Q4	Projections 2013:Q4	Projections 2014:Q4
Real GDP															
Advanced Economies	**2.8**	**2.6**	**3.0**	**2.8**	**0.1**	**−3.5**	**3.0**	**1.6**	**1.2**	**1.2**	**2.2**	**2.5**	**0.8**	**2.0**	**2.3**
United States	3.3	3.1	2.7	1.9	−0.3	−3.1	2.4	1.8	2.2	1.9	3.0	2.9	1.7	2.2	3.4
Euro Area	2.2	1.7	3.2	3.0	0.4	−4.4	2.0	1.4	−0.6	−0.3	1.1	1.6	−0.9	0.6	1.1
Germany	1.3	0.8	3.9	3.4	0.8	−5.1	4.0	3.1	0.9	0.6	1.5	1.2	0.4	1.5	1.1
France	2.2	1.8	2.5	2.3	−0.1	−3.1	1.7	1.7	0.0	−0.1	0.9	1.9	−0.3	0.4	1.0
Italy	1.6	0.9	2.2	1.7	−1.2	−5.5	1.7	0.4	−2.4	−1.5	0.5	1.2	−2.8	−0.4	0.6
Spain	3.7	3.6	4.1	3.5	0.9	−3.7	−0.3	0.4	−1.4	−1.6	0.7	1.6	−1.9	−0.7	1.1
Netherlands	2.8	2.0	3.4	3.9	1.8	−3.7	1.6	1.0	−0.9	−0.5	1.1	2.1	−0.9	0.5	1.0
Belgium	2.3	1.8	2.7	2.9	1.0	−2.8	2.4	1.8	−0.2	0.2	1.2	1.6	−0.4	0.7	1.6
Austria	2.4	2.4	3.7	3.7	1.4	−3.8	2.1	2.7	0.8	0.8	1.6	1.3	0.5	1.5	1.6
Greece	3.7	2.3	5.5	3.5	−0.2	−3.1	−4.9	−7.1	−6.4	−4.2	0.6	3.3	−5.6	−1.0	1.6
Portugal	2.7	0.8	1.4	2.4	0.0	−2.9	1.9	−1.6	−3.2	−2.3	0.6	1.8	−3.8	−0.1	0.8
Finland	3.8	2.9	4.4	5.3	0.3	−8.5	3.3	2.8	−0.2	0.5	1.2	2.0	−1.4	2.0	0.6
Ireland	8.0	5.9	5.4	5.4	−2.1	−5.5	−0.8	1.4	0.9	1.1	2.2	2.7	0.0	0.8	2.3
Slovak Republic	4.3	6.7	8.3	10.5	5.8	−4.9	4.4	3.2	2.0	1.4	2.7	3.5	1.2	2.1	2.5
Slovenia	4.0	4.0	5.8	7.0	3.4	−7.8	1.2	0.6	−2.3	−2.0	1.5	2.0	−2.8	0.7	2.2
Luxembourg	4.5	5.3	4.9	6.6	−0.7	−4.1	2.9	1.7	0.1	0.1	1.3	2.2	0.0	0.7	1.4
Estonia	6.5	8.9	10.1	7.5	−4.2	−14.1	3.3	8.3	3.2	3.0	3.2	3.7	3.3	2.6	3.2
Cyprus[3]	4.1	3.9	4.1	5.1	3.6	−1.9	1.3	0.5	−2.4	. . .	. . .	. . .	−3.3	. . .	. . .
Malta	. . .	3.6	2.6	4.1	3.9	−2.6	2.9	1.7	0.8	1.3	1.8	1.9	0.8	0.2	1.1
Japan	1.1	1.3	1.7	2.2	−1.0	−5.5	4.7	−0.6	2.0	1.6	1.4	1.1	0.4	3.8	−0.1
United Kingdom	3.3	2.8	2.6	3.6	−1.0	−4.0	1.8	0.9	0.2	0.7	1.5	2.5	0.3	1.1	1.5
Canada	3.3	3.1	2.7	2.1	1.1	−2.8	3.2	2.6	1.8	1.5	2.4	2.2	1.1	2.0	2.5
Korea	5.3	4.0	5.2	5.1	2.3	0.3	6.3	3.6	2.0	2.8	3.9	4.0	1.6	4.2	3.1
Australia	3.8	3.1	2.7	4.6	2.7	1.4	2.6	2.4	3.6	3.0	3.3	3.2	3.1	3.4	3.2
Taiwan Province of China	4.6	4.7	5.4	6.0	0.7	−1.8	10.8	4.1	1.3	3.0	3.9	5.0	4.0	1.8	5.4
Sweden	3.2	3.2	4.6	3.4	−0.8	−5.0	6.3	3.8	1.2	1.0	2.2	2.4	1.5	1.0	3.0
Hong Kong SAR	2.9	7.4	7.0	6.5	2.1	−2.5	6.8	4.9	1.4	3.0	4.4	4.5	2.3	2.8	5.3
Switzerland	1.5	2.7	3.8	3.8	2.2	−1.9	3.0	1.9	1.0	1.3	1.8	1.9	1.2	1.4	2.0
Singapore	5.3	7.4	8.6	9.0	1.7	−0.8	14.8	5.2	1.3	2.0	5.1	3.9	1.5	4.7	3.9
Czech Republic	. . .	6.8	7.0	5.7	3.1	−4.5	2.5	1.9	−1.2	0.3	1.6	3.0	−1.6	1.4	1.7
Norway	3.1	2.6	2.3	2.7	0.0	−1.4	0.2	1.3	3.0	2.5	2.2	2.1	1.9	3.6	1.4
Israel	4.1	4.7	5.8	5.9	4.1	1.1	5.0	4.6	3.1	3.6	3.9	3.5	2.6	4.4	3.4
Denmark	2.1	2.4	3.4	1.6	−0.8	−5.7	1.6	1.1	−0.6	0.8	1.3	1.5	−1.0	1.8	1.7
New Zealand	3.5	3.1	3.0	3.5	−0.8	−1.6	1.8	1.4	2.5	2.7	2.6	2.5	3.0	1.4	4.4
Iceland	3.9	7.2	4.7	6.0	1.2	−6.6	−4.1	2.9	1.6	1.9	2.1	2.3	1.4	4.2	0.5
San Marino	. . .	2.4	3.8	8.0	−5.1	−12.2	−7.5	−2.5	−4.0	−3.5	0.0	1.4	. . .	. . .	. . .
Memorandum															
Major Advanced Economies	2.5	2.3	2.6	2.3	−0.3	−3.8	2.8	1.5	1.4	1.3	2.2	2.3	0.8	2.0	2.2
Real Total Domestic Demand															
Advanced Economies	**2.9**	**2.6**	**2.8**	**2.4**	**−0.4**	**−3.8**	**2.9**	**1.3**	**1.0**	**1.0**	**2.0**	**2.4**	**0.6**	**1.7**	**2.1**
United States	3.7	3.2	2.6	1.2	−1.5	−4.0	2.8	1.7	2.1	1.7	3.0	3.0	1.4	2.2	3.5
Euro Area	. . .	1.8	3.1	2.8	0.3	−3.8	1.3	0.5	−2.2	−1.2	0.8	1.5	−2.2	−0.3	1.1
Germany	0.8	−0.2	2.7	1.9	1.2	−2.5	2.6	2.6	−0.4	0.3	1.3	1.2	−0.7	0.9	1.2
France	2.2	2.5	2.4	3.2	0.3	−2.6	1.6	1.7	−0.7	−0.5	1.0	1.6	−0.5	0.1	1.4
Italy	1.9	0.9	2.1	1.4	−1.2	−4.4	2.1	−1.0	−5.3	−2.9	0.2	0.9	−5.3	−1.2	0.5
Spain	4.2	5.0	5.2	4.1	−0.5	−6.2	−0.6	−1.9	−3.8	−4.1	−0.2	1.3	−4.6	−2.3	0.4
Japan	0.9	1.0	0.9	1.1	−1.3	−4.0	2.9	0.3	2.9	1.9	0.9	1.0	1.3	3.1	−0.3
United Kingdom	3.7	2.3	2.2	3.5	−1.8	−5.0	2.3	−0.6	1.2	1.1	1.6	2.2	1.5	1.5	1.4
Canada	3.1	4.5	3.9	3.6	2.7	−2.9	5.2	2.9	2.2	1.6	2.1	1.9	2.4	1.9	2.1
Other Advanced Economies[4]	3.5	3.4	4.0	4.9	1.6	−2.8	5.6	2.9	2.3	2.4	2.9	3.5	3.0	3.2	2.6
Memorandum															
Major Advanced Economies	2.7	2.3	2.3	1.7	−0.9	−3.8	2.8	1.3	1.3	1.2	2.1	2.2	0.7	1.8	2.2

[1]In this and other tables, when countries are not listed alphabetically, they are ordered on the basis of economic size.
[2]From the fourth quarter of the preceding year.
[3]Projections for Cyprus are excluded due to the ongoing crisis.
[4]In this table, Other Advanced Economies means advanced economies excluding the G7 (Canada, France, Germany, Italy, Japan, United Kingdom, United States) and Euro Area countries.

Table A3. Advanced Economies: Components of Real GDP

(Annual percent change)

	Averages		2005	2006	2007	2008	2009	2010	2011	2012	Projections	
	1995–2004	2005–14									2013	2014
Private Consumer Expenditure												
Advanced Economies	**3.0**	**1.4**	**2.7**	**2.5**	**2.4**	**0.0**	**−1.2**	**2.0**	**1.5**	**1.0**	**1.1**	**1.8**
United States	3.7	1.6	3.4	2.9	2.3	−0.6	−1.9	1.8	2.5	1.9	2.0	2.3
Euro Area	...	0.4	1.8	2.1	1.7	0.4	−1.0	0.9	0.1	−1.3	−1.0	0.8
Germany	1.1	0.7	0.2	1.5	−0.2	0.8	0.1	0.9	1.7	0.6	0.5	1.3
France	2.2	1.0	2.5	2.2	2.4	0.2	0.3	1.5	0.3	−0.1	−0.1	0.9
Italy	1.7	−0.4	1.2	1.4	1.1	−0.8	−1.6	1.5	0.1	−4.3	−2.6	0.0
Spain	3.6	0.2	4.1	4.0	3.5	−0.6	−3.8	0.7	−1.0	−2.2	−3.4	0.5
Japan	1.0	0.9	1.5	1.1	0.9	−0.9	−0.7	2.8	0.5	2.4	1.0	0.7
United Kingdom	4.0	0.5	2.5	1.5	2.7	−1.6	−3.1	1.3	−1.0	1.0	0.9	1.4
Canada	3.3	2.7	3.6	4.1	4.2	2.9	0.2	3.4	2.4	1.9	2.1	2.1
Other Advanced Economies[1]	3.8	2.8	3.6	3.7	4.7	1.1	0.2	3.8	2.9	2.0	2.6	3.1
Memorandum												
Major Advanced Economies	2.8	1.2	2.5	2.3	1.9	−0.4	−1.4	1.9	1.6	1.2	1.2	1.7
Public Consumption												
Advanced Economies	**2.2**	**1.1**	**1.2**	**1.6**	**1.8**	**2.1**	**3.3**	**1.2**	**−0.5**	**0.1**	**−0.7**	**0.7**
United States	2.1	0.4	0.6	1.0	1.3	2.2	4.3	0.9	−2.3	−1.3	−3.1	1.2
Euro Area	...	1.1	1.6	2.1	2.2	2.3	2.6	0.7	−0.1	0.0	−0.2	0.1
Germany	1.1	1.5	0.3	0.9	1.4	3.2	3.0	1.7	1.0	1.4	1.3	1.2
France	1.3	1.3	1.2	1.4	1.5	1.3	2.5	1.8	0.2	1.4	0.9	0.8
Italy	1.3	−0.3	1.9	0.5	1.0	0.6	0.8	−0.4	−1.2	−2.9	−1.8	−1.4
Spain	3.9	1.8	5.5	4.6	5.6	5.9	3.7	1.5	−0.5	−3.7	−3.2	−1.2
Japan	2.8	1.2	0.8	0.0	1.1	−0.1	2.3	1.9	1.5	2.7	1.9	0.4
United Kingdom	2.4	0.9	2.0	1.5	0.6	1.6	0.8	0.4	−0.1	2.6	0.4	−0.7
Canada	1.5	2.1	1.6	3.1	2.8	4.6	3.4	3.0	1.0	0.4	0.3	0.6
Other Advanced Economies[1]	2.9	2.4	2.0	2.9	3.1	2.8	3.6	2.6	1.7	1.8	2.0	1.3
Memorandum												
Major Advanced Economies	2.0	0.8	0.9	1.0	1.3	1.8	3.2	1.2	−0.9	0.0	−1.1	0.7
Gross Fixed Capital Formation												
Advanced Economies	**3.6**	**0.7**	**4.0**	**4.1**	**2.5**	**−2.9**	**−12.5**	**1.4**	**2.3**	**2.1**	**2.5**	**4.6**
United States	5.2	0.6	5.3	2.5	−1.4	−5.1	−15.3	−0.3	3.4	6.1	5.1	7.9
Euro Area	...	−0.5	3.2	5.6	5.2	−1.4	−12.7	−0.1	1.5	−4.1	−2.2	1.3
Germany	0.0	1.2	0.8	8.2	4.7	1.3	−11.6	5.9	6.2	−2.5	−1.0	1.5
France	3.0	0.8	4.4	4.0	6.3	0.4	−10.6	1.3	3.6	0.0	−1.4	1.6
Italy	3.1	−2.1	1.3	3.4	1.8	−3.7	−11.7	0.6	−1.8	−8.0	−2.9	1.3
Spain	6.3	−3.7	7.1	7.1	4.5	−4.7	−18.0	−6.2	−5.3	−9.1	−7.5	−1.7
Japan	−0.9	−0.2	0.8	1.5	0.3	−4.1	−10.6	−0.2	1.1	4.5	4.5	1.4
United Kingdom	4.6	0.9	2.4	6.3	8.2	−4.6	−13.7	3.5	−2.9	1.4	4.5	5.8
Canada	5.0	3.1	8.7	6.6	3.2	1.3	−11.9	10.4	5.0	3.3	2.4	3.4
Other Advanced Economies[1]	3.7	2.8	4.8	5.5	6.5	0.0	−6.2	6.9	3.1	2.2	2.5	3.7
Memorandum												
Major Advanced Economies	3.4	0.6	3.8	3.6	1.2	−3.5	−13.4	1.3	2.6	3.2	3.3	5.1

Table A3. Advanced Economies: Components of Real GDP *(concluded)*

(Annual percent change)

	Averages		2005	2006	2007	2008	2009	2010	2011	2012	Projections	
	1995–2004	2005–14									2013	2014
Final Domestic Demand												
Advanced Economies	**2.9**	**1.2**	**2.7**	**2.7**	**2.3**	**−0.2**	**−2.7**	**1.8**	**1.3**	**1.1**	**1.1**	**2.0**
United States	3.7	1.3	3.3	2.5	1.4	−1.0	−3.3	1.3	1.8	2.0	1.7	3.0
Euro Area	...	0.4	2.0	2.8	2.5	0.4	−2.8	0.7	0.3	−1.5	−1.1	0.7
Germany	0.9	1.0	0.3	2.6	1.1	1.3	−1.6	2.0	2.4	0.2	0.4	1.3
France	2.1	1.0	2.5	2.4	2.9	0.5	−1.4	1.5	0.9	0.3	−0.1	1.0
Italy	1.9	−0.7	1.3	1.6	1.2	−1.2	−3.2	0.9	−0.5	−4.7	−2.5	0.0
Spain	4.3	−0.4	5.2	5.0	4.1	−0.7	−6.2	−0.8	−1.8	−3.9	−4.1	−0.2
Japan	0.8	0.7	1.2	1.0	0.8	−1.6	−2.3	2.0	0.8	2.8	2.0	0.8
United Kingdom	3.7	0.7	2.4	2.2	3.1	−1.4	−4.0	1.4	−1.1	1.4	1.3	1.6
Canada	3.3	2.7	4.3	4.5	3.7	2.9	−2.0	4.9	2.7	1.9	1.8	2.1
Other Advanced Economies[1]	3.5	2.7	3.5	3.9	4.9	1.2	−0.8	4.2	2.7	2.1	2.5	2.9
Memorandum												
Major Advanced Economies	2.7	1.1	2.5	2.3	1.6	−0.6	−2.8	1.7	1.3	1.4	1.2	2.1
Stock Building[2]												
Advanced Economies	**0.0**	**0.0**	**−0.1**	**0.1**	**0.1**	**−0.2**	**−1.1**	**1.1**	**0.0**	**−0.1**	**0.0**	**0.0**
United States	0.0	0.0	−0.1	0.1	−0.2	−0.5	−0.8	1.5	−0.2	0.1	0.1	0.0
Euro Area	...	−0.1	−0.2	0.3	0.3	−0.1	−1.0	0.6	0.2	−0.6	−0.2	0.0
Germany	0.0	0.0	−0.4	0.1	0.8	−0.1	−0.7	0.6	0.2	−0.6	0.0	0.0
France	0.1	−0.2	0.0	0.1	0.2	−0.3	−1.2	0.1	0.8	−1.0	−0.3	0.0
Italy	0.0	−0.1	−0.4	0.5	0.2	0.0	−1.2	1.1	−0.5	−0.6	0.0	0.2
Spain	−0.1	0.0	−0.1	0.3	−0.1	0.1	0.0	0.0	0.1	0.1	0.0	0.0
Japan	0.1	−0.1	−0.3	−0.1	0.3	0.2	−1.5	0.9	−0.4	0.0	−0.1	0.1
United Kingdom	0.0	0.0	0.0	−0.1	0.4	−0.4	−1.0	0.9	0.3	−0.2	0.0	0.0
Canada	0.0	0.0	0.5	−0.2	0.1	−0.1	−0.8	0.3	0.2	0.2	−0.2	0.0
Other Advanced Economies[1]	0.0	0.0	−0.1	0.1	0.1	0.3	−1.9	1.2	0.1	0.1	0.0	−0.1
Memorandum												
Major Advanced Economies	0.0	0.0	−0.1	0.0	0.1	−0.3	−1.0	1.1	−0.1	−0.1	0.0	0.0
Foreign Balance[2]												
Advanced Economies	**−0.1**	**0.3**	**0.0**	**0.2**	**0.5**	**0.5**	**0.3**	**0.2**	**0.4**	**0.3**	**0.3**	**0.2**
United States	−0.5	0.2	−0.3	−0.1	0.6	1.2	1.1	−0.5	0.1	0.0	0.1	−0.2
Euro Area	...	0.4	−0.1	0.2	0.2	0.1	−0.7	0.7	0.9	1.6	0.9	0.3
Germany	0.4	0.4	0.8	1.1	1.5	0.0	−2.9	1.7	0.6	1.0	0.3	0.2
France	0.0	−0.1	−0.7	0.0	−0.9	−0.3	−0.5	0.0	0.0	0.8	0.4	−0.2
Italy	−0.2	0.5	0.0	0.1	0.3	0.0	−1.2	−0.4	1.5	2.8	1.4	0.3
Spain	−0.6	0.9	−1.7	−1.5	−0.9	1.5	2.9	0.2	2.4	2.4	2.4	0.9
Japan	0.1	0.1	0.3	0.8	1.0	0.2	−2.0	2.0	−0.8	−0.8	−0.3	0.6
United Kingdom	−0.5	0.2	0.3	0.2	−0.2	0.9	1.1	−0.6	1.2	−0.8	−0.5	0.0
Canada	0.1	−0.9	−1.5	−1.4	−1.5	−1.9	0.1	−2.1	−0.4	−0.4	−0.2	0.3
Other Advanced Economies[1]	0.5	0.7	1.0	1.0	0.7	0.3	1.5	0.7	0.7	0.0	0.4	0.8
Memorandum												
Major Advanced Economies	−0.2	0.2	−0.1	0.2	0.5	0.6	0.0	0.0	0.1	0.2	0.1	0.0

[1]In this table, Other Advanced Economies means advanced economies excluding the G7 (Canada, France, Germany, Italy, Japan, United Kingdom, United States) and Euro Area countries.
[2]Changes expressed as percent of GDP in the preceding period.

Table A4. Emerging Market and Developing Economies: Real GDP

(Annual percent change)

	Average 1995–2004	2005	2006	2007	2008	2009	2010	2011	2012	Projections 2013	2014	2018
Central and Eastern Europe[1]	**4.1**	**5.9**	**6.4**	**5.4**	**3.1**	**−3.6**	**4.6**	**5.2**	**1.6**	**2.2**	**2.8**	**3.8**
Albania	6.0	5.8	5.4	5.9	7.5	3.3	3.5	3.0	1.3	1.8	2.5	2.5
Bosnia and Herzegovina	. . .	3.9	6.0	6.1	5.6	−2.9	0.7	1.3	−0.7	0.5	2.0	4.0
Bulgaria	1.6	6.4	6.5	6.4	6.2	−5.5	0.4	1.8	0.8	1.2	2.3	3.5
Croatia	4.2	4.3	4.9	5.1	2.1	−6.9	−2.3	0.0	−2.0	−0.2	1.5	2.5
Hungary	3.5	4.1	3.9	0.1	0.7	−6.7	1.2	1.7	−1.7	0.0	1.2	1.6
Kosovo	. . .	3.8	3.4	6.3	6.9	2.9	3.9	5.0	2.1	2.9	4.3	4.6
Latvia	5.6	10.1	11.2	9.6	−3.3	−17.7	−0.9	5.5	5.6	4.2	4.2	4.0
Lithuania	. . .	7.8	7.8	9.8	2.9	−14.8	1.5	5.9	3.6	3.0	3.3	3.8
FYR Macedonia	1.7	4.4	5.0	6.1	5.0	−0.9	2.9	2.9	−0.3	2.0	3.1	4.2
Montenegro	. . .	4.2	8.6	10.7	6.9	−5.7	2.5	3.2	0.0	1.2	2.0	2.2
Poland	4.6	3.6	6.2	6.8	5.1	1.6	3.9	4.3	2.0	1.3	2.2	3.7
Romania	2.5	4.2	7.9	6.3	7.3	−6.6	−1.1	2.2	0.3	1.6	2.0	3.5
Serbia	. . .	5.4	3.6	5.4	3.8	−3.5	1.0	1.6	−1.8	2.0	2.0	3.0
Turkey	4.2	8.4	6.9	4.7	0.7	−4.8	9.2	8.5	2.6	3.4	3.7	4.5
Commonwealth of Independent States[1,2]	**2.9**	**6.7**	**8.8**	**8.9**	**5.3**	**−6.4**	**4.9**	**4.8**	**3.4**	**3.4**	**4.0**	**4.0**
Russia	2.8	6.4	8.2	8.5	5.2	−7.8	4.5	4.3	3.4	3.4	3.8	3.6
Excluding Russia	3.2	7.7	10.6	9.9	5.6	−3.1	6.0	6.1	3.3	3.5	4.6	4.8
Armenia	8.0	14.1	13.2	13.7	6.9	−14.1	2.2	4.7	7.2	4.3	4.1	4.3
Azerbaijan	5.5	26.4	34.5	25.0	10.8	9.3	5.0	0.1	2.2	4.1	5.8	4.0
Belarus	4.7	9.4	10.0	8.6	10.2	0.2	7.7	5.5	1.5	2.1	2.6	3.6
Georgia	5.8	9.6	9.4	12.3	2.3	−3.8	6.3	7.2	6.5	6.0	6.0	6.0
Kazakhstan	4.5	9.7	10.7	8.9	3.2	1.2	7.3	7.5	5.0	5.5	5.6	6.2
Kyrgyz Republic	4.1	−0.2	3.1	8.5	7.6	2.9	−0.5	6.0	−0.9	7.4	7.5	5.0
Moldova	1.3	7.5	4.8	3.0	7.8	−6.0	7.1	6.8	−0.8	4.0	4.0	5.0
Tajikistan	4.0	6.7	7.0	7.8	7.9	3.9	6.5	7.4	7.5	7.0	6.0	6.0
Turkmenistan	7.8	13.0	11.0	11.1	14.7	6.1	9.2	14.7	11.0	7.7	7.9	7.2
Ukraine	1.2	3.0	7.4	7.6	2.3	−14.8	4.1	5.2	0.2	0.0	2.8	3.5
Uzbekistan	3.8	7.0	7.5	9.5	9.0	8.1	8.5	8.3	8.0	7.0	6.5	5.5
Developing Asia	**7.1**	**9.5**	**10.4**	**11.6**	**7.9**	**6.9**	**9.9**	**8.1**	**6.6**	**7.1**	**7.3**	**7.7**
Bangladesh	5.3	6.3	6.5	6.3	6.0	5.9	6.4	6.5	6.1	6.0	6.4	7.2
Bhutan	6.9	7.1	6.8	17.9	4.7	6.7	11.7	8.5	9.7	6.3	8.6	10.0
Brunei Darussalam	2.1	0.4	4.4	0.2	−1.9	−1.8	2.6	2.2	1.3	1.2	6.0	3.7
Cambodia	7.7	13.3	10.8	10.2	6.7	0.1	6.1	7.1	6.5	6.7	7.2	7.5
China	9.2	11.3	12.7	14.2	9.6	9.2	10.4	9.3	7.8	8.0	8.2	8.5
Fiji	2.7	2.5	1.9	−0.9	1.0	−1.3	0.1	1.9	2.1	2.2	2.0	2.0
India	6.1	9.0	9.4	10.1	6.2	5.0	11.2	7.7	4.0	5.7	6.2	7.0
Indonesia	2.9	5.7	5.5	6.3	6.0	4.6	6.2	6.5	6.2	6.3	6.4	6.5
Kiribati	3.5	0.3	1.2	0.5	−2.4	−2.3	1.4	2.0	2.5	2.5	2.0	2.0
Lao P.D.R.	6.0	6.8	8.6	7.8	7.8	7.5	8.1	8.0	8.3	8.0	7.7	7.6
Malaysia	5.2	5.0	5.6	6.3	4.8	−1.5	7.2	5.1	5.6	5.1	5.2	5.2
Maldives	8.4	−8.7	19.6	10.6	12.2	−3.6	7.1	7.0	3.5	3.8	4.0	4.1
Marshall Islands	. . .	2.6	1.9	3.2	−1.9	−1.5	5.6	0.8	1.9	2.3	2.6	1.0
Micronesia	. . .	2.2	−0.2	−2.1	−2.6	1.0	2.5	2.1	1.4	0.7	0.6	0.6
Mongolia	4.5	7.3	8.6	10.2	8.9	−1.3	6.4	17.5	12.3	14.0	11.6	8.9
Myanmar	. . .	13.6	13.1	12.0	3.6	5.1	5.3	5.5	6.3	6.5	6.6	7.0
Nepal	4.2	3.5	3.4	3.4	6.1	4.5	4.8	3.9	4.6	3.0	4.0	4.1
Papua New Guinea	0.7	3.9	2.3	7.2	6.6	6.1	7.6	11.1	9.1	4.4	5.6	3.9
Philippines	4.1	4.8	5.2	6.6	4.2	1.1	7.6	3.9	6.6	6.0	5.5	5.5
Samoa	4.2	7.0	2.1	1.8	4.3	−5.1	0.4	2.0	1.2	0.9	3.1	2.5
Solomon Islands	−0.1	12.9	4.0	6.4	7.1	−4.7	7.8	10.7	5.5	4.0	3.8	3.4
Sri Lanka	4.6	6.2	7.7	6.8	6.0	3.5	8.0	8.2	6.4	6.3	6.7	6.5
Thailand	3.2	4.6	5.1	5.0	2.5	−2.3	7.8	0.1	6.4	5.9	4.2	4.7
Timor-Leste	. . .	6.5	−3.1	11.6	14.6	12.8	9.5	10.6	10.0	10.0	10.0	9.0
Tonga	2.1	0.7	−4.5	−2.4	0.5	0.9	1.6	1.5	1.4	1.5	1.8	0.9
Tuvalu	. . .	−3.8	2.6	5.5	7.6	−1.7	−2.9	1.1	1.2	1.3	1.2	1.0
Vanuatu	1.5	5.3	8.5	5.2	6.5	3.3	1.6	1.4	2.7	4.3	4.3	4.0
Vietnam	7.3	8.4	8.2	8.5	6.3	5.3	6.8	5.9	5.0	5.2	5.2	5.5

Table A4. Emerging Market and Developing Economies: Real GDP *(continued)*

(Annual percent change)

	Average 1995–2004	2005	2006	2007	2008	2009	2010	2011	2012	Projections 2013	Projections 2014	Projections 2018
Latin America and the Caribbean	**2.6**	**4.7**	**5.7**	**5.8**	**4.2**	**−1.5**	**6.1**	**4.6**	**3.0**	**3.4**	**3.9**	**3.9**
Antigua and Barbuda	2.7	7.2	12.7	7.1	1.5	−10.7	−8.5	−3.0	1.6	1.7	3.2	3.5
Argentina[3]	1.1	9.2	8.5	8.7	6.8	0.9	9.2	8.9	1.9	2.8	3.5	3.0
The Bahamas	4.0	3.4	2.5	1.4	−2.3	−4.9	0.2	1.6	2.5	2.7	2.5	2.5
Barbados	1.8	4.0	5.7	1.7	0.3	−4.1	0.2	0.6	0.0	0.5	1.0	2.4
Belize	5.5	2.6	5.1	1.2	3.8	0.0	2.7	1.9	5.3	2.5	2.5	2.5
Bolivia	3.3	4.4	4.8	4.6	6.1	3.4	4.1	5.2	5.2	4.8	5.0	5.0
Brazil	2.5	3.2	4.0	6.1	5.2	−0.3	7.5	2.7	0.9	3.0	4.0	4.2
Chile	4.7	6.3	5.8	5.2	3.1	−0.9	5.8	5.9	5.5	4.9	4.6	4.6
Colombia	2.3	4.7	6.7	6.9	3.5	1.7	4.0	6.6	4.0	4.1	4.5	4.5
Costa Rica	4.3	5.9	8.8	7.9	2.7	−1.0	4.7	4.2	5.0	4.2	4.4	4.5
Dominica	1.7	−1.7	3.7	3.9	7.8	−0.8	0.7	1.9	0.4	1.3	1.5	1.9
Dominican Republic	4.8	9.3	10.7	8.5	5.3	3.5	7.8	4.5	3.9	2.2	3.4	5.0
Ecuador	2.7	5.3	4.4	2.2	6.4	1.0	3.3	8.0	5.0	4.4	3.9	3.5
El Salvador	3.0	3.6	3.9	3.8	1.3	−3.1	1.4	2.0	1.6	1.6	1.6	2.0
Grenada	4.8	13.3	−4.0	6.1	0.9	−6.7	−0.4	1.0	−0.8	0.5	1.0	2.3
Guatemala	3.4	3.3	5.4	6.3	3.3	0.5	2.9	4.1	3.0	3.3	3.4	3.5
Guyana	2.3	−1.9	5.1	7.0	2.0	3.3	4.4	5.4	3.3	5.5	6.0	3.3
Haiti	1.7	1.8	2.2	3.3	0.8	2.9	−5.4	5.6	2.8	6.5	6.3	5.4
Honduras	3.6	6.1	6.6	6.2	4.2	−2.4	3.7	3.7	3.3	3.3	3.0	3.0
Jamaica	0.8	0.9	2.9	1.4	−0.8	−3.1	−1.4	1.5	0.1	0.5	1.2	2.6
Mexico	2.5	3.2	5.1	3.2	1.2	−6.0	5.3	3.9	3.9	3.4	3.4	3.3
Nicaragua	4.2	4.3	4.2	5.0	4.0	−2.2	3.6	5.4	5.2	4.0	4.0	4.0
Panama	4.4	7.2	8.5	12.1	10.1	3.9	7.5	10.8	10.7	9.0	7.2	6.0
Paraguay	1.6	2.1	4.8	5.4	6.4	−4.0	13.1	4.3	−1.2	11.0	4.6	4.7
Peru	3.5	6.8	7.7	8.9	9.8	0.9	8.8	6.9	6.3	6.3	6.1	6.0
St. Kitts and Nevis	3.4	8.4	4.7	4.8	3.9	−4.2	0.0	−1.9	−0.9	1.9	3.2	3.5
St. Lucia	1.8	−1.2	8.9	1.6	5.1	0.4	0.2	1.4	−0.4	1.1	2.2	2.3
St. Vincent and the Grenadines	4.3	3.0	6.0	3.0	−0.5	−2.2	−2.3	0.4	0.5	1.0	2.0	3.0
Suriname	3.0	4.9	5.8	5.1	4.1	3.0	4.1	4.7	4.5	4.5	4.5	4.9
Trinidad and Tobago	7.7	6.2	13.2	4.8	3.4	−4.4	0.2	−2.6	0.4	2.0	2.5	2.5
Uruguay	0.4	6.8	4.1	6.5	7.2	2.4	8.9	5.7	3.8	3.8	4.0	4.0
Venezuela	1.0	10.3	9.9	8.8	5.3	−3.2	−1.5	4.2	5.5	0.1	2.3	2.6
Middle East, North Africa, Afghanistan, and Pakistan	**4.6**	**6.1**	**6.7**	**6.3**	**5.0**	**2.9**	**5.3**	**3.9**	**4.7**	**3.1**	**3.7**	**4.5**
Afghanistan	...	11.2	5.6	13.7	3.6	21.0	8.4	7.0	10.2	3.1	4.8	4.8
Algeria	4.1	5.9	1.7	3.4	2.0	1.7	3.6	2.4	2.5	3.3	3.4	3.9
Bahrain	4.8	7.9	6.7	8.4	6.3	3.2	4.7	2.1	3.9	4.2	3.3	3.8
Djibouti	0.6	3.1	4.8	5.1	5.8	5.0	3.5	4.5	4.8	5.0	5.0	5.8
Egypt	4.8	4.5	6.8	7.1	7.2	4.7	5.1	1.8	2.2	2.0	3.3	6.5
Iran	4.9	4.7	6.2	6.4	0.6	3.9	5.9	3.0	−1.9	−1.3	1.1	2.4
Iraq	...	4.4	10.2	1.4	6.6	5.8	5.9	8.6	8.4	9.0	8.4	8.3
Jordan	4.6	8.1	8.1	8.2	7.2	5.5	2.3	2.6	2.8	3.3	3.5	4.5
Kuwait	4.1	10.1	7.5	6.0	2.5	−7.1	−2.4	6.3	5.1	1.1	3.1	3.9
Lebanon	4.1	0.7	1.4	8.4	8.6	9.0	7.0	1.5	1.5	2.0	4.0	4.0
Libya	0.6	11.9	6.5	6.4	2.7	−0.8	5.0	−62.1	104.5	20.2	10.1	5.0
Mauritania	3.7	5.4	11.4	1.0	3.5	−1.2	5.1	3.9	6.4	5.9	5.8	3.5
Morocco	3.4	3.0	7.8	2.7	5.6	4.8	3.6	5.0	3.0	4.5	4.8	5.8
Oman	3.2	4.0	5.5	6.7	13.2	3.3	5.6	4.5	5.0	4.2	3.5	3.8
Pakistan	4.2	9.0	5.8	6.8	3.7	1.7	3.1	3.0	3.7	3.5	3.3	3.0
Qatar	9.6	7.5	26.2	18.0	17.7	12.0	16.7	13.0	6.6	5.2	5.0	6.5
Saudi Arabia	2.7	7.3	5.6	6.0	8.4	1.8	7.4	8.5	6.8	4.4	4.2	4.3
Sudan[4]	15.8	0.4	8.9	8.5	3.0	5.2	2.5	−1.9	−4.4	1.2	2.6	4.0
Syria[5]	2.6	6.2	5.0	5.7	4.5	5.9	3.4	...	...	...	...	...
Tunisia	4.8	4.0	5.7	6.3	4.5	3.1	3.1	−1.9	3.6	4.0	4.5	4.8
United Arab Emirates	6.4	8.6	8.8	6.5	5.3	−4.8	1.3	5.2	3.9	3.1	3.6	3.7
Yemen	4.7	5.6	3.2	3.3	3.6	3.9	7.7	−10.5	0.1	4.4	5.4	6.0

Table A4. Emerging and Developing Economies: Real GDP *(concluded)*

(Annual percent change)

	Average 1995–2004	2005	2006	2007	2008	2009	2010	2011	2012	Projections 2013	2014	2018
Sub-Saharan Africa	**4.5**	**6.2**	**6.4**	**7.0**	**5.6**	**2.7**	**5.4**	**5.3**	**4.8**	**5.6**	**6.1**	**5.5**
Angola	7.7	20.6	20.7	22.6	13.8	2.4	3.4	3.9	8.4	6.2	7.3	6.0
Benin	4.8	2.9	3.8	4.6	5.0	2.7	2.6	3.5	3.8	4.1	4.1	4.6
Botswana	7.3	1.6	5.1	4.8	3.0	−4.7	7.0	5.1	3.8	4.1	4.2	4.6
Burkina Faso	6.3	8.7	6.3	4.1	5.8	3.0	7.9	4.2	8.0	7.0	7.0	6.7
Burundi	−0.3	4.4	5.4	4.8	5.0	3.5	3.8	4.2	4.0	4.5	5.1	5.5
Cameroon[6]	4.3	2.3	3.2	2.8	3.6	1.9	3.3	4.1	4.7	5.4	5.5	5.8
Cape Verde	7.0	6.5	10.1	8.6	6.2	3.7	5.2	5.0	4.3	4.1	4.5	5.0
Central African Republic	0.9	2.5	4.8	4.6	2.1	1.7	3.0	3.3	4.1	4.3	6.0	5.8
Chad	7.7	7.9	0.2	0.2	1.7	−1.2	13.0	0.5	5.0	8.1	10.5	2.4
Comoros	2.1	4.2	1.2	0.5	1.0	1.8	2.1	2.2	2.5	3.5	4.0	4.1
Democratic Republic of the Congo	−0.6	7.8	5.6	6.3	6.2	2.8	7.2	6.9	7.1	8.3	6.4	4.6
Republic of Congo	2.9	7.8	6.2	−1.6	5.6	7.5	8.8	3.4	3.8	6.4	5.8	5.1
Côte d'Ivoire	1.9	1.9	0.7	1.6	2.3	3.7	2.4	−4.7	9.8	8.0	8.0	7.0
Equatorial Guinea	39.3	9.7	1.3	18.7	13.8	−3.6	−2.6	4.5	2.0	−2.1	−0.8	−7.1
Eritrea	1.8	2.6	−1.0	1.4	−9.8	3.9	2.2	8.7	7.0	3.4	2.1	0.6
Ethiopia	4.8	12.6	11.5	11.8	11.2	10.0	8.0	7.5	7.0	6.5	6.5	6.5
Gabon	1.1	1.5	−1.9	5.2	1.0	−2.9	6.8	7.1	6.2	6.1	6.8	2.2
The Gambia	4.2	−0.9	1.1	3.6	5.7	6.4	6.5	−4.3	3.9	8.9	8.5	5.8
Ghana	4.7	6.0	6.1	6.5	8.4	4.0	8.0	14.4	7.0	6.9	6.8	5.7
Guinea	3.8	3.0	2.5	1.8	4.9	−0.3	1.9	3.9	3.9	4.5	5.2	18.2
Guinea-Bissau	0.2	4.3	2.1	3.2	3.2	3.0	3.5	5.3	−1.5	4.2	10.2	4.5
Kenya	2.7	6.0	6.3	7.0	1.5	2.7	5.8	4.4	4.7	5.8	6.2	6.1
Lesotho	3.3	2.9	4.1	4.9	5.1	4.8	6.3	5.7	4.0	3.5	3.1	4.0
Liberia	. . .	5.9	9.0	13.2	6.2	5.3	6.1	7.9	8.3	7.5	5.3	7.7
Madagascar	2.8	4.6	5.0	6.2	7.1	−4.1	0.4	1.8	1.9	2.6	3.8	5.1
Malawi	4.3	2.6	2.1	9.5	8.3	9.0	6.5	4.3	1.9	5.5	6.1	6.5
Mali	4.7	6.1	5.3	4.3	5.0	4.5	5.8	2.7	−1.2	4.8	6.3	4.8
Mauritius	4.4	1.5	4.5	5.9	5.5	3.0	4.1	3.8	3.3	3.7	4.4	4.5
Mozambique	8.5	8.4	8.7	7.3	6.8	6.3	7.1	7.3	7.5	8.4	8.0	7.8
Namibia	4.3	2.5	7.1	5.4	3.4	−1.1	6.6	4.8	4.0	4.2	4.0	4.3
Niger	2.8	8.4	5.8	0.6	9.6	−1.0	10.7	2.2	11.2	6.2	6.4	6.5
Nigeria	6.5	5.4	6.2	7.0	6.0	7.0	8.0	7.4	6.3	7.2	7.0	6.7
Rwanda	10.1	9.4	9.2	5.5	13.4	6.2	7.2	8.3	7.7	7.6	7.2	6.5
São Tomé and Príncipe	2.6	1.6	12.6	2.0	9.1	4.0	4.5	4.9	4.0	4.5	6.0	1.8
Senegal	4.4	5.6	2.4	5.0	3.7	2.2	4.3	2.6	3.5	4.0	4.6	5.2
Seychelles	2.0	9.0	9.4	10.1	−1.9	−0.2	5.6	5.0	2.8	3.2	3.9	3.5
Sierra Leone	−0.8	4.4	4.4	8.0	5.3	3.2	5.3	6.0	19.8	17.1	14.2	4.4
South Africa	3.1	5.3	5.6	5.5	3.6	−1.5	3.1	3.5	2.5	2.8	3.3	3.1
South Sudan	. . .	. . .	. . .	. . .	. . .	. . .	. . .	. . .	−53.0	32.1	49.2	11.7
Swaziland	2.8	2.2	2.9	2.8	3.1	1.2	1.9	0.3	−1.5	0.0	0.3	0.3
Tanzania	5.2	7.4	6.7	7.1	7.4	6.0	7.0	6.4	6.9	7.0	7.2	6.6
Togo	2.2	1.2	4.1	2.3	2.4	3.5	4.0	4.9	5.0	5.1	5.5	4.1
Uganda	7.1	8.6	9.5	8.6	7.7	7.1	5.6	6.7	2.6	4.8	6.2	7.0
Zambia	3.0	5.3	6.2	6.2	5.7	6.4	7.6	6.8	7.3	7.8	8.0	7.8
Zimbabwe[7]	. . .	−5.6	−3.4	−3.7	−17.8	8.9	9.6	10.6	4.4	5.0	5.7	5.5

[1]Data for some countries refer to real net material product (NMP) or are estimates based on NMP. The figures should be interpreted only as indicative of broad orders of magnitude because reliable, comparable data are not generally available. In particular, the growth of output of new private enterprises of the informal economy is not fully reflected in the recent figures.
[2]Georgia, which is not a member of the Commonwealth of Independent States, is included in this group for reasons of geography and similarity in economic structure.
[3]The data for Argentina are officially reported data. The IMF has, however, issued a declaration of censure and called on Argentina to adopt remedial measures to address the quality of the official GDP data. Alternative data sources have shown significantly lower real growth than the official data since 2008. In this context, the IMF is also using alternative estimates of GDP growth for the surveillance of macroeconomic developments in Argentina.
[4]Data for 2011 exclude South Sudan after July 9. Data for 2012 and onward pertain to the current Sudan.
[5]Data for Syria are excluded for 2011 onward due to the uncertain political situation.
[6]The percent changes in 2002 are calculated over a period of 18 months, reflecting a change in the fiscal year cycle (from July–June to January–December).
[7]The Zimbabwe dollar ceased circulating in early 2009. Data are based on IMF staff estimates of price and exchange rate developments in U.S. dollars. IMF staff estimates of U.S. dollar values may differ from authorities' estimates. Real GDP is in constant 2009 prices.

Table A5. Summary of Inflation

(Percent)

	Average 1995–2004	2005	2006	2007	2008	2009	2010	2011	2012	Projections 2013	2014	2018
GDP Deflators												
Advanced Economies	**1.7**	**2.1**	**2.1**	**2.2**	**1.9**	**0.7**	**1.1**	**1.4**	**1.3**	**1.4**	**1.8**	**1.9**
United States	1.9	3.3	3.2	2.9	2.2	0.9	1.3	2.1	1.8	1.6	2.0	2.1
Euro Area	2.0	1.9	1.8	2.4	2.0	1.0	0.8	1.2	1.2	1.5	1.3	1.6
Japan	−0.9	−1.3	−1.1	−0.9	−1.3	−0.5	−2.2	−1.9	−0.9	−0.7	1.8	1.3
Other Advanced Economies[1]	2.2	2.0	2.1	2.5	3.0	0.8	2.4	1.9	1.6	1.8	2.0	2.2
Consumer Prices												
Advanced Economies	**2.0**	**2.3**	**2.3**	**2.2**	**3.4**	**0.1**	**1.5**	**2.7**	**2.0**	**1.7**	**2.0**	**2.1**
United States	2.5	3.4	3.2	2.9	3.8	−0.3	1.6	3.1	2.1	1.8	1.7	2.3
Euro Area[2]	1.9	2.2	2.2	2.1	3.3	0.3	1.6	2.7	2.5	1.7	1.5	1.7
Japan	−0.1	−0.3	0.2	0.1	1.4	−1.3	−0.7	−0.3	0.0	0.1	3.0	2.0
Other Advanced Economies[1]	2.2	2.1	2.1	2.1	3.8	1.4	2.4	3.4	2.1	2.1	2.3	2.3
Emerging Market and Developing Economies	**13.1**	**5.9**	**5.6**	**6.5**	**9.2**	**5.1**	**6.0**	**7.2**	**5.9**	**5.9**	**5.6**	**4.8**
Regional Groups												
Central and Eastern Europe	31.1	5.9	5.9	6.0	8.1	4.7	5.3	5.3	5.8	4.4	3.6	3.6
Commonwealth of Independent States[3]	39.0	12.1	9.5	9.7	15.6	11.2	7.2	10.1	6.5	6.8	6.5	6.5
Developing Asia	5.0	3.6	4.0	5.4	7.3	2.6	5.6	6.4	4.5	5.0	5.0	3.9
Latin America and the Caribbean	13.0	6.3	5.3	5.4	7.9	5.9	6.0	6.6	6.0	6.1	5.7	5.1
Middle East, North Africa, Afghanistan, and Pakistan	7.1	7.1	8.2	10.3	12.4	7.3	6.9	9.7	10.7	9.4	9.0	7.7
Middle East and North Africa	7.1	6.9	8.2	10.6	12.5	6.2	6.5	9.2	10.7	9.6	9.0	7.3
Sub-Saharan Africa	16.5	8.8	7.1	6.4	12.9	9.4	7.4	9.3	9.1	7.2	6.3	5.6
Memorandum												
European Union	3.8	2.3	2.3	2.4	3.6	0.9	2.0	3.1	2.6	1.9	1.8	1.8
Analytical Groups												
By Source of Export Earnings												
Fuel	23.7	10.2	9.4	10.4	14.4	9.0	7.8	9.8	9.1	9.3	8.3	7.5
Nonfuel	10.6	4.8	4.7	5.6	7.9	4.2	5.6	6.6	5.2	5.2	5.1	4.2
Of Which, Primary Products	12.3	5.1	5.5	4.7	10.1	5.3	4.5	6.8	6.9	5.6	5.7	4.0
By External Financing Source												
Net Debtor Economies	13.9	5.9	5.9	6.2	9.2	7.3	7.2	7.7	7.2	6.9	6.7	5.3
Of Which, Official Financing	12.1	7.5	7.2	8.2	12.8	9.0	7.7	11.2	10.4	7.7	7.9	6.8
Net Debtor Economies by Debt-Servicing Experience												
Economies with Arrears and/or Rescheduling during 2007–11	14.8	7.9	9.0	7.9	11.9	6.7	8.0	11.9	12.1	9.0	8.5	7.3
Memorandum												
Median Inflation Rate												
Advanced Economies	2.2	2.1	2.3	2.2	3.9	0.6	2.0	3.1	2.6	1.9	1.9	2.0
Emerging Market and Developing Economies	5.8	5.4	6.1	6.2	10.4	4.0	4.2	5.6	4.9	4.7	4.6	4.0

[1]In this table, Other Advanced Economies means advanced economies excluding the United States, Euro Area countries, and Japan.
[2]Based on Eurostat's harmonized index of consumer prices.
[3]Georgia, which is not a member of the Commonwealth of Independent States, is included in this group for reasons of geography and similarity in economic structure.

Table A6. Advanced Economies: Consumer Prices[1]

(Annual percent change)

	Average 1995–2004	2005	2006	2007	2008	2009	2010	2011	2012	Projections 2013	Projections 2014	Projections 2018	End of Period[2] 2012	End of Period[2] Projections 2013	End of Period[2] Projections 2014
Advanced Economies	**2.0**	**2.3**	**2.3**	**2.2**	**3.4**	**0.1**	**1.5**	**2.7**	**2.0**	**1.7**	**2.0**	**2.1**	**2.0**	**1.7**	**2.1**
United States	2.5	3.4	3.2	2.9	3.8	−0.3	1.6	3.1	2.1	1.8	1.7	2.3	1.8	1.7	1.8
Euro Area[3]	1.9	2.2	2.2	2.1	3.3	0.3	1.6	2.7	2.5	1.7	1.5	1.7	2.2	1.6	1.4
Germany	1.3	1.9	1.8	2.3	2.8	0.2	1.2	2.5	2.1	1.6	1.7	1.9	2.0	1.6	1.7
France	1.6	1.8	1.7	1.5	2.8	0.1	1.5	2.1	2.0	1.6	1.5	1.8	1.3	1.6	1.5
Italy	2.7	2.2	2.2	2.0	3.5	0.8	1.6	2.9	3.3	2.0	1.4	1.5	2.4	2.0	0.8
Spain	3.0	3.4	3.6	2.8	4.1	−0.2	2.0	3.1	2.4	1.9	1.5	1.5	3.0	1.3	1.4
Netherlands	2.4	1.5	1.7	1.6	2.2	1.0	0.9	2.5	2.8	2.8	1.7	1.4	2.8	2.3	1.6
Belgium	1.7	2.5	2.3	1.8	4.5	0.0	2.3	3.4	2.6	1.7	1.4	1.2	2.1	1.5	1.2
Austria	1.5	2.1	1.7	2.2	3.2	0.4	1.7	3.6	2.6	2.2	1.9	1.9	2.9	2.2	1.9
Greece	4.6	3.5	3.3	3.0	4.2	1.3	4.7	3.1	1.0	−0.8	−0.4	1.3	0.3	−0.6	−0.1
Portugal	3.0	2.1	3.0	2.4	2.7	−0.9	1.4	3.6	2.8	0.7	1.0	1.5	2.1	0.7	1.5
Finland	1.5	0.8	1.3	1.6	3.9	1.6	1.7	3.3	3.2	2.9	2.5	2.0	3.5	2.8	2.5
Ireland	3.1	2.2	2.7	2.9	3.1	−1.7	−1.6	1.2	1.9	1.3	1.3	1.8	1.5	1.8	1.2
Slovak Republic	7.7	2.8	4.3	1.9	3.9	0.9	0.7	4.1	3.7	1.9	2.0	2.3	3.4	1.9	2.1
Slovenia	8.0	2.5	2.5	3.6	5.7	0.9	1.8	1.8	2.6	1.8	1.9	2.1	2.5	1.5	2.0
Luxembourg	2.0	3.8	3.0	2.7	4.1	0.0	2.8	3.7	2.9	1.9	1.9	2.0	2.5	2.0	2.3
Estonia	8.9	4.1	4.4	6.6	10.4	−0.1	2.9	5.1	4.2	3.2	2.8	2.5	3.8	3.2	2.8
Cyprus[4]	2.7	2.0	2.3	2.2	4.4	0.2	2.6	3.5	3.1	. . .	. . .	. . .	1.5	. . .	. . .
Malta	2.9	2.5	2.6	0.7	4.7	1.8	2.0	2.5	3.2	2.4	2.0	2.2	2.8	2.4	2.2
Japan	−0.1	−0.3	0.2	0.1	1.4	−1.3	−0.7	−0.3	0.0	0.1	3.0	2.0	−0.2	0.7	3.6
United Kingdom[3]	1.6	2.0	2.3	2.3	3.6	2.1	3.3	4.5	2.8	2.7	2.5	2.0	2.6	2.6	2.4
Canada	2.0	2.2	2.0	2.1	2.4	0.3	1.8	2.9	1.5	1.5	1.8	2.0	0.9	1.9	1.9
Korea	3.8	2.8	2.2	2.5	4.7	2.8	2.9	4.0	2.2	2.4	2.9	3.0	1.4	2.8	3.0
Australia	2.7	2.7	3.6	2.3	4.4	1.8	2.9	3.3	1.8	2.5	2.5	2.4	2.2	2.3	2.9
Taiwan Province of China	1.2	2.3	0.6	1.8	3.5	−0.9	1.0	1.4	1.9	2.0	2.0	2.0	15.3	2.0	2.0
Sweden	1.2	0.5	1.4	2.2	3.4	−0.5	1.2	3.0	0.9	0.3	2.3	2.0	1.0	−0.2	2.5
Hong Kong SAR	0.8	0.9	2.0	2.0	4.3	0.6	2.3	5.3	4.1	3.5	3.5	3.5	3.8	3.5	3.5
Switzerland	0.9	1.2	1.1	0.7	2.4	−0.5	0.7	0.2	−0.7	−0.2	0.2	1.0	−0.4	0.5	1.0
Singapore	0.9	0.5	1.0	2.1	6.6	0.6	2.8	5.2	4.6	4.0	3.4	2.3	4.0	4.0	3.5
Czech Republic	. . .	1.8	2.5	2.9	6.3	1.0	1.5	1.9	3.3	2.3	1.9	2.0	2.4	2.4	2.0
Norway	2.1	1.5	2.3	0.7	3.8	2.2	2.4	1.3	0.7	1.5	1.5	2.5	1.4	1.5	1.5
Israel	4.8	1.3	2.1	0.5	4.6	3.3	2.7	3.5	1.7	1.6	2.0	2.0	1.6	2.0	2.0
Denmark	2.1	1.8	1.9	1.7	3.4	1.3	2.3	2.8	2.4	2.0	2.0	2.0	2.0	2.0	2.0
New Zealand	2.0	3.0	3.4	2.4	4.0	2.1	2.3	4.0	1.1	1.4	2.2	2.0	0.9	2.2	2.2
Iceland	3.2	4.0	6.7	5.1	12.7	12.0	5.4	4.0	5.2	4.7	4.0	2.5	4.2	5.0	3.5
San Marino	. . .	1.7	2.1	2.5	4.1	2.4	2.6	2.0	2.8	1.6	0.9	1.5	2.8	1.6	0.9
Memorandum															
Major Advanced Economies	1.8	2.3	2.3	2.2	3.2	−0.1	1.4	2.6	1.9	1.6	1.9	2.1	1.6	1.6	2.0

[1]Movements in consumer prices are shown as annual averages.
[2]Monthly year-over-year changes and for several countries, on quarterly basis.
[3]Based on Eurostat's harmonized index of consumer prices.
[4]Projections for Cyprus are excluded due to the ongoing crisis.

Table A7. Emerging Market and Developing Economies: Consumer Prices[1]

(Annual percent change)

	Average 1995–2004	2005	2006	2007	2008	2009	2010	2011	2012	Projections 2013	Projections 2014	Projections 2018	End of Period[2] 2012	End of Period[2] Projections 2013	End of Period[2] Projections 2014
Central and Eastern Europe[3]	**31.1**	**5.9**	**5.9**	**6.0**	**8.1**	**4.7**	**5.3**	**5.3**	**5.8**	**4.4**	**3.6**	**3.6**	**4.7**	**3.8**	**3.4**
Albania	8.4	2.4	2.4	2.9	3.4	2.3	3.5	3.4	2.0	2.2	2.7	3.0	2.4	2.5	3.0
Bosnia and Herzegovina	...	3.6	6.1	1.5	7.4	−0.4	2.1	3.7	2.0	1.8	1.8	2.2	2.0	1.8	1.8
Bulgaria	52.8	6.0	7.4	7.6	12.0	2.5	3.0	3.4	2.4	2.1	1.9	3.0	2.8	1.8	2.0
Croatia	3.4	3.3	3.2	2.9	6.1	2.4	1.0	2.3	3.4	3.2	2.3	2.6	4.7	2.7	2.1
Hungary	12.7	3.6	3.9	7.9	6.1	4.2	4.8	3.9	5.7	3.2	3.5	3.0	5.0	4.0	3.3
Kosovo	...	−1.4	0.6	4.4	9.4	−2.4	3.5	7.3	2.5	2.4	1.5	1.5	3.7	1.5	1.7
Latvia	7.1	6.9	6.6	10.1	15.3	3.3	−1.2	4.2	2.3	1.8	2.1	2.3	1.6	2.9	0.8
Lithuania	...	2.7	3.8	5.8	11.1	4.2	1.2	4.1	3.2	2.1	2.5	2.4	2.9	2.7	2.3
FYR Macedonia	3.5	0.5	3.2	2.3	8.4	−0.8	1.5	3.9	3.3	2.5	2.1	2.0	4.7	2.2	2.0
Montenegro	...	3.4	2.1	3.5	9.0	3.6	0.7	3.1	3.6	2.7	2.2	1.5	5.1	2.1	2.0
Poland	10.1	2.1	1.0	2.5	4.2	3.4	2.6	4.3	3.7	1.9	2.0	2.5	2.4	2.0	2.0
Romania	42.1	9.0	6.6	4.8	7.8	5.6	6.1	5.8	3.3	4.6	2.9	2.5	5.0	3.7	3.0
Serbia	...	16.2	10.7	6.9	12.4	8.1	6.2	11.1	7.3	9.6	5.4	3.5	12.2	5.5	4.0
Turkey	57.0	8.2	9.6	8.8	10.4	6.3	8.6	6.5	8.9	6.6	5.3	5.0	6.4	5.5	5.0
Commonwealth of Independent States[3,4]	**39.0**	**12.1**	**9.5**	**9.7**	**15.6**	**11.2**	**7.2**	**10.1**	**6.5**	**6.8**	**6.5**	**6.5**	**6.3**	**6.6**	**6.6**
Russia	38.3	12.7	9.7	9.0	14.1	11.7	6.9	8.4	5.1	6.9	6.2	6.0	6.6	6.4	6.0
Excluding Russia	41.0	10.6	8.9	11.6	19.4	10.2	7.9	14.1	9.9	6.5	7.4	7.8	5.6	7.1	7.9
Armenia	16.8	0.6	3.0	4.6	9.0	3.5	7.3	7.7	2.5	4.2	4.0	4.0	3.2	4.0	4.0
Azerbaijan	22.7	9.7	8.4	16.6	20.8	1.6	5.7	7.9	1.1	3.4	6.7	6.0	−0.3	7.0	6.5
Belarus	104.7	10.3	7.0	8.4	14.8	13.0	7.7	53.2	59.2	20.5	15.5	20.1	21.8	16.8	18.8
Georgia	19.9	8.3	9.2	9.2	10.0	1.7	7.1	8.5	−0.9	1.0	4.6	5.0	−1.4	3.2	6.0
Kazakhstan	22.8	7.5	8.6	10.8	17.1	7.3	7.1	8.3	5.1	7.2	6.4	6.0	6.0	6.6	6.6
Kyrgyz Republic	17.2	4.3	5.6	10.2	24.5	6.8	7.8	16.6	2.8	8.6	7.2	5.4	7.5	7.0	7.0
Moldova	17.7	11.9	12.7	12.4	12.7	0.0	7.4	7.6	4.7	4.6	5.0	5.0	4.1	5.0	5.0
Tajikistan	78.4	7.3	10.0	13.2	20.4	6.5	6.5	12.4	5.8	7.7	7.0	6.0	6.4	7.0	7.0
Turkmenistan	85.0	10.7	8.2	6.3	14.5	−2.7	4.4	5.3	4.9	5.6	5.5	5.0	5.3	6.0	5.0
Ukraine	36.5	13.5	9.1	12.8	25.2	15.9	9.4	8.0	0.6	0.5	4.7	5.0	−0.2	2.8	4.7
Uzbekistan	45.6	10.0	14.2	12.3	12.7	14.1	9.4	12.8	12.1	10.9	11.0	11.0	10.4	11.0	11.0
Developing Asia	**5.0**	**3.6**	**4.0**	**5.4**	**7.3**	**2.6**	**5.6**	**6.4**	**4.5**	**5.0**	**5.0**	**3.9**	**4.7**	**5.1**	**4.8**
Bangladesh	5.2	7.0	6.8	9.1	8.9	5.4	8.1	10.7	8.7	6.5	6.2	5.5	7.4	6.0	6.1
Bhutan	6.3	5.3	5.0	5.2	8.3	4.4	7.0	8.9	9.7	10.2	9.1	6.0	13.0	9.3	8.2
Brunei Darussalam	1.0	1.1	0.2	1.0	2.1	1.0	0.4	2.0	0.5	1.5	2.0	1.4	0.5	1.5	2.0
Cambodia	4.5	6.3	6.1	7.7	25.0	−0.7	4.0	5.5	2.9	3.1	4.3	3.0	2.5	4.6	4.0
China	3.0	1.8	1.5	4.8	5.9	−0.7	3.3	5.4	2.6	3.0	3.0	3.0	2.5	3.1	3.0
Fiji	2.9	2.3	2.5	4.8	7.7	3.7	5.5	8.7	4.3	3.0	3.0	3.0	1.5	3.0	3.0
India	6.3	4.2	6.2	6.4	8.3	10.9	12.0	8.9	9.3	10.8	10.7	6.7	11.2	10.6	10.2
Indonesia	13.4	10.5	13.1	6.7	9.8	4.8	5.1	5.4	4.3	5.6	5.6	4.5	4.3	6.0	5.3
Kiribati	2.0	−0.3	−1.5	4.2	11.0	8.8	−2.8	1.2	2.0	2.5	2.5	2.5	2.0	2.5	2.5
Lao P.D.R.	30.0	7.2	6.8	4.5	7.6	0.0	6.0	7.6	4.3	7.3	4.7	4.0	4.7	6.4	4.8
Malaysia	2.5	3.0	3.6	2.0	5.4	0.6	1.7	3.2	1.7	2.2	2.4	2.2	1.7	2.2	2.4
Maldives	2.4	2.5	3.5	6.8	12.0	4.5	6.1	11.3	10.9	5.8	5.1	4.4	5.4	4.7	4.5
Marshall Islands	...	3.5	5.3	2.6	14.7	0.5	1.8	5.4	5.7	3.9	2.0	2.0	5.7	3.9	2.0
Micronesia	...	4.3	4.6	3.3	8.5	5.0	6.3	4.6	5.6	4.2	3.5	2.0	5.6	4.2	3.5
Mongolia	17.5	12.5	4.5	8.2	26.8	6.3	10.2	7.7	15.0	11.1	9.3	6.5	14.2	10.0	8.5
Myanmar	...	10.7	26.3	32.9	22.5	8.2	8.2	4.0	6.1	6.5	5.1	4.8	6.1	5.3	5.0
Nepal	6.0	4.5	8.0	6.2	6.7	12.6	9.5	9.6	8.3	9.6	8.3	5.5	11.5	9.0	7.9
Papua New Guinea	11.4	1.8	2.4	0.9	10.8	6.9	6.0	8.4	4.0	7.9	6.0	6.0	6.4	6.8	6.0
Philippines	5.8	6.6	5.5	2.9	8.2	4.2	3.8	4.7	3.1	3.1	3.2	3.1	2.9	3.7	3.0
Samoa	3.6	7.8	3.5	4.7	6.3	14.6	−0.2	2.9	6.2	2.0	1.5	4.0	5.5	4.5	−2.0
Solomon Islands	9.1	7.5	11.2	7.7	17.3	7.1	0.9	7.4	5.1	5.4	4.4	5.2	6.2	4.7	4.1
Sri Lanka	9.5	11.0	10.0	15.8	22.4	3.5	6.2	6.7	7.5	7.9	7.1	5.5	9.2	7.9	6.7
Thailand	3.4	4.5	4.6	2.2	5.5	−0.9	3.3	3.8	3.0	3.0	3.4	1.9	3.6	3.8	2.4
Timor-Leste	...	1.1	3.9	10.3	9.0	0.7	6.8	13.5	11.8	8.0	8.0	8.0	11.7	8.0	8.0
Tonga	5.8	8.5	6.1	7.4	7.4	3.5	3.9	5.3	4.5	5.3	6.0	2.9	4.5	6.0	6.0
Tuvalu	...	3.2	4.2	2.3	10.4	−0.3	−1.9	0.5	1.4	2.7	2.7	2.7	...	...	...
Vanuatu	2.4	1.1	2.0	3.8	4.2	5.2	2.7	0.7	1.4	1.7	2.2	3.0	0.8	1.6	2.0
Vietnam	5.0	8.4	7.5	8.3	23.1	6.7	9.2	18.7	9.1	8.8	8.0	6.7	6.8	8.2	9.1

Table A7. Emerging Market and Developing Economies: Consumer Prices[1] *(continued)*

(Annual percent change)

	Average 1995–2004	2005	2006	2007	2008	2009	2010	2011	2012	Projections 2013	2014	2018	End of Period[2] 2012	Projections 2013	2014
Latin America and the Caribbean	**13.0**	**6.3**	**5.3**	**5.4**	**7.9**	**5.9**	**6.0**	**6.6**	**6.0**	**6.1**	**5.7**	**5.1**	**5.9**	**6.1**	**5.5**
Antigua and Barbuda	1.8	2.1	1.8	1.4	5.3	−0.6	3.4	3.5	3.4	3.0	3.0	2.5	1.8	3.1	3.1
Argentina[5]	4.3	9.6	10.9	8.8	8.6	6.3	10.5	9.8	10.0	9.8	10.1	10.1	10.8	10.1	10.1
The Bahamas	1.6	2.1	2.1	2.5	4.7	1.9	1.3	3.2	2.3	2.0	2.0	2.0	2.3	2.0	2.0
Barbados	1.9	6.1	7.3	4.0	8.1	3.7	5.8	9.4	4.6	4.9	4.5	4.5	1.2	−0.3	−0.7
Belize	1.8	3.7	4.2	2.3	6.4	−1.1	0.9	1.5	1.4	1.3	2.0	2.0	0.6	2.0	2.0
Bolivia	5.1	5.4	2.3	8.7	14.0	3.3	2.5	9.9	4.5	4.6	4.3	4.0	4.5	4.4	4.2
Brazil	12.9	6.9	4.2	3.6	5.7	4.9	5.0	6.6	5.4	6.1	4.7	4.5	5.8	5.5	4.5
Chile	4.4	3.1	3.4	4.4	8.7	1.5	1.4	3.3	3.0	2.1	3.0	3.0	1.5	3.0	3.0
Colombia	12.5	5.0	4.3	5.6	7.0	4.2	2.3	3.4	3.2	2.2	3.0	3.0	2.4	2.4	3.0
Costa Rica	12.8	13.8	11.5	9.4	13.4	7.8	5.7	4.9	4.5	4.7	5.0	5.0	4.6	5.0	5.0
Dominica	1.4	1.6	2.6	3.2	6.4	0.0	2.8	1.4	2.3	2.3	1.6	2.7	3.6	1.5	1.6
Dominican Republic	13.1	4.2	7.6	6.1	10.6	1.4	6.3	8.5	3.7	4.5	4.8	4.0	3.9	5.0	4.5
Ecuador	30.1	2.1	3.3	2.3	8.4	5.2	3.6	4.5	5.1	4.7	4.1	3.0	4.2	6.1	2.1
El Salvador	4.1	4.7	4.0	4.6	7.3	0.5	1.2	5.1	1.7	1.9	2.4	2.6	0.8	2.3	2.6
Grenada	1.6	3.5	4.3	3.9	8.0	−0.3	3.4	3.0	2.4	2.6	2.6	2.6	1.8	2.6	2.6
Guatemala	7.5	9.1	6.6	6.8	11.4	1.9	3.9	6.2	3.8	4.3	4.4	4.0	3.4	4.5	4.8
Guyana	5.9	6.9	6.7	12.2	8.1	3.0	3.7	5.0	3.0	5.6	5.7	4.0	4.6	6.0	5.5
Haiti	17.8	16.8	14.2	9.0	14.4	3.4	4.1	7.4	6.8	6.7	3.9	3.1	6.5	5.0	4.5
Honduras	14.1	8.8	5.6	6.9	11.4	5.5	4.7	6.8	5.2	5.7	5.8	5.5	5.4	5.9	5.7
Jamaica	11.5	15.1	8.5	9.3	22.0	9.6	12.6	7.5	7.3	8.5	6.7	6.7	7.4	8.3	6.2
Mexico	14.8	4.0	3.6	4.0	5.1	5.3	4.2	3.4	4.1	3.7	3.2	3.0	4.0	3.6	3.3
Nicaragua	8.4	9.2	9.7	9.3	16.8	11.6	3.0	7.4	7.9	7.0	7.6	7.0	7.2	7.7	7.1
Panama	0.9	2.9	2.5	4.2	8.8	2.4	3.5	5.9	5.7	5.2	4.8	3.2	4.6	4.8	4.5
Paraguay	9.3	6.8	9.6	8.1	10.2	2.6	4.7	8.3	3.8	3.6	5.0	4.0	4.0	5.0	5.0
Peru	5.3	1.6	2.0	1.8	5.8	2.9	1.5	3.4	3.7	2.1	2.3	2.0	2.6	2.1	2.0
St. Kitts and Nevis	3.1	3.4	8.5	4.5	5.3	2.1	0.6	7.1	1.4	3.0	2.5	2.5	0.3	3.4	2.5
St. Lucia	2.5	3.9	3.6	2.8	5.5	−0.2	3.3	2.8	4.3	4.8	3.2	3.3	6.2	2.4	2.8
St. Vincent and the Grenadines	1.5	3.4	3.0	7.0	10.1	0.4	0.8	3.2	2.6	1.7	2.3	2.5	0.8	2.4	2.5
Suriname	39.5	9.6	11.1	6.6	15.0	0.0	6.9	17.7	5.0	4.8	4.0	4.0	4.1	4.5	4.0
Trinidad and Tobago	4.2	6.9	8.3	7.9	12.0	7.0	10.5	5.1	9.3	5.6	4.0	4.0	7.2	4.0	4.0
Uruguay	15.3	4.7	6.4	8.1	7.9	7.1	6.7	8.1	8.1	7.3	7.2	5.6	7.5	7.8	7.0
Venezuela	35.3	16.0	13.7	18.7	30.4	27.1	28.2	26.1	21.1	27.3	27.6	20.5	20.1	28.0	27.3
Middle East, North Africa, Afghanistan, and Pakistan	**7.1**	**7.1**	**8.2**	**10.3**	**12.4**	**7.3**	**6.9**	**9.7**	**10.7**	**9.4**	**9.0**	**7.7**	**10.9**	**8.7**	**8.8**
Afghanistan	. . .	9.7	5.3	12.5	23.4	−10.0	7.1	10.4	4.4	6.1	5.8	5.0	5.7	5.0	5.0
Algeria	7.3	1.4	2.3	3.7	4.9	5.7	3.9	4.5	8.9	5.0	4.5	4.0	9.0	5.0	4.0
Bahrain	0.7	2.6	2.0	3.3	3.5	2.8	2.0	−0.4	1.2	2.6	2.1	2.0	2.6	2.0	2.0
Djibouti	2.2	3.1	3.5	5.0	12.0	1.7	4.0	5.1	3.7	2.5	2.5	2.5	2.5	1.1	2.3
Egypt	5.0	8.8	4.2	11.0	11.7	16.2	11.7	11.1	8.6	8.2	13.7	6.3	7.3	9.6	13.1
Iran	19.5	10.4	11.9	18.4	25.4	10.8	12.4	21.5	30.6	27.2	21.1	20.6	31.9	22.0	20.0
Iraq	. . .	37.0	53.2	30.8	2.7	−2.2	2.4	5.6	6.1	4.3	5.5	5.5	3.6	5.0	5.5
Jordan	2.5	3.5	6.3	4.7	13.9	−0.7	5.0	4.4	4.8	5.9	3.2	2.1	7.2	3.2	2.6
Kuwait	1.6	4.1	3.1	5.5	10.6	4.0	4.0	4.7	2.9	3.3	3.8	4.0	2.9	3.3	3.8
Lebanon	3.5	−0.7	5.6	4.1	10.8	1.2	4.5	5.0	6.6	6.7	2.4	2.0	10.1	2.8	2.0
Libya	−0.2	2.7	1.5	6.2	10.4	2.4	2.5	15.9	6.1	2.0	5.2	3.5	−3.7	6.9	3.8
Mauritania	5.5	12.1	6.2	7.3	7.5	2.1	6.3	5.7	4.9	4.7	5.2	5.5	3.4	5.1	5.3
Morocco	2.1	1.0	3.3	2.0	3.9	1.0	1.0	0.9	1.3	2.5	2.5	2.6	2.6	2.5	2.5
Oman	−0.2	1.9	3.4	5.9	12.6	3.5	3.3	4.0	2.9	3.3	3.3	3.5	2.9	3.3	3.3
Pakistan	6.7	9.3	8.0	7.8	10.8	17.6	10.1	13.7	11.0	8.2	9.5	11.8	11.3	9.0	10.0
Qatar	3.0	8.8	11.8	13.8	15.0	−4.9	−2.4	1.9	1.9	3.0	4.0	5.0	1.9	3.0	4.0
Saudi Arabia	0.1	0.5	1.9	5.0	6.1	4.1	3.8	3.7	2.9	3.7	3.6	3.5	3.7	3.6	3.5
Sudan[6]	27.3	8.5	7.2	8.0	14.3	11.3	13.0	18.1	35.5	28.4	29.4	5.0	44.4	24.8	33.0
Syria[7]	2.2	7.2	10.4	4.7	15.2	2.8	4.4	. . .	. . .	. . .	. . .	. . .	. . .	. . .	. . .
Tunisia	3.3	2.0	4.1	3.4	4.9	3.5	4.4	3.5	5.6	6.0	4.7	4.0	5.9	5.3	5.0
United Arab Emirates	3.0	6.2	9.3	11.1	12.3	1.6	0.9	0.9	0.7	1.6	1.9	2.0	1.1	1.7	1.9
Yemen	17.4	9.9	10.8	7.9	19.0	3.7	11.2	19.5	11.0	7.5	8.7	7.3	5.5	7.5	10.0

Table A7. Emerging Market and Developing Economies: Consumer Prices[1] *(concluded)*

(Annual percent change)

	Average 1995–2004	2005	2006	2007	2008	2009	2010	2011	2012	Projections 2013	Projections 2014	Projections 2018	End of Period[2] 2012	End of Period[2] Projections 2013	End of Period[2] Projections 2014
Sub-Saharan Africa	**16.5**	**8.8**	**7.1**	**6.4**	**12.9**	**9.4**	**7.4**	**9.3**	**9.1**	**7.2**	**6.3**	**5.6**	**7.9**	**6.9**	**5.8**
Angola	320.9	23.0	13.3	12.2	12.5	13.7	14.5	13.5	10.3	9.4	8.4	7.0	9.0	9.2	7.8
Benin	4.2	5.4	3.8	1.3	7.4	0.9	2.2	2.7	6.7	3.5	2.8	2.8	6.8	3.3	3.1
Botswana	8.3	8.6	11.6	7.1	12.6	8.1	6.9	8.5	7.5	7.2	6.9	6.4	7.4	7.0	6.7
Burkina Faso	2.9	6.4	2.4	−0.2	10.7	2.6	−0.6	2.7	3.6	2.0	2.0	2.0	2.0	2.0	2.0
Burundi	14.3	1.2	9.1	14.4	26.0	4.6	4.1	14.9	11.8	9.0	5.9	5.1	11.8	9.0	5.9
Cameroon[8]	4.7	2.0	4.9	1.1	5.3	3.0	1.3	2.9	3.0	3.0	2.5	2.5	3.0	3.0	2.5
Cape Verde	3.4	0.4	4.8	4.4	6.8	1.0	2.1	4.5	2.5	4.0	3.3	2.5	4.1	3.5	3.1
Central African Republic	3.1	2.9	6.7	0.9	9.3	3.5	1.5	1.2	5.2	2.0	2.3	2.0	1.7	2.4	2.3
Chad	3.1	3.7	7.7	−7.4	8.3	10.1	−2.1	1.9	7.7	1.5	3.0	3.0	2.1	3.0	3.0
Comoros	3.2	3.0	3.4	4.5	4.8	4.8	3.9	6.8	6.0	4.3	3.4	3.6	5.0	3.6	3.2
Democratic Republic of the Congo	180.3	21.4	13.2	16.7	18.0	46.2	23.5	15.5	9.3	6.8	8.0	6.7	5.7	8.0	8.0
Republic of Congo	4.1	2.5	4.7	2.6	6.0	4.3	5.0	1.8	5.0	4.5	3.0	2.6	7.5	4.1	2.9
Côte d'Ivoire	4.0	3.9	2.5	1.9	6.3	1.0	1.4	4.9	1.3	3.1	2.5	2.5	3.4	1.9	2.5
Equatorial Guinea	6.7	5.6	4.5	2.8	4.7	5.7	5.3	4.8	5.5	5.0	5.4	4.6	5.9	5.2	5.1
Eritrea	14.1	12.5	15.1	9.3	19.9	33.0	12.7	13.3	12.3	12.3	12.3	12.3	12.3	12.3	12.3
Ethiopia	3.4	11.7	13.6	17.2	44.4	8.5	8.1	33.2	22.8	8.3	9.6	9.0	12.9	10.8	9.0
Gabon	1.9	1.2	−1.4	5.0	5.3	1.9	1.4	1.3	3.0	3.0	3.0	3.0	3.1	3.0	3.0
The Gambia	6.0	5.0	2.1	5.4	4.5	4.6	5.0	4.8	4.6	5.5	5.5	5.0	4.9	6.0	5.0
Ghana	26.5	15.1	10.2	10.7	16.5	19.3	10.7	8.7	9.2	8.4	8.2	7.0	8.8	8.1	8.1
Guinea	6.3	31.4	34.7	22.9	18.4	4.7	15.5	21.4	15.2	11.2	8.1	6.0	12.8	9.7	7.0
Guinea-Bissau	14.6	3.2	0.7	4.6	10.4	−1.6	1.1	5.1	2.2	3.0	2.5	2.0	2.1	1.7	3.5
Kenya	7.3	9.9	6.0	4.3	15.1	10.6	4.1	14.0	9.4	5.2	5.0	5.0	7.0	7.0	5.0
Lesotho	8.2	3.4	6.1	8.0	10.7	7.4	3.6	5.6	5.3	4.9	4.7	7.1	4.3	5.5	3.8
Liberia	. . .	6.9	7.2	13.7	17.5	7.4	7.3	8.5	6.8	6.4	5.0	5.0	7.7	5.1	5.0
Madagascar	12.7	18.4	10.8	10.4	9.2	9.0	9.3	10.0	6.5	7.0	6.5	5.0	7.7	7.0	6.5
Malawi	27.7	15.5	13.9	7.9	8.7	8.4	7.4	7.6	21.3	20.2	8.1	3.0	34.6	11.8	5.8
Mali	2.4	6.4	1.5	1.5	9.1	2.2	1.3	3.1	5.3	2.9	2.9	2.8	2.4	5.3	3.7
Mauritius	5.7	4.8	8.7	8.6	9.7	2.5	2.9	6.5	3.9	5.7	4.6	5.0	3.2	6.0	5.1
Mozambique	16.3	6.4	13.2	8.2	10.3	3.3	12.7	10.4	2.1	5.4	5.6	5.6	2.2	4.5	5.6
Namibia	8.3	2.3	5.1	6.7	10.4	8.8	4.5	3.1	6.7	6.0	5.4	4.5	6.2	5.7	5.2
Niger	2.9	7.8	0.1	0.1	10.5	1.1	0.9	2.9	0.5	1.7	1.6	1.9	0.7	1.6	1.2
Nigeria	18.3	17.9	8.2	5.4	11.6	12.5	13.7	10.8	12.2	10.7	8.2	7.0	12.0	9.5	7.0
Rwanda	9.9	9.1	8.8	9.1	15.4	10.3	2.3	5.7	6.3	4.9	5.7	5.0	3.9	6.0	5.5
São Tomé and Príncipe	24.0	17.2	23.1	18.6	32.0	17.0	13.3	14.3	10.6	9.3	5.8	3.0	10.4	8.0	4.0
Senegal	2.1	1.7	2.1	5.9	5.8	−1.7	1.2	3.4	1.1	1.5	1.6	1.7	1.1	1.6	1.6
Seychelles	2.8	0.6	−1.9	5.3	37.0	31.7	−2.4	2.6	7.1	4.6	3.3	3.0	5.8	4.7	3.3
Sierra Leone	14.6	12.0	9.5	11.6	14.8	9.2	17.8	18.5	13.8	8.7	8.2	5.4	12.0	9.0	7.5
South Africa	6.4	3.4	4.7	7.1	11.5	7.1	4.3	5.0	5.7	5.8	5.5	5.0	5.6	5.6	5.4
South Sudan	. . .	. . .	. . .	. . .	. . .	. . .	. . .	. . .	45.1	15.5	5.9	5.0	25.2	8.6	3.9
Swaziland	7.6	1.8	5.2	8.1	12.7	7.4	4.5	6.1	8.9	8.1	6.1	5.0	8.3	9.8	2.2
Tanzania	10.3	4.4	7.3	7.0	10.3	12.1	7.2	12.7	16.0	9.0	5.9	5.0	12.1	7.0	5.0
Togo	3.4	6.8	2.2	0.9	8.7	1.9	3.2	3.6	2.6	4.2	3.5	2.4	2.8	6.4	4.1
Uganda	4.9	8.6	7.2	6.1	12.0	13.1	4.0	18.7	14.1	5.5	5.0	5.0	5.9	5.0	5.0
Zambia	26.1	18.3	9.0	10.7	12.4	13.4	8.5	8.7	6.6	6.5	5.5	5.0	7.3	6.0	5.0
Zimbabwe[9]	. . .	−31.5	33.0	−72.7	157.0	6.2	3.0	3.5	3.7	4.5	4.2	4.0	2.9	4.6	4.0

[1]Movements in consumer prices are shown as annual averages.

[2]Monthly year-over-year changes and for several countries, on quarterly basis.

[3]For many countries, inflation for the earlier years is measured on the basis of a retail price index. Consumer price index (CPI) inflation data with broader and more up-to-date coverage are typically used for more recent years.

[4]Georgia, which is not a member of the Commonwealth of Independent States, is included in this group for reasons of geography and similarity in economic structure.

[5]The data for Argentina are officially reported data. The IMF has, however, issued a declaration of censure and called on Argentina to adopt remedial measures to address the quality of the official CPI-GBA data. Alternative data sources have shown considerably higher inflation rates than the official data since 2007. In this context, the IMF is also using alternative estimates of CPI inflation for the surveillance of macroeconomic developments in Argentina.

[6]Data for 2011 exclude South Sudan after July 9. Data for 2012 and onward pertain to the current Sudan.

[7]Data for Syria are excluded for 2011 onward due to the uncertain political situation.

[8]The percent changes in 2002 are calculated over a period of 18 months, reflecting a change in the fiscal year cycle (from July–June to January–December).

[9]The Zimbabwe dollar ceased circulating in early 2009. Data are based on IMF staff estimates of price and exchange rate developments in U.S. dollars. IMF staff estimates of U.S. dollar values may differ from authorities' estimates.

Table A8. Major Advanced Economies: General Government Fiscal Balances and Debt[1]

(Percent of GDP unless noted otherwise)

	Average 1997–2006	2007	2008	2009	2010	2011	2012	Projections 2013	2014	2018
Major Advanced Economies										
Net Lending/Borrowing	−2.7	−2.1	−4.5	−10.2	−9.0	−7.7	−7.0	−5.7	−4.7	−3.2
Output Gap[2]	0.4	1.1	−0.6	−5.3	−3.6	−3.3	−3.1	−3.3	−2.8	−0.2
Structural Balance[2]	−3.0	−2.7	−4.1	−6.6	−6.9	−6.2	−5.4	−4.1	−3.3	−3.0
United States										
Net Lending/Borrowing	−1.7	−2.7	−6.7	−13.3	−11.1	−10.0	−8.5	−6.5	−5.4	−4.2
Output Gap[2]	0.8	0.3	−1.8	−6.1	−5.0	−4.7	−4.3	−4.4	−3.6	0.0
Structural Balance[2]	−2.0	−2.8	−5.1	−8.1	−8.5	−7.7	−6.4	−4.6	−3.9	−4.2
Net Debt	43.0	48.0	54.0	66.7	75.1	82.4	87.9	89.0	89.7	86.6
Gross Debt	62.2	66.5	75.5	89.1	98.2	102.5	106.5	108.1	109.2	106.7
Euro Area										
Net Lending/Borrowing	−2.1	−0.7	−2.1	−6.4	−6.2	−4.1	−3.6	−2.9	−2.6	−1.2
Output Gap[2]	0.3	2.8	1.9	−3.3	−2.1	−1.3	−2.2	−3.0	−2.6	−0.3
Structural Balance[2]	−2.5	−2.4	−3.0	−4.4	−4.4	−3.4	−2.0	−1.2	−1.1	−0.9
Net Debt	55.1	52.1	54.0	62.3	65.5	67.8	71.9	73.9	74.5	72.0
Gross Debt	70.1	66.5	70.3	80.0	85.6	88.1	92.9	95.0	95.3	90.0
Germany[3]										
Net Lending/Borrowing	−2.5	0.2	−0.1	−3.1	−4.1	−0.8	0.2	−0.3	−0.1	0.1
Output Gap[2]	−0.3	2.7	2.3	−3.7	−1.2	0.6	0.1	−0.6	−0.4	−0.3
Structural Balance[2,4]	−2.5	−1.1	−0.9	−1.1	−2.3	−0.9	0.2	0.0	0.1	0.2
Net Debt	46.4	50.6	50.1	56.7	56.3	55.3	57.2	56.2	54.7	51.4
Gross Debt	62.9	65.4	66.8	74.5	82.5	80.5	82.0	80.4	78.3	68.7
France										
Net Lending/Borrowing	−2.7	−2.8	−3.3	−7.6	−7.1	−5.2	−4.6	−3.7	−3.5	−0.6
Output Gap[2]	0.2	0.7	−0.6	−4.6	−3.8	−2.7	−3.1	−3.8	−3.6	−0.7
Structural Balance[2,4]	−2.8	−3.0	−3.0	−4.6	−4.6	−3.5	−2.4	−1.2	−1.0	0.0
Net Debt	54.8	59.6	62.3	72.0	76.1	78.8	84.1	86.5	87.8	81.8
Gross Debt	61.0	64.2	68.2	79.2	82.3	86.0	90.3	92.7	94.0	88.1
Italy										
Net Lending/Borrowing	−3.0	−1.6	−2.7	−5.4	−4.3	−3.7	−3.0	−2.6	−2.3	−1.1
Output Gap[2]	1.1	3.1	1.6	−3.7	−1.9	−1.8	−3.4	−4.5	−3.9	−0.3
Structural Balance[2,5]	−4.3	−3.5	−3.8	−4.1	−3.6	−3.5	−1.3	−0.2	−0.3	−1.0
Net Debt	93.0	86.9	88.8	97.2	99.2	99.7	103.2	105.8	106.0	100.8
Gross Debt	108.7	103.3	106.1	116.4	119.3	120.8	127.0	130.6	130.8	123.4
Japan										
Net Lending/Borrowing	−6.2	−2.1	−4.1	−10.4	−9.3	−9.9	−10.2	−9.8	−7.0	−5.4
Output Gap[2]	−1.0	0.6	−1.1	−6.8	−2.8	−3.6	−2.1	−1.2	−0.5	0.1
Structural Balance[2]	−6.0	−2.2	−3.5	−7.5	−7.9	−8.5	−9.3	−9.5	−6.9	−5.4
Net Debt	65.6	80.5	95.3	106.2	113.1	127.4	134.3	143.4	146.7	154.8
Gross Debt[6]	153.6	183.0	191.8	210.2	216.0	230.3	237.9	245.4	244.6	242.8
United Kingdom										
Net Lending/Borrowing	−1.2	−2.9	−5.1	−11.4	−10.1	−7.9	−8.3	−7.0	−6.4	−2.6
Output Gap[2]	1.5	3.6	1.7	−2.1	−1.8	−2.5	−3.0	−3.9	−3.9	−2.2
Structural Balance[2]	−2.1	−5.2	−7.3	−9.7	−8.6	−6.5	−5.4	−4.3	−3.4	−0.7
Net Debt	36.7	38.0	48.1	63.2	72.9	77.7	82.8	86.1	89.6	91.1
Gross Debt	41.9	43.7	52.2	68.1	79.4	85.4	90.3	93.6	97.1	98.2
Canada										
Net Lending/Borrowing	1.1	1.5	−0.3	−4.8	−5.2	−4.0	−3.2	−2.8	−2.3	−0.8
Output Gap[2]	1.0	1.7	0.8	−3.3	−1.9	−1.1	−1.1	−1.7	−1.4	−0.2
Structural Balance[2]	0.6	0.5	−0.8	−2.8	−4.1	−3.4	−2.6	−1.9	−1.5	−0.7
Net Debt	44.6	22.9	22.4	27.7	29.7	32.3	34.6	35.9	36.6	34.9
Gross Debt	81.9	66.5	71.3	81.4	83.0	83.4	85.6	87.0	84.6	78.2

Note: The methodology and specific assumptions for each country are discussed in Box A1. The country group composites for fiscal data are calculated as the sum of the U.S. dollar values for the relevant individual countries.

[1]Debt data refer to the end of the year. Debt data are not always comparable across countries.
[2]Percent of potential GDP.
[3]Beginning in 1995, the debt and debt-services obligations of the Treuhandanstalt (and of various other agencies) were taken over by the general government. This debt is equivalent to 8 percent of GDP, and the associated debt service to 0.5 to 1 percent of GDP.
[4]Excludes sizable one-time receipts from the sale of assets, including licenses.
[5]Excludes one-time measures based on the authorities' data and, in the absence of the latter, receipts from the sale of assets.
[6]Includes equity shares.

Table A9. Summary of World Trade Volumes and Prices

(Annual percent change)

	Averages		2005	2006	2007	2008	2009	2010	2011	2012	Projections	
	1995–2004	2005–14									2013	2014
Trade in Goods and Services												
World Trade[1]												
Volume	7.0	4.5	7.7	9.2	8.0	3.1	−10.6	12.5	6.0	2.5	3.6	5.3
Price Deflator												
In U.S. Dollars	0.9	3.3	5.5	5.2	7.6	11.3	−10.6	5.8	11.3	−1.7	1.3	−0.3
In SDRs	0.6	3.1	5.7	5.6	3.4	7.8	−8.4	6.9	7.5	1.3	2.1	0.1
Volume of Trade												
Exports												
Advanced Economies	6.3	3.8	6.3	8.8	7.0	2.4	−11.6	12.1	5.6	1.9	2.8	4.6
Emerging Market and Developing Economies	8.7	6.1	11.1	11.0	9.8	4.3	−7.9	13.3	6.4	3.7	4.8	6.5
Imports												
Advanced Economies	6.8	3.0	6.4	7.7	5.5	1.0	−12.1	11.5	4.7	1.0	2.2	4.1
Emerging Market and Developing Economies	8.2	7.9	11.9	12.3	14.8	8.4	−8.3	14.8	8.6	4.9	6.2	7.3
Terms of Trade												
Advanced Economies	0.0	−0.5	−1.4	−1.2	0.4	−1.8	2.5	−1.0	−1.6	−0.7	0.2	−0.1
Emerging Market and Developing Economies	1.1	1.3	5.4	3.4	1.6	2.7	−4.8	2.7	3.3	0.2	−0.5	−0.9
Trade in Goods												
World Trade[1]												
Volume	7.2	4.4	7.6	9.1	7.3	2.5	−11.7	14.0	6.3	2.4	3.5	5.3
Price Deflator												
In U.S. Dollars	0.8	3.6	5.9	5.8	7.8	12.3	−11.9	6.6	12.6	−1.9	1.1	−0.4
In SDRs	0.5	3.3	6.2	6.2	3.6	8.7	−9.7	7.8	8.8	1.2	1.9	0.0
World Trade Prices in U.S. Dollars[2]												
Manufactures	0.2	2.0	2.8	2.5	5.7	6.3	−6.4	2.4	6.7	−0.5	1.0	0.5
Oil	9.0	10.0	41.3	20.5	10.7	36.4	−36.3	27.9	31.6	1.0	−2.3	−4.9
Nonfuel Primary Commodities	0.1	5.6	6.2	23.2	14.0	7.5	−15.7	26.3	17.8	−9.8	−0.9	−4.3
Food	0.2	4.8	−0.8	10.4	15.2	23.4	−14.7	11.5	19.7	−1.8	−2.4	−6.1
Beverages	−3.8	5.8	18.1	8.4	13.8	23.3	1.6	14.1	16.6	−18.6	−11.9	1.1
Agricultural Raw Materials	−1.6	2.8	0.7	8.7	5.0	−0.7	−17.1	33.2	22.7	−12.7	−1.1	−0.9
Metal	2.7	8.7	22.4	56.2	17.4	−7.8	−19.2	48.2	13.5	−16.8	3.2	−4.3
World Trade Prices in SDRs[2]												
Manufactures	−0.1	1.8	3.0	3.0	1.5	3.0	−4.1	3.5	3.1	2.6	1.8	0.9
Oil	8.6	9.7	41.6	21.0	6.4	32.1	−34.8	29.3	27.2	4.1	−1.5	−4.5
Nonfuel Primary Commodities	−0.3	5.4	6.4	23.7	9.6	4.1	−13.6	27.7	13.8	−7.0	0.0	−3.9
Food	−0.2	4.5	−0.6	10.9	10.7	19.5	−12.5	12.7	15.7	1.2	−1.6	−5.7
Beverages	−4.1	5.6	18.3	8.8	9.4	19.4	4.1	15.4	12.7	−16.1	−11.2	1.5
Agricultural Raw Materials	−1.9	2.6	0.9	9.2	0.9	−3.8	−15.1	34.6	18.6	−10.0	−0.3	−0.5
Metal	2.4	8.5	22.7	56.9	12.8	−10.7	−17.2	49.8	9.7	−14.3	4.1	−3.9
World Trade Prices in Euros[2]												
Manufactures	−0.2	1.4	2.6	1.7	−3.2	−1.0	−1.1	7.5	1.8	7.7	−2.3	1.3
Oil	8.5	9.3	41.0	19.5	1.4	27.1	−32.7	34.3	25.5	9.2	−5.4	−4.1
Nonfuel Primary Commodities	−0.4	5.0	5.9	22.2	4.5	0.1	−10.9	32.6	12.3	−2.4	−4.1	−3.6
Food	−0.3	4.2	−1.0	9.5	5.5	14.9	−9.8	17.0	14.2	6.2	−5.6	−5.3
Beverages	−4.2	5.2	17.8	7.5	4.2	14.8	7.3	19.8	11.2	−11.9	−14.8	1.9
Agricultural Raw Materials	−2.0	2.2	0.5	7.9	−3.8	−7.5	−12.5	39.8	17.0	−5.5	−4.3	−0.1
Metal	2.2	8.1	22.2	55.0	7.5	−14.1	−14.6	55.5	8.3	−10.0	−0.1	−3.5

Table A9. Summary of World Trade Volumes and Prices (concluded)
(Annual percent change)

	Averages		2005	2006	2007	2008	2009	2010	2011	2012	Projections	
	1995–2004	2005–14									2013	2014
Trade in Goods												
Volume of Trade												
Exports												
Advanced Economies	6.4	3.5	5.8	8.7	6.0	1.8	−13.4	14.1	5.9	1.8	2.4	4.3
Emerging Market and Developing Economies	8.8	6.0	11.1	10.3	8.8	3.6	−8.1	13.9	6.3	4.2	4.7	6.3
Fuel Exporters	4.6	2.6	6.7	4.0	4.3	2.9	−7.0	3.8	3.5	4.0	1.5	2.6
Nonfuel Exporters	10.3	7.3	12.8	13.1	10.8	3.8	−8.7	17.8	7.4	4.2	6.2	7.8
Imports												
Advanced Economies	7.1	3.0	6.7	8.0	5.1	0.4	−13.1	13.3	5.0	0.6	2.1	4.3
Emerging Market and Developing Economies	8.3	7.7	11.3	11.8	14.1	7.8	−9.5	15.4	9.5	4.6	6.5	7.5
Fuel Exporters	7.3	8.5	15.1	12.7	23.6	14.1	−12.2	7.9	8.9	7.6	5.1	5.6
Nonfuel Exporters	8.5	7.5	10.5	11.6	12.1	6.3	−8.9	17.3	9.7	3.9	6.8	8.0
Price Deflators in SDRs												
Exports												
Advanced Economies	−0.1	2.2	3.6	4.1	3.5	5.4	−6.9	4.5	6.3	−0.2	2.6	0.3
Emerging Market and Developing Economies	2.8	5.7	13.7	11.4	5.5	14.7	−13.9	14.0	13.5	2.4	0.7	−0.9
Fuel Exporters	6.6	9.0	31.4	18.9	7.9	25.7	−26.2	24.5	24.0	3.3	−1.6	−3.4
Nonfuel Exporters	1.4	4.4	7.2	8.2	4.4	10.0	−7.9	9.9	9.3	2.1	1.7	0.2
Imports												
Advanced Economies	0.0	2.7	5.2	5.5	2.9	7.8	−10.3	5.8	8.3	0.9	2.4	0.1
Emerging Market and Developing Economies	1.7	4.4	7.5	7.3	3.8	11.3	−8.9	11.1	9.0	2.6	1.3	0.4
Fuel Exporters	0.9	4.2	8.3	8.3	4.1	9.1	−5.1	7.5	7.2	2.4	0.4	0.5
Nonfuel Exporters	1.8	4.4	7.3	7.1	3.7	11.8	−9.8	12.0	9.4	2.7	1.6	0.4
Terms of Trade												
Advanced Economies	−0.1	−0.5	−1.5	−1.3	0.6	−2.3	3.9	−1.2	−1.8	−1.1	0.2	0.2
Emerging Market and Developing Economies	1.1	1.3	5.8	3.8	1.6	3.1	−5.4	2.6	4.1	−0.2	−0.6	−1.3
Regional Groups												
Central and Eastern Europe	0.8	−0.6	−2.3	−1.1	1.8	−2.7	3.4	−3.8	−1.8	−0.8	1.0	0.3
Commonwealth of Independent States[3]	3.5	3.8	14.8	8.7	2.4	14.6	−19.1	15.1	10.7	−0.3	−1.2	−2.0
Developing Asia	−1.3	−0.8	−0.9	−0.4	0.4	−3.0	4.5	−6.5	−2.0	0.8	−0.1	0.0
Latin America and the Caribbean	1.1	2.3	4.5	7.0	2.2	3.8	−7.6	11.3	7.9	−3.1	0.9	−2.5
Middle East, North Africa, Afghanistan, and Pakistan	5.4	4.1	21.0	8.0	2.5	11.9	−18.4	12.1	14.6	0.0	−2.1	−3.4
Middle East and North Africa	5.7	4.2	21.8	8.2	2.4	12.5	−18.8	12.4	14.8	0.5	−2.1	−3.5
Sub-Saharan Africa	...	2.7	9.7	7.0	4.8	9.1	−12.9	10.5	8.5	−1.6	−3.2	−2.0
Analytical Groups												
By Source of Export Earnings												
Fuel Exporters	5.6	4.7	21.4	9.8	3.7	15.3	−22.2	15.8	15.6	0.9	−1.9	−3.9
Nonfuel Exporters	−0.4	−0.1	−0.1	1.0	0.6	−1.6	2.1	−1.9	0.0	−0.6	0.2	−0.2
Memorandum												
World Exports in Billions of U.S. Dollars												
Goods and Services	7,835	19,273	12,961	14,917	17,366	19,887	15,889	18,904	22,276	22,413	23,487	24,633
Goods	6,320	15,558	10,436	12,061	13,971	16,054	12,489	15,175	18,154	18,255	19,056	19,932
Average Oil Price[4]	9.0	10.0	41.3	20.5	10.7	36.4	−36.3	27.9	31.6	1.0	−2.3	−4.9
In U.S. Dollars a Barrel	23.21	83.58	53.35	64.27	71.13	97.04	61.78	79.03	104.01	105.01	102.60	97.58
Export Unit Value of Manufactures[5]	0.2	2.0	2.8	2.5	5.7	6.3	−6.4	2.4	6.7	−0.5	1.0	0.5

[1]Average of annual percent change for world exports and imports.
[2]As represented, respectively, by the export unit value index for manufactures of the advanced economies and accounting for 83 percent of the advanced economies' trade (export of goods) weights; the average of U.K. Brent, Dubai Fateh, and West Texas Intermediate crude oil prices; and the average of world market prices for nonfuel primary commodities weighted by their 2002–04 shares in world commodity exports.
[3]Georgia, which is not a member of the Commonwealth of Independent States, is included in this group for reasons of geography and similarity in economic structure.
[4]Percent change of average of U.K. Brent, Dubai Fateh, and West Texas Intermediate crude oil prices.
[5]Percent change for manufactures exported by the advanced economies.

Table A10. Summary of Balances on Current Account
(Billions of U.S. dollars)

	2005	2006	2007	2008	2009	2010	2011	2012	Projections 2013	Projections 2014	Projections 2018
Advanced Economies	**−383.2**	**−426.2**	**−317.7**	**−478.8**	**−54.0**	**−9.0**	**−77.3**	**−58.1**	**−50.0**	**−56.5**	**−163.1**
United States	−745.8	−800.6	−710.3	−677.1	−381.9	−442.0	−465.9	−475.0	−473.5	−516.7	−739.1
Euro Area[1,2]	50.3	53.6	46.1	−96.9	30.6	64.5	78.4	221.4	294.9	302.5	361.1
Japan	166.1	170.9	212.1	159.9	146.6	204.0	119.3	59.0	63.5	97.8	102.9
Other Advanced Economies[3]	146.1	149.9	134.3	135.3	150.7	164.4	190.9	136.5	65.1	59.8	112.0
Emerging Market and Developing Economies	**414.5**	**635.8**	**619.1**	**675.8**	**268.9**	**334.9**	**486.8**	**394.4**	**296.3**	**215.8**	**248.9**
Regional Groups											
Central and Eastern Europe	−61.3	−88.9	−136.7	−160.0	−49.6	−82.9	−119.5	−79.3	−92.9	−101.7	−159.8
Commonwealth of Independent States[4]	87.5	96.1	71.2	108.4	42.1	71.9	112.3	85.3	53.8	29.6	−15.0
Developing Asia	142.0	271.4	402.8	426.9	288.1	232.0	178.8	130.4	145.0	188.9	504.5
Latin America and the Caribbean	36.1	47.9	7.3	−38.8	−28.8	−60.7	−75.5	−99.5	−102.3	−126.6	−191.1
Middle East, North Africa, Afghanistan, and Pakistan	212.0	281.6	264.5	341.7	44.7	189.1	408.3	393.1	338.8	281.7	189.9
Sub-Saharan Africa	−1.8	27.8	9.9	−2.4	−27.5	−14.4	−17.6	−35.6	−46.2	−56.1	−79.6
Memorandum											
European Union	7.0	−27.8	−61.7	−167.3	10.8	19.4	61.9	161.7	209.1	219.3	310.1
Analytical Groups											
By Source of Export Earnings											
Fuel	354.6	480.6	430.8	591.6	142.6	332.5	622.0	595.8	498.3	414.1	245.3
Nonfuel	59.9	155.2	188.2	84.2	126.3	2.4	−138.5	−200.7	−202.0	−200.3	−0.9
Of Which, Primary Products	−4.4	6.6	4.5	−19.7	−7.1	−8.4	−19.2	−41.5	−41.2	−45.6	−47.0
By External Financing Source											
Net Debtor Economies	−92.8	−125.5	−238.2	−379.9	−200.4	−293.9	−379.7	−417.5	−440.0	−489.5	−622.9
Of Which, Official Financing	−16.9	−18.3	−21.3	−35.9	−20.3	−13.8	−12.3	−22.8	−18.7	−22.3	−30.5
Net Debtor Economies by Debt-Servicing Experience											
Economies with Arrears and/or Rescheduling during 2007–11	−6.6	−4.4	−14.3	−26.7	−22.0	−32.5	−41.6	−52.4	−50.8	−56.1	−63.7
World[1]	**31.3**	**209.6**	**301.3**	**197.0**	**214.9**	**326.0**	**409.5**	**336.3**	**246.4**	**159.3**	**85.8**

Table A10. Summary of Balances on Current Account (concluded)
(Percent of GDP)

	2005	2006	2007	2008	2009	2010	2011	2012	Projections 2013	Projections 2014	Projections 2018
Advanced Economies	**−1.1**	**−1.2**	**−0.8**	**−1.1**	**−0.1**	**0.0**	**−0.2**	**−0.1**	**−0.1**	**−0.1**	**−0.3**
United States	−5.9	−6.0	−5.1	−4.7	−2.7	−3.0	−3.1	−3.0	−2.9	−3.0	−3.5
Euro Area[1,2]	0.5	0.5	0.4	−0.7	0.2	0.5	0.6	1.8	2.3	2.3	2.5
Japan	3.6	3.9	4.9	3.3	2.9	3.7	2.0	1.0	1.2	1.9	1.7
Other Advanced Economies[3]	2.0	1.9	1.5	1.4	1.8	1.8	1.8	1.3	0.6	0.5	0.8
Emerging Market and Developing Economies	**3.8**	**4.9**	**3.9**	**3.5**	**1.5**	**1.5**	**1.9**	**1.4**	**1.0**	**0.7**	**0.6**
Regional Groups											
Central and Eastern Europe	−5.2	−6.8	−8.4	−8.3	−3.1	−4.7	−6.3	−4.3	−4.7	−4.9	−5.9
Commonwealth of Independent States[4]	8.7	7.4	4.2	5.0	2.6	3.6	4.5	3.2	1.9	0.9	−0.4
Developing Asia	3.6	5.8	6.8	5.8	3.7	2.5	1.6	1.1	1.1	1.3	2.3
Latin America and the Caribbean	1.4	1.5	0.2	−0.9	−0.7	−1.2	−1.3	−1.7	−1.7	−2.0	−2.4
Middle East, North Africa, Afghanistan, and Pakistan	14.2	16.0	12.7	13.2	1.9	7.0	13.0	11.5	9.9	8.2	4.4
Middle East and North Africa	15.5	17.6	14.1	14.7	2.5	7.7	14.0	12.5	10.8	8.9	4.7
Sub-Saharan Africa	−0.3	3.9	1.2	−0.3	−3.1	−1.3	−1.4	−2.8	−3.5	−3.9	−4.2
Memorandum											
European Union	0.1	−0.2	−0.4	−0.9	0.1	0.1	0.4	1.0	1.2	1.2	1.6
Analytical Groups											
By Source of Export Earnings											
Fuel	15.2	16.5	12.0	12.9	3.8	7.3	11.5	10.1	8.2	6.6	3.0
Nonfuel	0.7	1.6	1.5	0.6	0.9	0.0	−0.7	−0.9	−0.9	−0.8	0.0
Of Which, Primary Products	−1.2	1.5	0.9	−3.4	−1.3	−1.2	−2.5	−5.0	−4.6	−4.6	−3.4
By External Financing Source											
Net Debtor Economies	−1.6	−1.9	−3.0	−4.2	−2.4	−2.9	−3.3	−3.6	−3.6	−3.8	−3.6
Of Which, Official Financing	−3.6	−3.5	−3.4	−4.9	−2.8	−1.8	−1.5	−2.7	−2.1	−2.3	−2.4
Net Debtor Economies by Debt-Servicing Experience											
Economies with Arrears and/or Rescheduling during 2007–11	−1.3	−0.8	−2.1	−3.2	−2.7	−3.5	−3.9	−4.6	−4.2	−4.4	−3.9
World[1]	**0.1**	**0.4**	**0.5**	**0.3**	**0.4**	**0.5**	**0.6**	**0.5**	**0.3**	**0.2**	**0.1**
Memorandum											
In Percent of Total World Current Account											
Transactions	0.1	0.7	0.9	0.5	0.7	0.9	0.9	0.8	0.5	0.3	0.1
In Percent of World GDP	0.1	0.4	0.5	0.3	0.4	0.5	0.6	0.5	0.3	0.2	0.1

[1]Reflects errors, omissions, and asymmetries in balance of payments statistics on current account, as well as the exclusion of data for international organizations and a limited number of countries. See "Classification of Countries" in the introduction to this Statistical Appendix.
[2]Calculated as the sum of the balances of individual Euro Area countries.
[3]In this table, Other Advanced Economies means advanced economies excluding the United States, Euro Area countries, and Japan.
[4]Georgia, which is not a member of the Commonwealth of Independent States, is included in this group for reasons of geography and similarity in economic structure.

Table A11. Advanced Economies: Balance on Current Account

(Percent of GDP)

	2005	2006	2007	2008	2009	2010	2011	2012	Projections 2013	2014	2018
Advanced Economies	**−1.1**	**−1.2**	**−0.8**	**−1.1**	**−0.1**	**0.0**	**−0.2**	**−0.1**	**−0.1**	**−0.1**	**−0.3**
United States	−5.9	−6.0	−5.1	−4.7	−2.7	−3.0	−3.1	−3.0	−2.9	−3.0	−3.5
Euro Area[1]	0.5	0.5	0.4	−0.7	0.2	0.5	0.6	1.8	2.3	2.3	2.5
Germany	5.1	6.3	7.4	6.2	6.0	6.2	6.2	7.0	6.1	5.7	4.7
France	−0.5	−0.6	−1.0	−1.7	−1.3	−1.6	−1.9	−2.4	−1.3	−1.4	0.0
Italy	−0.9	−1.5	−1.3	−2.9	−2.0	−3.5	−3.1	−0.5	0.3	0.3	0.1
Spain	−7.4	−9.0	−10.0	−9.6	−4.8	−4.5	−3.7	−1.1	1.1	2.2	3.6
Netherlands	7.4	9.3	6.7	4.3	5.2	7.7	9.7	8.3	8.7	9.0	8.6
Belgium	2.0	1.9	1.9	−1.3	−1.4	1.9	−1.4	−0.5	−0.1	0.2	1.1
Austria	2.2	2.8	3.5	4.9	2.7	3.4	0.6	2.0	2.2	2.3	2.3
Greece	−7.6	−11.4	−14.6	−14.9	−11.2	−10.1	−9.9	−2.9	−0.3	0.4	1.4
Portugal	−10.3	−10.7	−10.1	−12.6	−10.9	−10.6	−7.0	−1.5	0.1	−0.1	1.1
Finland	3.4	4.2	4.3	2.6	1.8	1.5	−1.6	−1.7	−1.7	−1.8	−1.8
Ireland	−3.5	−3.5	−5.4	−5.7	−2.3	1.1	1.1	4.9	3.4	3.9	4.0
Slovak Republic	−8.5	−7.8	−5.3	−6.6	−2.6	−3.7	−2.1	2.3	2.2	2.7	3.3
Slovenia	−1.7	−2.5	−4.8	−6.2	−0.7	−0.6	0.0	2.3	2.7	2.5	1.3
Luxembourg	11.5	10.4	10.1	5.4	7.2	8.2	7.1	6.0	6.6	6.8	5.8
Estonia	−10.0	−15.3	−15.9	−9.2	3.4	2.9	2.1	−1.2	0.0	0.1	1.4
Cyprus[2]	−5.9	−7.0	−11.8	−15.6	−10.7	−9.8	−4.7	−4.9	...	...	...
Malta	−8.5	−9.7	−4.0	−4.9	−7.8	−4.6	−0.5	0.3	0.5	0.8	0.6
Japan	3.6	3.9	4.9	3.3	2.9	3.7	2.0	1.0	1.2	1.9	1.7
United Kingdom	−2.1	−2.9	−2.3	−1.0	−1.3	−2.5	−1.3	−3.5	−4.4	−4.3	−2.6
Canada	1.9	1.4	0.8	0.1	−3.0	−3.6	−3.0	−3.7	−3.5	−3.4	−2.5
Korea	2.2	1.5	2.1	0.3	3.9	2.9	2.3	3.7	2.7	2.4	1.1
Australia	−5.7	−5.3	−6.2	−4.5	−4.2	−3.0	−2.3	−3.7	−5.5	−6.0	−5.6
Taiwan Province of China	4.8	7.0	8.9	6.9	11.4	9.3	8.9	10.5	10.3	9.8	8.7
Sweden	6.8	8.3	9.1	9.0	6.7	6.9	7.0	7.1	6.0	6.8	7.8
Hong Kong SAR	11.1	11.9	12.1	13.4	8.4	5.4	5.2	2.3	2.0	2.5	5.0
Switzerland	13.6	14.4	8.6	2.1	10.5	14.3	8.4	13.4	12.6	12.3	11.6
Singapore	21.4	24.8	26.1	15.1	17.7	26.8	24.6	18.6	16.9	17.2	14.4
Czech Republic	−0.9	−2.1	−4.4	−2.1	−2.5	−3.8	−2.9	−2.7	−2.1	−1.8	−1.8
Norway	16.5	16.4	12.5	16.0	11.7	11.9	12.8	14.2	11.7	10.9	8.2
Israel	3.1	4.8	2.7	1.1	3.8	3.7	1.4	−0.1	1.7	2.5	2.3
Denmark	4.3	3.0	1.4	2.9	3.4	5.9	5.6	5.3	4.7	4.7	4.8
New Zealand	−7.9	−8.3	−8.1	−8.7	−2.5	−3.2	−4.1	−5.0	−5.8	−6.0	−7.1
Iceland	−16.1	−25.6	−15.7	−28.4	−11.6	−8.4	−5.6	−4.9	−2.8	−1.7	−0.1
San Marino	...	...	...	...	...	...	...	...	...	...	...
Memorandum											
Major Advanced Economies	−1.8	−1.9	−1.2	−1.3	−0.6	−0.8	−1.0	−1.2	−1.1	−1.2	−1.4
Euro Area[3]	0.1	−0.1	0.1	−1.5	−0.1	0.0	0.1	1.2	2.3	2.3	2.5

[1]Calculated as the sum of the balances of individual Euro Area countries.
[2]Projections for Cyprus are excluded due to the ongoing crisis.
[3]Corrected for reporting discrepancies in intra-area transactions.

Table A12. Emerging Market and Developing Economies: Balance on Current Account

(Percent of GDP)

	2005	2006	2007	2008	2009	2010	2011	2012	Projections 2013	2014	2018
Central and Eastern Europe	**−5.2**	**−6.8**	**−8.4**	**−8.3**	**−3.1**	**−4.7**	**−6.3**	**−4.3**	**−4.7**	**−4.9**	**−5.9**
Albania	−6.1	−5.6	−10.4	−15.2	−14.0	−11.4	−12.0	−10.1	−9.4	−9.0	−5.5
Bosnia and Herzegovina	−17.1	−7.9	−9.1	−14.2	−6.6	−5.6	−9.5	−9.7	−8.7	−7.9	−5.0
Bulgaria	−11.6	−17.6	−25.2	−23.0	−8.9	−1.5	0.3	−0.7	−1.9	−2.1	−3.4
Croatia	−5.3	−6.7	−7.3	−9.0	−5.1	−1.1	−1.0	−0.1	0.0	−0.5	−2.5
Hungary	−7.5	−7.4	−7.3	−7.4	−0.2	1.1	0.9	1.7	2.1	1.8	−1.8
Kosovo	−7.4	−6.7	−8.3	−15.3	−15.4	−17.4	−20.4	−20.3	−20.0	−17.6	−14.8
Latvia	−12.6	−22.6	−22.4	−13.2	8.7	2.9	−2.1	−1.7	−1.8	−1.9	−2.0
Lithuania	−7.0	−10.6	−14.5	−13.3	3.9	0.0	−3.7	−0.9	−1.3	−1.7	−1.8
FYR Macedonia	−2.5	−0.4	−7.1	−12.8	−6.8	−2.1	−3.0	−3.9	−4.7	−6.2	−4.9
Montenegro	−16.6	−31.3	−39.5	−49.8	−27.9	−22.9	−17.7	−17.6	−16.8	−16.9	−16.2
Poland	−2.4	−3.8	−6.2	−6.6	−4.0	−5.1	−4.9	−3.6	−3.6	−3.5	−3.6
Romania	−8.6	−10.4	−13.4	−11.6	−4.2	−4.4	−4.5	−3.8	−4.2	−4.5	−4.9
Serbia	−8.8	−10.1	−17.8	−21.7	−6.6	−6.8	−9.2	−10.9	−8.7	−8.6	−9.8
Turkey	−4.6	−6.1	−5.9	−5.7	−2.2	−6.2	−9.7	−5.9	−6.8	−7.3	−8.4
Commonwealth of Independent States[1]	**8.7**	**7.4**	**4.2**	**5.0**	**2.6**	**3.6**	**4.5**	**3.2**	**1.9**	**0.9**	**−0.4**
Russia	11.1	9.5	5.9	6.2	4.1	4.6	5.2	4.0	2.5	1.6	0.1
Excluding Russia	1.3	0.6	−1.4	0.9	−1.8	0.4	2.3	0.6	−0.4	−1.2	−1.7
Armenia	−1.0	−1.8	−6.4	−11.8	−15.8	−14.8	−10.9	−10.6	−9.6	−8.2	−6.4
Azerbaijan	1.3	17.6	27.3	35.5	23.0	28.0	26.5	20.3	10.6	6.0	−0.1
Belarus	1.4	−3.9	−6.7	−8.2	−12.6	−15.0	−9.7	−2.9	−5.2	−5.5	−6.5
Georgia	−11.1	−15.2	−19.8	−22.0	−10.5	−10.2	−12.8	−12.0	−10.0	−8.4	−7.6
Kazakhstan	−1.8	−2.5	−8.1	4.7	−3.6	1.2	7.4	4.6	4.0	2.2	2.0
Kyrgyz Republic	2.8	−3.1	−6.2	−15.5	−2.5	−6.4	−6.0	−12.7	−7.6	−6.1	−3.1
Moldova	−7.6	−11.3	−15.2	−16.1	−8.2	−7.7	−11.3	−9.4	−10.0	−9.7	−8.3
Tajikistan	−1.6	−2.8	−8.6	−7.6	−5.9	−1.2	−4.7	−1.9	−2.2	−2.4	−2.2
Turkmenistan	5.1	15.7	15.5	16.5	−14.7	−10.6	2.0	1.7	2.5	2.8	4.1
Ukraine	2.9	−1.5	−3.7	−7.1	−1.5	−2.2	−6.3	−8.2	−7.9	−7.8	−7.5
Uzbekistan	7.7	9.2	7.3	8.7	2.2	6.2	5.8	2.7	3.5	4.2	2.1
Developing Asia	**3.6**	**5.8**	**6.8**	**5.8**	**3.7**	**2.5**	**1.6**	**1.1**	**1.1**	**1.3**	**2.3**
Bangladesh	0.0	1.2	0.8	1.4	2.8	0.5	−1.2	0.4	0.3	−0.5	−0.6
Bhutan	−29.5	−4.1	13.3	−2.1	−1.9	−9.5	−21.9	−18.7	−20.1	−18.6	−19.2
Brunei Darussalam	47.3	50.1	47.8	48.9	40.2	45.5	32.4	48.5	45.1	44.5	44.2
Cambodia	−3.8	−0.6	−1.9	−5.7	−4.5	−3.9	−8.1	−10.0	−9.9	−7.7	−5.9
China	5.9	8.5	10.1	9.3	4.9	4.0	2.8	2.6	2.6	2.9	4.3
Fiji	−7.4	−14.9	−10.1	−15.0	−4.2	−7.5	−7.8	−6.8	−22.5	−8.1	−8.5
India	−1.3	−1.0	−0.7	−2.4	−2.1	−3.2	−3.4	−5.1	−4.9	−4.6	−3.4
Indonesia	0.6	2.7	1.6	0.1	2.0	0.7	0.2	−2.8	−3.3	−3.3	−3.3
Kiribati	−16.3	−3.1	5.5	5.0	−19.6	−14.7	−26.2	−6.7	−21.2	−22.0	−26.3
Lao P.D.R.	−18.1	−9.9	−15.7	−18.5	−21.0	−18.3	−21.4	−21.8	−23.4	−23.3	−16.8
Malaysia	14.4	16.1	15.4	17.1	15.5	11.1	11.0	6.4	6.0	5.7	4.5
Maldives	−27.5	−23.2	−14.7	−32.4	−11.1	−9.2	−21.4	−26.5	−27.8	−27.0	−34.8
Marshall Islands	−1.4	−3.5	−4.2	−1.8	−16.9	−28.1	−6.2	−6.3	−2.5	−1.3	−5.1
Micronesia	−6.7	−11.6	−7.3	−16.7	−18.5	−16.6	−18.9	−15.0	−14.0	−14.8	−13.7
Mongolia	1.2	6.5	6.3	−12.9	−9.0	−14.9	−31.7	−31.3	−26.3	−21.2	−7.0
Myanmar	3.7	7.1	−0.5	−3.3	−2.8	−1.3	−2.6	−4.2	−4.5	−5.1	−5.8
Nepal	2.0	2.1	−0.1	2.7	4.2	−2.4	−1.0	4.7	−0.1	−1.4	−2.3
Papua New Guinea	14.0	−1.7	4.0	8.4	−16.4	−26.2	−2.1	−17.7	−10.7	−5.1	6.5
Philippines	1.9	4.4	4.8	2.1	5.6	4.5	3.2	2.9	2.4	2.0	1.2
Samoa	−9.6	−10.2	−15.5	−6.4	−6.2	−7.6	−4.5	−10.0	−13.8	−16.3	−11.8
Solomon Islands	−6.7	−9.1	−15.7	−20.5	−21.4	−30.8	−6.0	−5.8	−10.6	−8.7	−9.9
Sri Lanka	−2.5	−5.3	−4.3	−9.5	−0.5	−2.2	−7.8	−6.0	−5.3	−5.1	−4.9
Thailand	−4.3	1.1	6.3	0.8	8.3	3.1	1.7	0.7	1.0	1.1	−0.1
Timor-Leste	31.0	41.7	60.2	61.5	52.5	48.6	57.8	45.9	38.3	31.1	12.0
Tonga	−5.0	−5.5	−5.5	−8.1	−7.8	−3.9	−4.0	−4.2	−3.1	−3.6	−3.3
Tuvalu	24.7	27.2	14.2	−13.2	27.8	−3.8	−29.2	−8.5	−3.3	1.9	4.4
Vanuatu	−8.7	−6.2	−6.4	−9.3	−3.1	−4.9	−6.3	−6.6	−6.3	−6.3	−6.2
Vietnam	−1.1	−0.3	−9.8	−11.9	−6.6	−4.1	0.2	7.4	7.9	6.3	−1.3

Table A12. Emerging Market and Developing Economies: Balance on Current Account *(continued)*

(Percent of GDP)

| | 2005 | 2006 | 2007 | 2008 | 2009 | 2010 | 2011 | 2012 | Projections | | |
									2013	2014	2018
Latin America and the Caribbean	**1.4**	**1.5**	**0.2**	**−0.9**	**−0.7**	**−1.2**	**−1.3**	**−1.7**	**−1.7**	**−2.0**	**−2.4**
Antigua and Barbuda	−17.2	−26.3	−29.9	−25.9	−19.4	−14.7	−10.8	−12.8	−13.1	−14.0	−14.7
Argentina[2]	2.6	3.4	2.6	1.8	2.5	0.6	−0.4	0.1	−0.1	−0.5	−1.6
The Bahamas	−8.4	−17.7	−11.5	−10.6	−10.5	−10.5	−14.0	−14.1	−13.7	−12.8	−9.8
Barbados	−7.5	−4.8	−2.7	−9.6	−5.6	−8.2	−8.7	−5.7	−6.1	−5.8	−4.8
Belize	−13.6	−2.1	−4.1	−10.6	−5.7	−2.8	−1.1	−2.6	−3.2	−3.6	−5.5
Bolivia	5.9	11.2	11.4	11.9	4.3	4.9	2.2	7.5	4.8	3.5	2.0
Brazil	1.6	1.3	0.1	−1.7	−1.5	−2.2	−2.1	−2.3	−2.4	−3.2	−3.4
Chile	1.5	4.6	4.1	−3.2	2.0	1.5	−1.3	−3.5	−4.0	−3.6	−2.8
Colombia	−1.3	−1.9	−2.8	−2.9	−2.1	−3.1	−3.0	−3.4	−3.4	−2.9	−2.4
Costa Rica	−4.9	−4.5	−6.3	−9.3	−2.0	−3.5	−5.3	−5.3	−5.5	−5.4	−6.0
Dominica	−21.4	−13.0	−21.1	−27.5	−21.2	−16.2	−12.8	−13.5	−13.8	−13.9	−16.7
Dominican Republic	−1.6	−3.6	−5.3	−9.9	−5.0	−8.4	−7.9	−7.2	−4.6	−3.3	−3.7
Ecuador	1.1	3.7	3.7	2.9	0.4	−2.6	−0.2	−0.5	−1.3	−1.5	−2.7
El Salvador	−3.6	−4.1	−6.1	−7.1	−1.5	−2.7	−4.6	−5.1	−4.9	−4.5	−4.3
Grenada	−24.6	−29.6	−27.7	−25.3	−23.6	−24.1	−23.3	−23.0	−23.4	−23.4	−22.9
Guatemala	−4.6	−5.0	−5.2	−4.3	0.0	−1.5	−3.6	−3.5	−3.7	−3.6	−3.5
Guyana	−9.5	−13.7	−9.6	−13.4	−9.0	−9.6	−13.4	−13.2	−14.1	−20.0	−5.6
Haiti	0.7	−1.5	−1.5	−4.4	−3.5	−12.5	−4.6	−4.0	−5.6	−5.3	−4.7
Honduras	−3.0	−3.7	−9.1	−15.4	−4.0	−5.3	−8.5	−9.9	−11.2	−8.7	−8.0
Jamaica	−9.2	−9.9	−16.6	−17.9	−10.9	−8.7	−12.6	−11.9	−10.3	−8.7	−4.8
Mexico	−0.7	−0.6	−1.3	−1.7	−0.7	−0.2	−0.8	−0.8	−1.0	−1.0	−1.2
Nicaragua	−11.0	−10.4	−13.5	−18.4	−9.3	−11.0	−13.7	−15.8	−13.7	−13.3	−9.9
Panama	−4.9	−3.1	−7.9	−10.9	−0.7	−10.2	−12.2	−9.0	−8.9	−8.7	−5.9
Paraguay	0.2	1.2	1.3	−1.7	0.4	−3.1	−1.1	−2.0	−2.4	−2.9	−3.3
Peru	1.5	3.2	1.4	−4.2	−0.6	−2.5	−1.9	−3.6	−3.5	−3.4	−2.8
St. Kitts and Nevis	−14.9	−14.1	−18.2	−27.6	−27.4	−22.4	−15.6	−13.5	−15.9	−17.2	−15.0
St. Lucia	−14.3	−30.6	−30.6	−29.2	−11.7	−16.9	−20.1	−19.1	−18.2	−17.2	−15.7
St. Vincent and the Grenadines	−18.6	−19.5	−28.0	−33.1	−29.3	−30.6	−28.8	−27.9	−26.8	−25.2	−17.5
Suriname	−11.7	4.5	8.1	6.6	−0.6	6.4	5.8	6.4	3.9	1.8	7.0
Trinidad and Tobago	22.5	39.6	23.9	30.5	8.5	20.3	11.1	12.1	11.0	11.2	10.3
Uruguay	0.2	−2.0	−0.9	−5.7	−1.3	−1.9	−2.8	−3.4	−2.9	−2.5	−2.7
Venezuela	17.5	14.4	6.9	10.2	0.7	2.2	7.7	2.9	6.2	7.7	3.3
Middle East, North Africa, Afghanistan, and Pakistan	**14.2**	**16.0**	**12.7**	**13.2**	**1.9**	**7.0**	**13.0**	**11.5**	**9.9**	**8.2**	**4.4**
Afghanistan	3.1	−1.1	5.8	5.1	1.6	2.8	2.2	4.0	1.6	0.3	−0.9
Algeria	20.5	24.7	22.6	20.1	0.3	7.5	10.0	5.9	6.1	4.5	3.2
Bahrain	11.0	13.8	15.7	10.2	2.9	3.6	12.6	15.4	13.6	11.6	6.7
Djibouti	−3.2	−11.5	−21.4	−24.3	−9.3	−5.8	−12.6	−13.4	−11.0	−9.3	−8.3
Egypt	3.2	1.6	2.1	0.5	−2.3	−2.0	−2.6	−3.1	−2.1	−1.6	−0.8
Iran	7.6	8.5	10.6	6.5	2.6	6.5	12.0	4.9	3.6	1.9	−1.8
Iraq	3.9	12.9	7.7	12.8	−8.3	3.0	12.5	7.0	3.6	2.9	4.3
Jordan	−18.0	−11.5	−16.8	−9.3	−3.3	−5.3	−12.0	−18.1	−10.0	−9.1	−4.7
Kuwait	37.2	44.6	36.8	40.9	26.7	31.9	44.0	45.0	40.8	37.6	30.1
Lebanon	−13.6	−5.3	−6.8	−9.3	−9.8	−9.6	−12.5	−16.1	−16.1	−14.6	−10.9
Libya	36.8	51.1	44.1	42.5	14.9	19.5	9.1	35.9	25.8	17.7	−0.4
Mauritania	−47.2	−1.3	−17.2	−14.8	−10.7	−8.7	−7.3	−25.8	−20.5	−3.2	−0.5
Morocco	1.8	2.2	−0.1	−5.2	−5.4	−4.1	−8.1	−9.6	−7.0	−5.8	−4.7
Oman	16.8	15.4	5.9	8.3	−1.2	8.7	17.7	15.6	9.9	4.7	−9.0
Pakistan	−1.4	−3.9	−4.8	−8.4	−5.7	−2.2	0.1	−2.0	−0.7	−0.8	−0.5
Qatar	29.9	25.1	25.3	28.7	10.2	26.8	30.4	29.5	29.3	23.7	6.2
Saudi Arabia	27.4	26.3	22.4	25.5	4.9	12.7	23.7	24.4	19.2	16.1	11.4
Sudan[3]	−10.0	−8.8	−5.9	−1.5	−9.6	−2.1	−0.4	−11.2	−6.9	−5.9	−4.5
Syria[4]	−2.2	1.4	−0.2	−1.3	−2.9	−2.9	...	...	...	...	...
Tunisia	−0.9	−1.8	−2.4	−3.8	−2.8	−4.8	−7.4	−8.0	−7.3	−6.6	−3.7
United Arab Emirates	12.4	16.3	6.9	7.9	3.5	3.2	9.7	8.2	8.4	7.9	7.3
Yemen	3.8	1.1	−7.0	−4.6	−10.2	−3.7	−4.0	−0.4	−4.3	−4.1	−4.6

Table A12. Emerging Market and Developing Economies: Balance on Current Account *(concluded)*

(Percent of GDP)

	2005	2006	2007	2008	2009	2010	2011	2012	Projections 2013	Projections 2014	Projections 2018
Sub-Saharan Africa	**−0.3**	**3.9**	**1.2**	**−0.3**	**−3.1**	**−1.3**	**−1.4**	**−2.8**	**−3.5**	**−3.9**	**−4.2**
Angola	18.2	25.6	19.9	10.3	−9.9	8.1	12.6	9.6	3.5	1.3	−2.8
Benin	−6.3	−5.3	−10.2	−8.1	−8.9	−7.3	−10.0	−9.8	−7.5	−7.1	−6.4
Botswana	15.2	17.2	15.0	6.9	−5.2	1.0	2.2	4.9	3.9	3.3	5.1
Burkina Faso	−11.6	−9.5	−8.3	−11.5	−4.7	−2.3	−1.1	−4.7	−3.7	−3.3	−1.6
Burundi	−4.9	−21.5	−5.4	−1.0	1.8	−12.2	−13.7	−15.6	−16.3	−16.0	−11.2
Cameroon	−3.4	1.6	1.4	−1.2	−3.3	−3.0	−3.0	−4.4	−3.5	−3.4	−4.6
Cape Verde	−3.5	−5.4	−14.7	−15.7	−15.6	−12.5	−16.0	−11.1	−13.2	−11.4	−4.3
Central African Republic	−6.6	−3.0	−6.2	−10.0	−9.2	−10.2	−7.6	−6.2	−5.4	−5.1	−3.0
Chad	1.2	6.0	11.6	8.9	−4.1	−5.0	−1.0	−2.1	−4.2	−1.8	0.1
Comoros	−7.4	−6.0	−5.7	−12.1	−7.8	−5.7	−9.0	−5.4	−6.7	−7.4	−5.7
Democratic Republic of the Congo	−13.3	−2.7	−1.1	−17.5	−10.5	−8.1	−11.6	−12.4	−12.0	−13.3	−8.5
Republic of Congo	3.7	3.6	−6.5	2.3	−7.4	5.1	0.7	3.6	2.8	−0.1	2.3
Côte d'Ivoire	0.2	2.8	−0.2	2.3	7.6	2.5	12.9	−1.8	−2.7	−3.3	−4.2
Equatorial Guinea	−7.7	−1.1	−3.0	−1.2	−17.8	−24.0	−10.8	−14.7	−11.2	−11.9	−13.3
Eritrea	0.3	−3.6	−6.1	−5.5	−7.6	−5.6	0.6	2.3	2.0	1.7	−4.6
Ethiopia	−6.3	−9.1	−4.5	−5.6	−5.0	−4.0	0.6	−5.8	−7.5	−6.5	−5.8
Gabon	22.7	15.6	14.9	23.3	7.5	8.9	14.2	12.6	10.5	7.1	−0.8
The Gambia	−10.3	−6.9	−8.3	−12.3	−12.3	−16.0	−15.3	−17.0	−15.8	−14.2	−12.6
Ghana	−7.0	−8.2	−8.7	−11.9	−5.4	−8.6	−9.2	−12.6	−11.6	−10.1	−7.9
Guinea	−1.0	−4.6	−11.6	−10.6	−8.6	−11.5	−20.5	−34.1	−25.2	−46.9	−4.6
Guinea-Bissau	−2.1	−5.6	−3.4	−4.9	−6.7	−8.6	−1.1	−6.1	−5.7	−4.9	−3.0
Kenya	−1.5	−2.3	−4.0	−6.6	−5.8	−6.5	−9.7	−9.1	−7.4	−8.1	−5.4
Lesotho	1.4	11.5	8.2	10.0	0.2	−11.9	−22.0	−14.1	−12.7	−11.2	0.0
Liberia	−30.5	−11.4	−22.4	−43.3	−28.8	−32.8	−34.1	−36.7	−51.3	−57.0	−26.7
Madagascar	−11.6	−9.9	−12.7	−20.6	−21.1	−9.7	−6.9	−7.7	−5.2	−3.5	3.8
Malawi	−11.9	−11.3	1.0	−9.7	−4.8	−1.3	−5.9	−3.7	−1.6	−1.8	−3.8
Mali	−8.5	−4.1	−6.9	−12.2	−7.3	−12.6	−6.1	−3.4	−6.9	−9.1	−7.6
Mauritius	−5.0	−9.1	−5.4	−10.1	−7.4	−10.3	−12.6	−10.0	−9.8	−9.1	−7.3
Mozambique	−17.2	−8.6	−10.9	−12.9	−12.2	−17.4	−25.8	−26.1	−25.4	−40.6	−30.8
Namibia	4.7	13.8	9.1	2.8	−0.4	0.3	−1.7	−1.6	−3.7	−3.3	−0.5
Niger	−8.9	−8.6	−8.3	−13.0	−24.7	−19.9	−24.7	−17.7	−19.0	−20.0	−10.2
Nigeria	8.9	25.3	16.8	14.1	8.3	5.9	3.6	6.6	5.5	4.8	−0.5
Rwanda	1.0	−4.3	−2.2	−4.9	−7.3	−5.9	−7.3	−10.9	−10.2	−9.0	−6.6
São Tomé and Príncipe	−21.4	−32.3	−29.7	−34.9	−23.6	−22.5	−27.4	−26.6	−24.7	−20.8	13.8
Senegal	−8.9	−9.2	−11.6	−14.1	−6.7	−4.4	−7.9	−9.8	−8.5	−7.8	−6.4
Seychelles	−22.7	−16.1	−15.4	−20.1	−9.7	−19.9	−22.5	−22.0	−18.1	−17.2	−10.6
Sierra Leone	−5.3	−4.3	−4.3	−9.0	−6.4	−19.3	−52.9	−20.8	−9.7	−7.0	−5.7
South Africa	−3.5	−5.3	−7.0	−7.2	−4.0	−2.8	−3.4	−6.3	−6.4	−6.5	−6.0
South Sudan	. . .	. . .	. . .	. . .	. . .	. . .	18.3	−6.0	0.2	11.0	16.4
Swaziland	−4.1	−7.4	−2.2	−8.2	−14.0	−10.5	−8.6	0.3	−1.2	−5.4	−6.8
Tanzania	−6.6	−9.6	−11.0	−10.2	−9.8	−9.3	−13.6	−15.8	−14.8	−13.3	−10.3
Togo	−9.9	−8.4	−8.7	−6.8	−6.6	−6.7	−7.0	−7.9	−6.9	−5.7	−4.1
Uganda	−1.3	−3.1	−2.9	−7.7	−9.4	−10.2	−11.5	−10.9	−12.9	−14.8	−12.1
Zambia	−8.5	−0.4	−6.5	−7.2	4.2	7.1	1.5	−3.5	−2.3	−0.4	−1.5
Zimbabwe[5]	−10.2	−8.3	−7.0	−21.1	−22.3	−26.1	−36.6	−24.1	−23.0	−19.4	−8.9

[1]Georgia, which is not a member of the Commonwealth of Independent States, is included in this group for reasons of geography and similarity in economic structure.
[2]Calculations are based on Argentina's official GDP data. See footnote to Table A4.
[3]Data for 2011 exclude South Sudan after July 9. Data for 2012 and onward pertain to the current Sudan.
[4]Data for Syria are excluded for 2011 onward due to the uncertain political situation.
[5]The Zimbabwe dollar ceased circulating in early 2009. Data are based on IMF staff estimates of price and exchange rate developments in U.S. dollars. IMF staff estimates of U.S. dollar values may differ from authorities' estimates.

Table A13. Emerging Market and Developing Economies: Net Financial Flows[1]

(Billions of U.S. dollars)

	Average 2002–04	2005	2006	2007	2008	2009	2010	2011	2012	Projections 2013	Projections 2014
Emerging Market and Developing Economies											
Private Financial Flows, Net	168.8	312.2	308.6	691.0	278.8	320.9	600.0	495.3	144.9	336.3	413.2
Private Direct Investment, Net	167.7	277.3	301.1	439.3	479.8	334.5	400.9	473.2	446.3	477.4	506.5
Private Portfolio Flows, Net	20.3	36.7	−30.7	106.7	−70.2	90.4	224.5	96.7	164.9	142.3	148.3
Other Private Financial Flows, Net	−19.1	−1.8	38.2	144.9	−130.8	−104.0	−25.5	−74.5	−466.4	−283.4	−241.6
Official Financial Flows, Net[2]	−41.3	−86.3	−181.5	−79.8	−97.9	139.2	68.2	−59.5	−41.7	−48.8	−15.9
Change in Reserves[3]	−281.1	−591.7	−758.4	−1,219.9	−734.5	−520.6	−843.1	−747.7	−402.3	−634.6	−637.1
Memorandum											
Current Account[4]	144.5	414.5	635.8	619.1	675.8	268.9	334.9	486.8	394.4	296.3	215.8
Central and Eastern Europe											
Private Financial Flows, Net	35.0	103.6	116.0	183.8	157.1	30.9	83.1	93.9	66.8	62.2	64.6
Private Direct Investment, Net	19.0	37.3	64.0	74.7	67.5	30.7	24.7	39.4	21.5	29.8	32.4
Private Portfolio Flows, Net	7.0	20.8	0.8	−4.1	−10.4	8.6	26.9	33.8	45.0	35.7	31.1
Other Private Financial Flows, Net	9.0	45.5	51.2	113.2	99.9	−8.5	31.5	20.7	0.3	−3.2	1.2
Official Flows, Net[2]	9.9	1.4	5.2	−6.7	20.1	49.5	35.3	22.4	17.0	22.4	27.4
Change in Reserves[3]	−11.0	−43.6	−30.7	−37.4	−7.0	−33.8	−37.1	−12.5	−30.6	−9.5	−8.3
Commonwealth of Independent States[5]											
Private Financial Flows, Net	8.7	29.3	51.5	130.2	−98.0	−63.4	−25.4	−64.9	−57.9	−56.7	−36.0
Private Direct Investment, Net	7.8	11.4	21.1	27.9	49.8	15.7	9.7	14.1	15.7	20.0	28.8
Private Portfolio Flows, Net	2.6	3.9	4.9	19.4	−31.7	−9.2	8.5	−28.6	−14.1	−2.6	5.2
Other Private Financial Flows, Net	−1.7	14.0	25.6	82.8	−116.2	−69.9	−43.6	−50.4	−59.5	−74.1	−70.0
Official Flows, Net[2]	−5.4	−18.6	−25.4	−6.5	−19.4	42.4	1.4	−16.9	−3.8	20.6	16.1
Change in Reserves[3]	−34.2	−77.0	−127.5	−167.7	26.7	−7.2	−52.1	−23.8	−24.3	−16.1	−8.0
Developing Asia											
Private Financial Flows, Net	96.2	123.0	83.4	197.1	68.2	206.2	409.0	311.9	14.4	193.3	210.7
Private Direct Investment, Net	64.6	114.9	125.5	166.4	158.0	117.4	223.4	222.3	223.5	223.0	216.2
Private Portfolio Flows, Net	16.6	16.3	−46.4	63.0	1.9	46.6	102.2	43.3	73.0	76.0	80.3
Other Private Financial Flows, Net	15.0	−8.2	4.3	−32.3	−91.7	42.1	83.5	46.4	−282.0	−105.8	−85.8
Official Flows, Net[2]	−13.3	−2.7	6.5	1.9	−7.7	19.2	17.0	10.0	10.0	9.1	12.9
Change in Reserves[3]	−168.4	−281.0	−362.3	−617.1	−505.0	−460.0	−567.7	−443.2	−126.3	−341.8	−408.1
Latin America and the Caribbean											
Private Financial Flows, Net	14.4	37.8	34.0	85.8	84.9	61.9	128.9	200.0	136.3	126.0	134.2
Private Direct Investment, Net	47.4	57.5	33.3	93.9	100.3	70.7	78.2	133.2	121.4	135.1	148.0
Private Portfolio Flows, Net	−12.4	−0.7	7.3	33.1	−4.9	31.8	58.1	49.3	26.9	3.9	6.3
Other Private Financial Flows, Net	−20.6	−19.0	−6.6	−41.1	−10.6	−40.5	−7.4	17.5	−12.0	−13.0	−20.1
Official Flows, Net[2]	9.5	−34.0	−49.6	3.3	−1.5	46.2	47.7	23.5	55.1	40.7	24.5
Change in Reserves[3]	−18.1	−36.2	−53.4	−134.9	−52.6	−50.4	−88.7	−111.6	−59.5	−60.7	−33.4
Middle East, North Africa, Afghanistan, and Pakistan											
Private Financial Flows, Net	10.0	0.9	15.6	77.2	44.4	71.9	19.0	−43.8	−35.2	−10.1	−0.4
Private Direct Investment, Net	17.3	37.7	48.6	54.2	65.1	68.0	41.6	27.2	31.4	31.9	39.7
Private Portfolio Flows, Net	7.5	−3.5	−3.5	−5.0	2.7	15.9	29.7	8.1	27.0	26.2	21.0
Other Private Financial Flows, Net	−14.8	−33.3	−29.5	28.0	−23.4	−12.0	−52.3	−79.1	−93.6	−68.3	−61.0
Official Flows, Net[2]	−43.1	−28.8	−85.4	−76.7	−100.8	−38.0	−65.4	−128.5	−148.3	−177.9	−129.0
Change in Reserves[3]	−43.7	−131.2	−153.6	−234.3	−181.7	22.6	−95.9	−135.3	−141.3	−189.3	−156.5
Sub-Saharan Africa											
Private Financial Flows, Net	4.5	17.7	8.1	16.8	22.3	13.5	−14.7	−1.7	20.4	21.7	40.0
Private Direct Investment, Net	11.6	18.5	8.6	22.2	39.0	32.0	23.2	37.0	32.8	37.6	41.5
Private Portfolio Flows, Net	−1.0	0.0	6.2	0.3	−27.9	−3.3	−0.9	−9.1	7.1	3.1	4.4
Other Private Financial Flows, Net	−6.1	−0.8	−6.7	−5.7	11.2	−15.2	−37.1	−29.5	−19.6	−19.1	−5.9
Official Flows, Net[2]	1.1	−3.6	−32.7	5.0	11.3	20.0	32.2	30.0	28.4	36.3	32.2
Change in Reserves[3]	−5.7	−22.8	−30.8	−28.5	−15.0	8.3	−1.7	−21.4	−20.3	−17.2	−22.6
Memorandum											
Fuel Exporting Countries											
Private Financial Flows, Net	7.9	0.0	26.3	123.9	−138.0	−54.6	−83.3	−167.4	−159.7	−122.7	−97.8
Other Countries											
Private Financial Flows, Net	160.9	312.2	282.3	567.1	416.8	375.5	683.3	662.8	304.9	459.6	511.9

[1]Net financial flows comprise net direct investment, net portfolio investment, other net official and private financial flows, and changes in reserves.
[2]Excludes grants and includes transactions in external assets and liabilities of official agencies.
[3]A minus sign indicates an increase.
[4]The sum of the current account balance, net private financial flows, net official flows, and the change in reserves equals, with the opposite sign, the sum of the capital account and errors and omissions.
[5]Georgia, which is not a member of the Commonwealth of Independent States, is included in this group for reasons of geography and similarity in economic structure.

Table A14. Emerging Market and Developing Economies: Private Financial Flows[1]

(Billions of U.S. dollars)

	Average 2002–04	2005	2006	2007	2008	2009	2010	2011	2012	Projections 2013	Projections 2014
Emerging Market and Developing Economies											
Private Financial Flows, Net	168.8	312.2	308.6	691.0	278.8	320.9	600.0	495.3	144.9	336.3	413.2
Assets	−161.5	−345.2	−632.9	−830.4	−610.1	−301.2	−643.2	−703.3	−734.1	−775.4	−719.7
Liabilities	330.1	650.6	938.2	1,514.9	889.8	620.8	1,240.9	1,196.3	876.7	1,107.2	1,127.3
Central and Eastern Europe											
Private Financial Flows, Net	35.0	103.6	116.0	183.8	157.1	30.9	83.1	93.9	66.8	62.2	64.6
Assets	−14.4	−17.8	−57.0	−44.5	−29.3	−9.9	−8.2	9.7	0.2	−2.6	−11.0
Liabilities	49.4	121.3	172.6	227.2	185.3	41.4	91.4	84.3	66.7	65.1	75.9
Commonwealth of Independent States[2]											
Private Financial Flows, Net	8.7	29.3	51.5	130.2	−98.0	−63.4	−25.4	−64.9	−57.9	−56.7	−36.0
Assets	−33.8	−80.3	−100.1	−160.6	−264.5	−75.0	−104.9	−165.0	−168.6	−164.7	−161.7
Liabilities	42.5	109.4	151.6	290.7	166.6	11.7	79.4	100.0	110.7	107.9	125.7
Developing Asia											
Private Financial Flows, Net	96.2	123.0	83.4	197.1	68.2	206.2	409.0	311.9	14.4	193.3	210.7
Assets	−36.1	−117.6	−233.7	−257.9	−170.8	−92.4	−252.2	−283.3	−332.8	−391.4	−352.8
Liabilities	132.2	235.0	314.0	449.4	242.4	297.0	659.9	594.2	347.4	581.3	559.4
Latin America and the Caribbean											
Private Financial Flows, Net	14.4	37.8	34.0	85.8	84.9	61.9	128.9	200.0	136.3	126.0	134.2
Assets	−34.8	−51.1	−91.2	−114.6	−77.9	−100.8	−167.0	−115.4	−149.7	−115.1	−99.9
Liabilities	48.9	88.0	125.2	200.5	161.7	162.1	295.0	314.6	283.8	240.4	232.6
Middle East, North Africa, Afghanistan, and Pakistan											
Private Financial Flows, Net	10.0	0.9	15.6	77.2	44.4	71.9	19.0	−43.8	−35.2	−10.1	−0.4
Assets	−32.6	−62.9	−118.4	−219.5	−50.2	−7.7	−82.1	−117.9	−63.6	−76.8	−74.3
Liabilities	42.6	63.8	133.9	296.6	94.7	79.7	101.2	74.3	29.1	67.3	74.4
Sub-Saharan Africa											
Private Financial Flows, Net	4.5	17.7	8.1	16.8	22.3	13.5	−14.7	−1.7	20.4	21.7	40.0
Assets	−9.7	−15.5	−32.6	−33.4	−17.3	−15.3	−28.8	−31.4	−19.6	−24.8	−20.1
Liabilities	14.5	33.2	40.9	50.4	39.1	28.9	13.9	29.0	38.9	45.2	59.3

[1]Private financial flows comprise direct investment, portfolio investment, and other long- and short-term investment flows.
[2]Georgia, which is not a member of the Commonwealth of Independent States, is included in this group for reasons of geography and similarity in economic structure.

Table A15. Summary of Sources and Uses of World Savings

(Percent of GDP)

| | Averages | | | | | | | | Projections | | |
| | | | | | | | | | | | Average |
	1991–98	1999–2006	2007	2008	2009	2010	2011	2012	2013	2014	2015–18
World											
Savings	22.1	22.0	24.3	24.2	21.9	23.3	23.8	23.9	24.4	24.8	25.9
Investment	22.7	22.1	23.9	23.9	21.8	23.0	23.4	23.6	24.2	24.7	25.8
Advanced Economies											
Savings	21.7	20.4	20.8	19.9	17.2	18.2	18.3	18.4	18.7	19.1	20.1
Investment	22.0	21.1	21.7	21.1	17.8	18.5	18.8	18.8	19.0	19.4	20.5
Net Lending	–0.3	–0.7	–0.9	–1.2	–0.6	–0.3	–0.4	–0.3	–0.3	–0.3	–0.4
Current Transfers	–0.4	–0.6	–0.8	–0.8	–0.9	–0.9	–0.9	–0.8	–0.8	–0.8	–0.8
Factor Income	–0.4	0.5	0.5	0.5	0.3	0.7	0.8	0.8	0.6	0.5	0.3
Resource Balance	0.6	–0.5	–0.5	–0.8	0.1	0.0	–0.2	–0.2	0.1	0.2	0.2
United States											
Savings	16.4	16.0	14.6	13.4	11.1	12.2	12.2	13.1	13.8	14.6	16.4
Investment	18.5	19.9	19.6	18.1	14.7	15.5	15.5	16.2	16.8	17.6	19.7
Net Lending	–2.1	–3.9	–5.0	–4.7	–3.6	–3.3	–3.3	–3.0	–2.9	–3.0	–3.3
Current Transfers	–0.5	–0.7	–0.8	–0.9	–0.9	–0.9	–0.9	–0.9	–0.8	–0.8	–0.7
Factor Income	–0.4	1.1	0.8	1.0	0.0	1.1	1.3	1.3	1.2	1.0	0.6
Resource Balance	–1.2	–4.3	–5.0	–4.9	–2.7	–3.4	–3.7	–3.4	–3.3	–3.2	–3.2
Euro Area											
Savings	21.4	21.6	23.0	21.5	19.1	19.8	20.2	20.2	20.3	20.5	21.2
Investment	21.7	21.1	22.6	22.2	18.8	19.3	19.6	18.3	17.8	18.0	18.5
Net Lending	–0.3	0.5	0.4	–0.7	0.3	0.5	0.6	1.9	2.5	2.5	2.7
Current Transfers[1]	–0.6	–0.8	–1.1	–1.1	–1.2	–1.3	–1.2	–1.2	–1.2	–1.2	–1.2
Factor Income[1]	–0.5	–0.3	–0.2	–0.6	–0.1	0.3	0.2	0.2	–0.3	–0.4	–0.5
Resource Balance[1]	1.3	1.6	1.6	1.0	1.5	1.5	1.6	2.8	3.7	3.9	4.2
Germany											
Savings	21.4	21.3	26.7	25.5	22.4	23.7	24.5	24.2	23.5	23.2	23.2
Investment	22.4	19.2	19.3	19.3	16.5	17.5	18.3	17.2	17.4	17.5	18.2
Net Lending	–1.0	2.1	7.4	6.2	6.0	6.2	6.2	7.0	6.1	5.7	5.0
Current Transfers	–1.6	–1.3	–1.3	–1.3	–1.4	–1.6	–1.4	–1.3	–1.3	–1.3	–1.3
Factor Income	0.2	0.1	1.8	1.3	2.5	2.2	2.3	2.4	1.2	0.9	0.9
Resource Balance	0.4	3.3	7.0	6.2	4.9	5.7	5.3	5.9	6.2	6.1	5.4
France											
Savings	19.1	20.4	21.0	20.2	17.6	17.7	18.7	17.6	17.9	18.0	19.4
Investment	18.1	19.4	22.0	21.9	19.0	19.3	20.6	19.9	19.2	19.5	19.9
Net Lending	1.0	1.0	–1.0	–1.7	–1.3	–1.6	–1.9	–2.3	–1.3	–1.4	–0.5
Current Transfers	–0.7	–1.1	–1.2	–1.3	–1.8	–1.7	–1.8	–1.8	–1.5	–1.5	–1.5
Factor Income	–0.2	1.3	1.7	1.7	1.7	2.1	2.1	1.3	1.5	1.5	1.5
Resource Balance	1.9	0.8	–1.4	–2.2	–1.3	–1.9	–2.2	–1.8	–1.3	–1.4	–0.5
Italy											
Savings	21.0	20.6	20.8	18.8	16.9	16.5	16.4	17.1	17.9	18.5	19.1
Investment	20.2	21.0	22.1	21.6	18.9	20.1	19.5	17.6	17.6	18.2	18.9
Net Lending	0.7	–0.4	–1.3	–2.9	–2.0	–3.5	–3.1	–0.5	0.3	0.3	0.2
Current Transfers	–0.5	–0.6	–1.0	–0.9	–0.8	–1.0	–1.0	–1.2	–1.5	–1.5	–1.5
Factor Income	–1.6	–0.5	–0.1	–1.2	–0.7	–0.5	–0.6	–0.6	–0.7	–0.7	–1.0
Resource Balance	2.9	0.7	–0.3	–0.7	–0.5	–1.9	–1.5	1.3	2.5	2.5	2.7
Japan											
Savings	31.2	26.4	27.8	26.3	22.6	23.5	22.0	21.6	22.4	23.1	23.7
Investment	28.9	23.3	22.9	23.0	19.7	19.8	20.0	20.6	21.2	21.3	21.8
Net Lending	2.3	3.1	4.9	3.3	2.9	3.7	2.0	1.0	1.2	1.9	1.9
Current Transfers	–0.2	–0.2	–0.3	–0.3	–0.2	–0.2	–0.2	–0.2	–0.2	–0.2	–0.2
Factor Income	0.9	1.8	3.2	3.2	2.7	2.6	3.0	3.0	3.1	3.1	2.9
Resource Balance	1.6	1.5	1.9	0.4	0.5	1.4	–0.7	–1.8	–1.6	–1.0	–0.8
United Kingdom											
Savings	16.0	15.0	16.0	16.1	12.9	12.5	13.3	10.8	10.7	11.2	13.6
Investment	16.8	17.3	18.3	17.1	14.1	15.0	14.6	14.3	15.1	15.5	17.0
Net Lending	–0.8	–2.4	–2.3	–1.0	–1.3	–2.5	–1.3	–3.5	–4.4	–4.3	–3.4
Current Transfers	–0.7	–0.9	–1.0	–1.0	–1.1	–1.4	–1.4	–1.4	–1.5	–1.5	–1.5
Factor Income	–0.2	0.8	1.3	2.2	1.3	1.0	1.7	0.3	0.6	0.6	0.6
Resource Balance	0.1	–2.3	–2.7	–2.3	–1.5	–2.1	–1.6	–2.3	–3.5	–3.5	–2.5

Table A15. Summary of Sources and Uses of World Savings *(continued)*
(Percent of GDP)

	Averages								Projections		Average
	1991–98	1999–2006	2007	2008	2009	2010	2011	2012	2013	2014	2015–18
Canada											
Savings	17.0	22.9	24.8	24.1	18.8	19.7	20.6	20.8	20.8	21.1	22.1
Investment	19.7	21.2	24.0	24.0	21.8	23.3	23.6	24.5	24.3	24.5	24.8
Net Lending	−2.7	1.6	0.8	0.1	−3.0	−3.6	−3.0	−3.7	−3.5	−3.4	−2.7
Current Transfers	−0.1	0.0	−0.1	0.0	−0.2	−0.2	−0.2	−0.2	−0.2	−0.2	−0.2
Factor Income	−4.0	−2.6	−1.2	−1.6	−1.3	−1.5	−1.5	−1.5	−1.5	−1.7	−2.4
Resource Balance	1.4	4.3	2.1	1.7	−1.5	−1.9	−1.3	−2.0	−1.9	−1.5	0.0
Emerging Market and Developing Economies											
Savings	23.6	27.6	33.2	33.7	32.1	32.9	33.3	32.8	33.1	33.2	33.6
Investment	26.0	25.6	29.4	30.3	30.7	31.5	31.5	31.5	32.2	32.6	33.1
Net Lending	−2.1	2.0	3.9	3.4	1.5	1.5	1.8	1.4	1.0	0.7	0.5
Current Transfers	0.7	1.4	1.6	1.5	1.4	1.2	1.1	0.9	1.0	1.0	1.0
Factor Income	−1.7	−2.0	−1.6	−1.5	−1.5	−1.9	−1.8	−1.7	−1.6	−1.5	−1.2
Resource Balance	−1.1	2.6	4.0	3.6	1.6	2.2	2.6	2.2	1.6	1.1	0.7
Memorandum											
Acquisition of Foreign Assets	1.7	5.9	12.5	7.0	4.9	7.0	6.2	4.3	4.6	4.0	3.7
Change in Reserves	1.0	3.1	7.7	3.8	2.9	3.8	2.9	1.5	2.2	2.0	2.2
Regional Groups											
Central and Eastern Europe											
Savings	19.6	16.8	16.3	16.7	15.9	15.9	16.7	17.0	16.9	17.3	17.4
Investment	21.7	21.1	24.7	25.0	18.9	20.5	22.9	21.2	21.5	22.1	22.8
Net Lending	−2.0	−4.3	−8.4	−8.3	−3.0	−4.7	−6.3	−4.3	−4.6	−4.8	−5.4
Current Transfers	1.8	2.0	1.6	1.5	1.7	1.5	1.6	1.5	1.5	1.4	1.2
Factor Income	−1.2	−1.7	−2.9	−2.4	−2.3	−2.4	−2.7	−2.5	−2.3	−2.3	−2.3
Resource Balance	−2.6	−4.7	−7.2	−7.5	−2.5	−4.0	−5.3	−3.3	−3.9	−4.0	−4.3
Memorandum											
Acquisition of Foreign Assets	0.9	3.3	4.8	1.9	2.1	2.8	−0.4	1.1	0.3	0.5	0.4
Change in Reserves	0.8	1.6	2.3	0.4	2.1	2.1	0.7	1.7	0.5	0.4	0.3
Commonwealth of Independent States[2]											
Savings	. . .	28.9	30.7	30.0	22.0	26.3	28.9	27.6	27.7	27.2	25.7
Investment	. . .	20.7	26.7	25.2	19.2	22.5	24.4	24.4	25.9	26.2	26.0
Net Lending	. . .	8.1	4.0	4.9	2.8	3.7	4.5	3.2	1.8	0.9	−0.2
Current Transfers	. . .	0.5	0.3	0.4	0.4	0.3	0.3	0.2	0.2	0.3	0.3
Factor Income	. . .	−2.9	−2.9	−3.4	−3.6	−3.7	−3.9	−3.7	−3.4	−2.8	−1.8
Resource Balance	. . .	10.4	6.8	8.0	5.8	7.0	8.2	6.8	5.2	3.6	1.5
Memorandum											
Acquisition of Foreign Assets	. . .	11.2	17.5	10.0	1.6	6.0	6.0	5.0	4.2	3.4	3.0
Change in Reserves	. . .	5.7	9.8	−1.2	0.4	2.6	1.0	0.9	0.6	0.3	0.3
Developing Asia											
Savings	32.7	36.1	44.2	44.6	45.7	44.8	43.6	43.0	43.2	43.6	44.5
Investment	33.9	33.3	37.3	38.7	41.9	42.3	41.9	41.9	42.1	42.3	42.5
Net Lending	−1.2	2.8	6.8	5.8	3.7	2.5	1.6	1.0	1.1	1.3	2.0
Current Transfers	0.9	1.7	1.9	1.9	1.6	1.5	1.3	1.1	1.2	1.3	1.3
Factor Income	−1.6	−1.4	−0.5	−0.2	−0.6	−0.9	−0.7	−0.9	−0.7	−0.7	−0.6
Resource Balance	−0.6	2.5	5.4	4.1	2.7	1.9	1.0	0.8	0.6	0.7	1.3
Memorandum											
Acquisition of Foreign Assets	3.7	6.4	13.6	7.8	7.0	8.8	6.2	3.3	4.8	4.5	4.5
Change in Reserves	1.9	4.5	10.4	6.9	5.9	6.0	3.9	1.0	2.5	2.8	3.4

Table A15. Summary of Sources and Uses of World Savings *(continued)*

(Percent of GDP)

| | Averages | | | | | | | | Projections | | |
	1991–98	1999–2006	2007	2008	2009	2010	2011	2012	2013	2014	Average 2015–18
Latin America and the Caribbean											
Savings	18.6	19.8	22.8	22.7	19.9	20.4	20.6	19.5	19.9	19.3	19.0
Investment	21.3	20.4	22.5	23.7	20.6	21.7	22.2	21.4	21.8	21.5	21.3
Net Lending	−2.8	−0.6	0.3	−1.0	−0.7	−1.4	−1.6	−1.9	−1.9	−2.1	−2.3
Current Transfers	0.8	1.6	1.8	1.6	1.4	1.2	1.1	1.1	1.1	1.1	1.0
Factor Income	−2.5	−3.0	−2.7	−2.6	−2.2	−3.0	−2.8	−2.3	−2.3	−2.3	−2.2
Resource Balance	−1.1	0.8	1.1	0.1	0.0	0.4	0.1	−0.7	−0.6	−0.9	−1.1
Memorandum											
Acquisition of Foreign Assets	1.2	2.6	5.6	2.3	4.2	5.1	4.7	3.6	2.5	1.7	1.3
Change in Reserves	0.7	0.7	3.6	1.2	1.2	1.8	2.0	1.0	1.0	0.5	0.3
Middle East, North Africa, Afghanistan, and Pakistan											
Savings	21.5	31.6	39.6	41.4	31.0	35.7	37.8	36.2	35.8	35.1	32.7
Investment	24.0	23.3	27.6	28.2	29.5	29.1	25.1	25.0	26.3	27.3	27.6
Net Lending	−2.6	8.5	12.9	13.2	2.3	7.2	13.1	11.8	10.4	8.6	5.4
Current Transfers	−1.6	−0.1	0.0	0.0	−0.5	−0.4	−0.6	−0.6	−0.6	−0.8	−0.9
Factor Income	0.8	−0.2	0.7	0.4	−0.1	−0.4	−0.4	−0.4	−0.2	0.1	1.1
Resource Balance	−1.8	8.6	12.1	12.9	2.5	7.7	14.0	12.4	10.7	8.9	5.2
Memorandum											
Acquisition of Foreign Assets	−0.4	10.9	25.3	14.9	4.0	9.2	14.1	11.0	10.9	9.4	7.4
Change in Reserves	0.8	4.3	11.3	7.0	−1.0	3.6	4.3	4.1	5.6	4.5	3.3
Sub-Saharan Africa											
Savings	15.0	18.0	23.6	22.3	20.2	20.9	19.8	18.9	19.4	19.3	18.9
Investment	17.1	19.2	22.3	22.4	23.1	22.1	21.2	21.7	22.8	23.2	23.2
Net Lending	−2.1	−1.1	1.3	0.0	−2.9	−1.2	−1.5	−2.8	−3.4	−3.9	−4.3
Current Transfers	2.0	2.6	4.6	4.6	4.7	4.2	4.0	3.8	3.9	3.7	3.4
Factor Income	−3.2	−4.9	−5.4	−6.2	−4.3	−4.8	−5.5	−5.4	−5.2	−4.9	−4.4
Resource Balance	−0.7	1.2	2.1	1.4	−3.3	−0.7	0.3	−1.2	−2.1	−2.6	−3.2
Memorandum											
Acquisition of Foreign Assets	1.1	3.3	7.8	4.9	2.6	3.3	2.9	2.2	2.8	2.6	2.0
Change in Reserves	0.7	1.8	3.4	1.6	−0.9	0.2	1.7	1.6	1.3	1.6	0.9
Analytical Groups											
By Source of Export Earnings											
Fuel Exporters											
Savings	22.5	33.1	38.6	39.1	29.4	33.4	36.2	35.0	34.6	33.4	30.5
Investment	25.5	22.9	27.2	26.3	25.8	26.3	24.9	25.2	26.7	27.1	26.8
Net Lending	−2.0	10.3	11.9	12.7	4.1	7.4	11.4	10.1	8.3	6.6	3.7
Current Transfers	−3.1	−1.4	−0.7	−0.6	−1.0	−1.0	−1.1	−1.1	−1.2	−1.2	−1.1
Factor Income	−0.3	−1.9	−1.6	−2.2	−1.8	−3.1	−2.8	−2.5	−2.3	−1.9	−0.8
Resource Balance	1.5	13.5	14.2	15.7	6.5	11.2	15.3	13.6	11.6	9.6	5.8
Memorandum											
Acquisition of Foreign Assets	−0.2	12.3	22.9	14.5	3.4	7.9	12.0	9.9	9.0	7.5	5.7
Change in Reserves	−0.1	5.0	10.7	3.6	−1.5	2.4	3.2	3.5	3.6	2.7	1.8
Nonfuel Exporters											
Savings	23.7	26.3	31.6	32.1	32.8	32.8	32.5	32.2	32.7	33.2	34.4
Investment	25.9	26.2	30.0	31.5	31.9	32.8	33.2	33.1	33.6	34.0	34.6
Net Lending	−2.1	0.1	1.6	0.6	0.9	0.0	−0.7	−0.9	−0.9	−0.8	−0.2
Current Transfers	1.4	2.1	2.2	2.1	2.0	1.8	1.6	1.5	1.6	1.6	1.5
Factor Income	−1.9	−2.0	−1.6	−1.3	−1.4	−1.6	−1.5	−1.5	−1.4	−1.4	−1.2
Resource Balance	−1.6	0.0	0.9	−0.2	0.3	−0.2	−0.8	−1.0	−1.1	−1.0	−0.5
Memorandum											
Acquisition of Foreign Assets	2.0	4.3	9.4	4.7	5.2	6.8	4.6	2.7	3.4	3.1	3.2
Change in Reserves	1.3	2.7	6.8	3.9	4.0	4.2	2.8	0.9	1.8	1.9	2.2

Table A15. Summary of Sources and Uses of World Savings *(concluded)*
(Percent of GDP)

	Averages								Projections		Average
	1991–98	1999–2006	2007	2008	2009	2010	2011	2012	2013	2014	2015–18
By External Financing Source											
Net Debtor Economies											
Savings	18.9	19.9	22.7	21.8	20.9	21.5	21.2	20.0	20.4	20.5	21.0
Investment	21.5	21.6	25.7	25.9	23.2	24.4	24.5	23.6	24.0	24.3	24.6
Net Lending	−2.5	−1.8	−2.9	−4.1	−2.3	−2.9	−3.3	−3.6	−3.6	−3.7	−3.6
Current Transfers	1.8	2.6	2.8	2.7	2.8	2.5	2.4	2.5	2.5	2.5	2.4
Factor Income	−2.0	−2.4	−2.5	−2.5	−2.3	−2.4	−2.6	−2.5	−2.5	−2.4	−2.4
Resource Balance	−2.4	−2.0	−3.1	−4.4	−2.9	−3.1	−3.2	−3.7	−3.7	−3.8	−3.6
Memorandum											
Acquisition of Foreign Assets	1.1	2.8	5.8	1.6	2.8	3.9	2.4	2.0	1.6	1.2	1.1
Change in Reserves	0.8	1.4	4.0	0.8	1.4	1.8	1.1	0.7	0.7	0.5	0.4
Official Financing											
Savings	16.1	19.2	20.3	19.1	18.5	20.0	20.2	19.2	20.4	20.0	19.4
Investment	20.3	21.5	23.1	23.5	21.0	21.3	21.1	21.4	22.0	21.8	21.9
Net Lending	−4.1	−2.3	−2.8	−4.4	−2.5	−1.3	−0.8	−2.2	−1.6	−1.9	−2.5
Current Transfers	4.0	5.7	6.8	6.6	7.2	7.4	7.9	8.1	8.3	8.1	7.7
Factor Income	−3.3	−3.3	−3.3	−3.4	−3.0	−2.7	−2.4	−2.4	−2.6	−2.7	−3.2
Resource Balance	−4.9	−4.8	−6.3	−7.6	−6.7	−6.0	−6.2	−7.8	−7.4	−7.3	−7.0
Memorandum											
Acquisition of Foreign Assets	1.2	1.6	3.0	2.7	1.9	2.0	1.3	−1.7	−0.6	−0.8	0.2
Change in Reserves	1.2	1.4	1.6	1.6	2.9	1.9	0.9	−0.3	0.6	0.9	1.0
Net Debtor Economies by Debt-Servicing Experience											
Economies with Arrears and/or Rescheduling during 2007–11											
Savings	14.7	18.0	22.1	21.4	19.1	19.5	19.8	19.1	20.2	20.0	19.7
Investment	19.2	19.2	24.1	24.9	21.7	23.7	24.9	24.5	25.0	24.9	24.2
Net Lending	−4.5	−1.2	−2.0	−3.6	−2.6	−4.3	−5.1	−5.3	−4.8	−4.9	−4.5
Current Transfers	1.7	4.4	5.1	4.6	4.8	4.3	3.8	3.6	3.6	3.5	3.2
Factor Income	−3.2	−3.9	−2.9	−3.3	−3.0	−3.9	−4.3	−3.5	−3.4	−3.4	−3.2
Resource Balance	−3.0	−1.7	−4.2	−5.0	−4.4	−4.8	−4.7	−5.4	−5.0	−5.0	−4.6
Memorandum											
Acquisition of Foreign Assets	3.1	3.0	6.2	2.2	1.7	2.9	2.7	0.3	1.2	0.2	0.5
Change in Reserves	0.7	0.8	3.8	0.6	1.7	1.3	0.4	−0.1	0.6	0.5	0.5

Note: The estimates in this table are based on individual countries' national accounts and balance of payments statistics. Country group composites are calculated as the sum of the U.S. dollar values for the relevant individual countries. This differs from the calculations in the April 2005 and earlier issues of the *World Economic Outlook,* where the composites were weighted by GDP valued at purchasing power parities as a share of total world GDP. For many countries, the estimates of national savings are built up from national accounts data on gross domestic investment and from balance-of-payments-based data on net foreign investment. The latter, which is equivalent to the current account balance, comprises three components: current transfers, net factor income, and the resource balance. The mixing of data sources, which is dictated by availability, implies that the estimates for national savings that are derived incorporate the statistical discrepancies. Furthermore, errors, omissions, and asymmetries in balance of payments statistics affect the estimates for net lending; at the global level, net lending, which in theory would be zero, equals the world current account discrepancy. Despite these statistical shortcomings, flow of funds estimates, such as those presented in these tables, provide a useful framework for analyzing development in savings and investment, both over time and across regions and countries.

[1]Calculated from the data of individual Euro Area countries.

[2]Georgia, which is not a member of the Commonwealth of Independent States, is included in this group for reasons of geography and similarity in economic structure.

Table A16. Summary of World Medium-Term Baseline Scenario

| | Averages | | 2011 | 2012 | Projections | | | |
| | | | | | | | Averages | |
	1995–2002	2003–10	2011	2012	2013	2014	2011–14	2015–18
	Annual Percent Change							
World Real GDP	**3.4**	**3.9**	**4.0**	**3.2**	**3.3**	**4.0**	**3.6**	**4.5**
Advanced Economies	2.9	1.6	1.6	1.2	1.2	2.2	1.6	2.6
Emerging Market and Developing Economies	4.3	6.8	6.4	5.1	5.3	5.7	5.6	6.1
Memorandum								
Potential Output								
Major Advanced Economies	2.5	1.7	1.2	1.2	1.5	1.6	1.4	1.8
World Trade, Volume[1]	**6.7**	**5.6**	**6.0**	**2.5**	**3.6**	**5.3**	**4.3**	**6.3**
Imports								
Advanced Economies	6.8	4.0	4.7	1.0	2.2	4.1	3.0	5.3
Emerging Market and Developing Economies	7.2	9.7	8.6	4.9	6.2	7.3	6.7	7.9
Exports								
Advanced Economies	6.2	4.6	5.6	1.9	2.8	4.6	3.7	5.3
Emerging Market and Developing Economies	7.9	8.0	6.4	3.7	4.8	6.5	5.3	7.8
Terms of Trade								
Advanced Economies	0.0	–0.3	–1.6	–0.7	0.2	–0.1	–0.6	0.0
Emerging Market and Developing Economies	0.9	1.9	3.3	0.2	–0.5	–0.9	0.5	–0.4
World Prices in U.S. Dollars								
Manufactures	–1.2	3.1	6.7	–0.5	1.0	0.5	1.9	0.7
Oil	5.8	15.5	31.6	1.0	–2.3	–4.9	5.4	–2.7
Nonfuel Primary Commodities	–2.4	9.6	17.8	–9.8	–0.9	–4.3	0.2	–1.1
Consumer Prices								
Advanced Economies	2.0	2.0	2.7	2.0	1.7	2.0	2.1	2.0
Emerging Market and Developing Economies	14.8	6.4	7.2	5.9	5.9	5.6	6.2	5.0
	Percent							
Interest Rates								
Real Six-Month LIBOR[2]	3.3	0.4	–1.6	–1.1	–0.9	–1.0	–1.2	0.2
World Real Long-Term Interest Rate[3]	3.3	1.7	0.2	0.2	0.5	0.5	0.4	1.9
	Percent of GDP							
Balances on Current Account								
Advanced Economies	–0.3	–0.7	–0.2	–0.1	–0.1	–0.1	–0.1	–0.2
Emerging Market and Developing Economies	–0.3	2.9	1.9	1.4	1.0	0.7	1.3	0.6
Total External Debt								
Emerging Market and Developing Economies	36.8	28.5	23.4	24.4	24.6	24.4	24.2	23.1
Debt Service								
Emerging Market and Developing Economies	9.2	9.3	8.0	8.4	8.6	8.6	8.4	8.3

[1]Data refer to trade in goods and services.
[2]London interbank offered rate on U.S. dollar deposits minus percent change in U.S. GDP deflator.
[3]GDP-weighted average of 10-year (or nearest maturity) government bond rates for Canada, France, Germany, Italy, Japan, United Kingdom, and United States.

WORLD ECONOMIC OUTLOOK
SELECTED TOPICS

World Economic Outlook Archives

I. Methodology—Aggregation, Modeling, and Forecasting

II. Historical Surveys

III. Economic Growth—Sources and Patterns

IV. Inflation and Deflation, and Commodity Markets

V. Fiscal Policy

VI. Monetary Policy, Financial Markets, and Flow of Funds

VII. Labor Markets, Poverty, and Inequality

VIII. Exchange Rate Issues

IX. External Payments, Trade, Capital Movements, and Foreign Debt

X. Regional Issues

XI. Country-Specific Analyses

XII. Special Topics

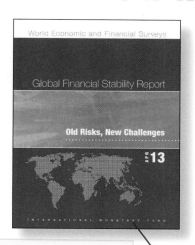

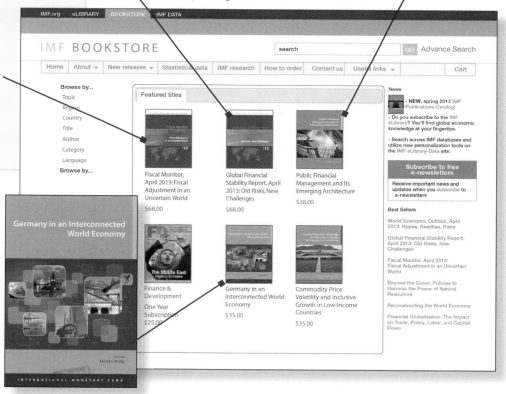